I love B movies. I love the way they make me think "What the hell is this?! That's crazy!" yet. still draw me in so that I watch the whole thing. I really like that feeling, and I like to bring a little of that kind of over-the-top flavor into my own manga. That was the initial idea that gave birth to volume 1 of this alchemy manga. Thank you for picking it up. As you read it, please criticize it by saying to yourself "What kind of alchemy is that?!"

—*Hiromu Arakawa, 2002*

Born in Hokkaido (northern Japan), Hiromu Arakawa first attracted national attention in 1999 with her award-winning manga **Stray Dog**. Her series **Fullmetal Alchemist** debuted in 2001 in Square Enix's monthly manga anthology **Shonen Gangan**.

FULLMETAL ALCHEMIST VOL. I

Story and Art by Hiromu Arakawa

English Adaptation/Egan Loo
Translation/Akira Watanabe
Touch-up Art & Lettering/Wayne Truman
Design/Amy Martin
Editor/Jason Thompson

Managing Editor/Annette Roman
Director of Production/Noboru Watanabe
Editorial Director/Alvin Lu
Sr. Director of Acquisitions/Rika Inouye
Vice President of Sales & Marketing/Liza Coppola
Executive Vice President/Hyoe Narita
Publisher/Seiji Horibuchi

Hagane no RenkinJutsushi vol. I ©2002 Hiromu Arakawa. First published in Japan in 2002 by SQUARE ENIX CO., LTD. English translation rights arranged with SQUARE ENIX CO., LTD. and VIZ, LLC. All rights reserved. The stories, characters and incidents mentioned in this publication are entirely fictional.

No portion of this book may be reproduced or transmitted in any form or by any means without written permission from the copyright holders.

CONTRA COSTA COUNTY LIBRARY

WITHDRAWN

3 1901 04254 2235

CONTENTS

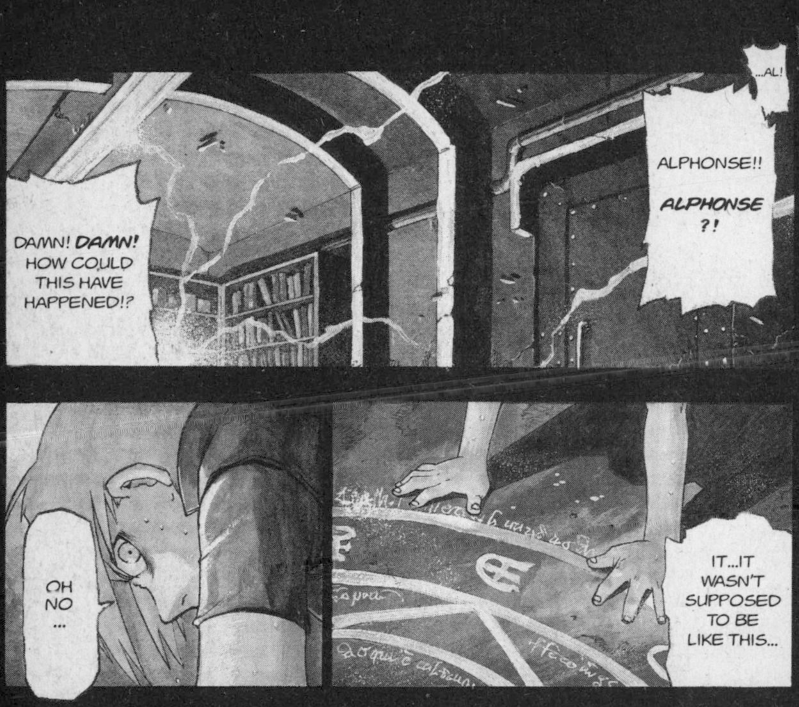
...
...AL!
ALPHONSE!! ALPHONSE ?!
DAMN! DAMN! HOW COULD THIS HAVE HAPPENED!?
IT...IT WASN'T SUPPOSED TO BE LIKE THIS...
OH NO ...

TEACHINGS THAT DO NOT SPEAK OF PAIN HAVE NO MEANING...

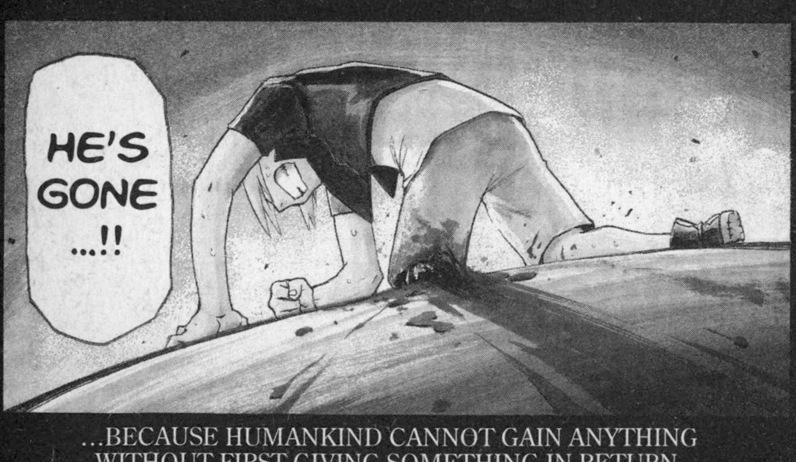
HE'S GONE ...!!

...BECAUSE HUMANKIND CANNOT GAIN ANYTHING WITHOUT FIRST GIVING SOMETHING IN RETURN.

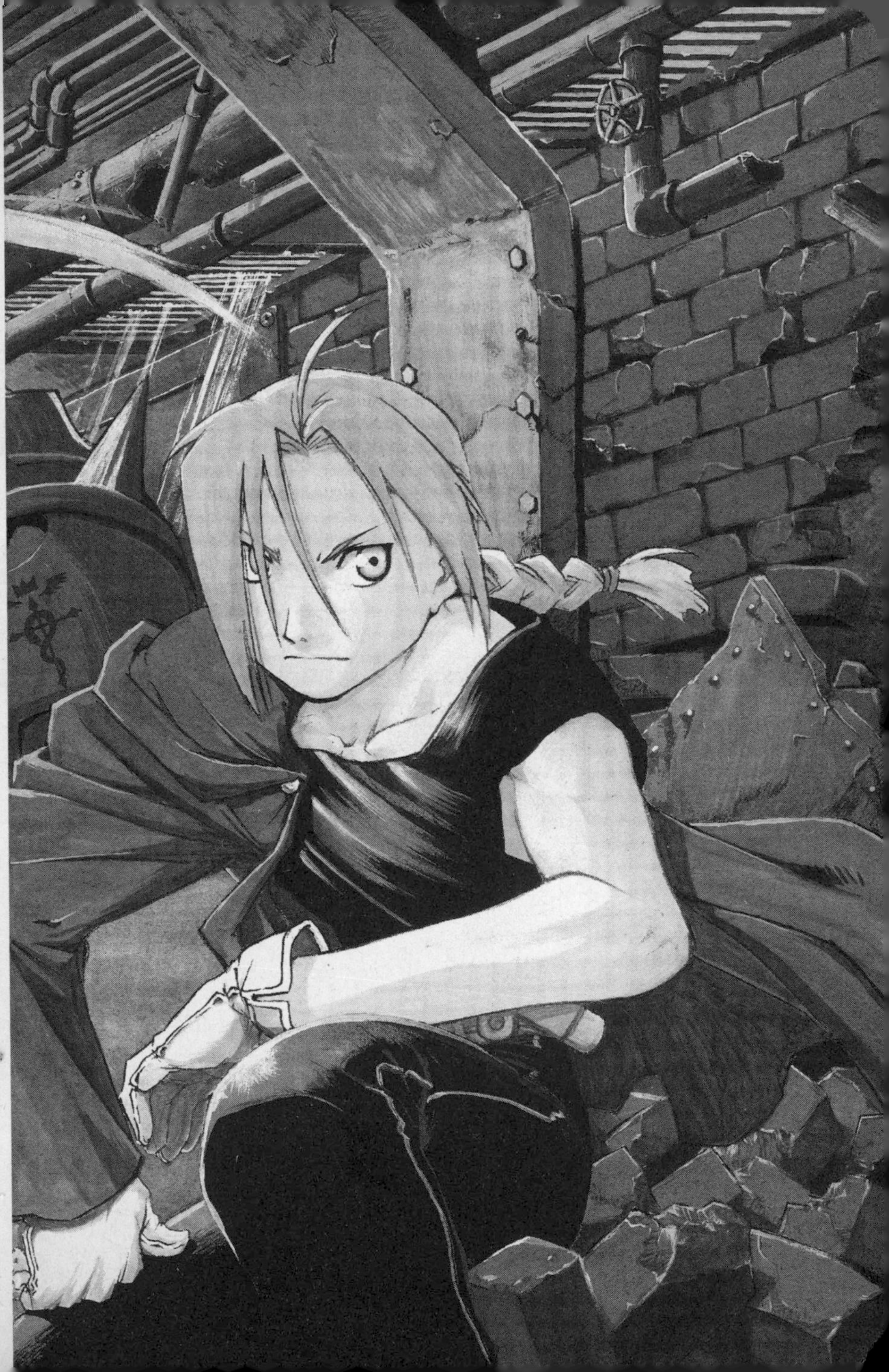

Chapter 1: The Two Alchemists

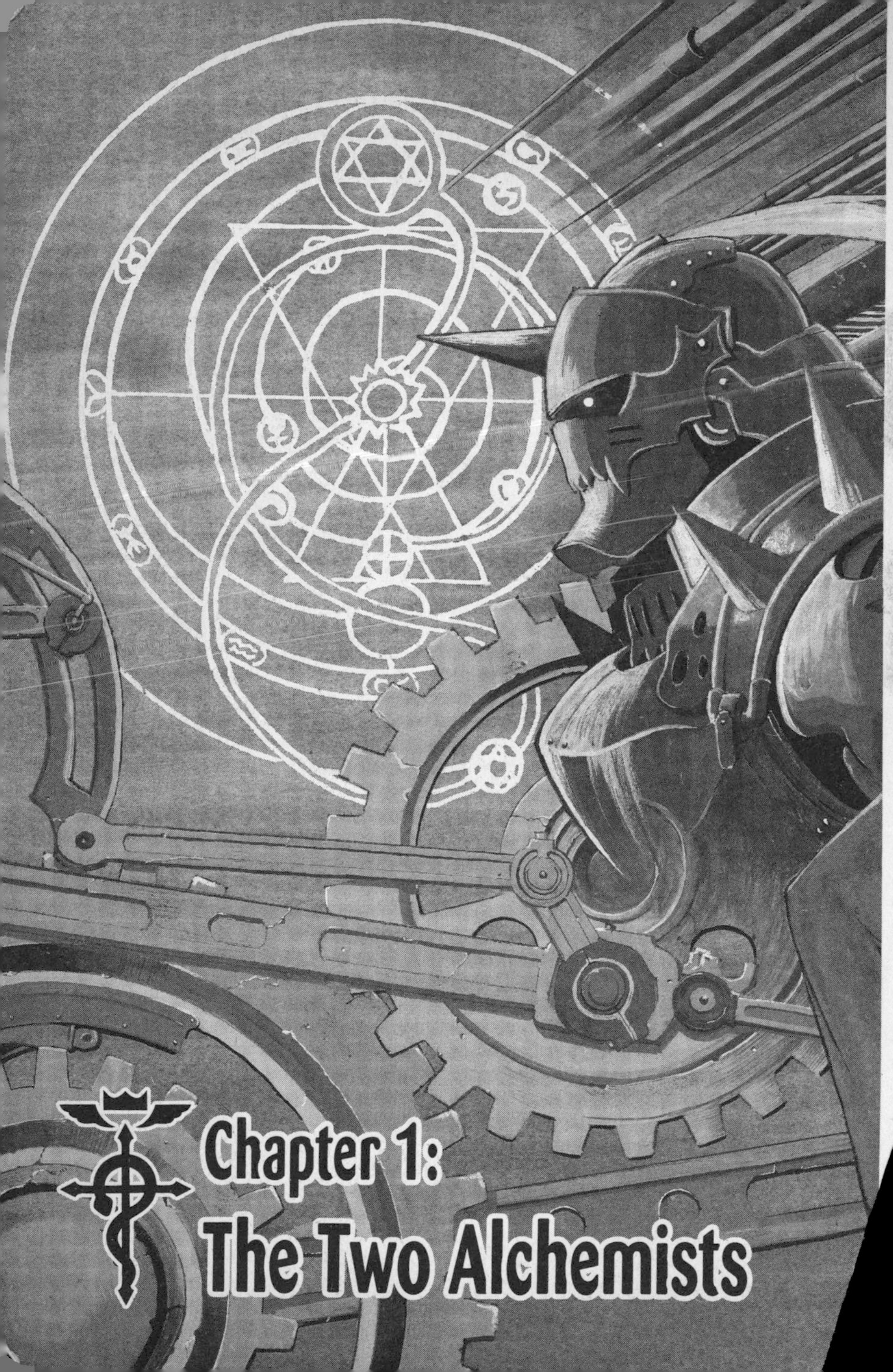

FULLMETAL
ALCHEMIST

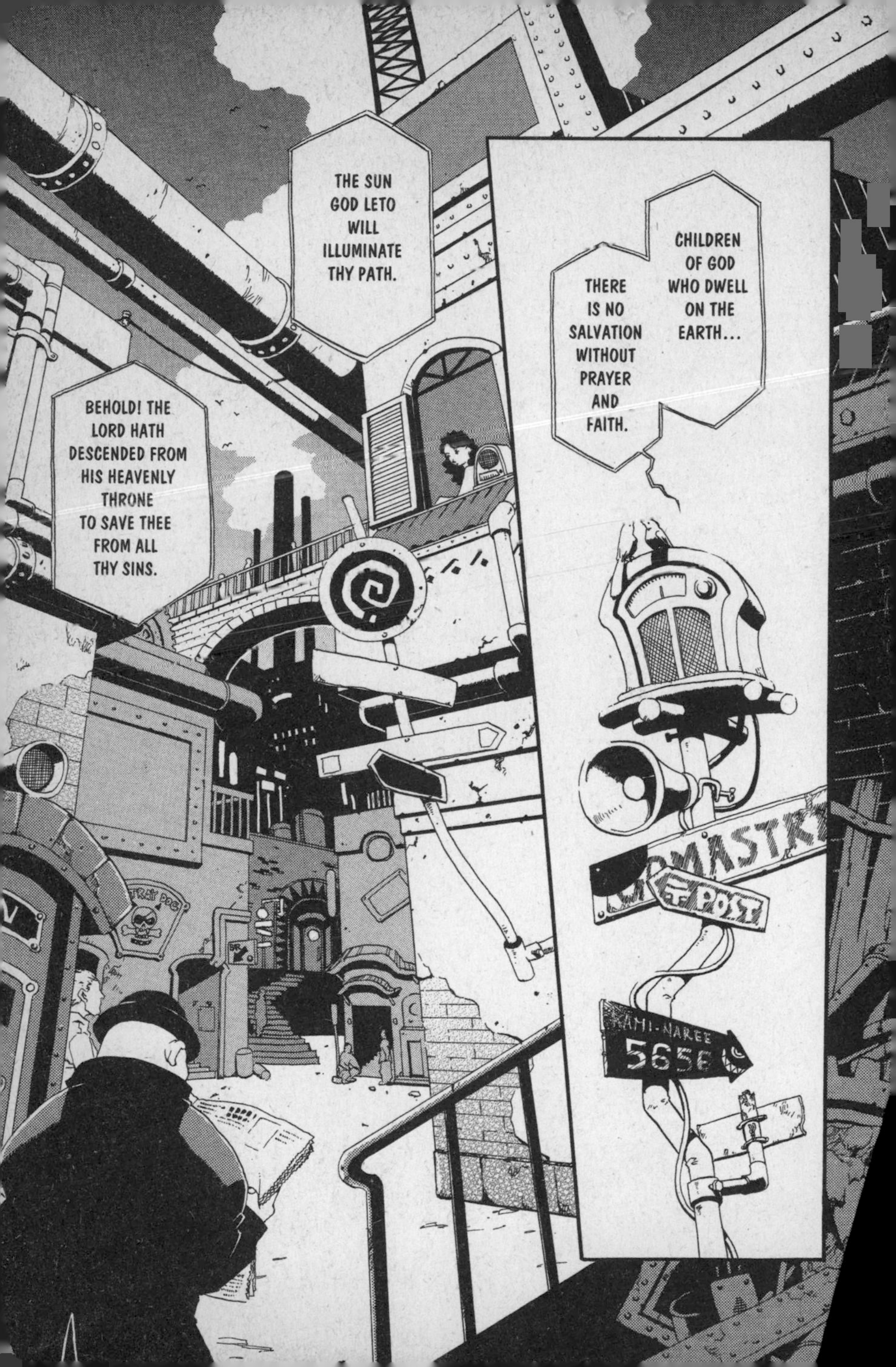

CHILDREN OF GOD WHO DWELL ON THE EARTH...
THERE IS NO SALVATION WITHOUT PRAYER AND FAITH.
THE SUN GOD LETO WILL ILLUMINATE THY PATH.
BEHOLD! THE LORD HATH DESCENDED FROM HIS HEAVENLY THRONE TO SAVE THEE FROM ALL THY SINS.
KAMI-NAREE
5656

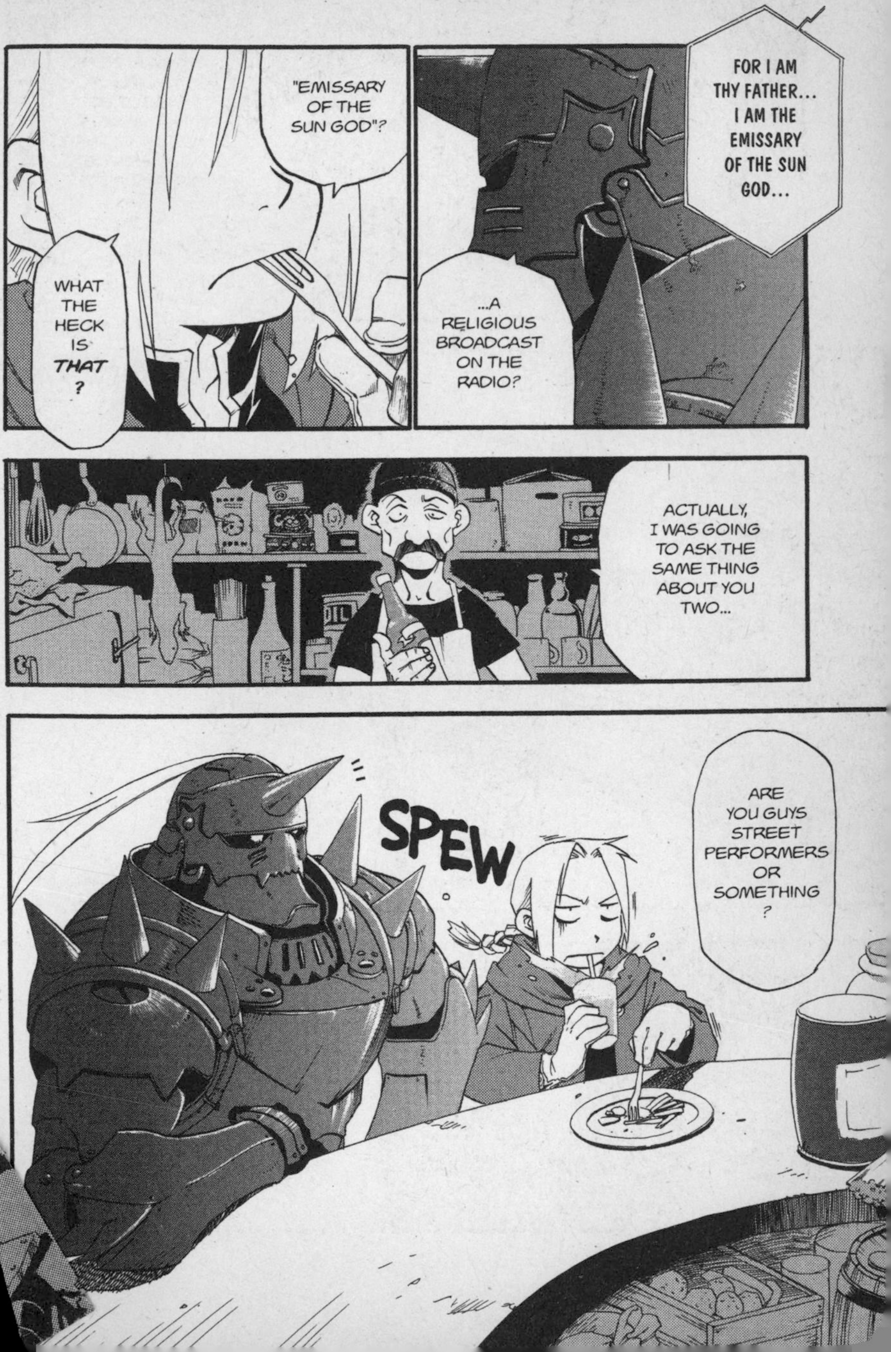
FOR I AM THY FATHER... I AM THE EMISSARY OF THE SUN GOD...
...A RELIGIOUS BROADCAST ON THE RADIO?
"EMISSARY OF THE SUN GOD"?
WHAT THE HECK IS *THAT*?
ACTUALLY, I WAS GOING TO ASK THE SAME THING ABOUT YOU TWO...
ARE YOU GUYS STREET PERFORMERS OR SOMETHING?
SPEW

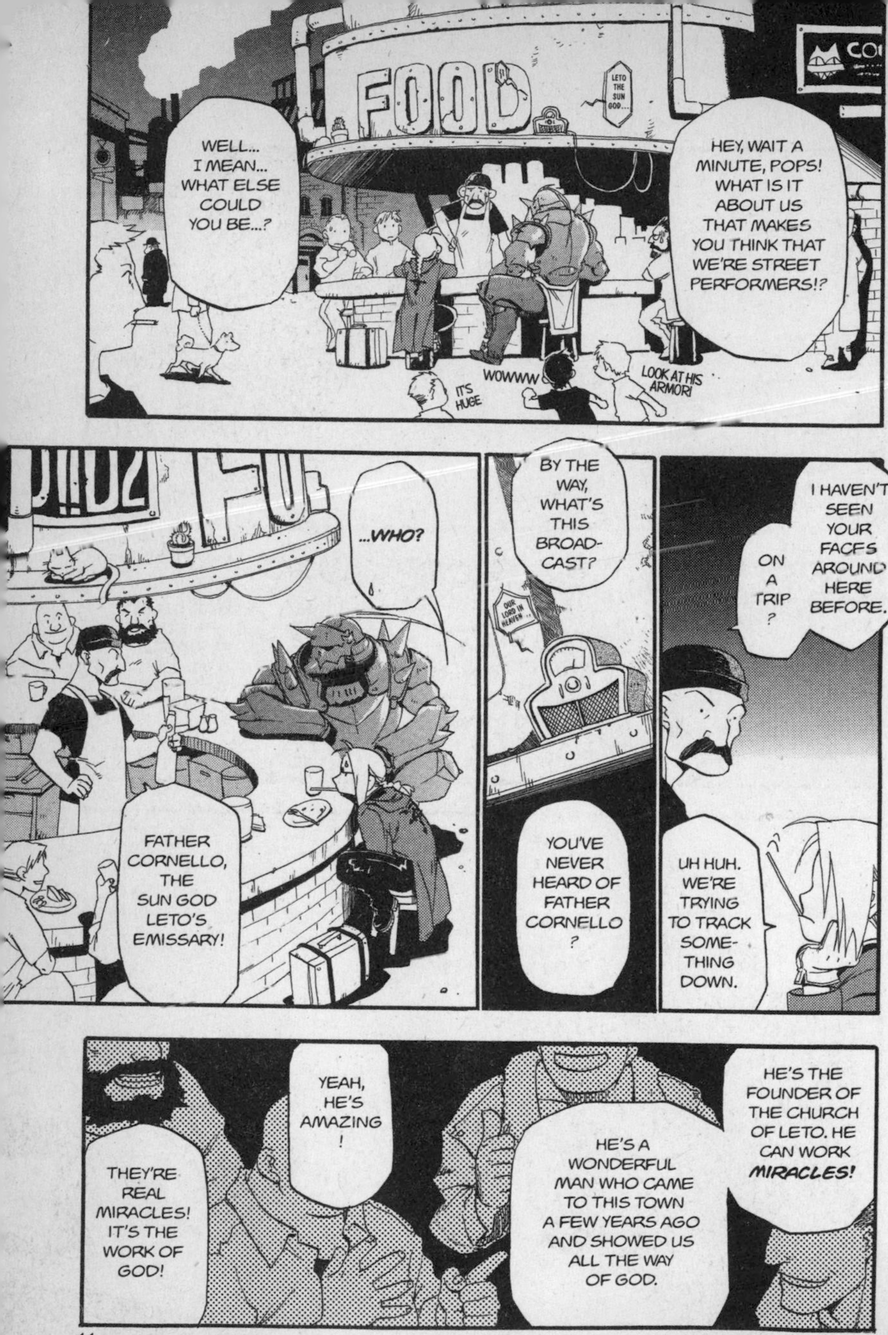
FOOD
LETO THE SUN GOD...
HEY, WAIT A MINUTE, POPS! WHAT IS IT ABOUT US THAT MAKES YOU THINK THAT WE'RE STREET PERFORMERS!?
WELL... I MEAN... WHAT ELSE COULD YOU BE...?
LOOK AT HIS ARMOR!
WOWWW
IT'S HUGE
I HAVEN'T SEEN YOUR FACES AROUND HERE BEFORE.
ON A TRIP?
UH HUH. WE'RE TRYING TO TRACK SOME-THING DOWN.
BY THE WAY, WHAT'S THIS BROAD-CAST?
OUR LORD IN HEAVEN...
YOU'VE NEVER HEARD OF FATHER CORNELLO?
...WHO?
FATHER CORNELLO, THE SUN GOD LETO'S EMISSARY!
HE'S THE FOUNDER OF THE CHURCH OF LETO. HE CAN WORK MIRACLES!
HE'S A WONDERFUL MAN WHO CAME TO THIS TOWN A FEW YEARS AGO AND SHOWED US ALL THE WAY OF GOD.
YEAH, HE'S AMAZING!
THEY'RE REAL MIRACLES! IT'S THE WORK OF GOD!

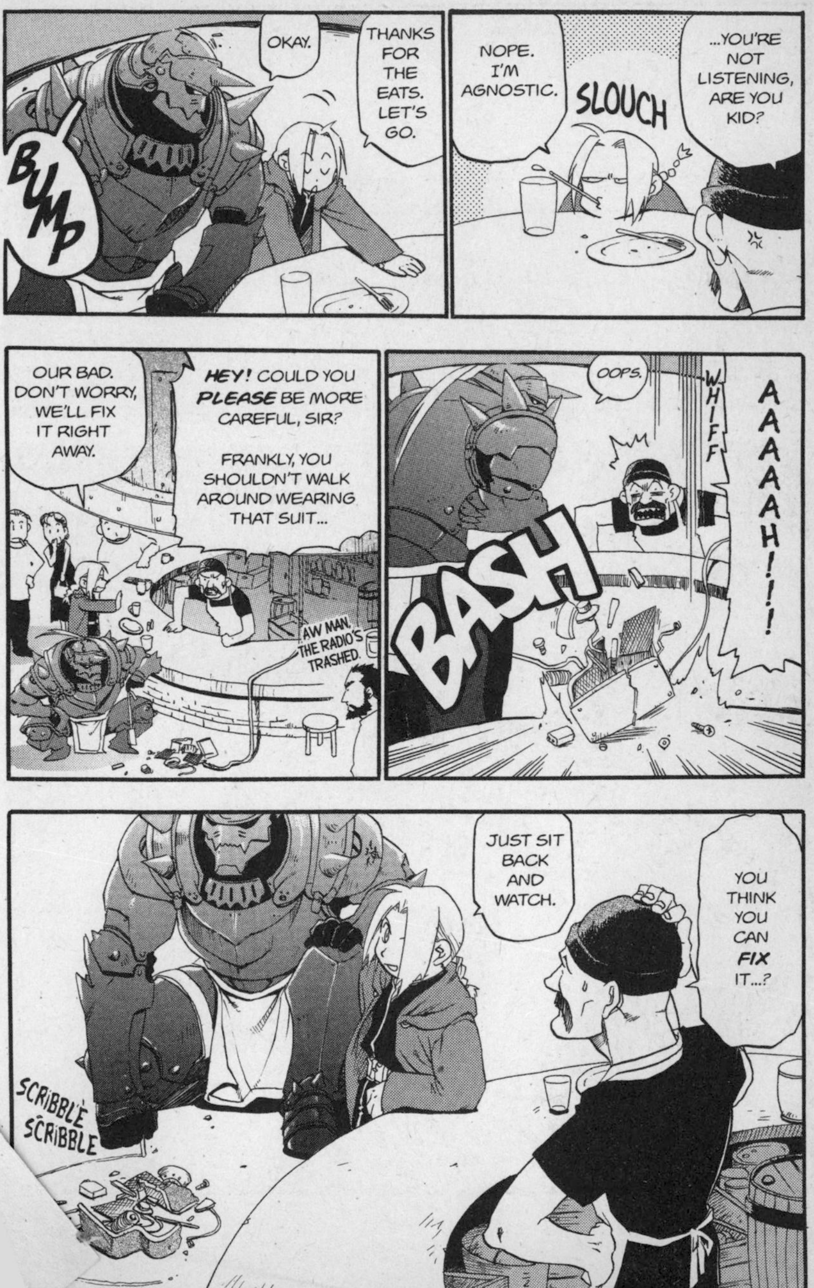
...YOU'RE NOT LISTENING, ARE YOU KID?
NOPE. I'M AGNOSTIC.
SLOUCH
THANKS FOR THE EATS. LET'S GO.
OKAY.
BUMP
AAAAAH!!!
WHIFF
OOPS.
BASH
HEY! COULD YOU PLEASE BE MORE CAREFUL, SIR?
FRANKLY, YOU SHOULDN'T WALK AROUND WEARING THAT SUIT...
OUR BAD. DON'T WORRY, WE'LL FIX IT RIGHT AWAY.
AW MAN, THE RADIO'S TRASHED.
YOU THINK YOU CAN FIX IT...?
JUST SIT BACK AND WATCH.
SCRIBBLE SCRIBBLE

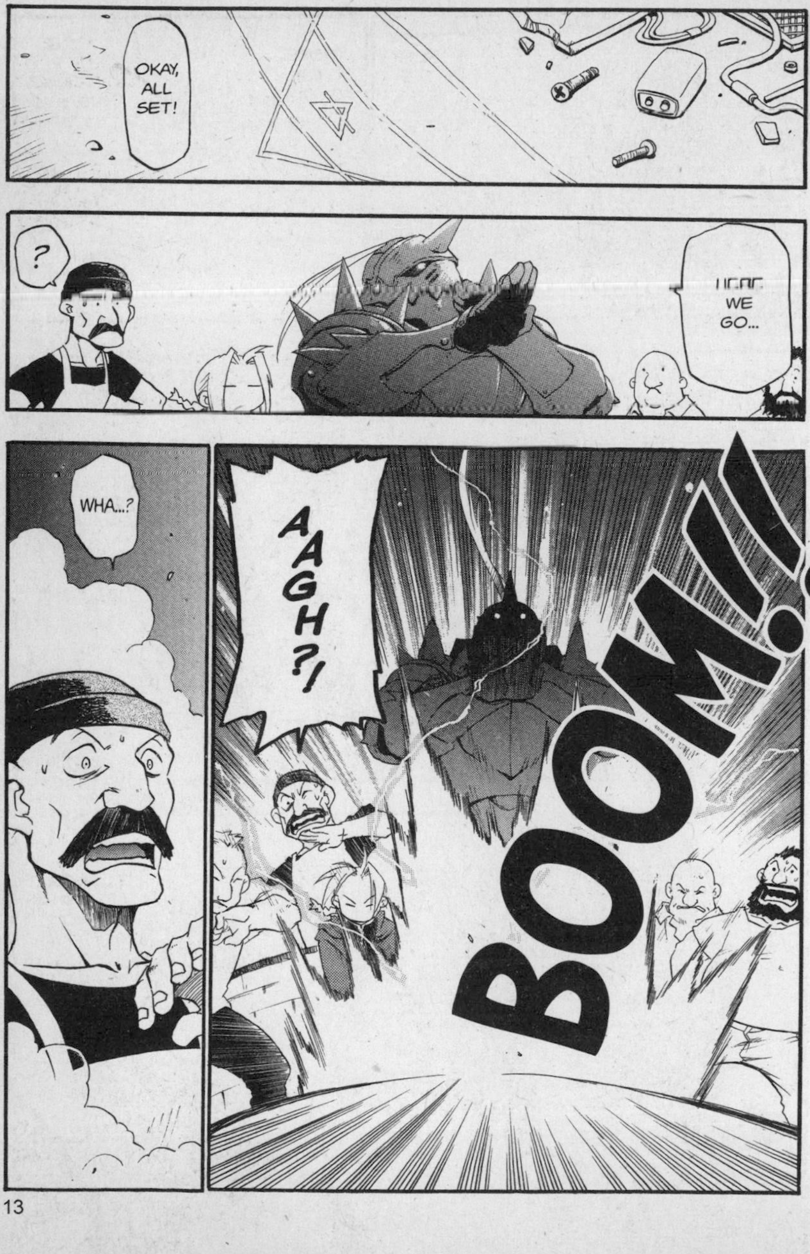

OKAY, ALL SET!
WE GO...
?
BOOM!!!
AAGH?!
WHA...?

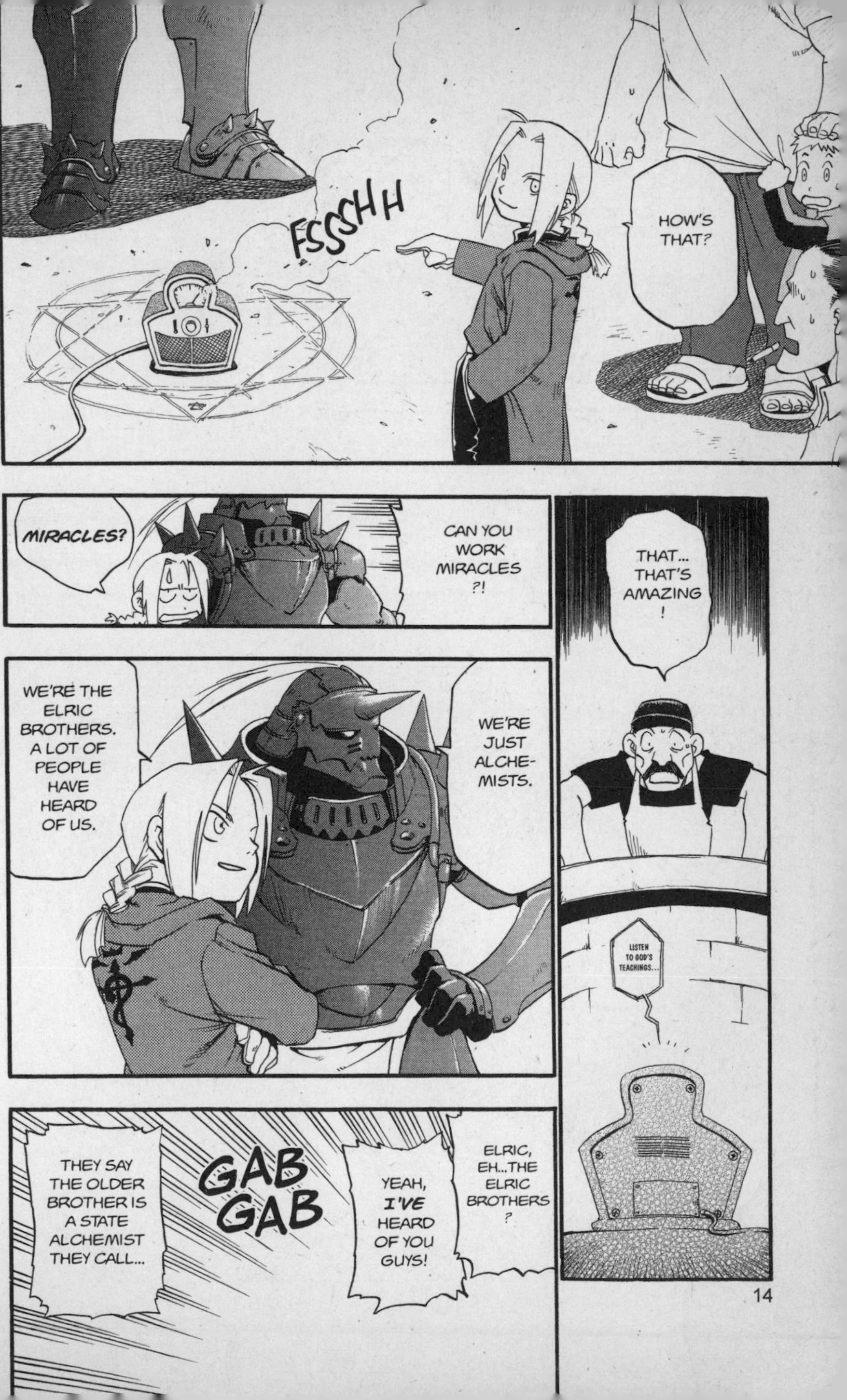
FSSSHH
HOW'S THAT?
THAT... THAT'S AMAZING!
LISTEN TO GOD'S TEACHINGS...
CAN YOU WORK MIRACLES?!
MIRACLES?
WE'RE JUST ALCHEMISTS.
WE'RE THE ELRIC BROTHERS. A LOT OF PEOPLE HAVE HEARD OF US.
ELRIC, EH...THE ELRIC BROTHERS?
YEAH, *I'VE* HEARD OF YOU GUYS!
GAB GAB
THEY SAY THE OLDER BROTHER IS A STATE ALCHEMIST THEY CALL...

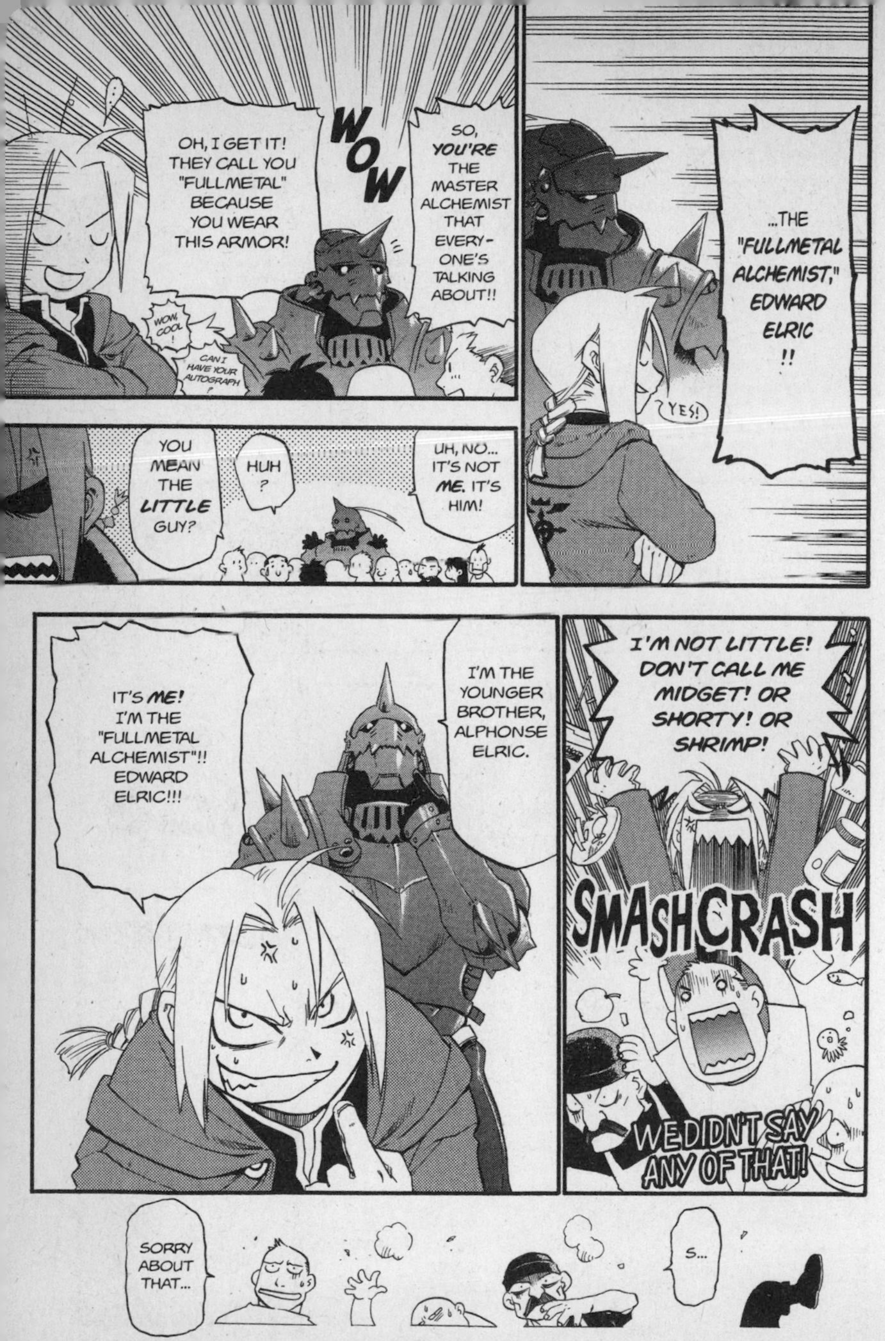
...THE "FULLMETAL ALCHEMIST," EDWARD ELRIC !!
YES!
SO, YOU'RE THE MASTER ALCHEMIST THAT EVERY-ONE'S TALKING ABOUT!!
WOW
OH, I GET IT! THEY CALL YOU "FULLMETAL" BECAUSE YOU WEAR THIS ARMOR!
WOW, COOL!
CAN I HAVE YOUR AUTOGRAPH?
UH, NO... IT'S NOT ME. IT'S HIM!
HUH?
YOU MEAN THE LITTLE GUY?
I'M NOT LITTLE! DON'T CALL ME MIDGET! OR SHORTY! OR SHRIMP!
SMASH CRASH
WE DIDN'T SAY ANY OF THAT!
I'M THE YOUNGER BROTHER, ALPHONSE ELRIC.
IT'S ME! I'M THE "FULLMETAL ALCHEMIST"!! EDWARD ELRIC!!!
S...
SORRY ABOUT THAT...

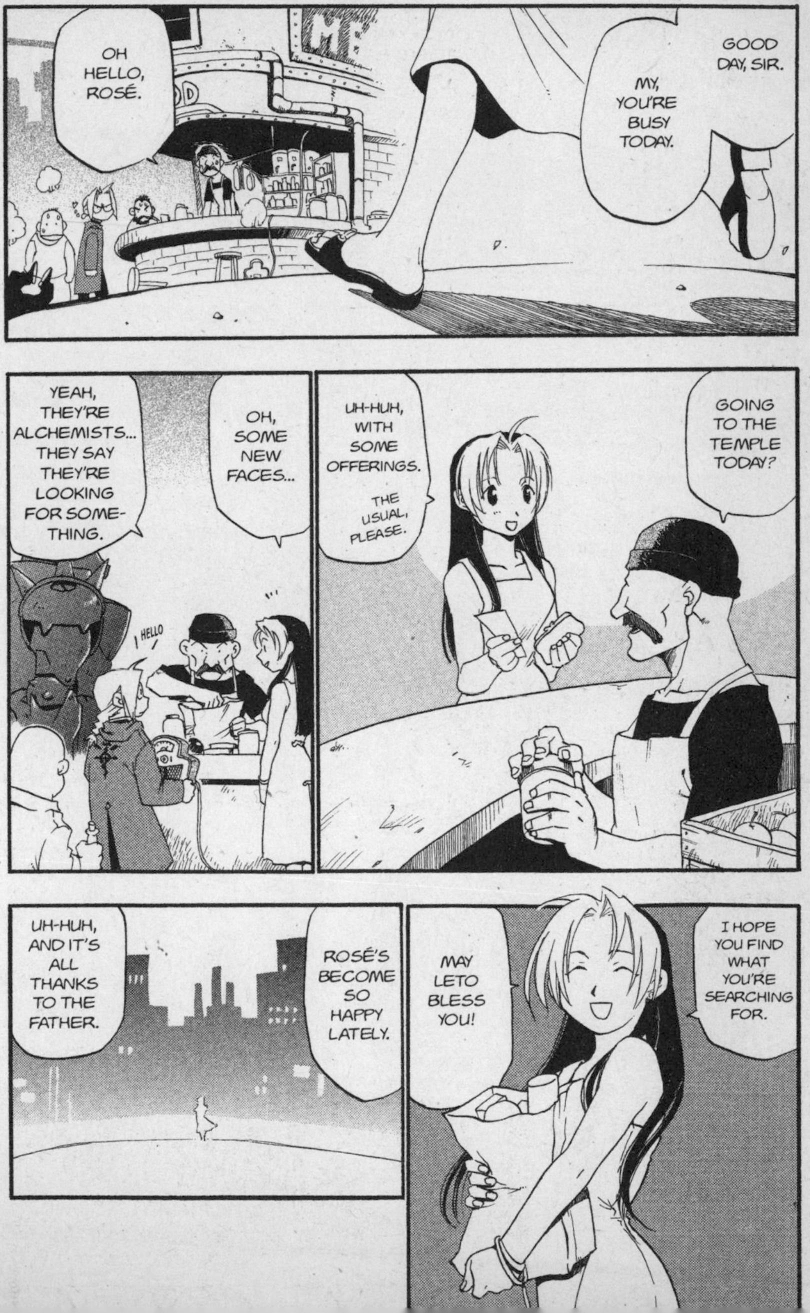
GOOD DAY, SIR.
MY, YOU'RE BUSY TODAY.
OH HELLO, ROSÉ.
GOING TO THE TEMPLE TODAY?
UH-HUH, WITH SOME OFFERINGS.
THE USUAL, PLEASE.
OH, SOME NEW FACES...
YEAH, THEY'RE ALCHEMISTS... THEY SAY THEY'RE LOOKING FOR SOME-THING.
HELLO
I HOPE YOU FIND WHAT YOU'RE SEARCHING FOR.
MAY LETO BLESS YOU!
ROSÉ'S BECOME SO HAPPY LATELY.
UH-HUH, AND IT'S ALL THANKS TO THE FATHER.

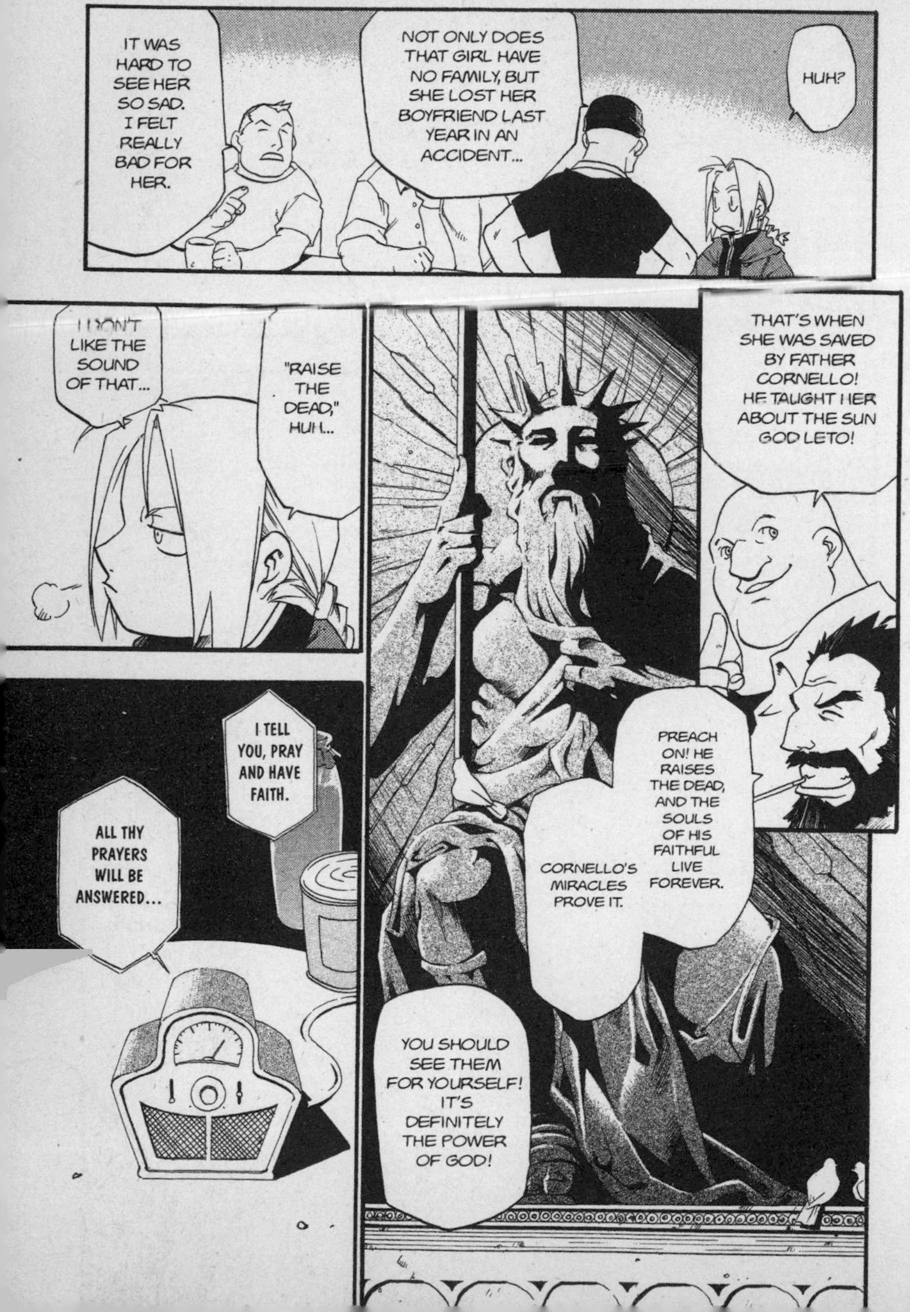
HUH?
NOT ONLY DOES THAT GIRL HAVE NO FAMILY, BUT SHE LOST HER BOYFRIEND LAST YEAR IN AN ACCIDENT...
IT WAS HARD TO SEE HER SO SAD. I FELT REALLY BAD FOR HER.
THAT'S WHEN SHE WAS SAVED BY FATHER CORNELLO! HE TAUGHT HER ABOUT THE SUN GOD LETO!
PREACH ON! HE RAISES THE DEAD, AND THE SOULS OF HIS FAITHFUL LIVE FOREVER.
CORNELLO'S MIRACLES PROVE IT.
YOU SHOULD SEE THEM FOR YOURSELF! IT'S DEFINITELY THE POWER OF GOD!
"RAISE THE DEAD," HUH...
I DON'T LIKE THE SOUND OF THAT...
I TELL YOU, PRAY AND HAVE FAITH.
ALL THY PRAYERS WILL BE ANSWERED...

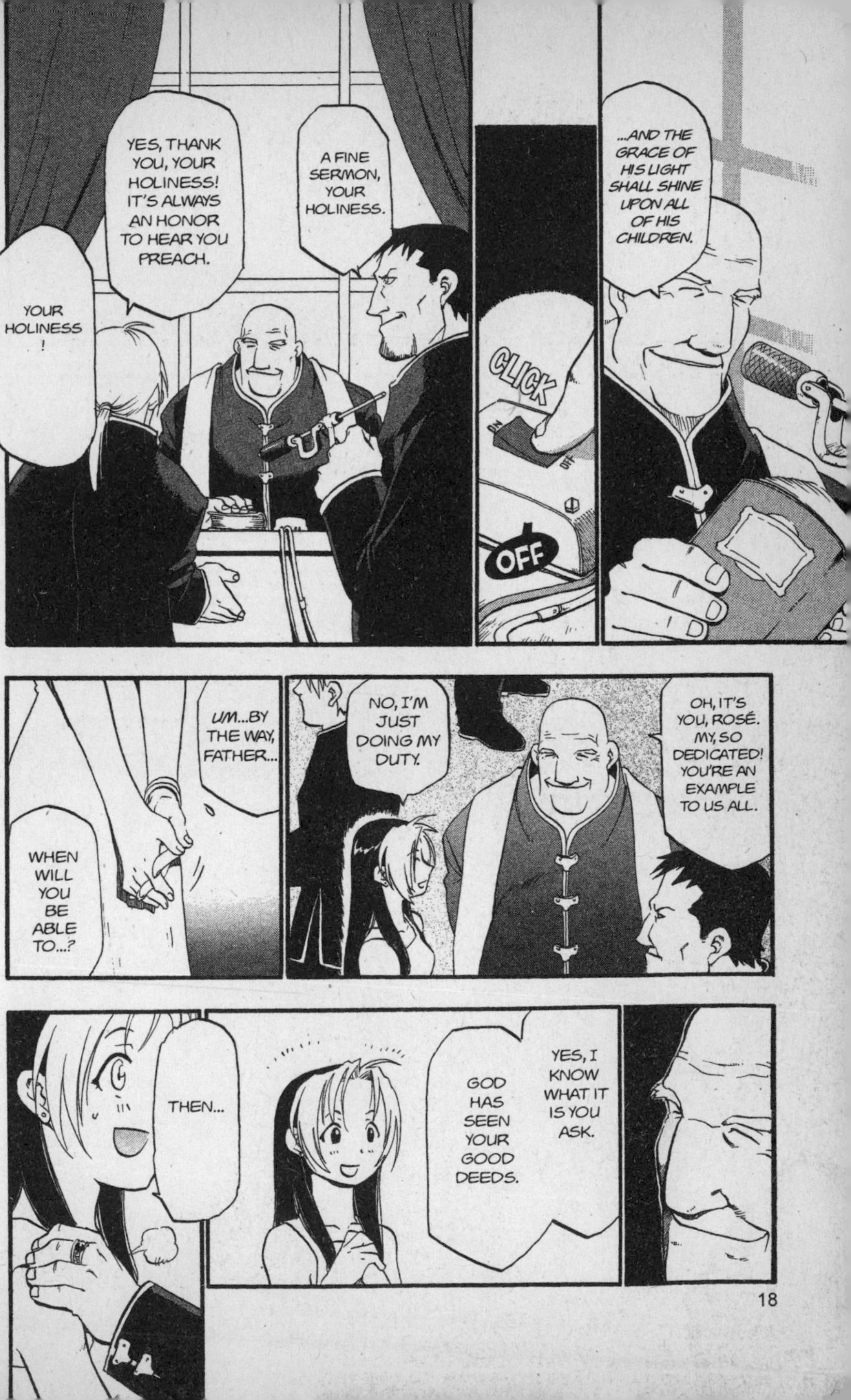

...AND THE GRACE OF HIS LIGHT SHALL SHINE UPON ALL OF HIS CHILDREN.
CLICK
ON
OFF
OFF
A FINE SERMON, YOUR HOLINESS.
YES, THANK YOU, YOUR HOLINESS! IT'S ALWAYS AN HONOR TO HEAR YOU PREACH.
YOUR HOLINESS!
OH, IT'S YOU, ROSÉ. MY, SO DEDICATED! YOU'RE AN EXAMPLE TO US ALL.
NO, I'M JUST DOING MY DUTY.
UM...BY THE WAY, FATHER...
WHEN WILL YOU BE ABLE TO...?
YES, I KNOW WHAT IT IS YOU ASK.
GOD HAS SEEN YOUR GOOD DEEDS.
THEN...

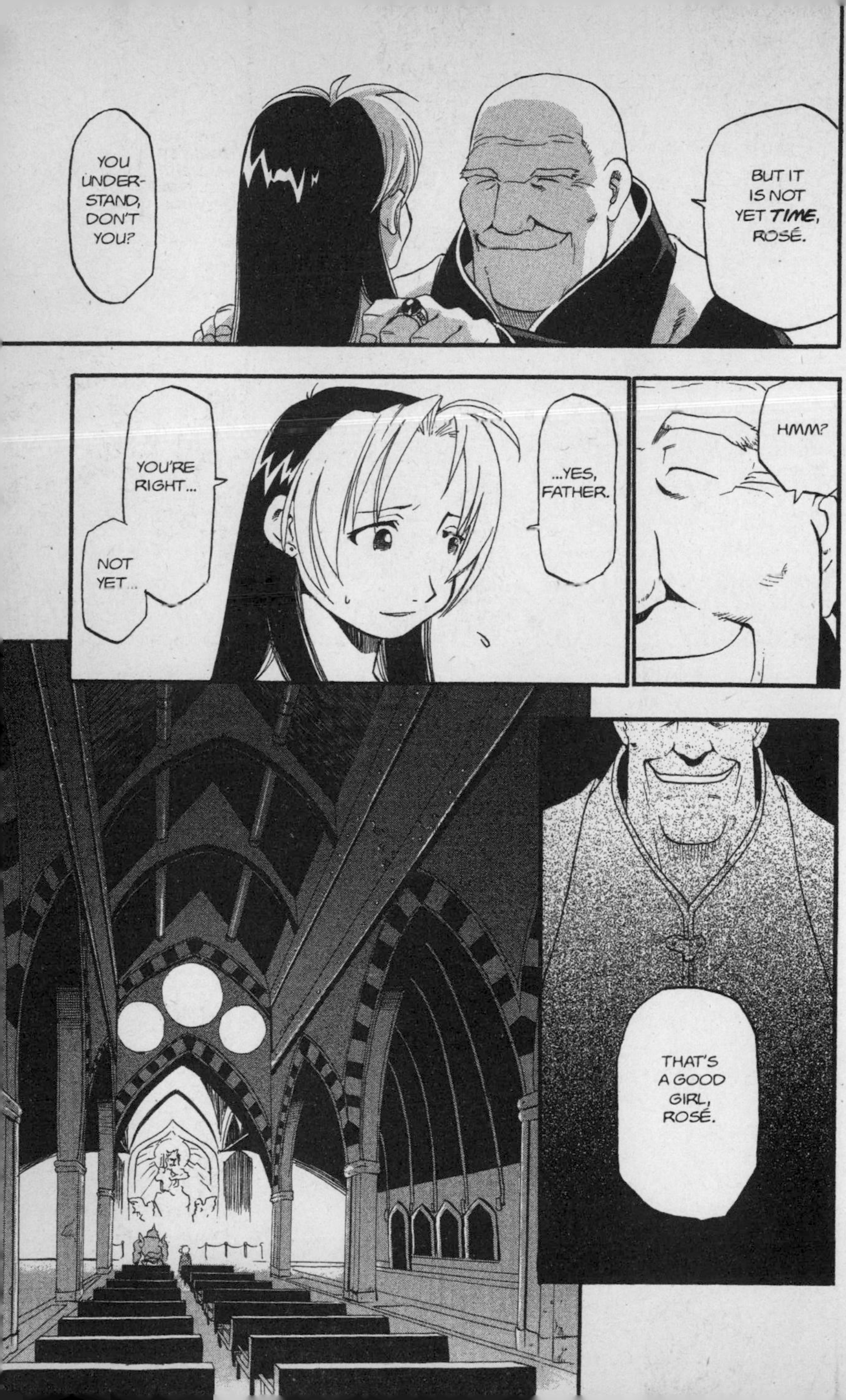
BUT IT IS NOT YET TIME, ROSÉ.
YOU UNDERSTAND, DON'T YOU?
HMM?
...YES, FATHER.
YOU'RE RIGHT...
NOT YET...
THAT'S A GOOD GIRL, ROSÉ.

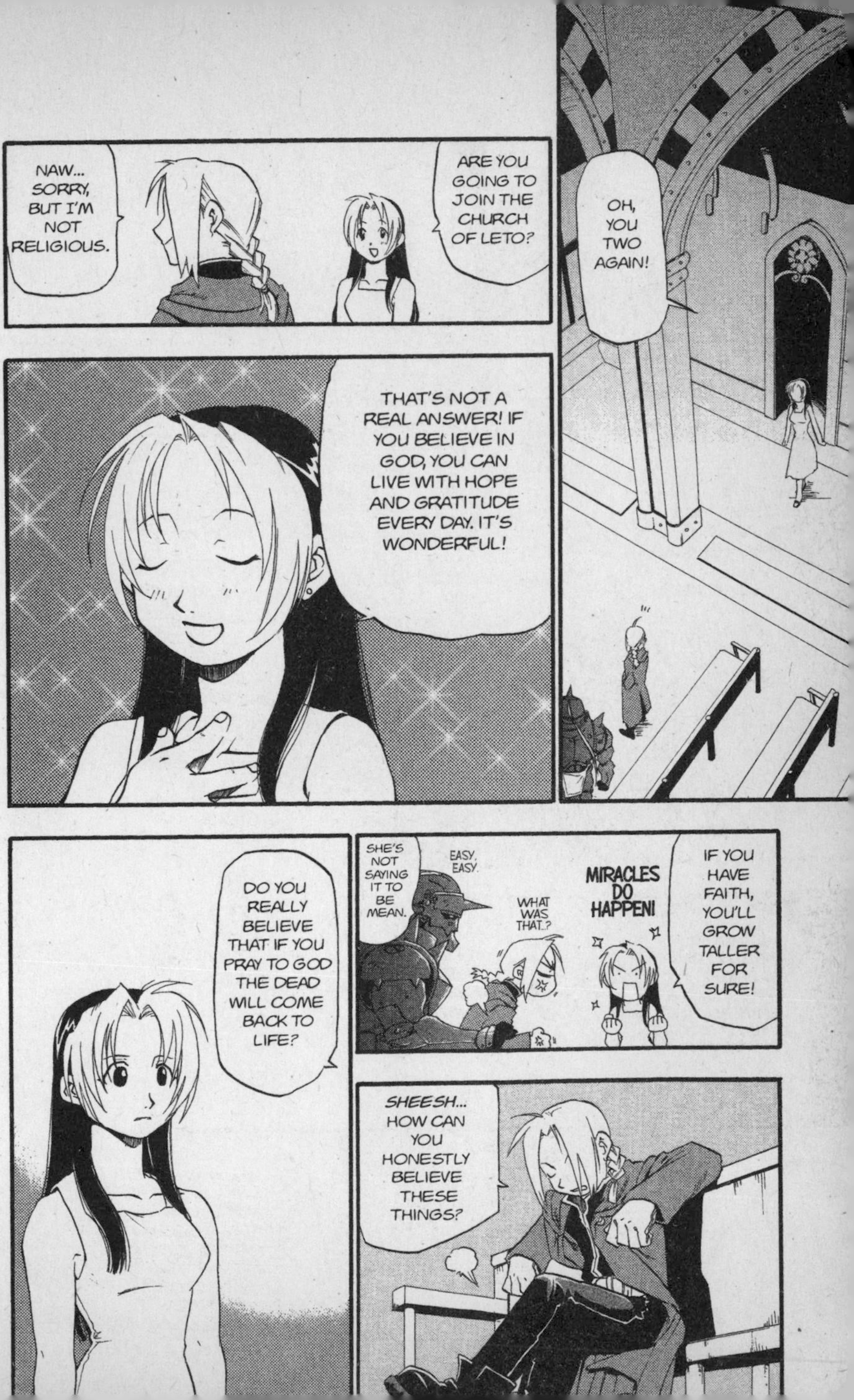
OH, YOU TWO AGAIN!
ARE YOU GOING TO JOIN THE CHURCH OF LETO?
NAW... SORRY, BUT I'M NOT RELIGIOUS.
THAT'S NOT A REAL ANSWER! IF YOU BELIEVE IN GOD, YOU CAN LIVE WITH HOPE AND GRATITUDE EVERY DAY. IT'S WONDERFUL!
IF YOU HAVE FAITH, YOU'LL GROW TALLER FOR SURE!
MIRACLES DO HAPPEN!
WHAT WAS THAT..?
EASY, EASY.
SHE'S NOT SAYING IT TO BE MEAN.
SHEESH... HOW CAN YOU HONESTLY BELIEVE THESE THINGS?
DO YOU REALLY BELIEVE THAT IF YOU PRAY TO GOD THE DEAD WILL COME BACK TO LIFE?

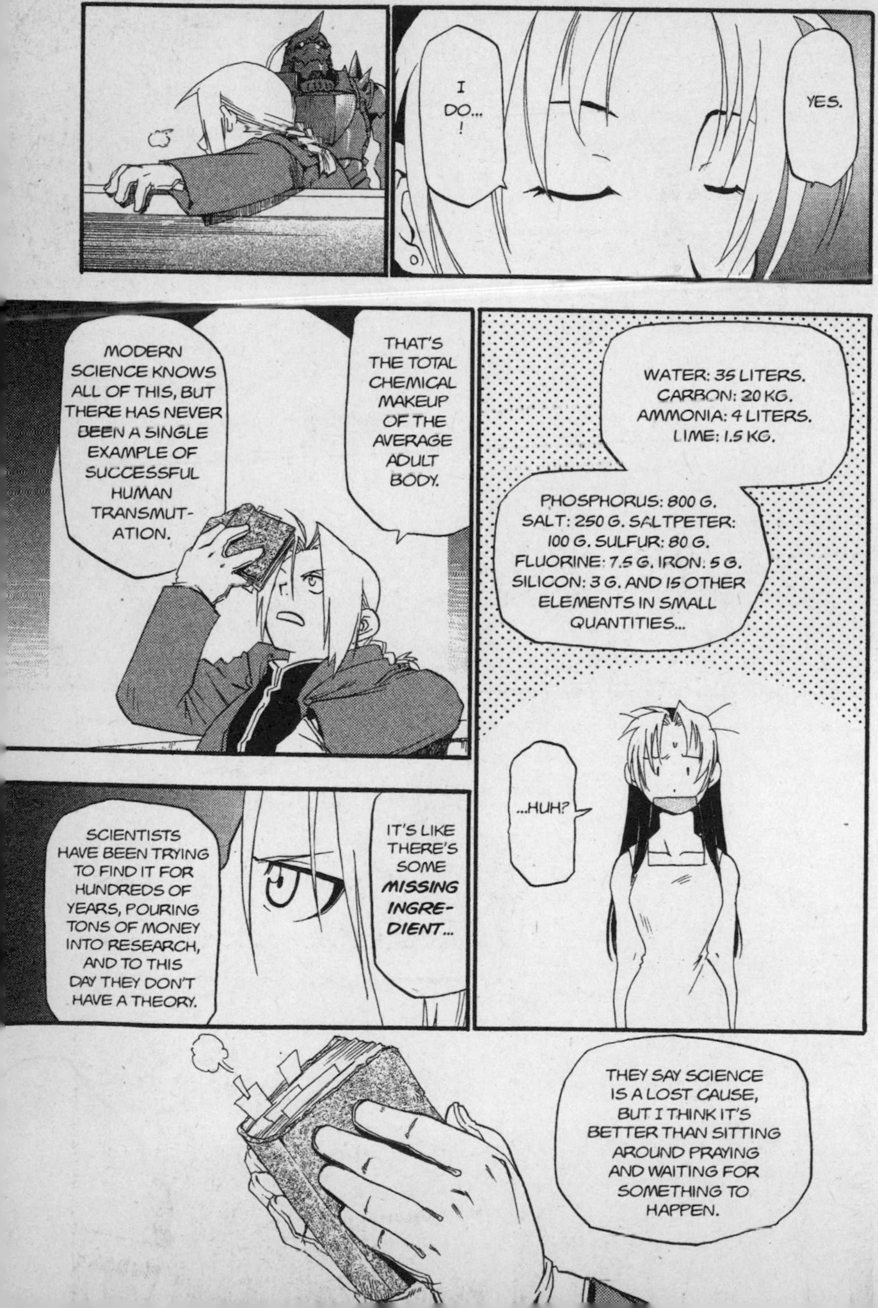
YES.
I DO...!
WATER: 35 LITERS. CARBON: 20 KG. AMMONIA: 4 LITERS. LIME: 1.5 KG.
PHOSPHORUS: 800 G. SALT: 250 G. SALTPETER: 100 G. SULFUR: 80 G. FLUORINE: 7.5 G. IRON: 5 G. SILICON: 3 G. AND 15 OTHER ELEMENTS IN SMALL QUANTITIES...
...HUH?
THAT'S THE TOTAL CHEMICAL MAKEUP OF THE AVERAGE ADULT BODY.
MODERN SCIENCE KNOWS ALL OF THIS, BUT THERE HAS NEVER BEEN A SINGLE EXAMPLE OF SUCCESSFUL HUMAN TRANSMUT-ATION.
IT'S LIKE THERE'S SOME *MISSING INGRE-DIENT*...
SCIENTISTS HAVE BEEN TRYING TO FIND IT FOR HUNDREDS OF YEARS, POURING TONS OF MONEY INTO RESEARCH, AND TO THIS DAY THEY DON'T HAVE A THEORY.
THEY SAY SCIENCE IS A LOST CAUSE, BUT I THINK IT'S BETTER THAN SITTING AROUND PRAYING AND WAITING FOR SOMETHING TO HAPPEN.

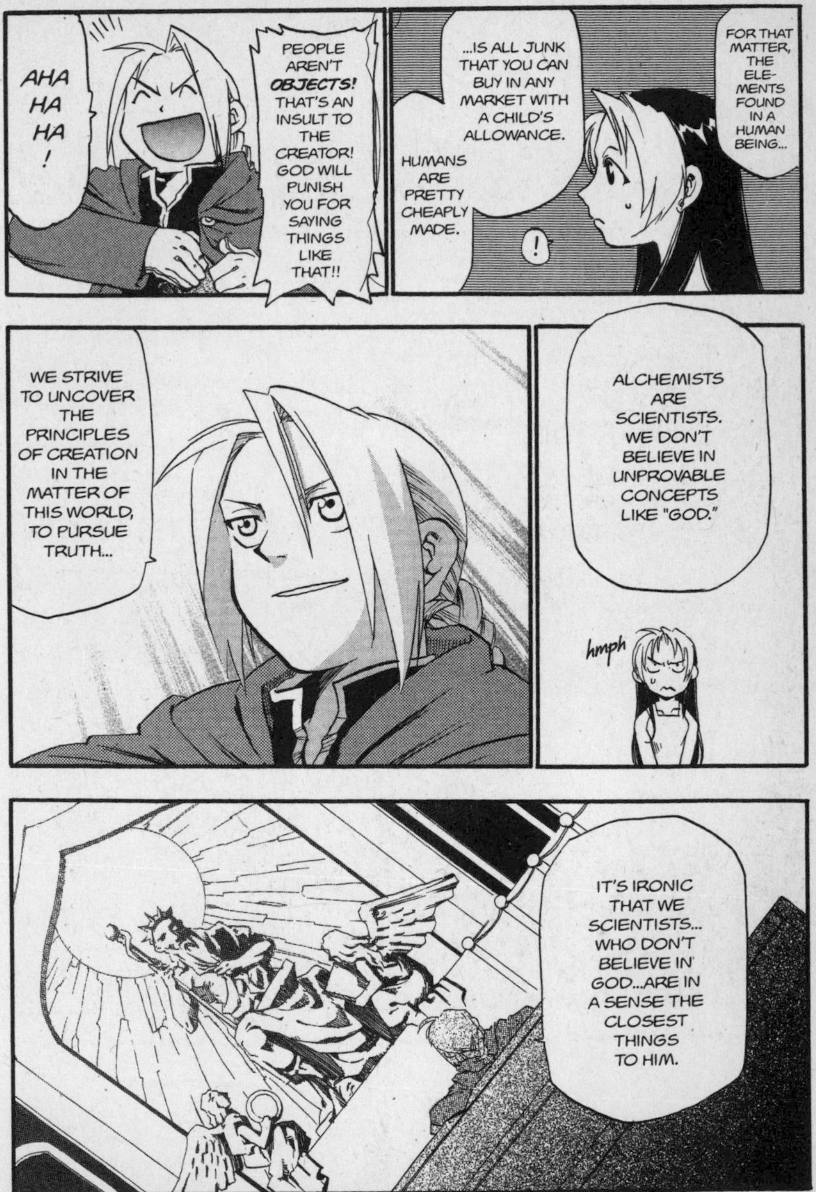
FOR THAT MATTER, THE ELE-MENTS FOUND IN A HUMAN BEING...
...IS ALL JUNK THAT YOU CAN BUY IN ANY MARKET WITH A CHILD'S ALLOWANCE.
HUMANS ARE PRETTY CHEAPLY MADE.
!
PEOPLE AREN'T ***OBJECTS!*** THAT'S AN INSULT TO THE CREATOR! GOD WILL PUNISH YOU FOR SAYING THINGS LIKE THAT!!
AHA HA HA!
ALCHEMISTS ARE SCIENTISTS. WE DON'T BELIEVE IN UNPROVABLE CONCEPTS LIKE "GOD."
hmph
WE STRIVE TO UNCOVER THE PRINCIPLES OF CREATION IN THE MATTER OF THIS WORLD, TO PURSUE TRUTH...
IT'S IRONIC THAT WE SCIENTISTS... WHO DON'T BELIEVE IN GOD...ARE IN A SENSE THE CLOSEST THINGS TO HIM.

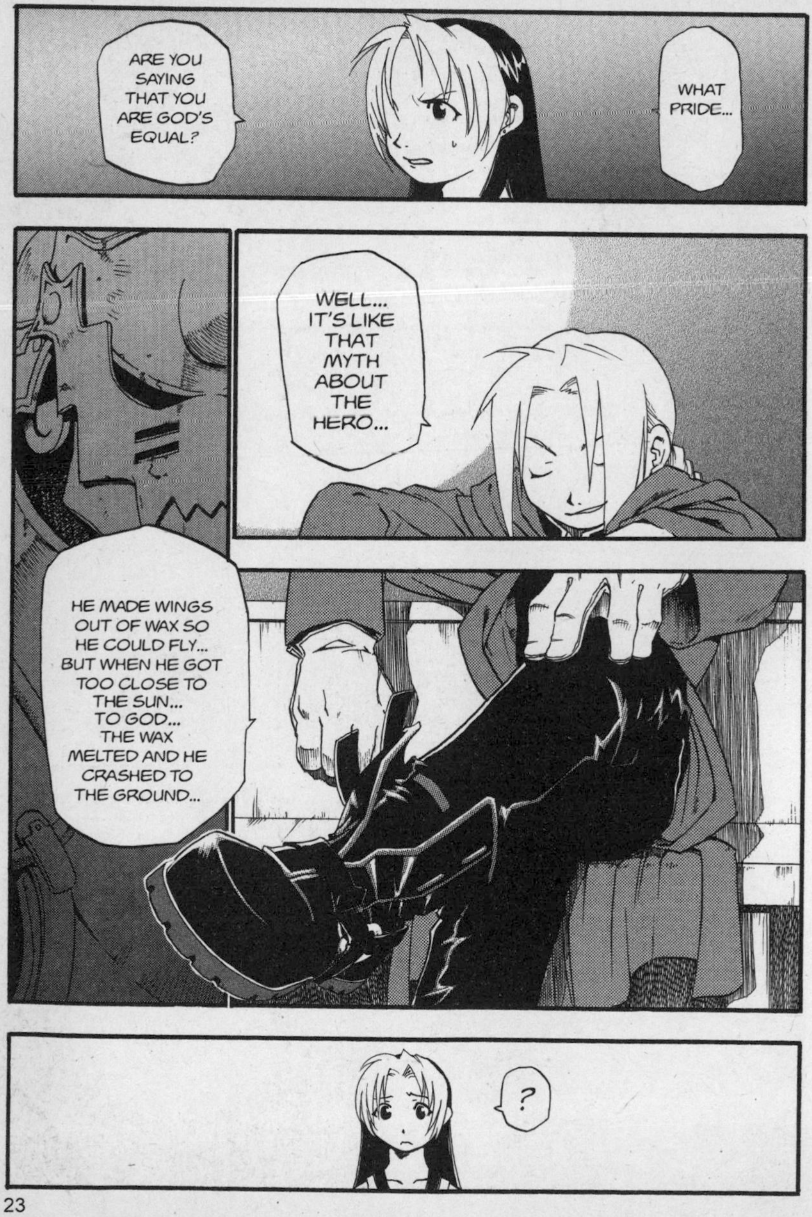
WHAT PRIDE...
ARE YOU SAYING THAT YOU ARE GOD'S EQUAL?
WELL... IT'S LIKE THAT MYTH ABOUT THE HERO...
HE MADE WINGS OUT OF WAX SO HE COULD FLY... BUT WHEN HE GOT TOO CLOSE TO THE SUN... TO GOD... THE WAX MELTED AND HE CRASHED TO THE GROUND...
?

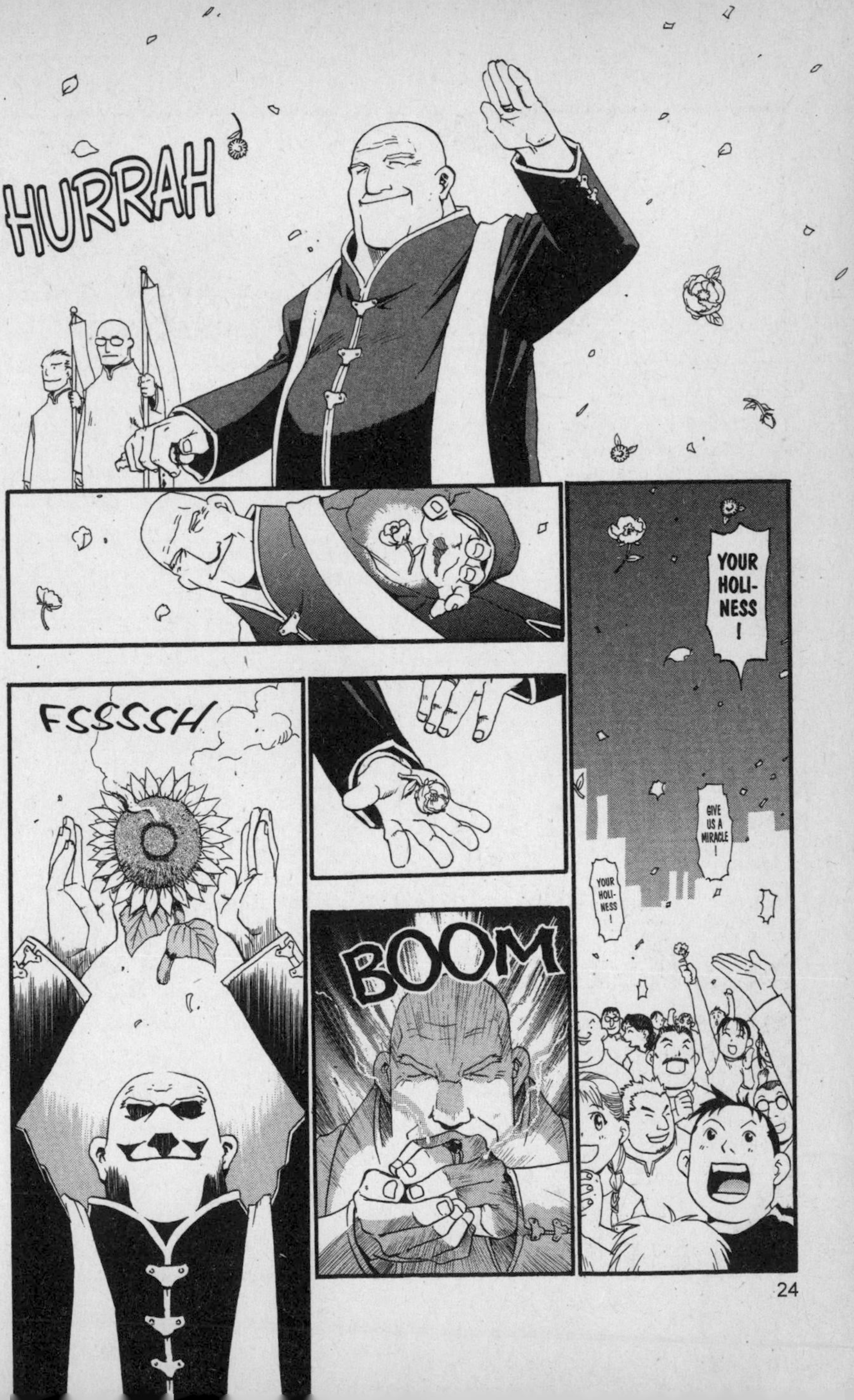
HURRAH
YOUR HOLI-NESS !
GIVE US A MIRACLE !
YOUR HOLI-NESS !
BOOM
FSSSSH

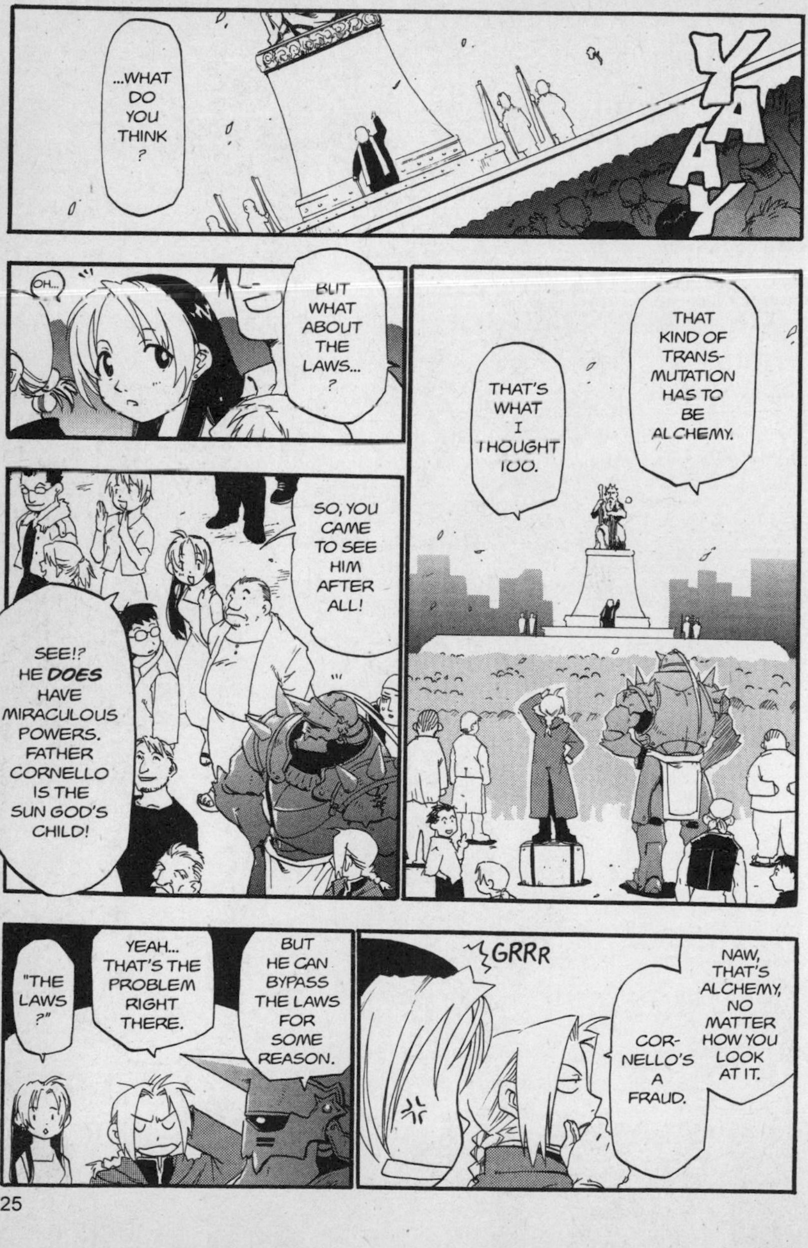
YAAY
...WHAT DO YOU THINK?
THAT KIND OF TRANSMUTATION HAS TO BE ALCHEMY.
THAT'S WHAT I THOUGHT TOO.
BUT WHAT ABOUT THE LAWS...?
OH...
SO, YOU CAME TO SEE HIM AFTER ALL!
SEE!? HE **DOES** HAVE MIRACULOUS POWERS. FATHER CORNELLO IS THE SUN GOD'S CHILD!
NAW, THAT'S ALCHEMY, NO MATTER HOW YOU LOOK AT IT.
GRRR
CORNELLO'S A FRAUD.
BUT HE CAN BYPASS THE LAWS FOR SOME REASON.
YEAH... THAT'S THE PROBLEM RIGHT THERE.
"THE LAWS?"

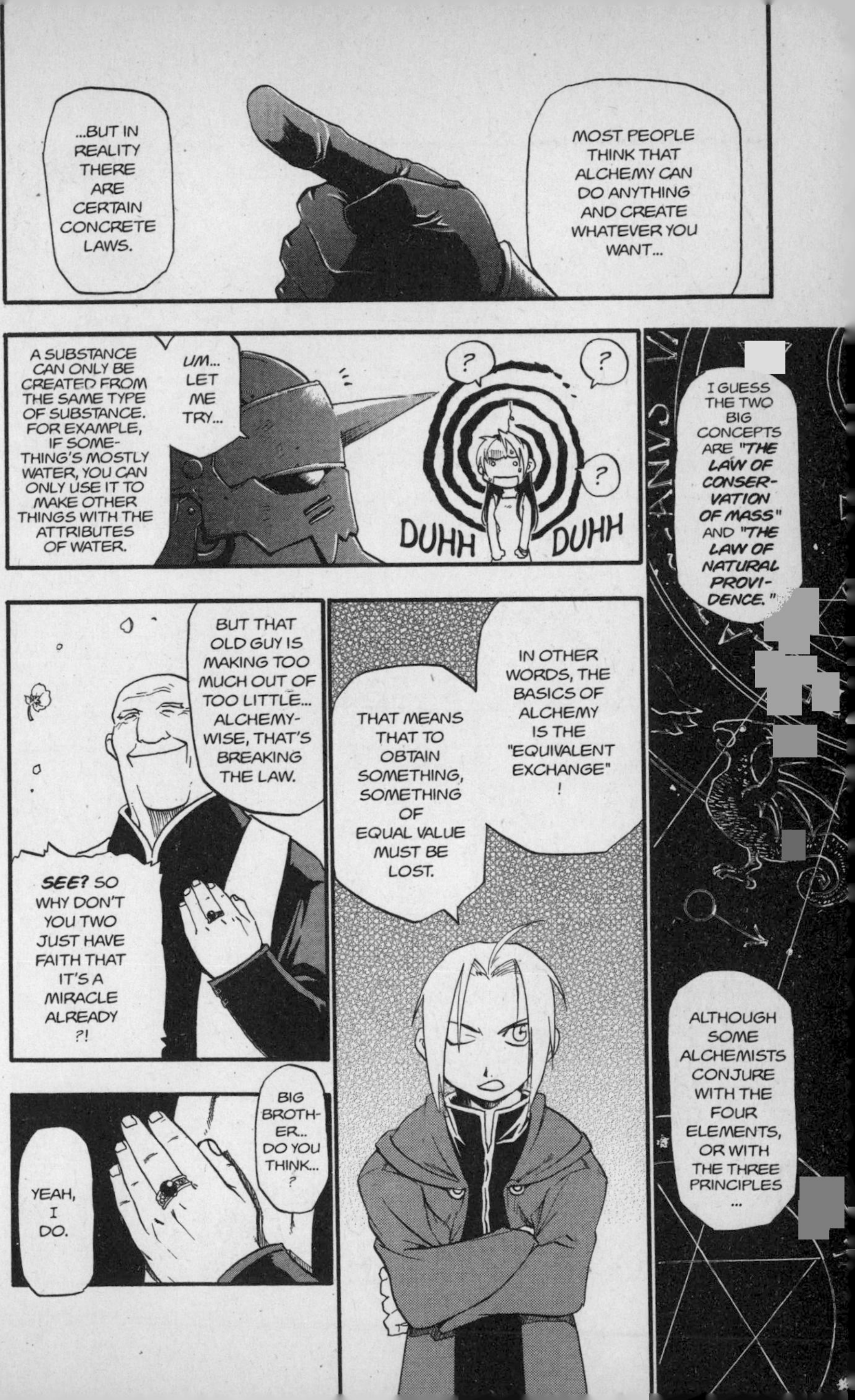
MOST PEOPLE THINK THAT ALCHEMY CAN DO ANYTHING AND CREATE WHATEVER YOU WANT...
...BUT IN REALITY THERE ARE CERTAIN CONCRETE LAWS.
I GUESS THE TWO BIG CONCEPTS ARE "THE LAW OF CONSERVATION OF MASS" AND "THE LAW OF NATURAL PROVIDENCE."
ALTHOUGH SOME ALCHEMISTS CONJURE WITH THE FOUR ELEMENTS, OR WITH THE THREE PRINCIPLES...
?
?
?
UM... LET ME TRY...
A SUBSTANCE CAN ONLY BE CREATED FROM THE SAME TYPE OF SUBSTANCE. FOR EXAMPLE, IF SOMETHING'S MOSTLY WATER, YOU CAN ONLY USE IT TO MAKE OTHER THINGS WITH THE ATTRIBUTES OF WATER.
DUHH
DUHH
IN OTHER WORDS, THE BASICS OF ALCHEMY IS THE "EQUIVALENT EXCHANGE"!
THAT MEANS THAT TO OBTAIN SOMETHING, SOMETHING OF EQUAL VALUE MUST BE LOST.
BUT THAT OLD GUY IS MAKING TOO MUCH OUT OF TOO LITTLE... ALCHEMY-WISE, THAT'S BREAKING THE LAW.
SEE? SO WHY DON'T YOU TWO JUST HAVE FAITH THAT IT'S A MIRACLE ALREADY?!
BIG BROTHER... DO YOU THINK...?
YEAH, I DO.

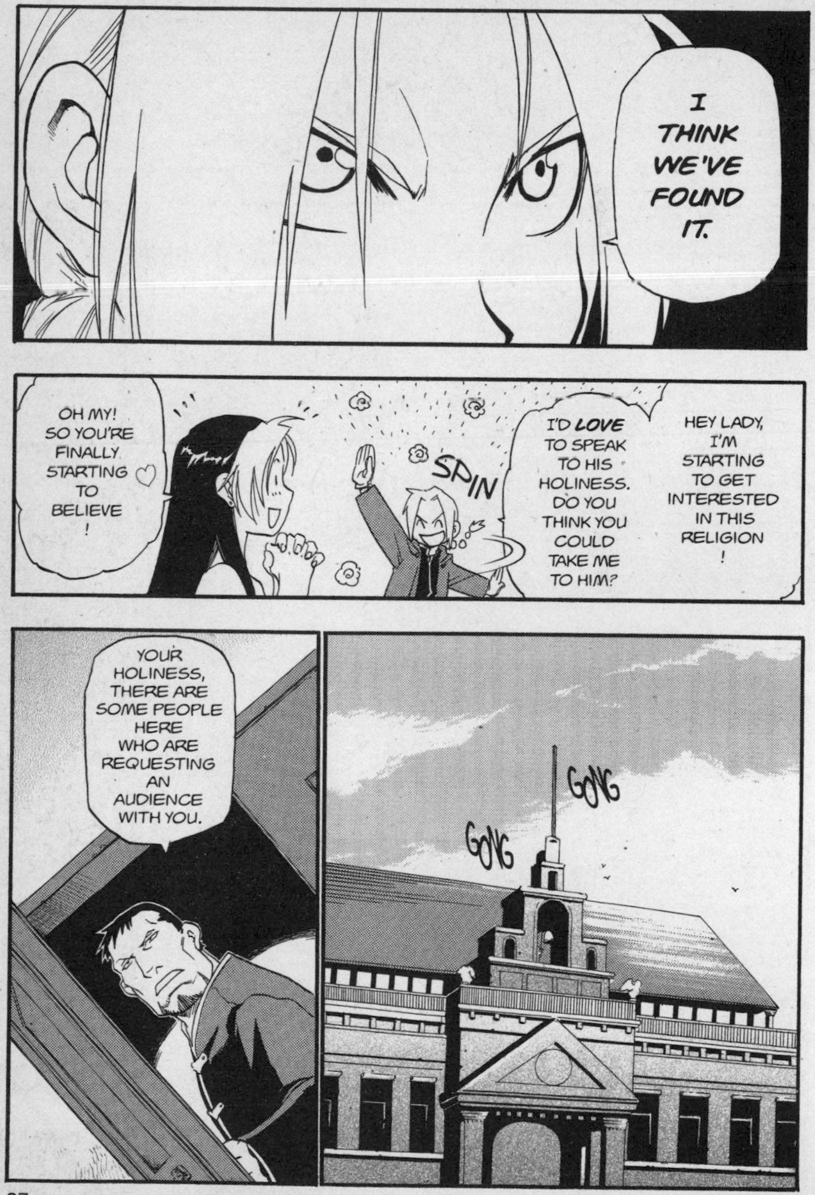
I THINK WE'VE FOUND IT.
HEY LADY, I'M STARTING TO GET INTERESTED IN THIS RELIGION!
I'D **LOVE** TO SPEAK TO HIS HOLINESS. DO YOU THINK YOU COULD TAKE ME TO HIM?
SPIN
OH MY! SO YOU'RE FINALLY STARTING TO BELIEVE ♡!
GONG
GONG
YOUR HOLINESS, THERE ARE SOME PEOPLE HERE WHO ARE REQUESTING AN AUDIENCE WITH YOU.

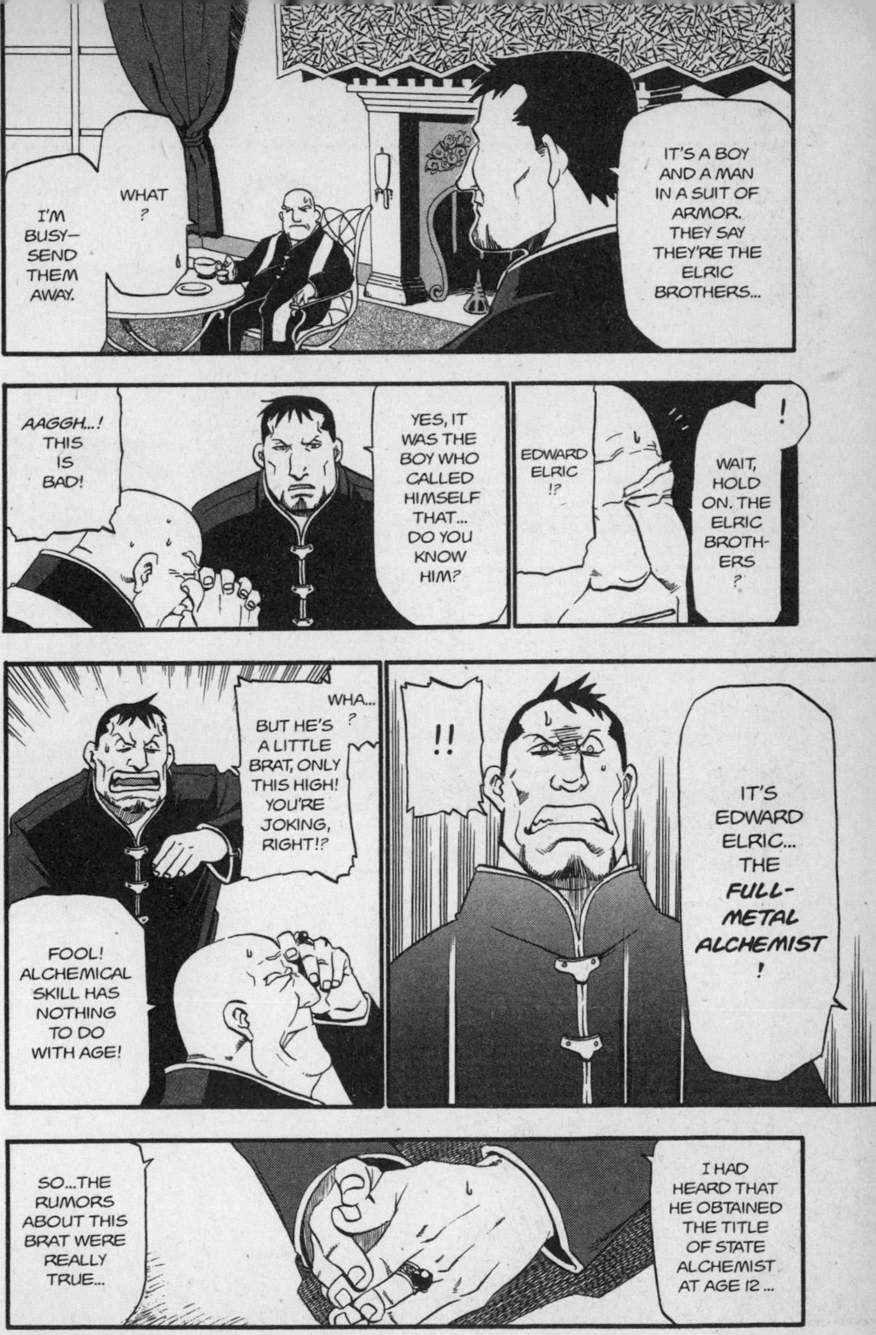
IT'S A BOY AND A MAN IN A SUIT OF ARMOR. THEY SAY THEY'RE THE ELRIC BROTHERS...
WHAT?
I'M BUSY— SEND THEM AWAY.
!
WAIT, HOLD ON. THE ELRIC BROTHERS?
EDWARD ELRIC!?
YES, IT WAS THE BOY WHO CALLED HIMSELF THAT... DO YOU KNOW HIM?
AAGGH...! THIS IS BAD!
IT'S EDWARD ELRIC... THE **FULL-METAL ALCHEMIST**!
!!
WHA...?
BUT HE'S A LITTLE BRAT, ONLY THIS HIGH! YOU'RE JOKING, RIGHT!?
FOOL! ALCHEMICAL SKILL HAS NOTHING TO DO WITH AGE!
I HAD HEARD THAT HE OBTAINED THE TITLE OF STATE ALCHEMIST AT AGE 12...
SO...THE RUMORS ABOUT THIS BRAT WERE REALLY TRUE...

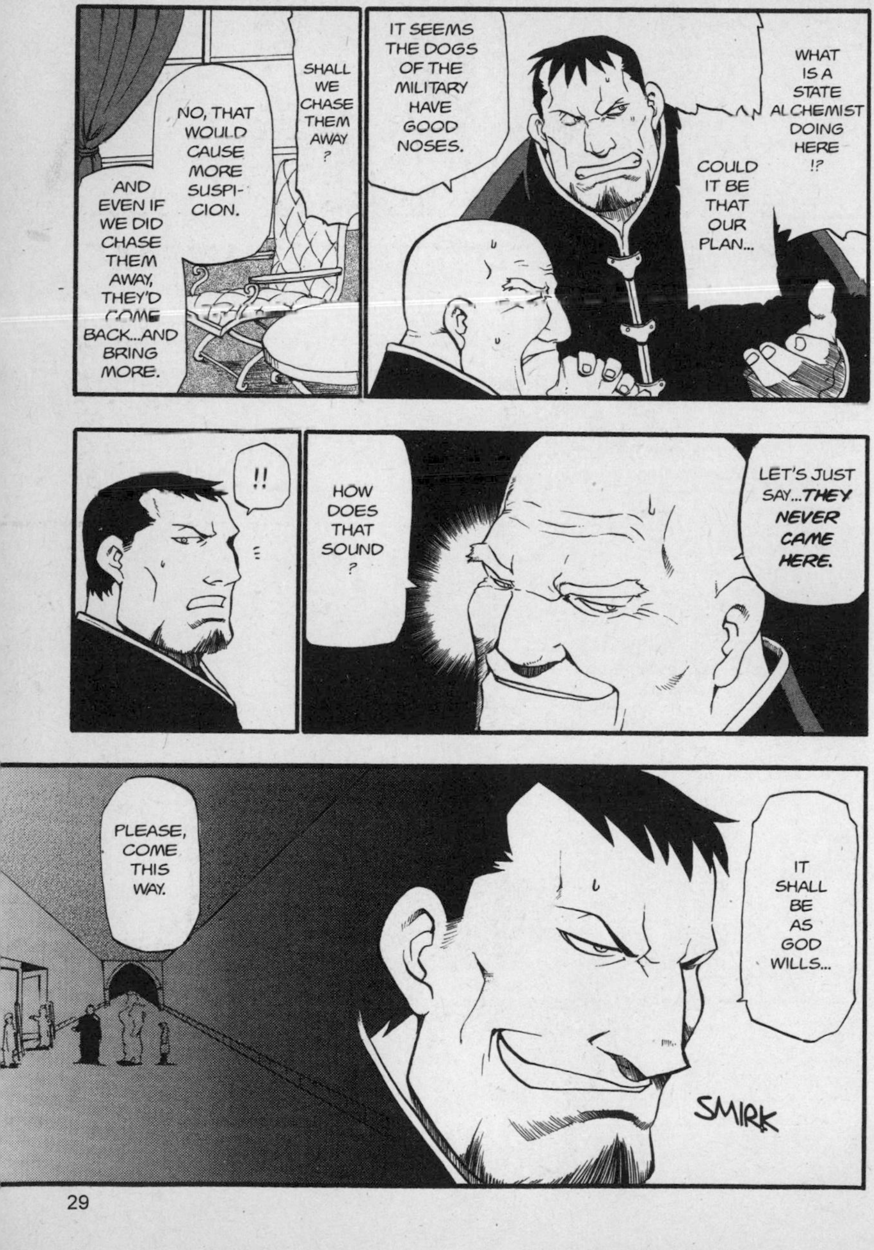
WHAT IS A STATE ALCHEMIST DOING HERE!?
COULD IT BE THAT OUR PLAN...
IT SEEMS THE DOGS OF THE MILITARY HAVE GOOD NOSES.
SHALL WE CHASE THEM AWAY?
NO, THAT WOULD CAUSE MORE SUSPICION.
AND EVEN IF WE DID CHASE THEM AWAY, THEY'D COME BACK...AND BRING MORE.
LET'S JUST SAY...*THEY NEVER CAME HERE.*
HOW DOES THAT SOUND?
!!
IT SHALL BE AS GOD WILLS...
SMIRK
PLEASE, COME THIS WAY.

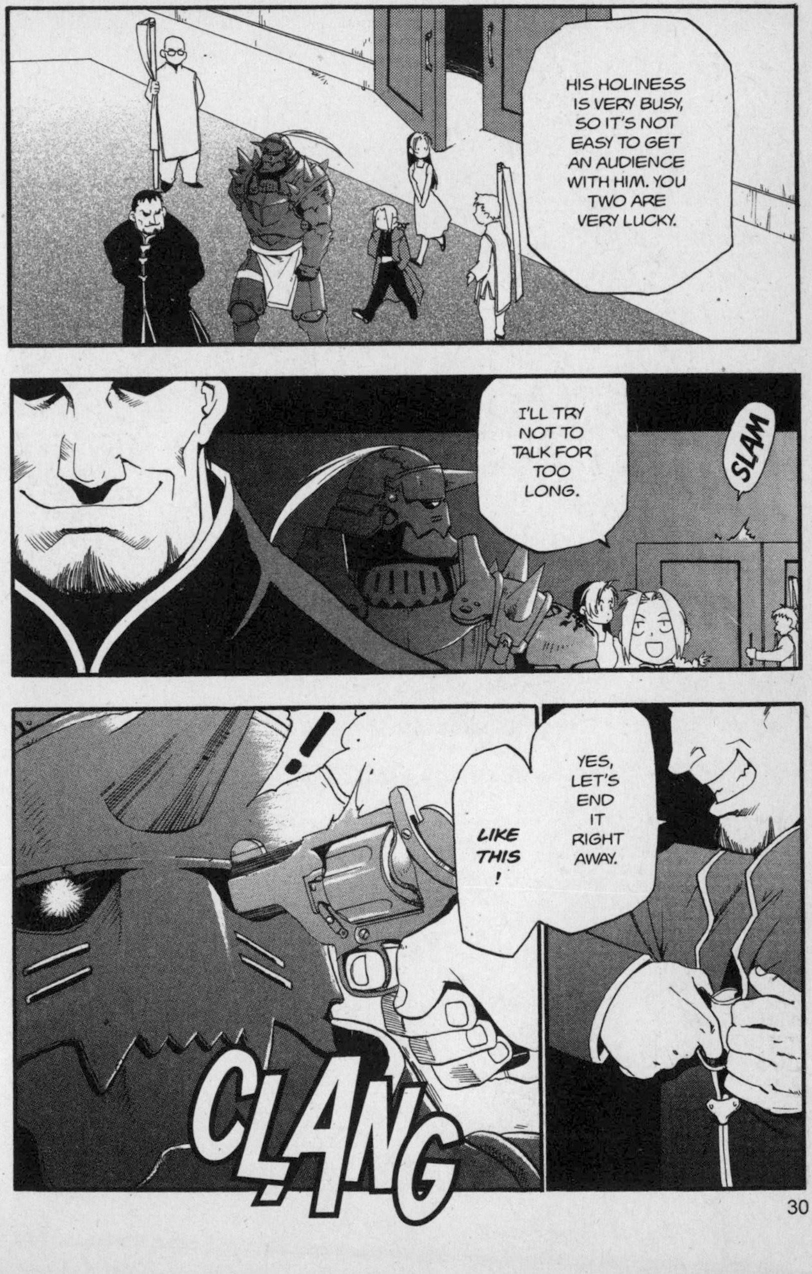
HIS HOLINESS IS VERY BUSY, SO IT'S NOT EASY TO GET AN AUDIENCE WITH HIM. YOU TWO ARE VERY LUCKY.
SLAM
I'LL TRY NOT TO TALK FOR TOO LONG.
YES, LET'S END IT RIGHT AWAY.
LIKE THIS!
!
CLANG

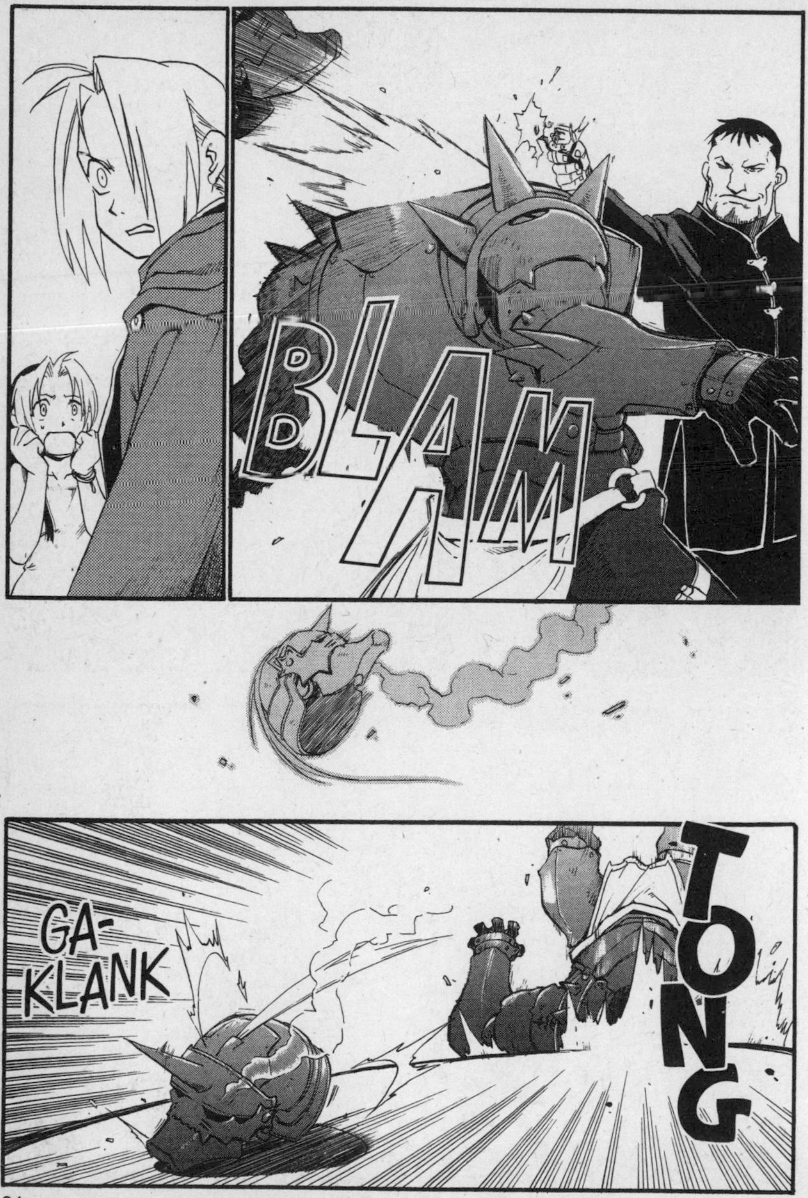
BLAM
TONG
GA-
KLANK

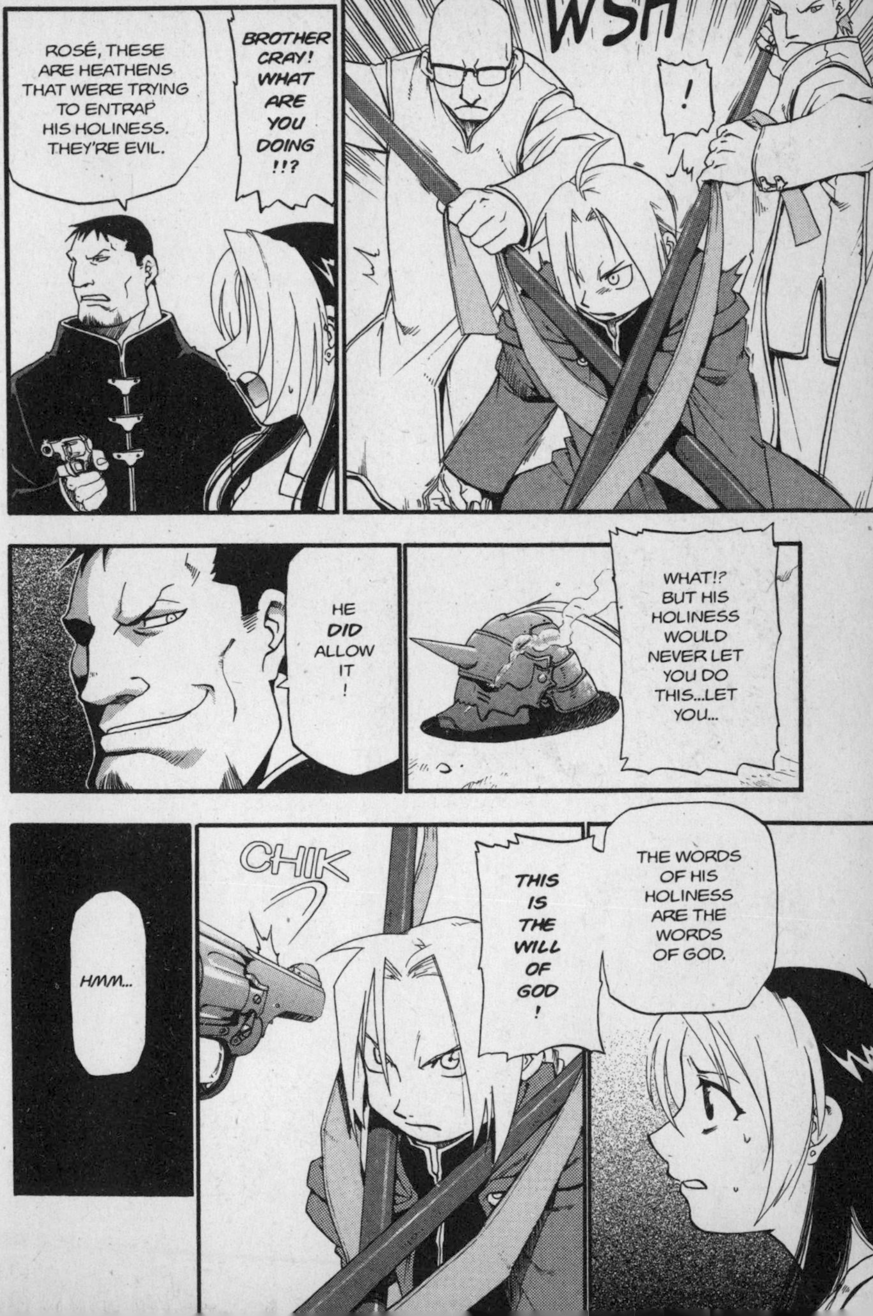
WSH
!
BROTHER CRAY! WHAT ARE YOU DOING!!?
ROSÉ, THESE ARE HEATHENS THAT WERE TRYING TO ENTRAP HIS HOLINESS. THEY'RE EVIL.
WHAT!? BUT HIS HOLINESS WOULD NEVER LET YOU DO THIS...LET YOU...
HE DID ALLOW IT!
THE WORDS OF HIS HOLINESS ARE THE WORDS OF GOD.
THIS IS THE WILL OF GOD!
CHIK
HMM...

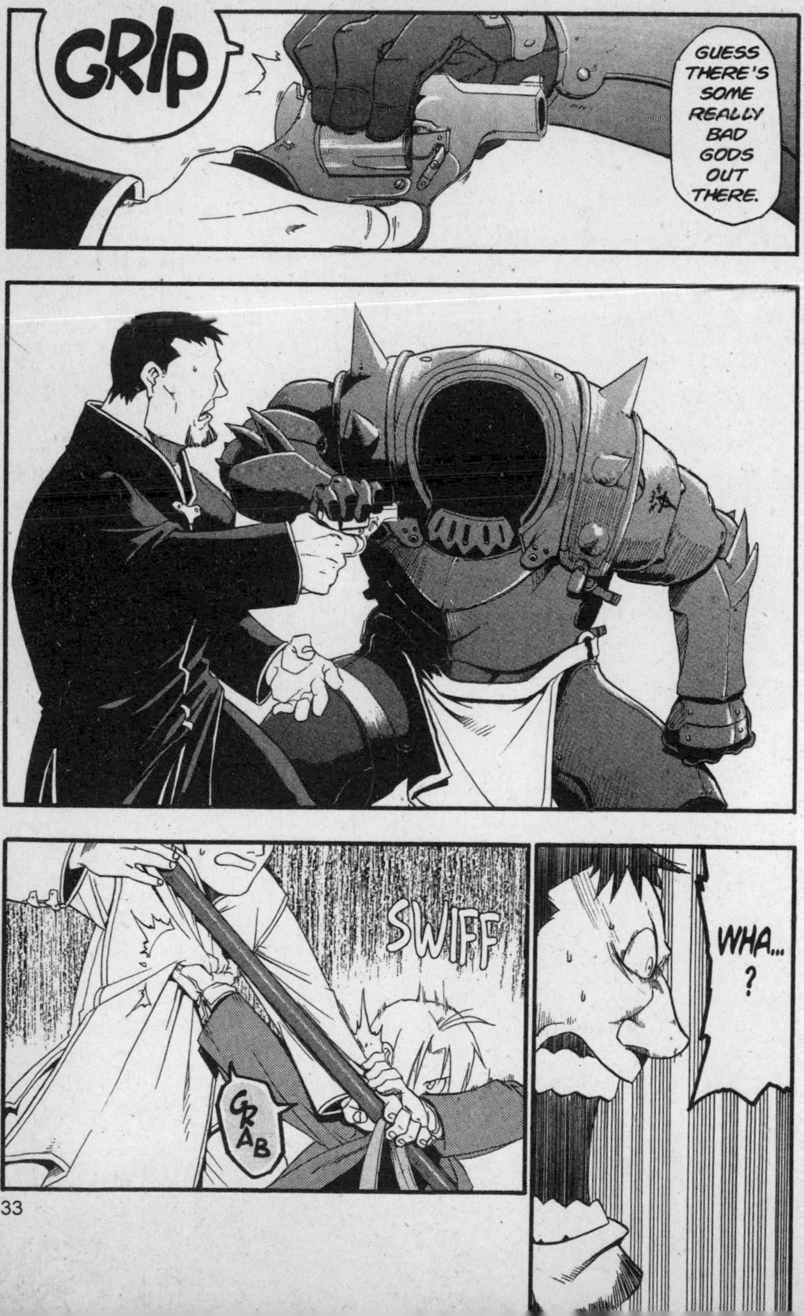
GUESS THERE'S SOME REALLY BAD GODS OUT THERE.
GRIP
WHA... ?
SWIFF
GRAB

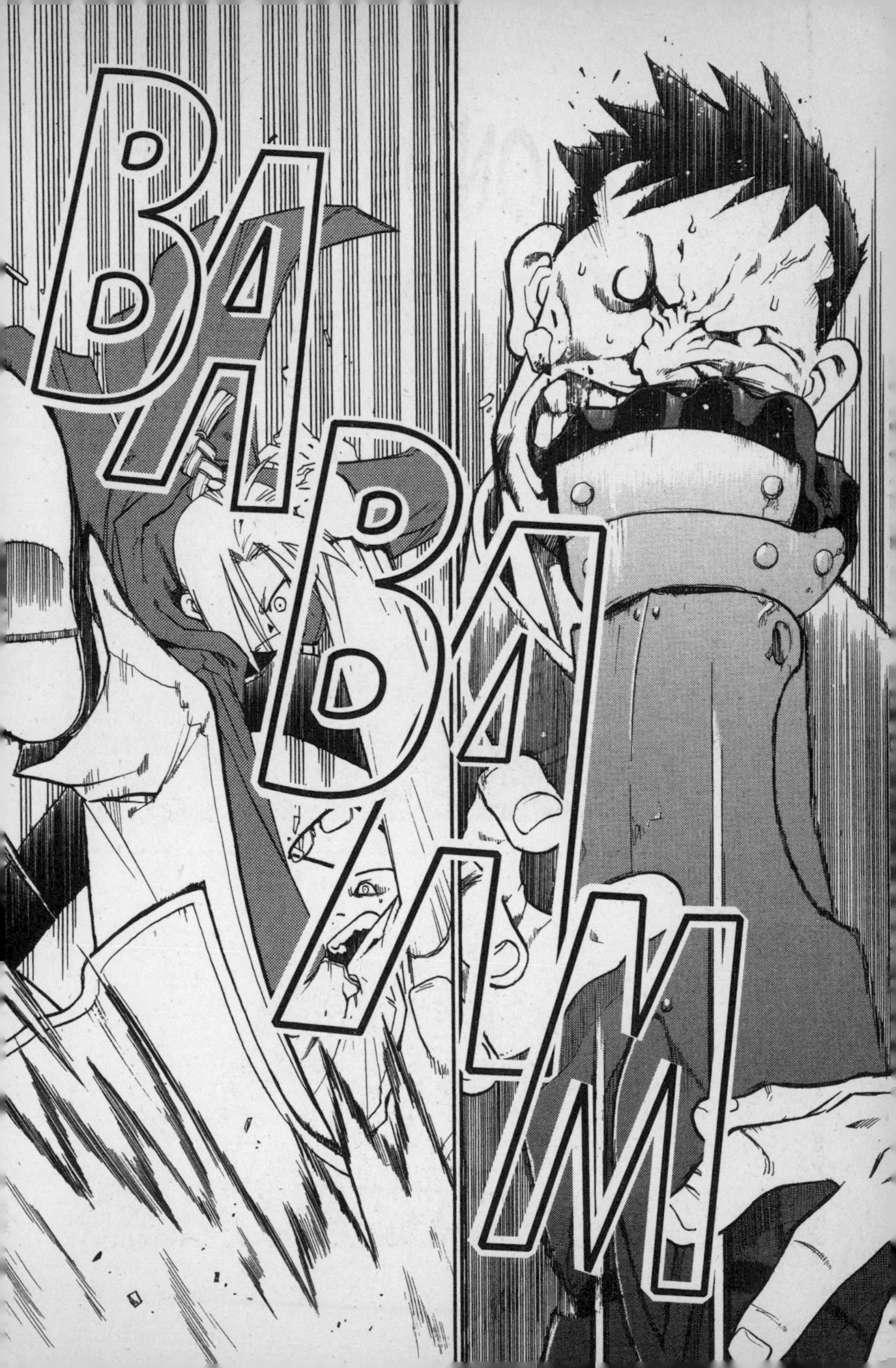
BABAM!

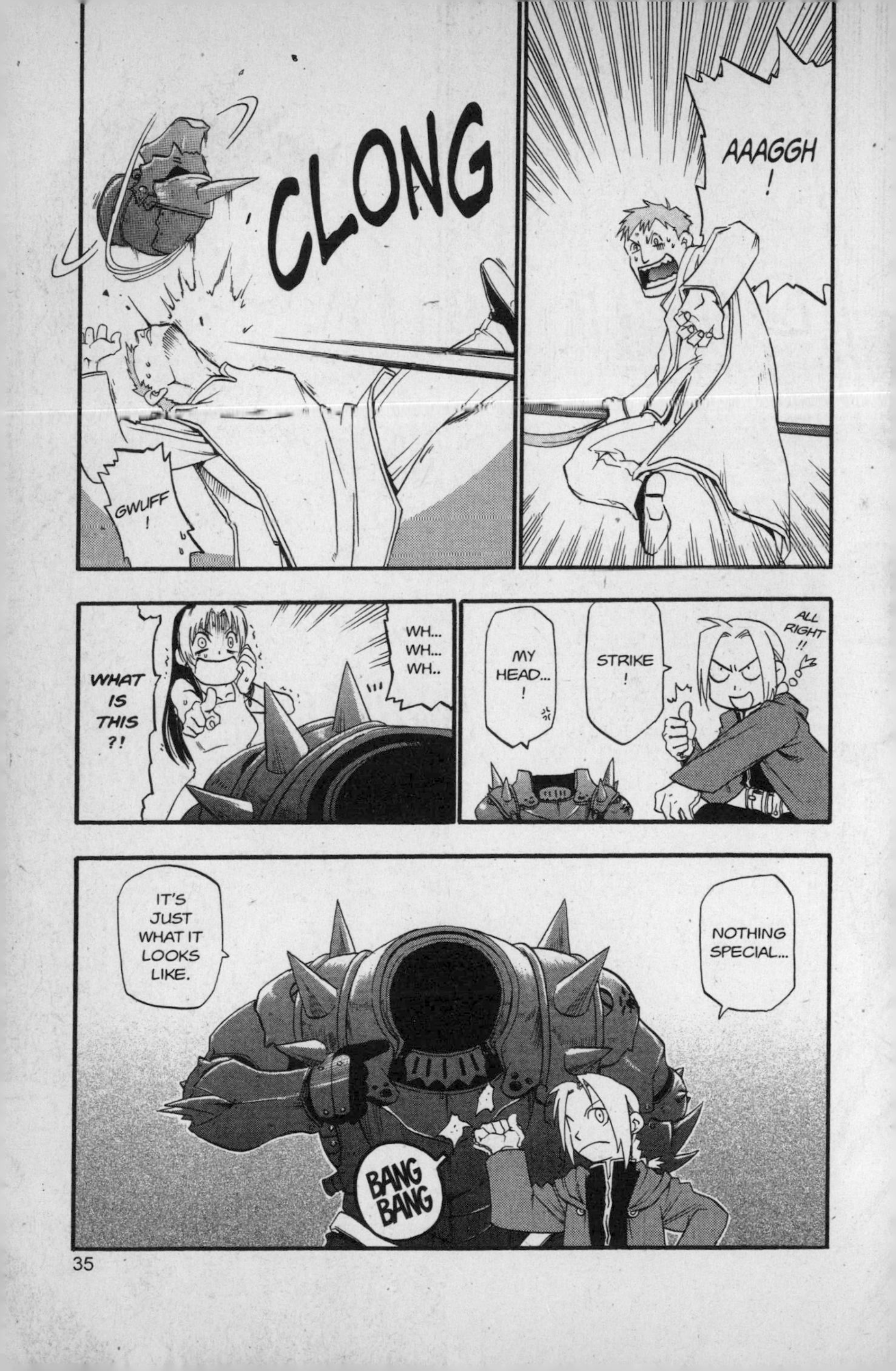
AAAGGH !
CLONG
GWUFF !
ALL RIGHT !!
STRIKE !
MY HEAD... !
WH... WH... WH..
WHAT IS THIS ?!
NOTHING SPECIAL...
IT'S JUST WHAT IT LOOKS LIKE.
BANG BANG

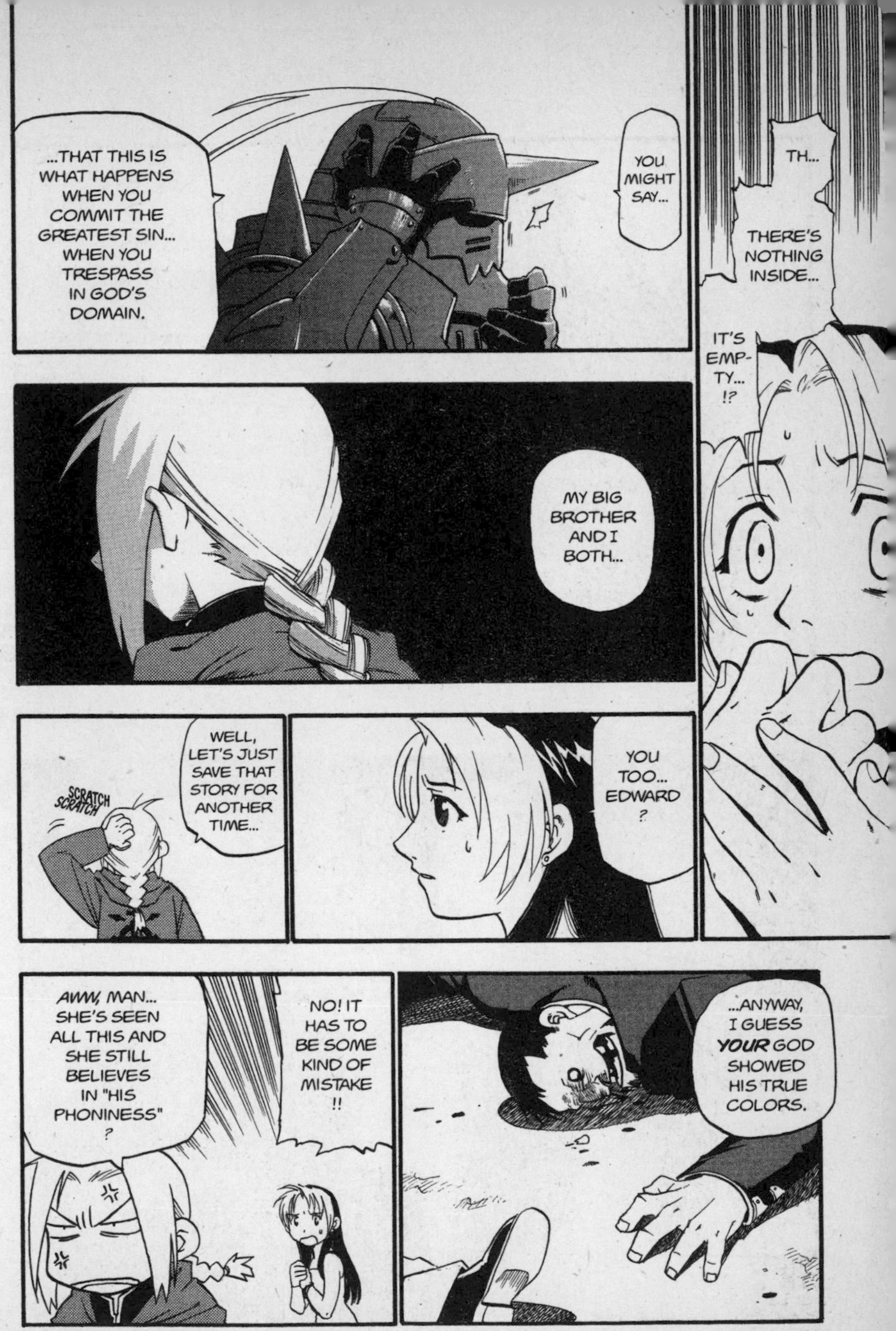
TH...
THERE'S NOTHING INSIDE...
IT'S EMPTY...!?
YOU MIGHT SAY...
...THAT THIS IS WHAT HAPPENS WHEN YOU COMMIT THE GREATEST SIN... WHEN YOU TRESPASS IN GOD'S DOMAIN.
MY BIG BROTHER AND I BOTH...
YOU TOO... EDWARD?
WELL, LET'S JUST SAVE THAT STORY FOR ANOTHER TIME...
SCRATCH SCRATCH
...ANYWAY, I GUESS **YOUR** GOD SHOWED HIS TRUE COLORS.
NO! IT HAS TO BE SOME KIND OF MISTAKE!!
AWW, MAN... SHE'S SEEN ALL THIS AND SHE STILL BELIEVES IN "HIS PHONINESS"?

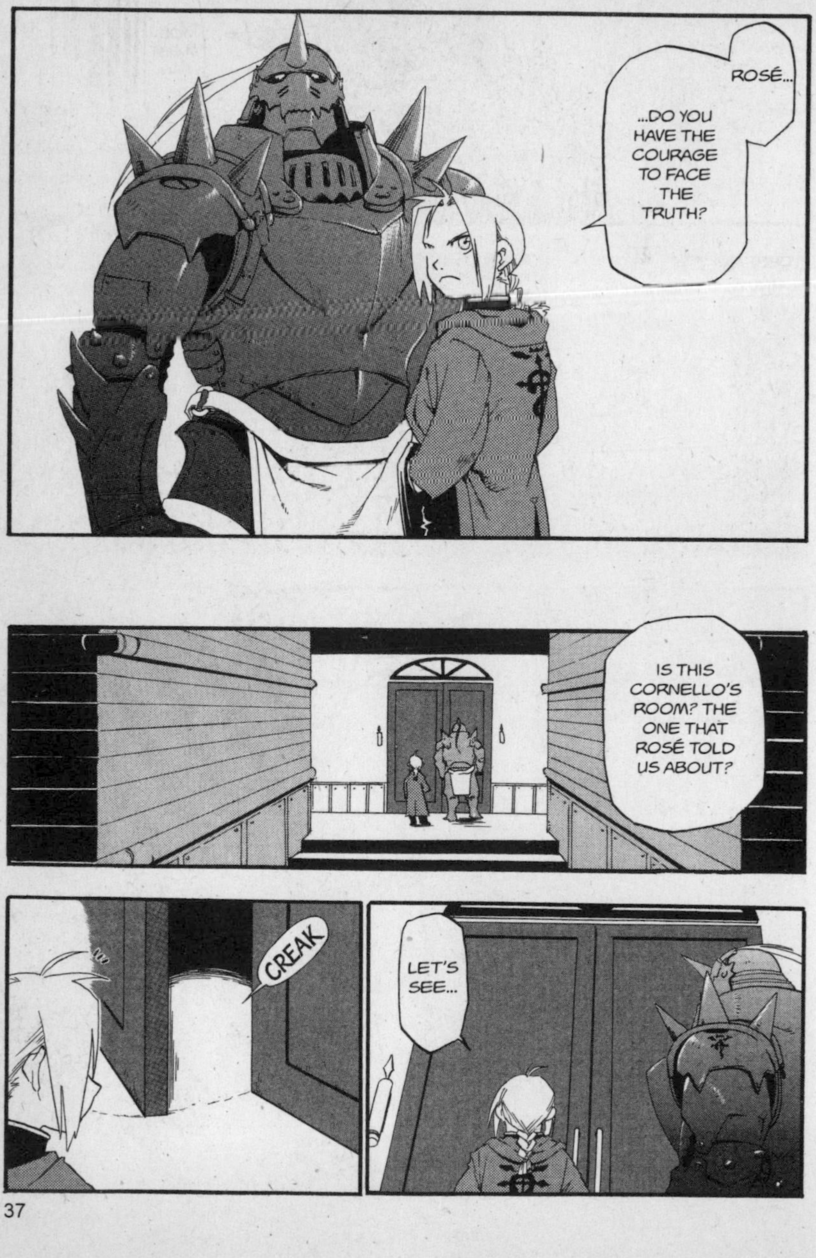
ROSÉ...
...DO YOU HAVE THE COURAGE TO FACE THE TRUTH?
IS THIS CORNELLO'S ROOM? THE ONE THAT ROSÉ TOLD US ABOUT?
LET'S SEE...
CREAK

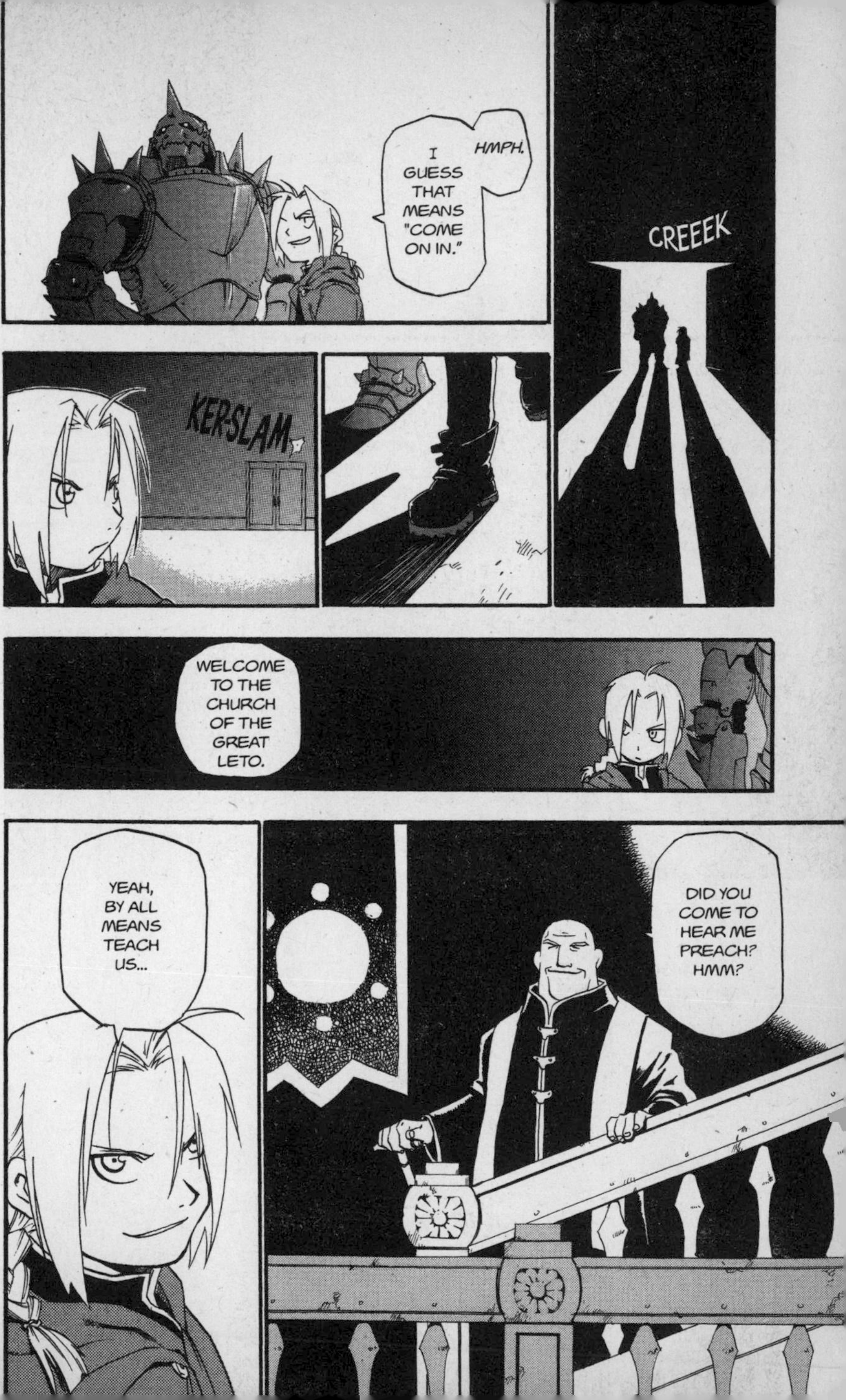
CREEEK
HMPH.
I GUESS THAT MEANS "COME ON IN."
KER-SLAM
WELCOME TO THE CHURCH OF THE GREAT LETO.
DID YOU COME TO HEAR ME PREACH? HMM?
YEAH, BY ALL MEANS TEACH US...

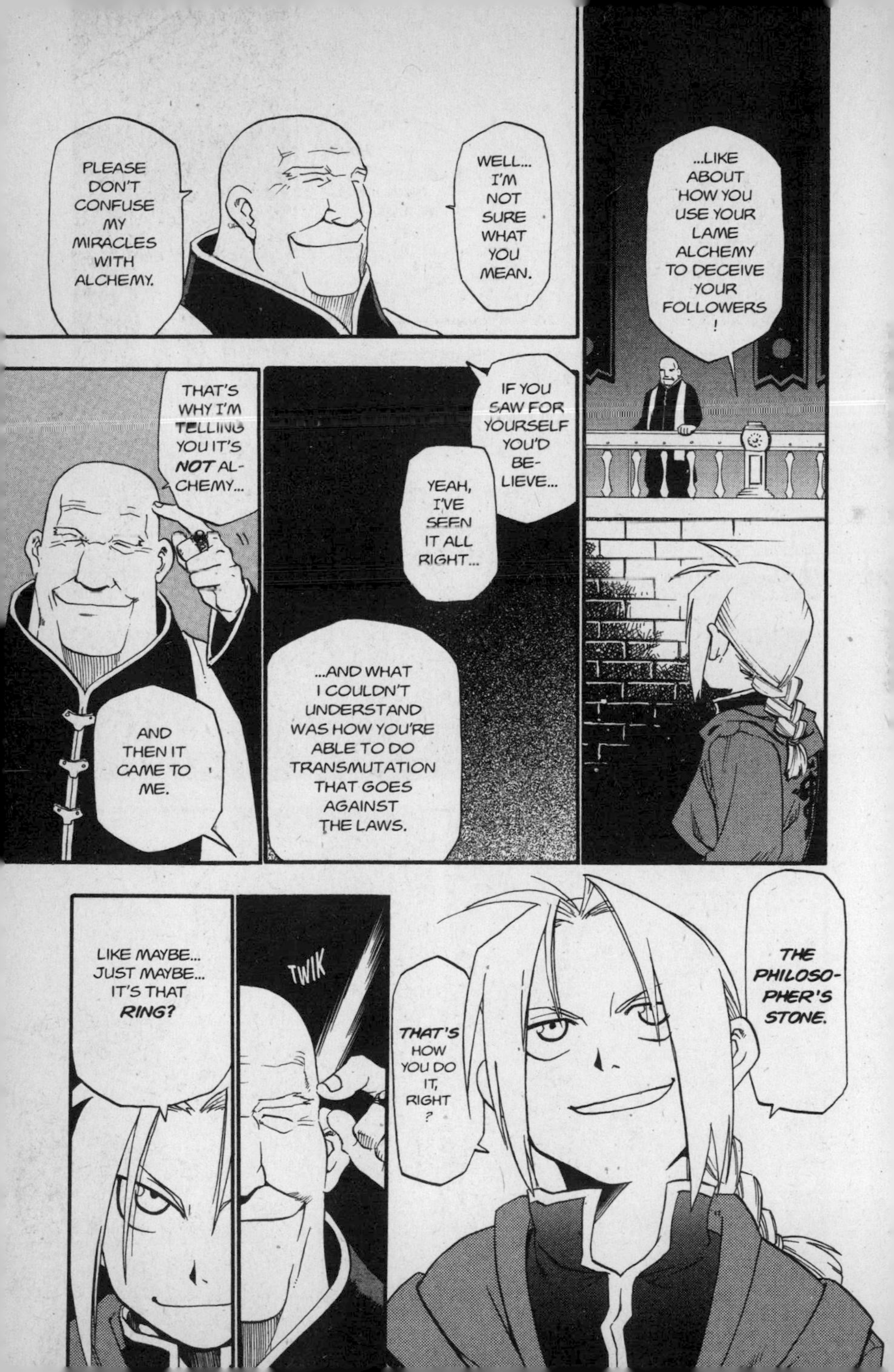
PLEASE DON'T CONFUSE MY MIRACLES WITH ALCHEMY.
WELL... I'M NOT SURE WHAT YOU MEAN.
...LIKE ABOUT HOW YOU USE YOUR LAME ALCHEMY TO DECEIVE YOUR FOLLOWERS!
THAT'S WHY I'M TELLING YOU IT'S ***NOT*** ALCHEMY...
AND THEN IT CAME TO ME.
IF YOU SAW FOR YOURSELF YOU'D BELIEVE...
YEAH, I'VE SEEN IT ALL RIGHT...
...AND WHAT I COULDN'T UNDERSTAND WAS HOW YOU'RE ABLE TO DO TRANSMUTATION THAT GOES AGAINST THE LAWS.
LIKE MAYBE... JUST MAYBE... IT'S THAT ***RING?***
TWIK
THE PHILOSOPHER'S STONE.
THAT'S HOW YOU DO IT, RIGHT?

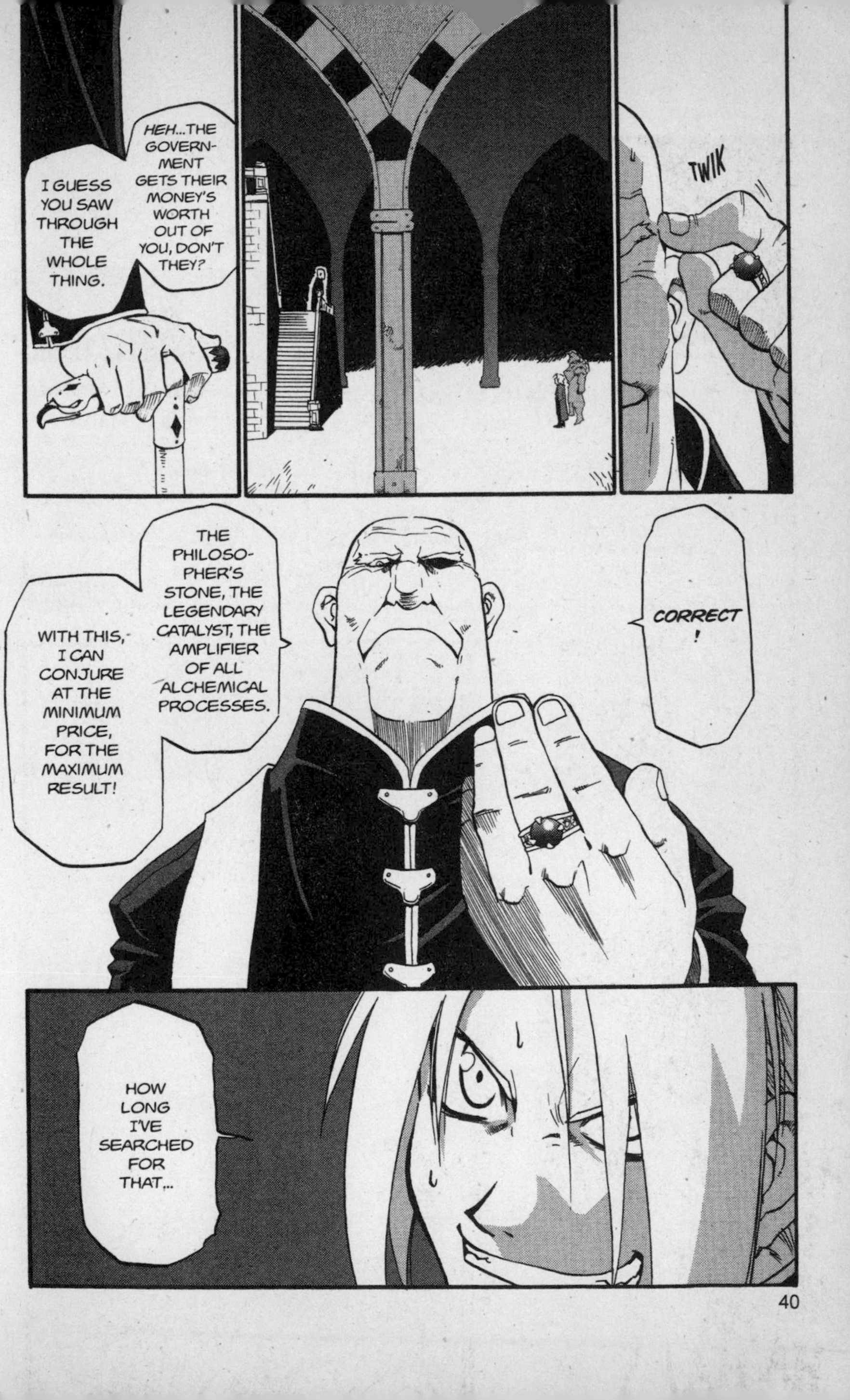
TWIK
HEH...THE GOVERNMENT GETS THEIR MONEY'S WORTH OUT OF YOU, DON'T THEY?
I GUESS YOU SAW THROUGH THE WHOLE THING.
CORRECT!
THE PHILOSOPHER'S STONE, THE LEGENDARY CATALYST, THE AMPLIFIER OF ALL ALCHEMICAL PROCESSES.
WITH THIS, I CAN CONJURE AT THE MINIMUM PRICE, FOR THE MAXIMUM RESULT!
HOW LONG I'VE SEARCHED FOR THAT...

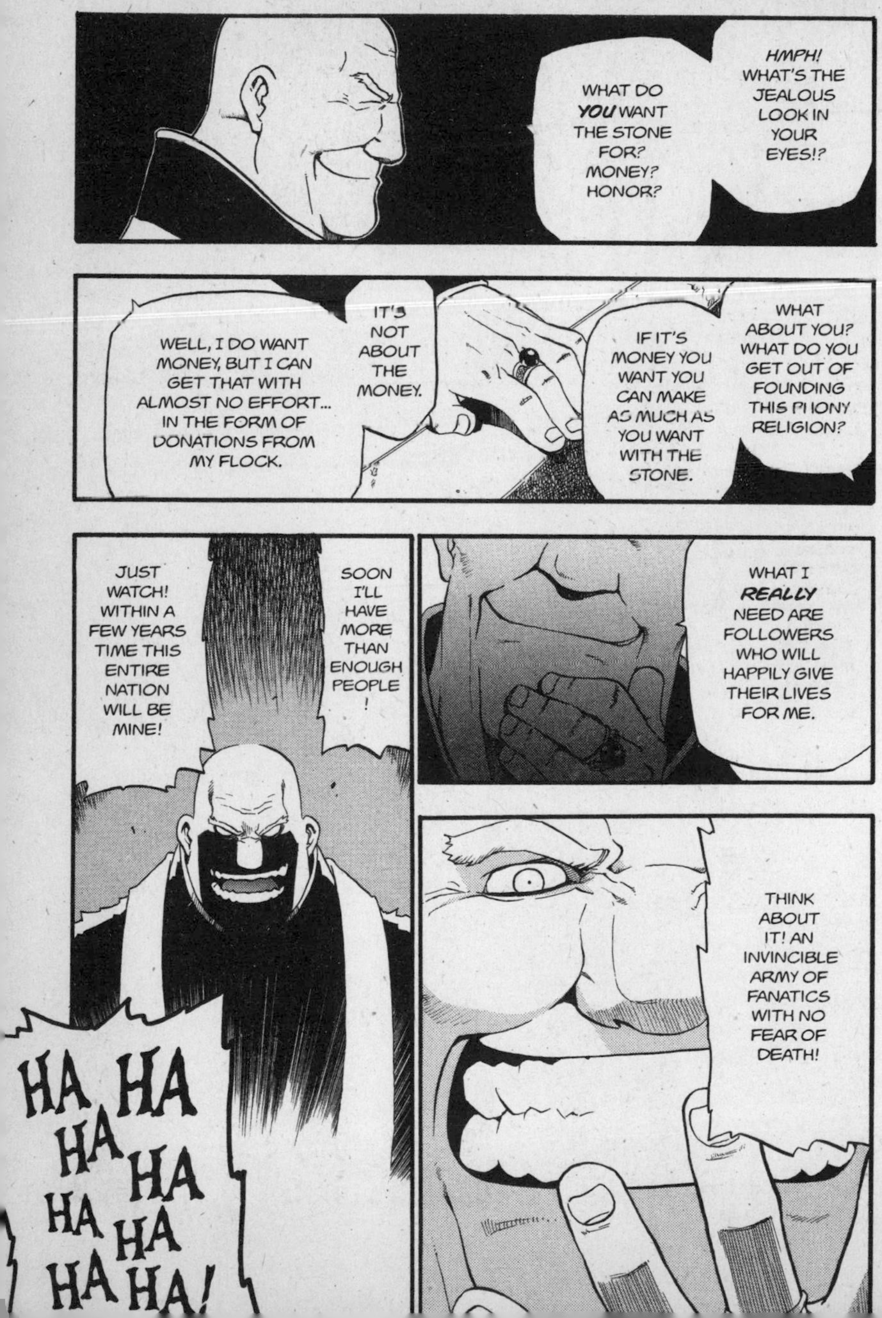
HMPH! WHAT'S THE JEALOUS LOOK IN YOUR EYES!?
WHAT DO YOU WANT THE STONE FOR? MONEY? HONOR?
WHAT ABOUT YOU? WHAT DO YOU GET OUT OF FOUNDING THIS PHONY RELIGION?
IF IT'S MONEY YOU WANT YOU CAN MAKE AS MUCH AS YOU WANT WITH THE STONE.
IT'S NOT ABOUT THE MONEY.
WELL, I DO WANT MONEY, BUT I CAN GET THAT WITH ALMOST NO EFFORT... IN THE FORM OF DONATIONS FROM MY FLOCK.
WHAT I REALLY NEED ARE FOLLOWERS WHO WILL HAPPILY GIVE THEIR LIVES FOR ME.
THINK ABOUT IT! AN INVINCIBLE ARMY OF FANATICS WITH NO FEAR OF DEATH!
SOON I'LL HAVE MORE THAN ENOUGH PEOPLE!
JUST WATCH! WITHIN A FEW YEARS TIME THIS ENTIRE NATION WILL BE MINE!
HA HA HA HA HA HA HA HA HA HA!

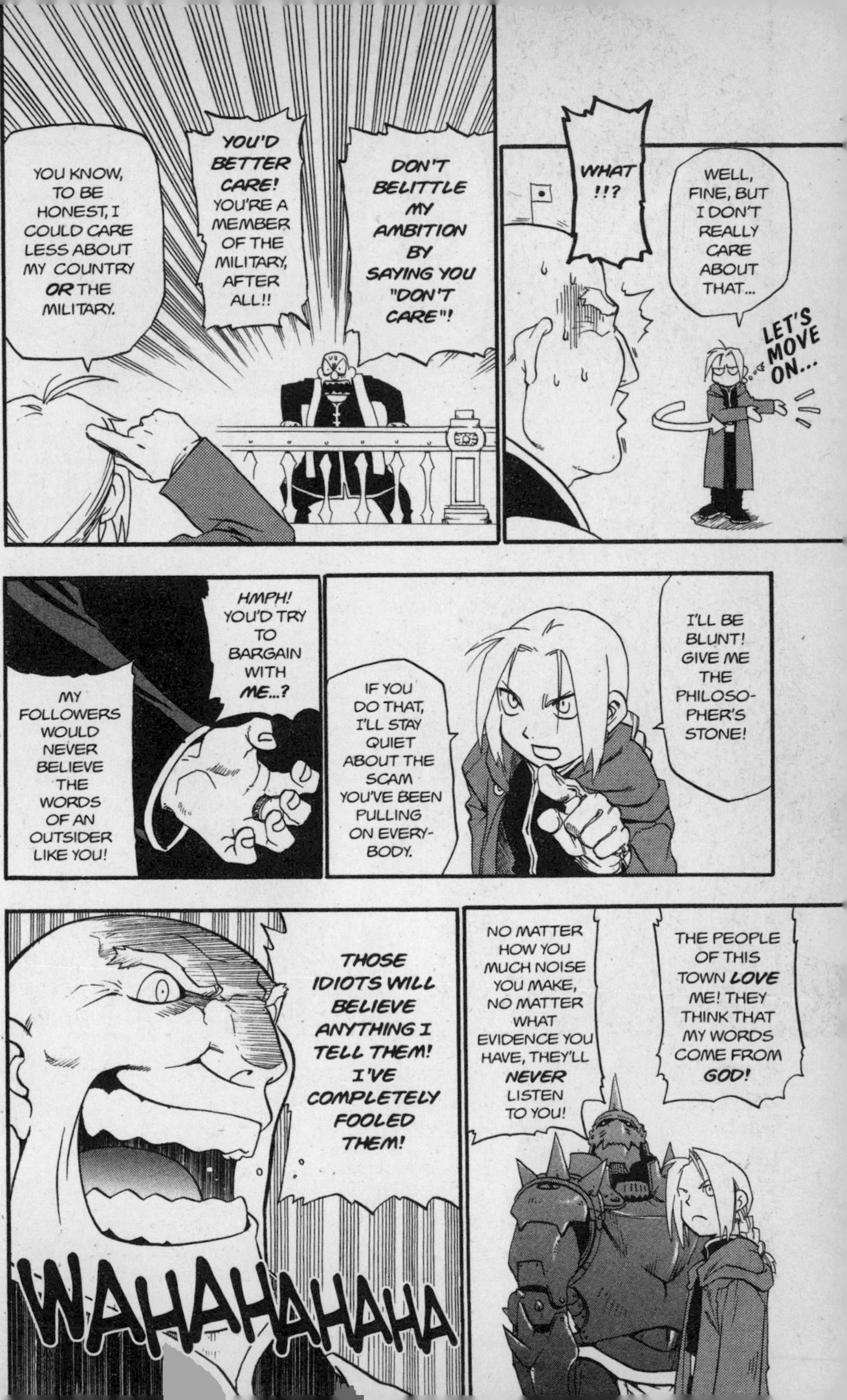
WELL, FINE, BUT I DON'T REALLY CARE ABOUT THAT...
LET'S MOVE ON...
WHAT !!?
DON'T BELITTLE MY AMBITION BY SAYING YOU "DON'T CARE"!
YOU'D BETTER CARE! YOU'RE A MEMBER OF THE MILITARY, AFTER ALL!!
YOU KNOW, TO BE HONEST, I COULD CARE LESS ABOUT MY COUNTRY OR THE MILITARY.
I'LL BE BLUNT! GIVE ME THE PHILOSO-PHER'S STONE!
IF YOU DO THAT, I'LL STAY QUIET ABOUT THE SCAM YOU'VE BEEN PULLING ON EVERY-BODY.
HMPH! YOU'D TRY TO BARGAIN WITH ME...?
MY FOLLOWERS WOULD NEVER BELIEVE THE WORDS OF AN OUTSIDER LIKE YOU!
THE PEOPLE OF THIS TOWN LOVE ME! THEY THINK THAT MY WORDS COME FROM GOD!
NO MATTER HOW YOU MUCH NOISE YOU MAKE, NO MATTER WHAT EVIDENCE YOU HAVE, THEY'LL NEVER LISTEN TO YOU!
THOSE IDIOTS WILL BELIEVE ANYTHING I TELL THEM! I'VE COMPLETELY FOOLED THEM!
WAHAHAHAHA

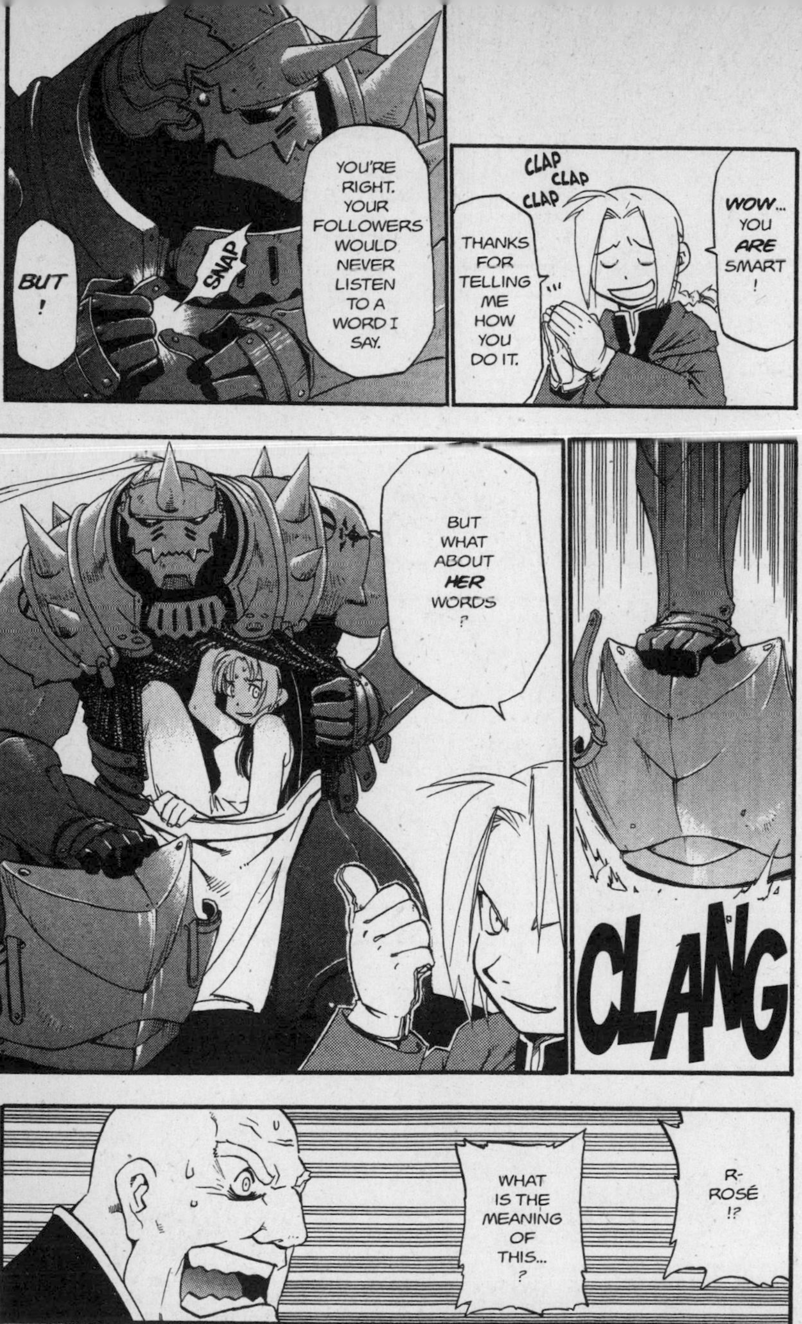

WOW... YOU ARE SMART!
CLAP CLAP CLAP
THANKS FOR TELLING ME HOW YOU DO IT.
YOU'RE RIGHT. YOUR FOLLOWERS WOULD NEVER LISTEN TO A WORD I SAY.
SNAP
BUT!
CLANG
BUT WHAT ABOUT HER WORDS?
R-ROSÉ!?
WHAT IS THE MEANING OF THIS...?

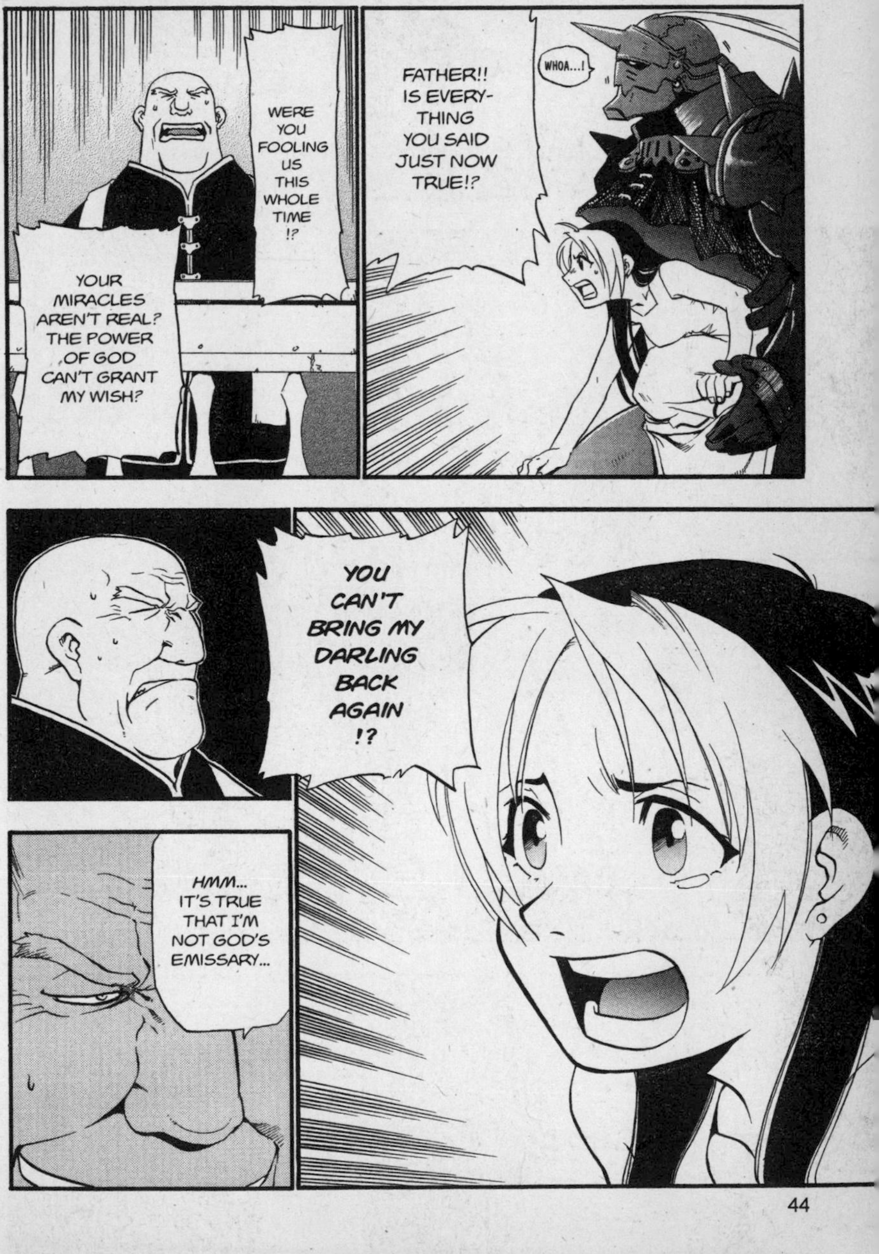
WHOA...!
FATHER!! IS EVERY-THING YOU SAID JUST NOW TRUE!?
WERE YOU FOOLING US THIS WHOLE TIME !?
YOUR MIRACLES AREN'T REAL? THE POWER OF GOD CAN'T GRANT MY WISH?
YOU CAN'T BRING MY DARLING BACK AGAIN !?
HMM... IT'S TRUE THAT I'M NOT GOD'S EMISSARY...

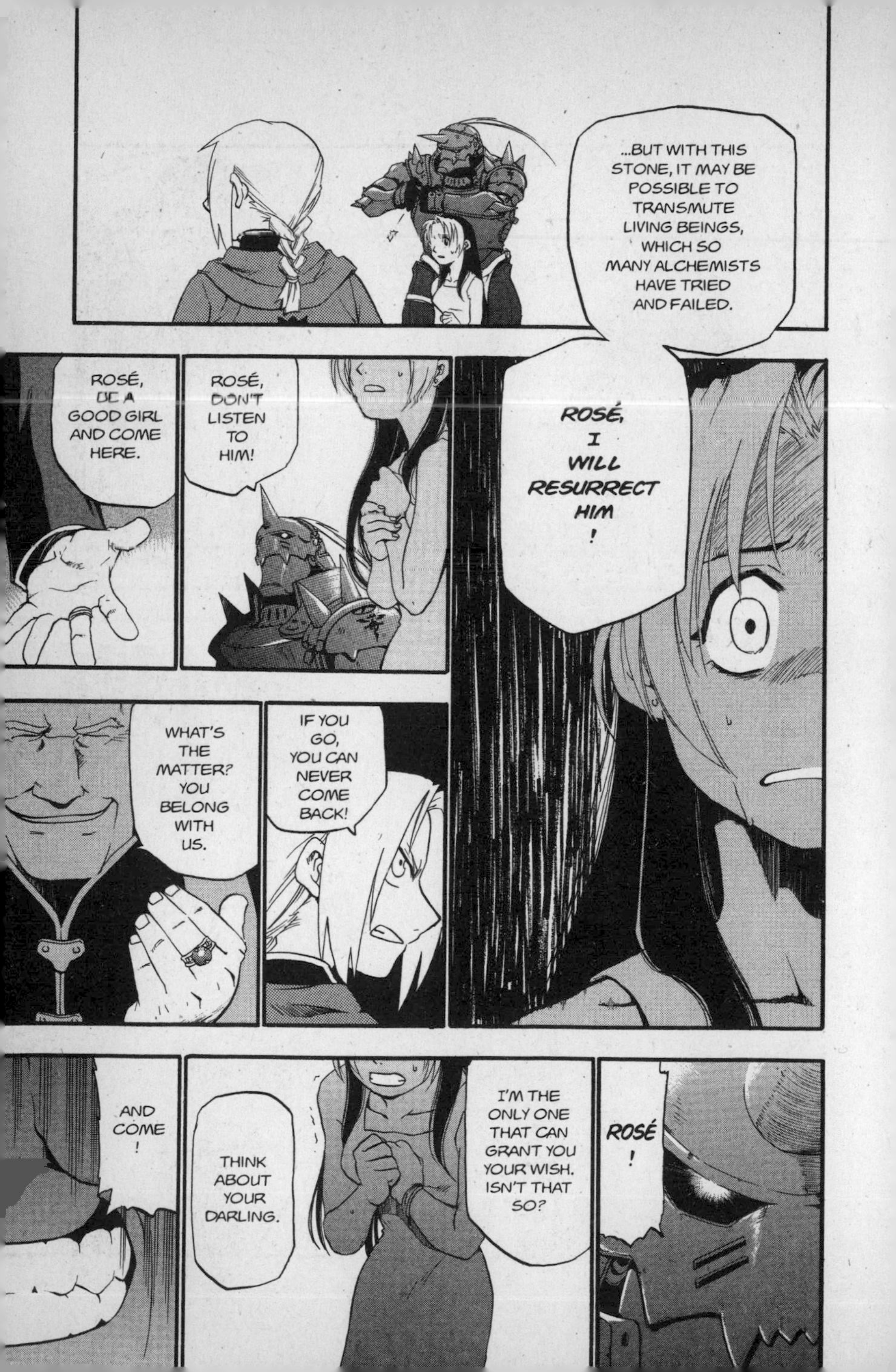
...BUT WITH THIS STONE, IT MAY BE POSSIBLE TO TRANSMUTE LIVING BEINGS, WHICH SO MANY ALCHEMISTS HAVE TRIED AND FAILED.
ROSÉ, I WILL RESURRECT HIM!
ROSÉ, DON'T LISTEN TO HIM!
ROSÉ, BE A GOOD GIRL AND COME HERE.
IF YOU GO, YOU CAN NEVER COME BACK!
WHAT'S THE MATTER? YOU BELONG WITH US.
ROSÉ!
I'M THE ONLY ONE THAT CAN GRANT YOU YOUR WISH. ISN'T THAT SO?
THINK ABOUT YOUR DARLING.
AND COME!

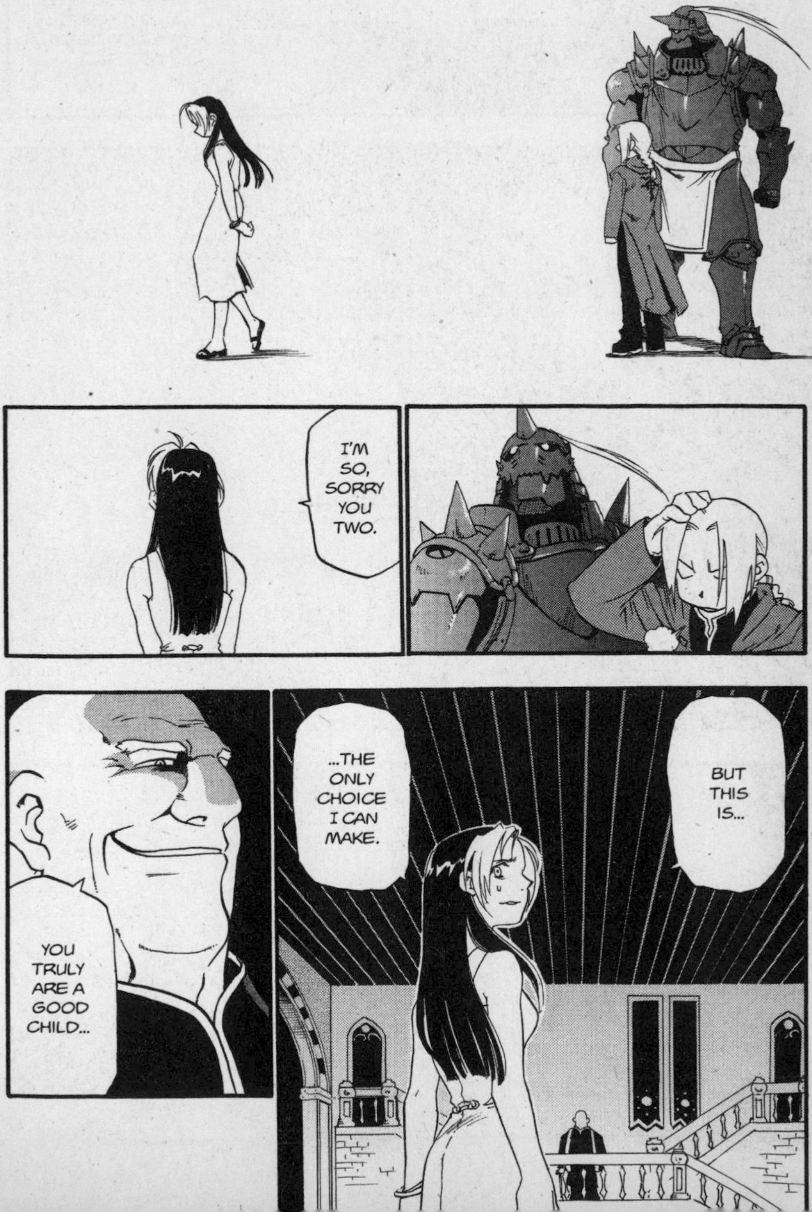
I'M SO, SORRY YOU TWO.
BUT THIS IS...
...THE ONLY CHOICE I CAN MAKE.
YOU TRULY ARE A GOOD CHILD...

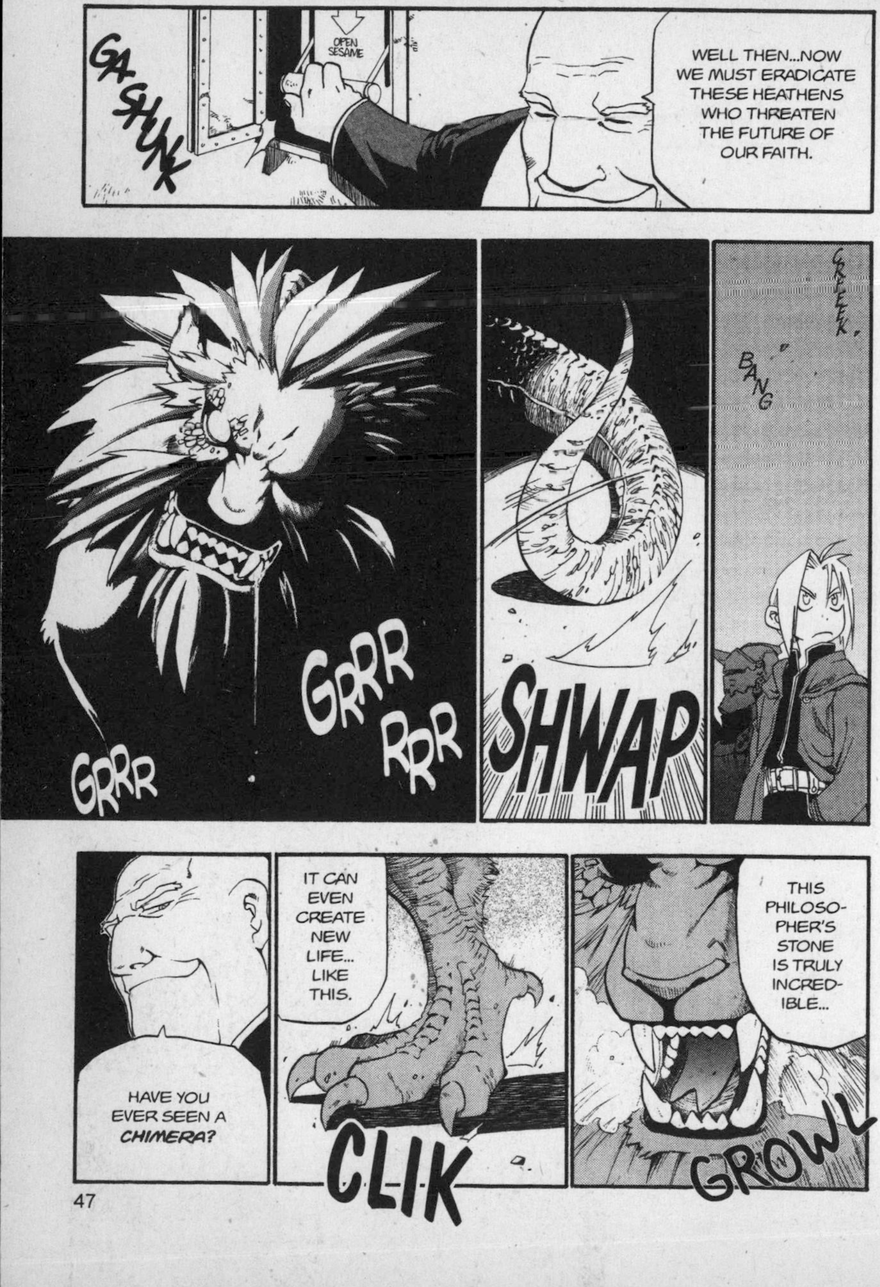

WELL THEN...NOW WE MUST ERADICATE THESE HEATHENS WHO THREATEN THE FUTURE OF OUR FAITH.
OPEN SESAME
GASHUNK
CREEEK
BANG
SHWAP
GRRR RRR
GRRR
THIS PHILOSOPHER'S STONE IS TRULY INCREDIBLE...
GROWL
IT CAN EVEN CREATE NEW LIFE... LIKE THIS.
CLIK
HAVE YOU EVER SEEN A *CHIMERA?*

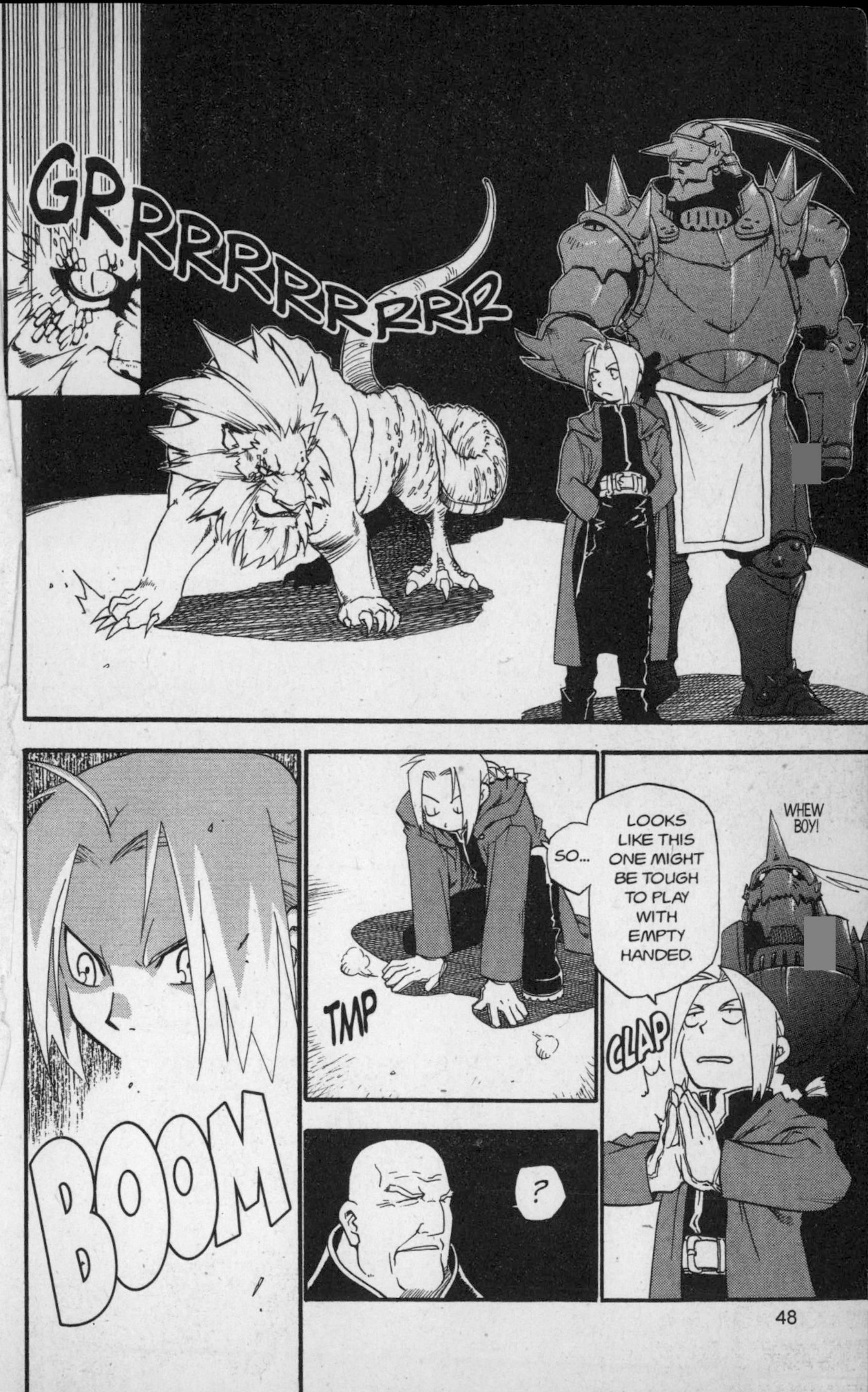
GRRRRRRRRRR
WHEW BOY!
SO...
LOOKS LIKE THIS ONE MIGHT BE TOUGH TO PLAY WITH EMPTY HANDED.
CLAP
TMP
?
BOOM

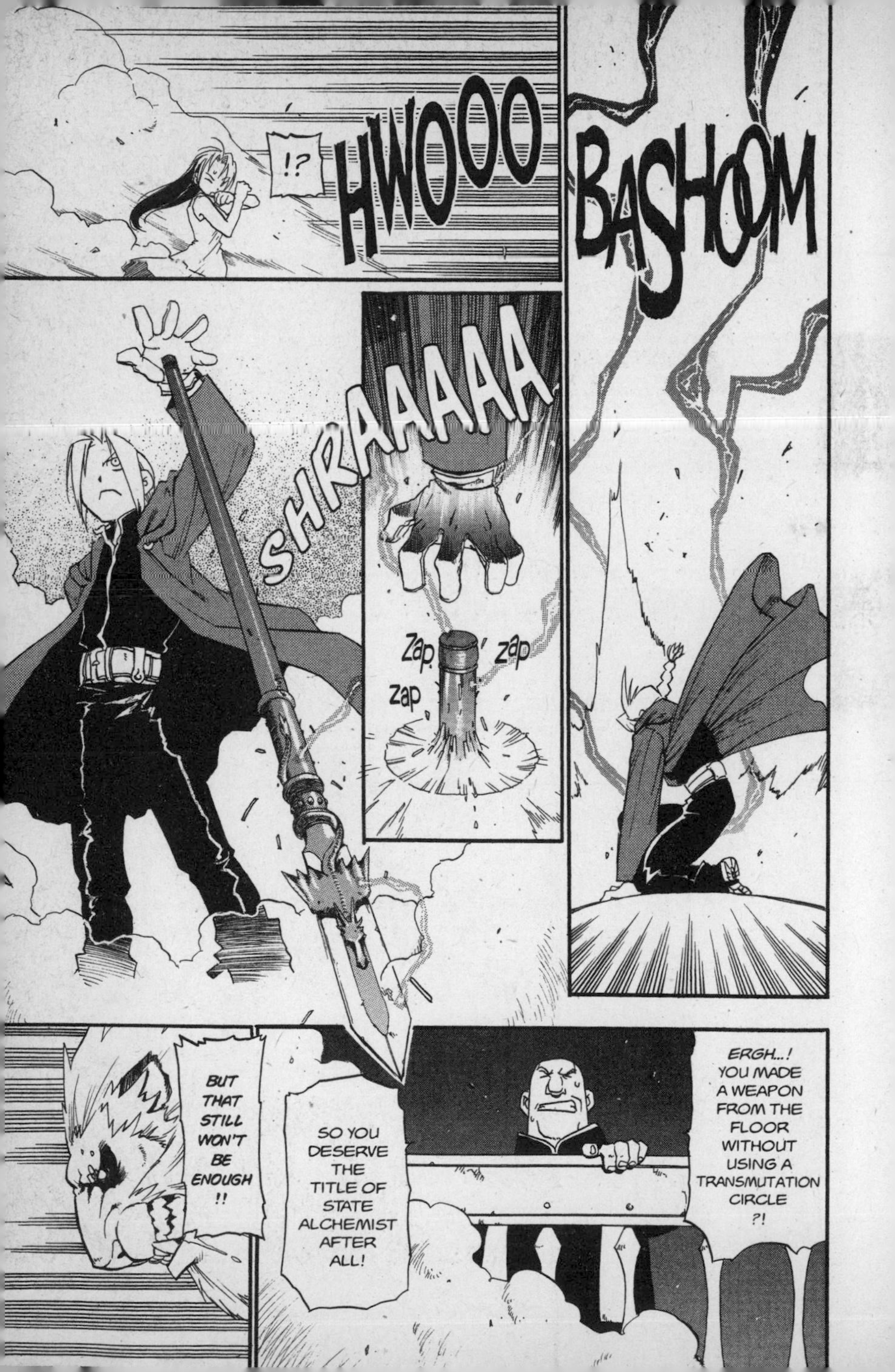
BASHOOM
HWOOO
!?
SHRAAAAA
zap
Zap
zap
ERGH...! YOU MADE A WEAPON FROM THE FLOOR WITHOUT USING A TRANSMUTATION CIRCLE ?!
SO YOU DESERVE THE TITLE OF STATE ALCHEMIST AFTER ALL!
BUT THAT STILL WON'T BE ENOUGH !!

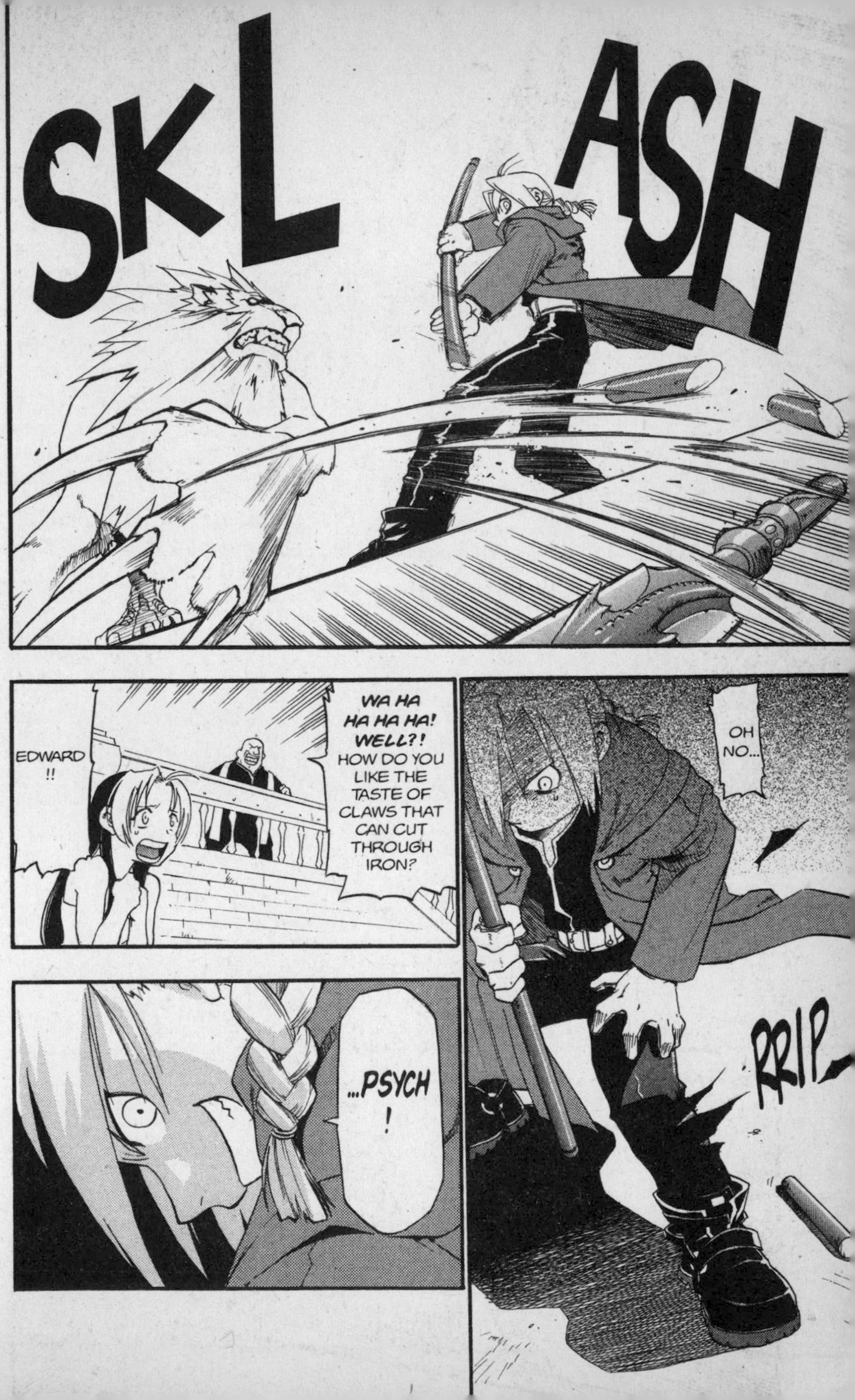
SKLASH
OH NO...
RRIP
WA HA HA HA HA! WELL?! HOW DO YOU LIKE THE TASTE OF CLAWS THAT CAN CUT THROUGH IRON?
EDWARD !!
...PSYCH !

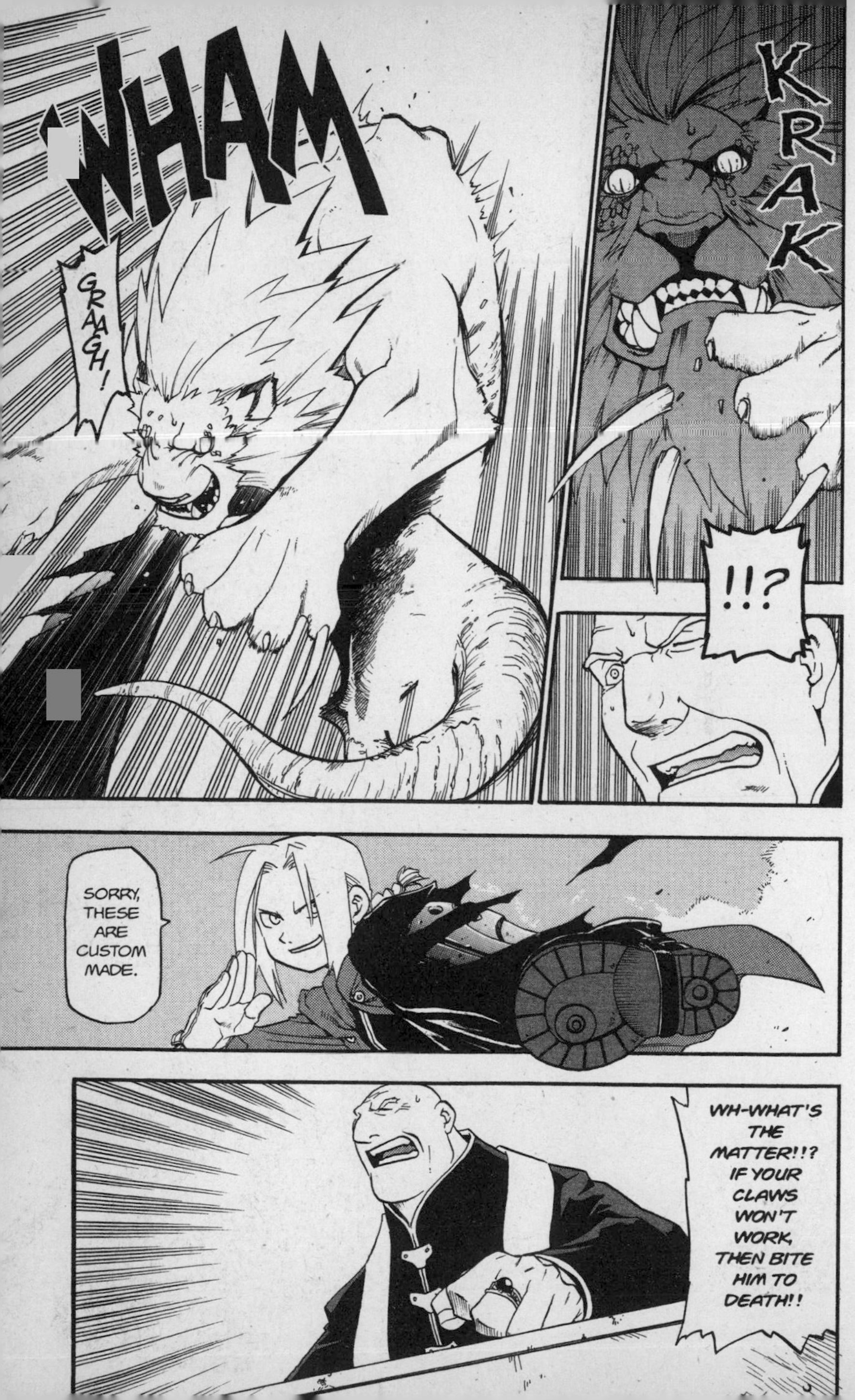
KRAK
!!?
WHAM
GRAAGH!
SORRY, THESE ARE CUSTOM MADE.
WH-WHAT'S THE MATTER!!? IF YOUR CLAWS WON'T WORK, THEN BITE HIM TO DEATH!!

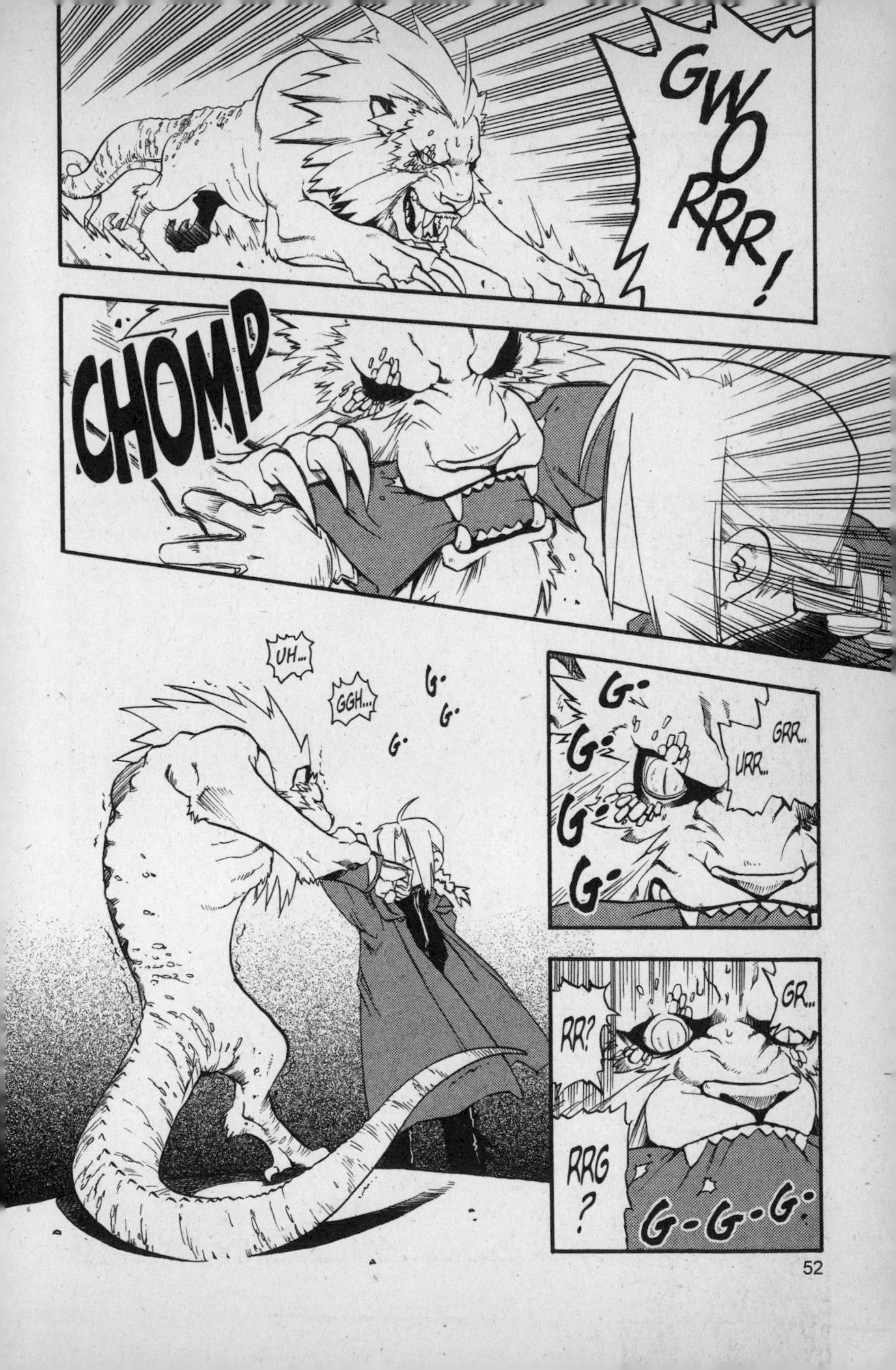

GWORRR!
CHOMP
GRR...
URR...
G G G G
GR...
RR?
RRG ?
G-G-G-G
UH...
GGH...
G G G

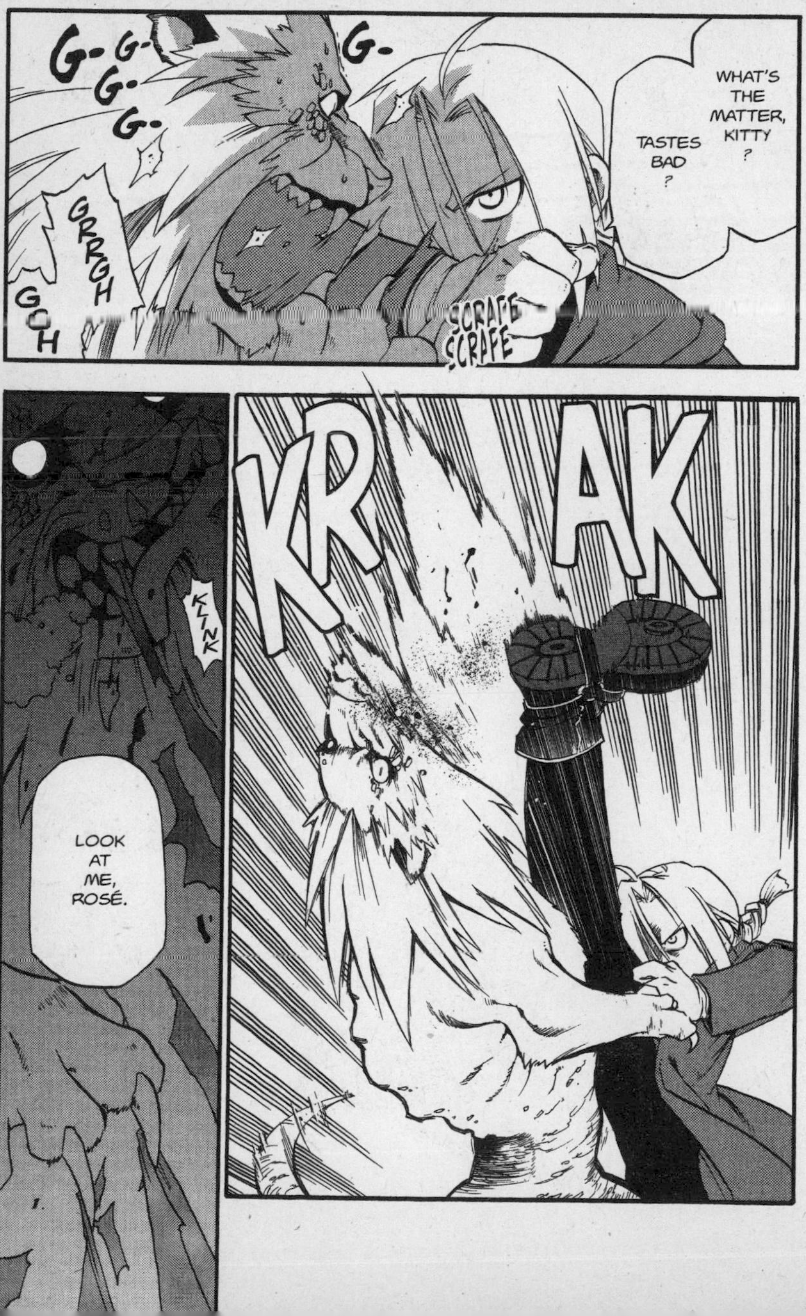
WHAT'S THE MATTER, KITTY?
TASTES BAD?
G-
G- G- G- G-
GRRGH
GOH
SCRAPE SCRAPE
KRAK
KLINK
LOOK AT ME, ROSÉ.

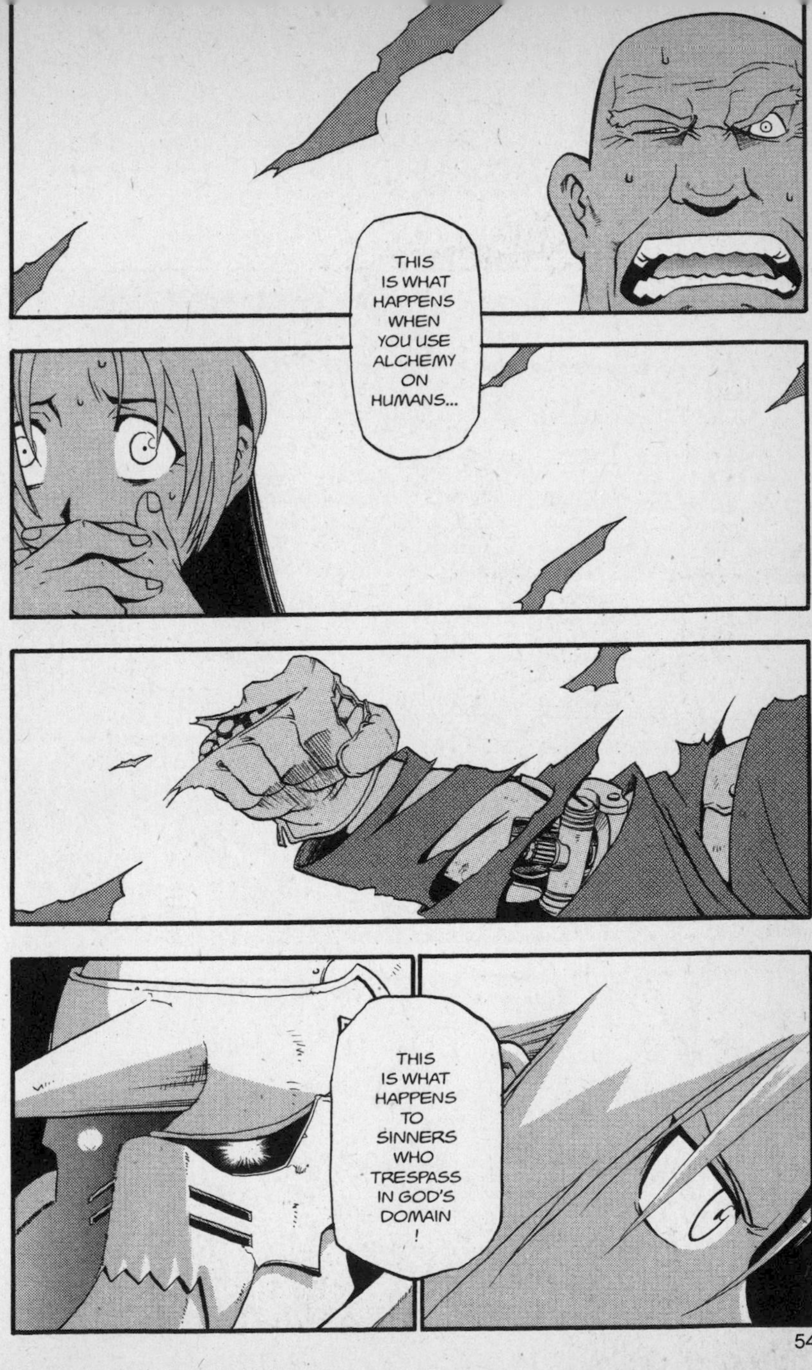
THIS IS WHAT HAPPENS WHEN YOU USE ALCHEMY ON HUMANS...
THIS IS WHAT HAPPENS TO SINNERS WHO TRESPASS IN GOD'S DOMAIN !

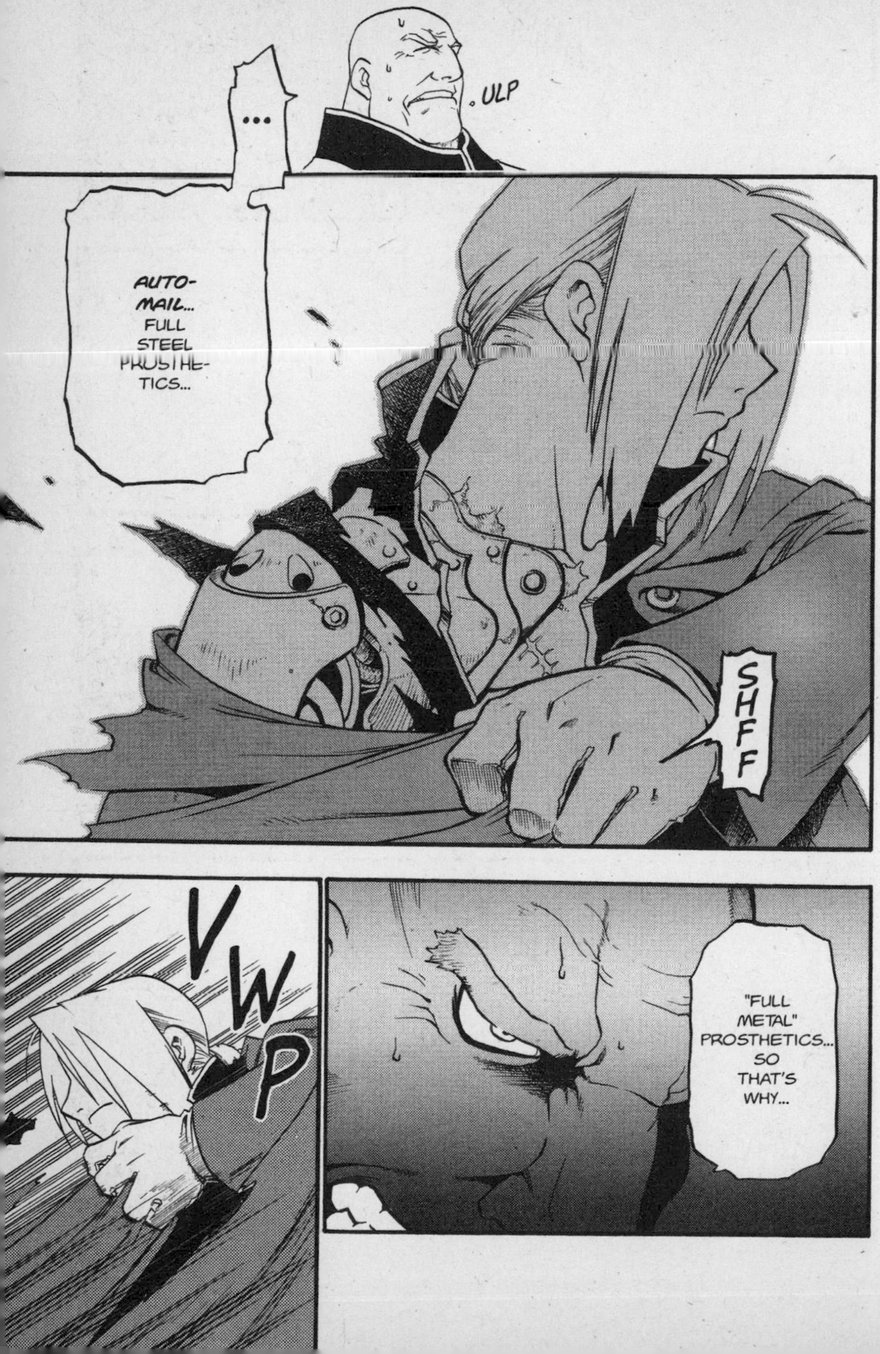
ULP
...
AUTO-MAIL... FULL STEEL PROSTHETICS...
SHFF
"FULL METAL" PROSTHETICS... SO THAT'S WHY...
VWP

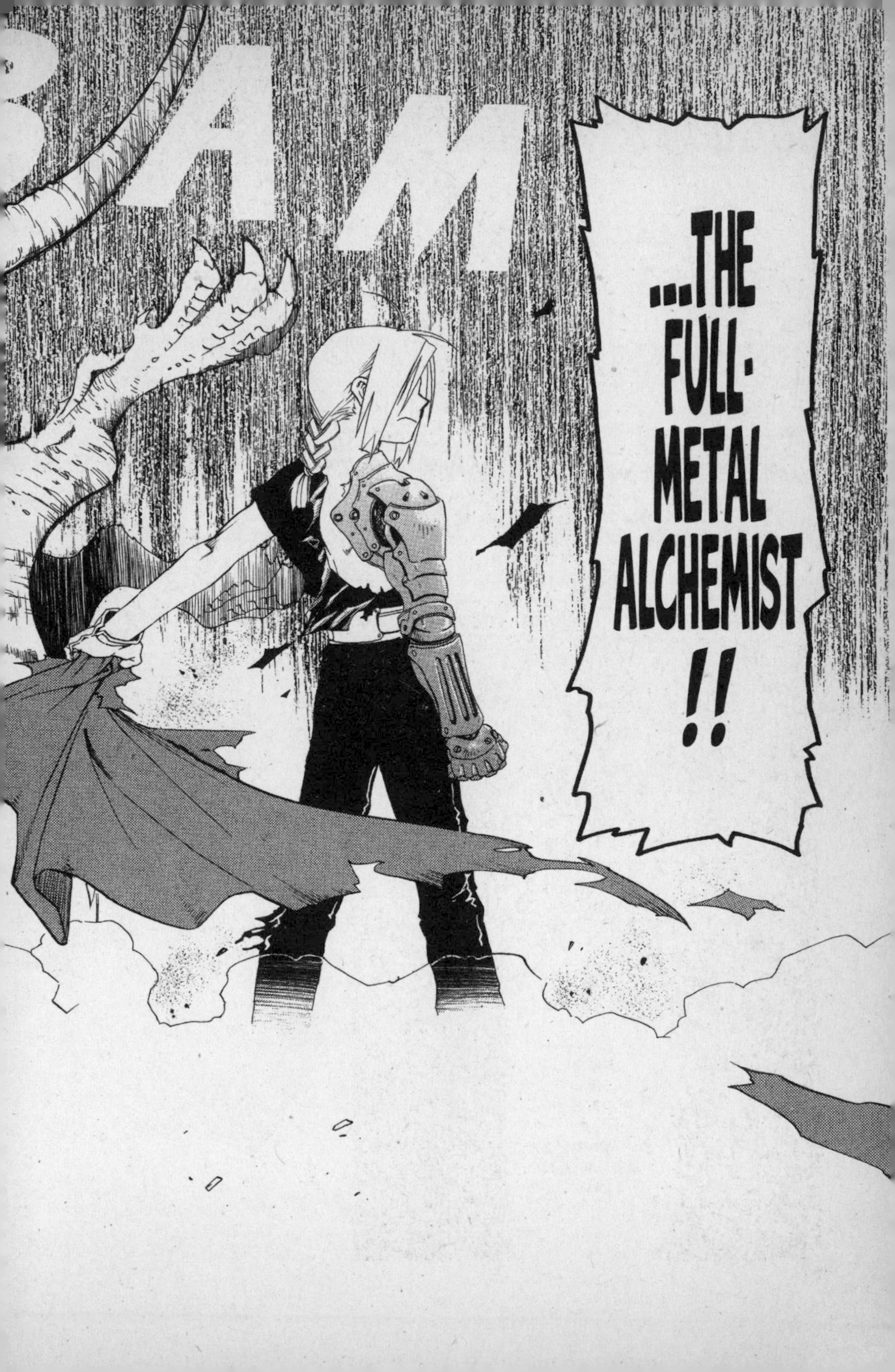
...THE FULL-METAL ALCHEMIST !!

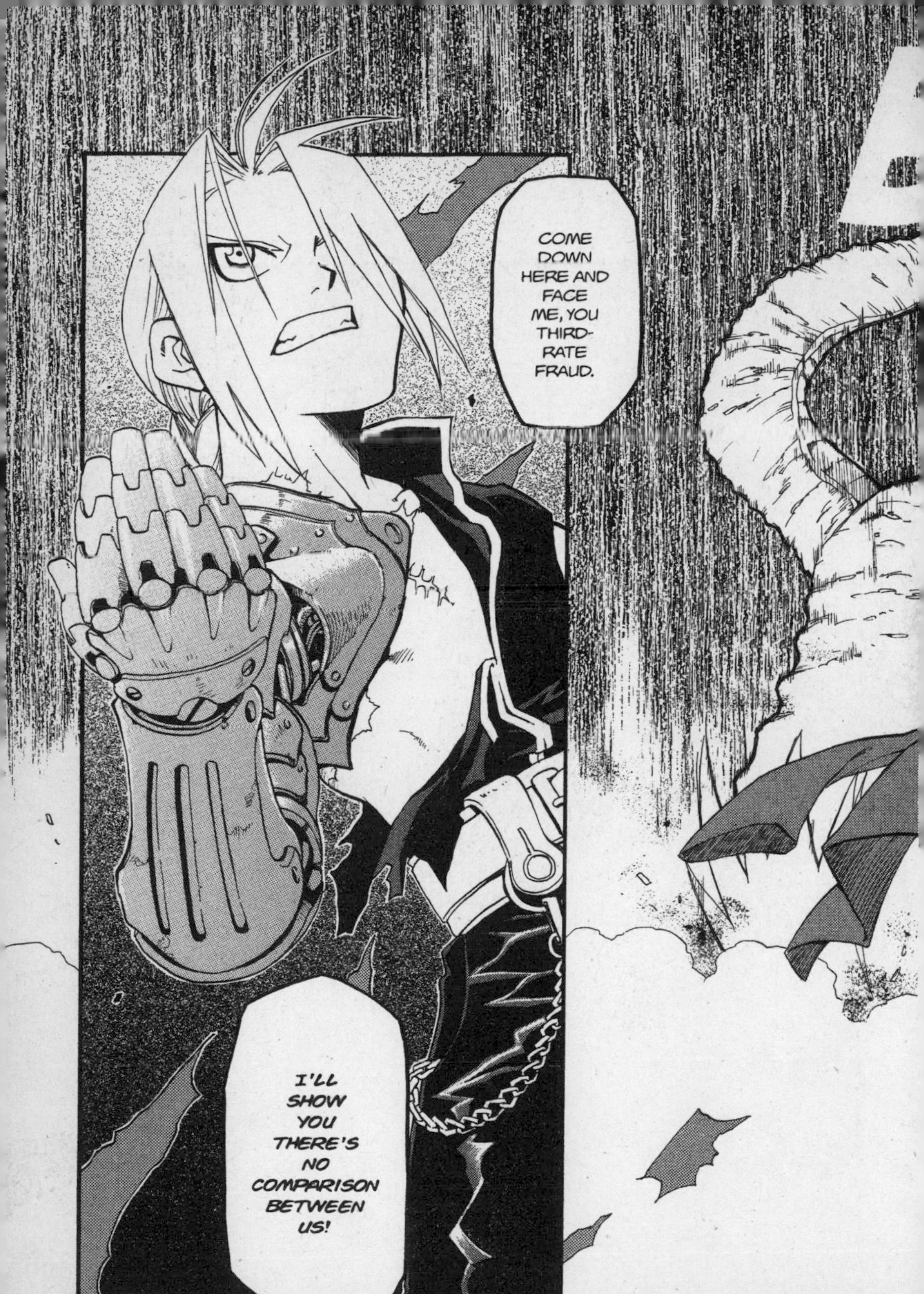
COME DOWN HERE AND FACE ME, YOU THIRD-RATE FRAUD.
I'LL SHOW YOU THERE'S NO COMPARISON BETWEEN US!

FULLMETAL
ALCHEMIST

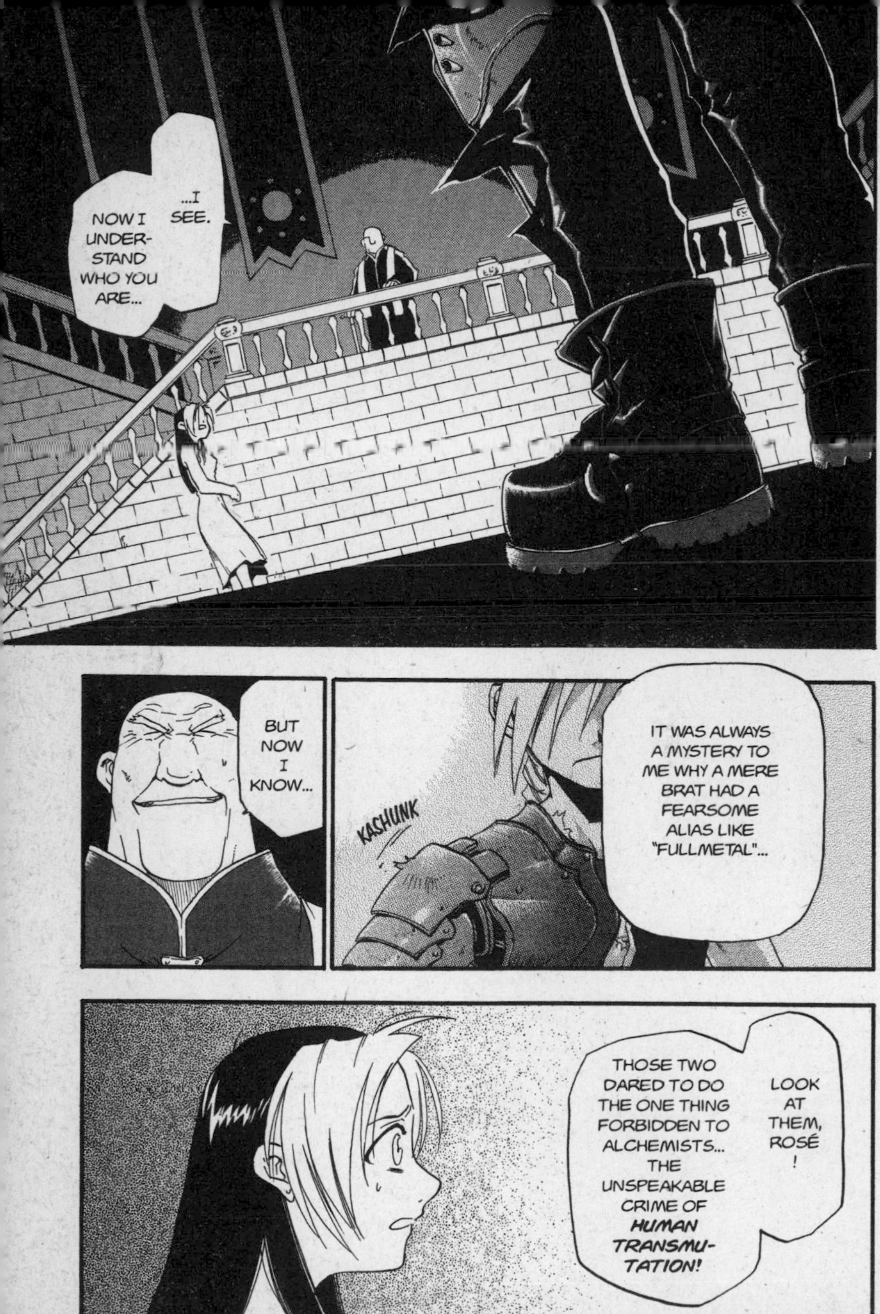
...I SEE.
NOW I UNDERSTAND WHO YOU ARE...
IT WAS ALWAYS A MYSTERY TO ME WHY A MERE BRAT HAD A FEARSOME ALIAS LIKE "FULLMETAL"...
KASHUNK
BUT NOW I KNOW...
LOOK AT THEM, ROSÉ!
THOSE TWO DARED TO DO THE ONE THING FORBIDDEN TO ALCHEMISTS... THE UNSPEAKABLE CRIME OF ***HUMAN TRANSMUTATION!***

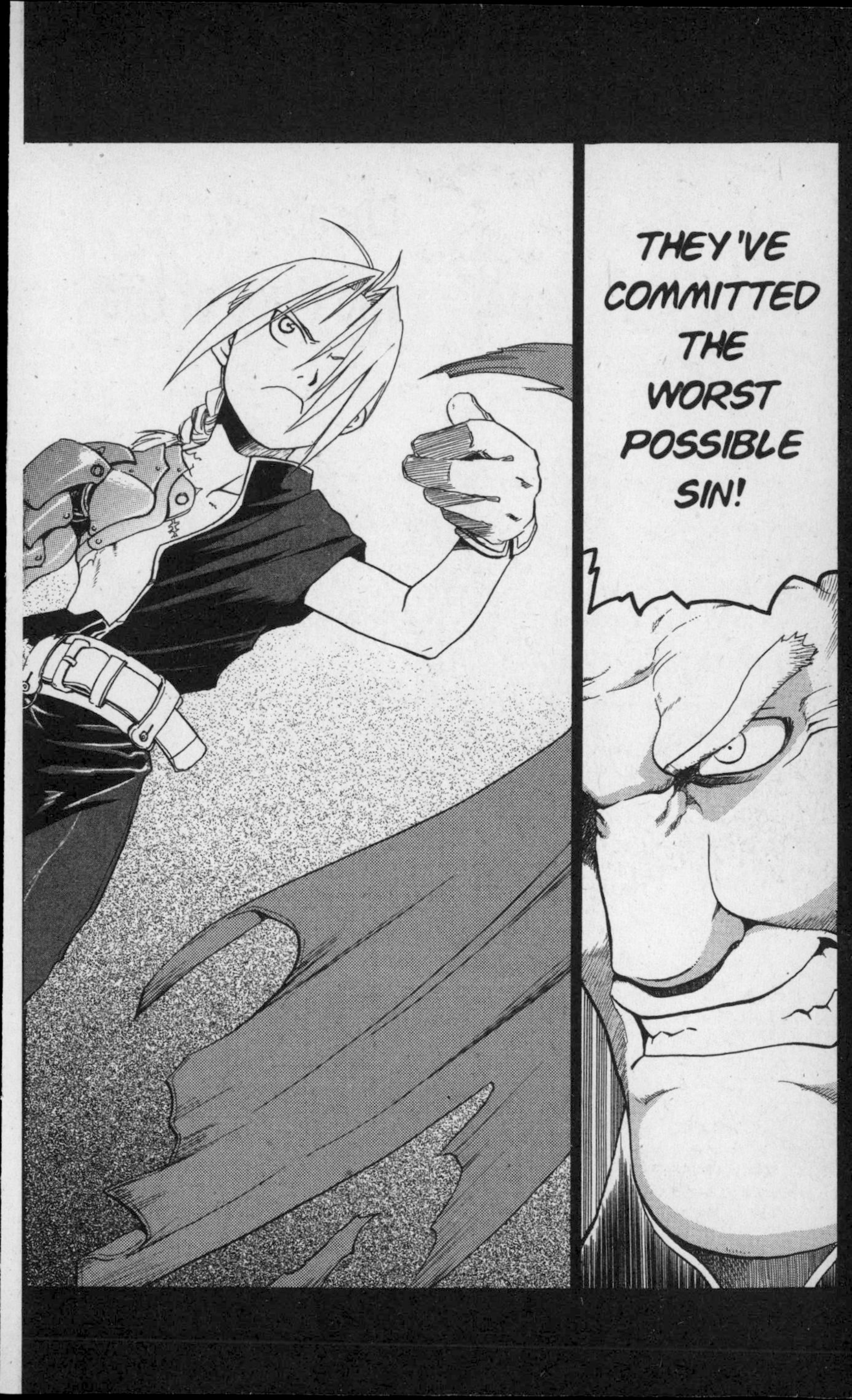
THEY'VE COMMITTED THE WORST POSSIBLE SIN!

...!

Chapter 2:
The Price of Life

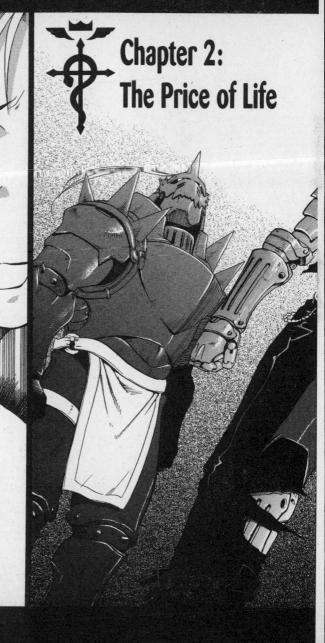

HE MADE WINGS OUT OF WAX SO HE COULD FLY... BUT WHEN HE GOT TOO CLOSE TO THE SUN... TO GOD... THE WAX MELTED AND HE CRASHED TO THE GROUND...

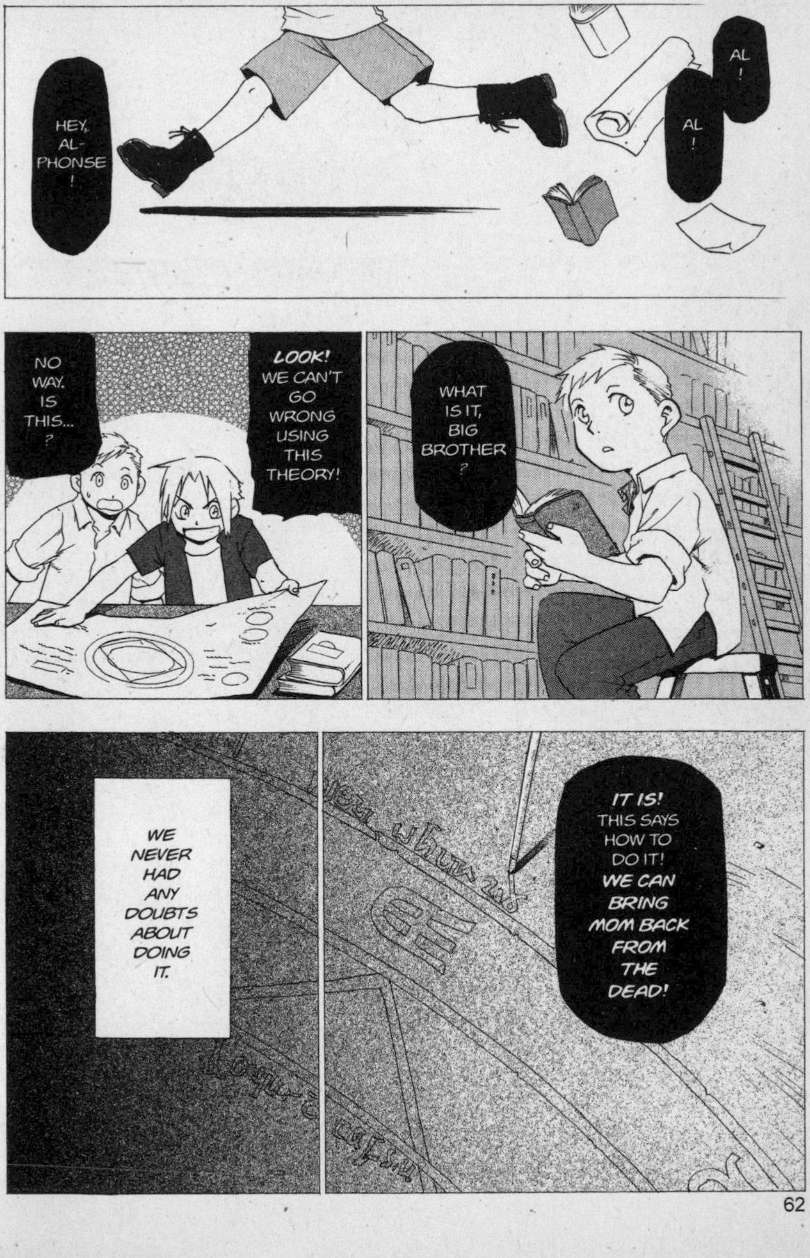
AL!
AL!
HEY, AL-PHONSE!
WHAT IS IT, BIG BROTHER?
LOOK! WE CAN'T GO WRONG USING THIS THEORY!
NO WAY. IS THIS...?
IT IS! THIS SAYS HOW TO DO IT! WE CAN BRING MOM BACK FROM THE DEAD!
WE NEVER HAD ANY DOUBTS ABOUT DOING IT.

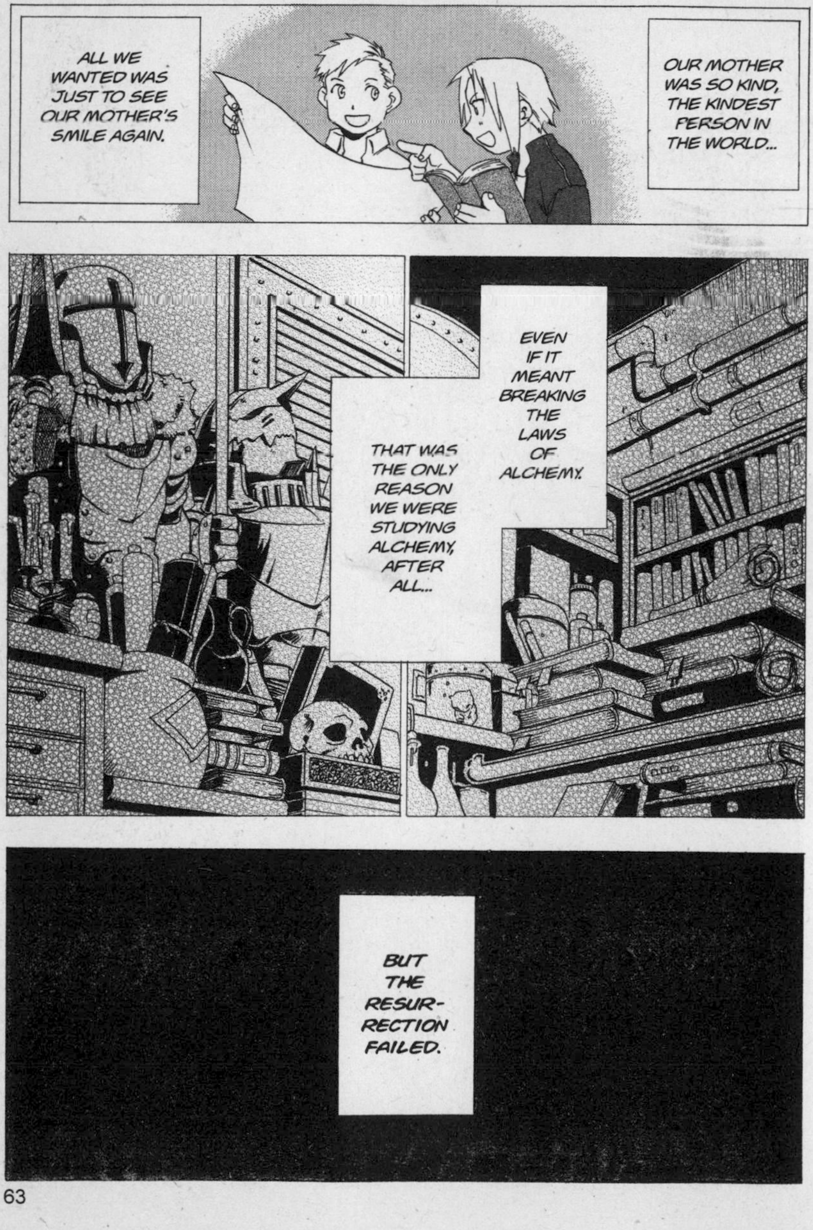
OUR MOTHER WAS SO KIND, THE KINDEST PERSON IN THE WORLD...
ALL WE WANTED WAS JUST TO SEE OUR MOTHER'S SMILE AGAIN.
EVEN IF IT MEANT BREAKING THE LAWS OF ALCHEMY.
THAT WAS THE ONLY REASON WE WERE STUDYING ALCHEMY, AFTER ALL...
BUT THE RESUR-RECTION FAILED.

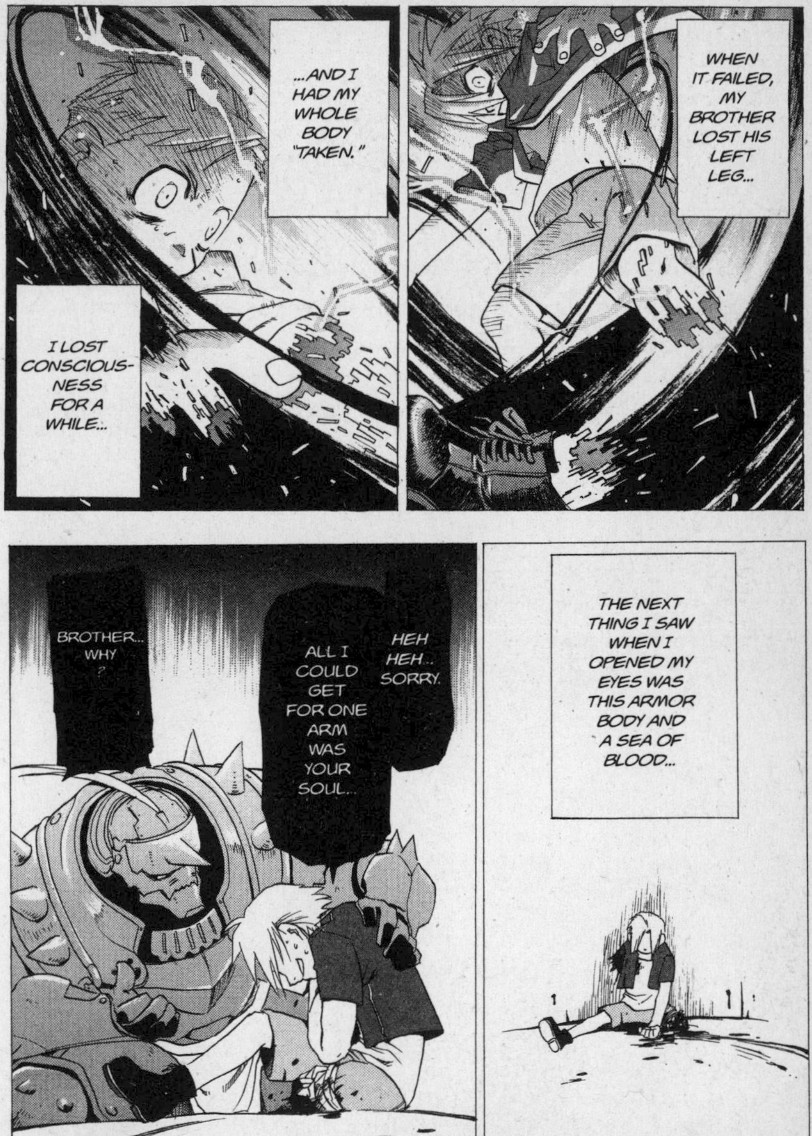
WHEN IT FAILED, MY BROTHER LOST HIS LEFT LEG...
...AND I HAD MY WHOLE BODY "TAKEN."
I LOST CONSCIOUS-NESS FOR A WHILE...
THE NEXT THING I SAW WHEN I OPENED MY EYES WAS THIS ARMOR BODY AND A SEA OF BLOOD...
HEH HEH... SORRY.
ALL I COULD GET FOR ONE ARM WAS YOUR SOUL...
BROTHER... WHY?

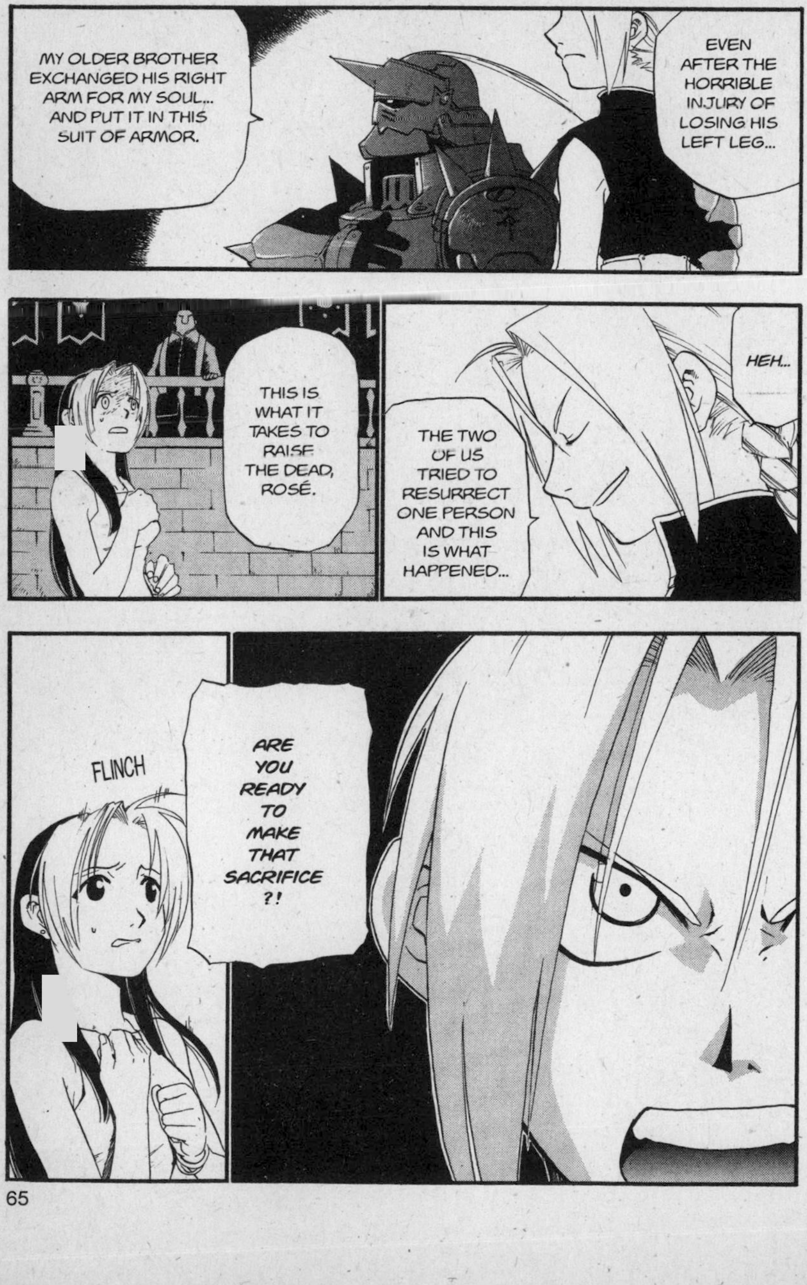
EVEN AFTER THE HORRIBLE INJURY OF LOSING HIS LEFT LEG...
MY OLDER BROTHER EXCHANGED HIS RIGHT ARM FOR MY SOUL... AND PUT IT IN THIS SUIT OF ARMOR.
HEH...
THE TWO OF US TRIED TO RESURRECT ONE PERSON AND THIS IS WHAT HAPPENED...
THIS IS WHAT IT TAKES TO RAISE THE DEAD, ROSÉ.
ARE YOU READY TO MAKE THAT SACRIFICE?!
FLINCH

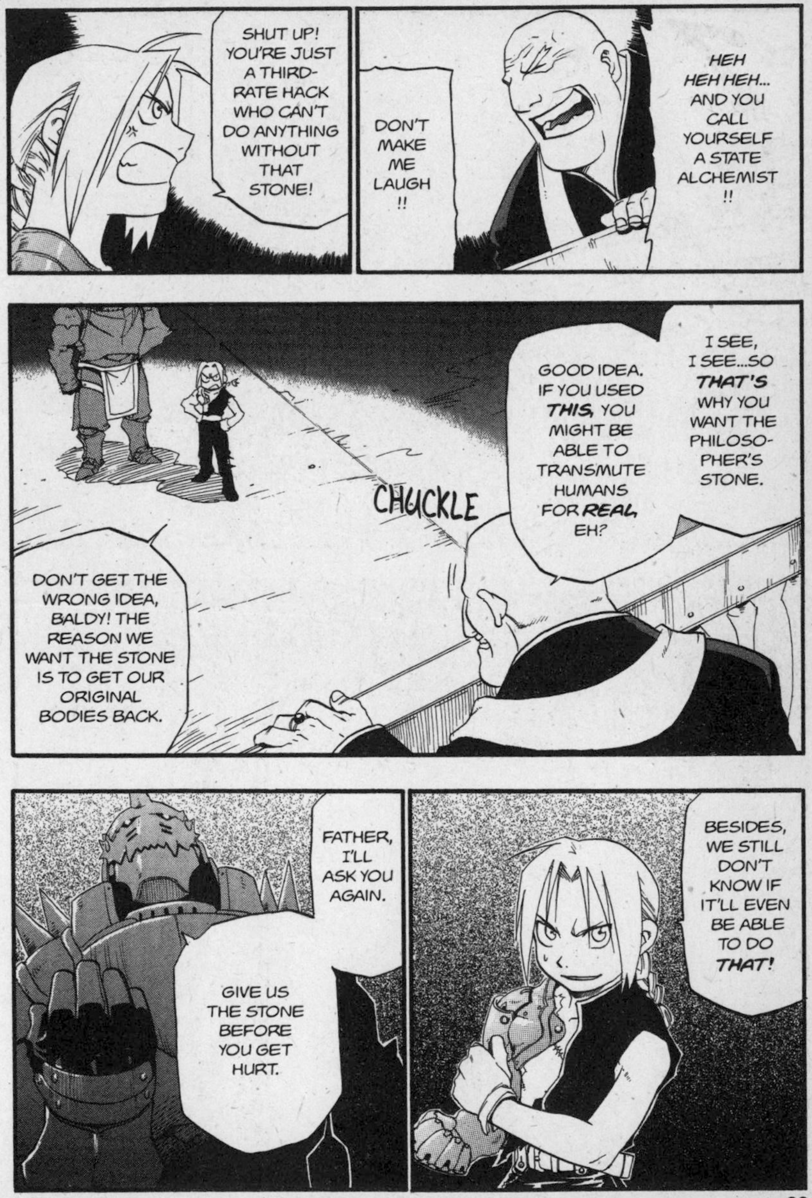
HEH HEH HEH... AND YOU CALL YOURSELF A STATE ALCHEMIST !!
DON'T MAKE ME LAUGH !!
SHUT UP! YOU'RE JUST A THIRD-RATE HACK WHO CAN'T DO ANYTHING WITHOUT THAT STONE!
I SEE, I SEE...SO THAT'S WHY YOU WANT THE PHILOSOPHER'S STONE.
GOOD IDEA. IF YOU USED THIS, YOU MIGHT BE ABLE TO TRANSMUTE HUMANS FOR REAL, EH?
CHUCKLE
DON'T GET THE WRONG IDEA, BALDY! THE REASON WE WANT THE STONE IS TO GET OUR ORIGINAL BODIES BACK.
BESIDES, WE STILL DON'T KNOW IF IT'LL EVEN BE ABLE TO DO THAT!
FATHER, I'LL ASK YOU AGAIN.
GIVE US THE STONE BEFORE YOU GET HURT.

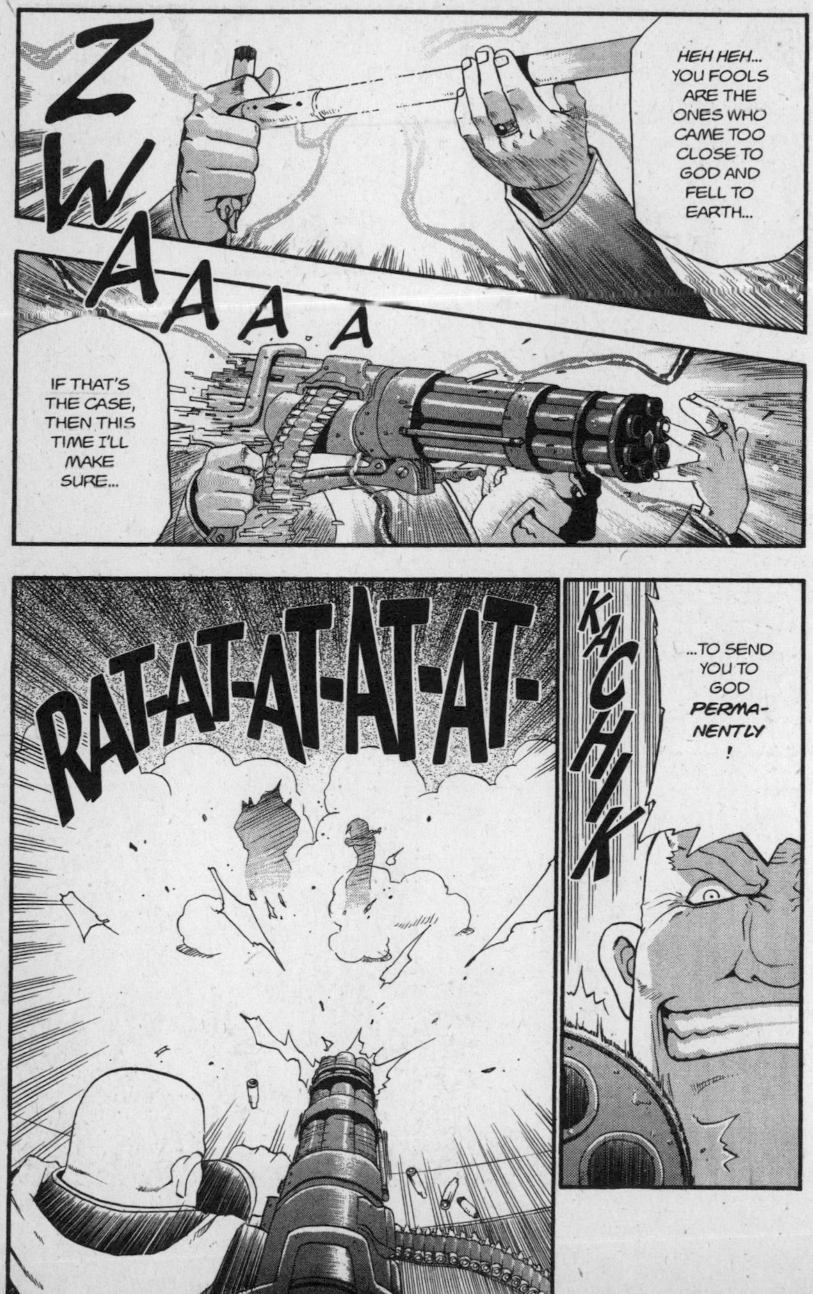

HEH HEH... YOU FOOLS ARE THE ONES WHO CAME TOO CLOSE TO GOD AND FELL TO EARTH...
ZWAAAAA
IF THAT'S THE CASE, THEN THIS TIME I'LL MAKE SURE...
KACHIK
...TO SEND YOU TO GOD *PERMANENTLY* !
RAT-AT-AT-AT-AT-

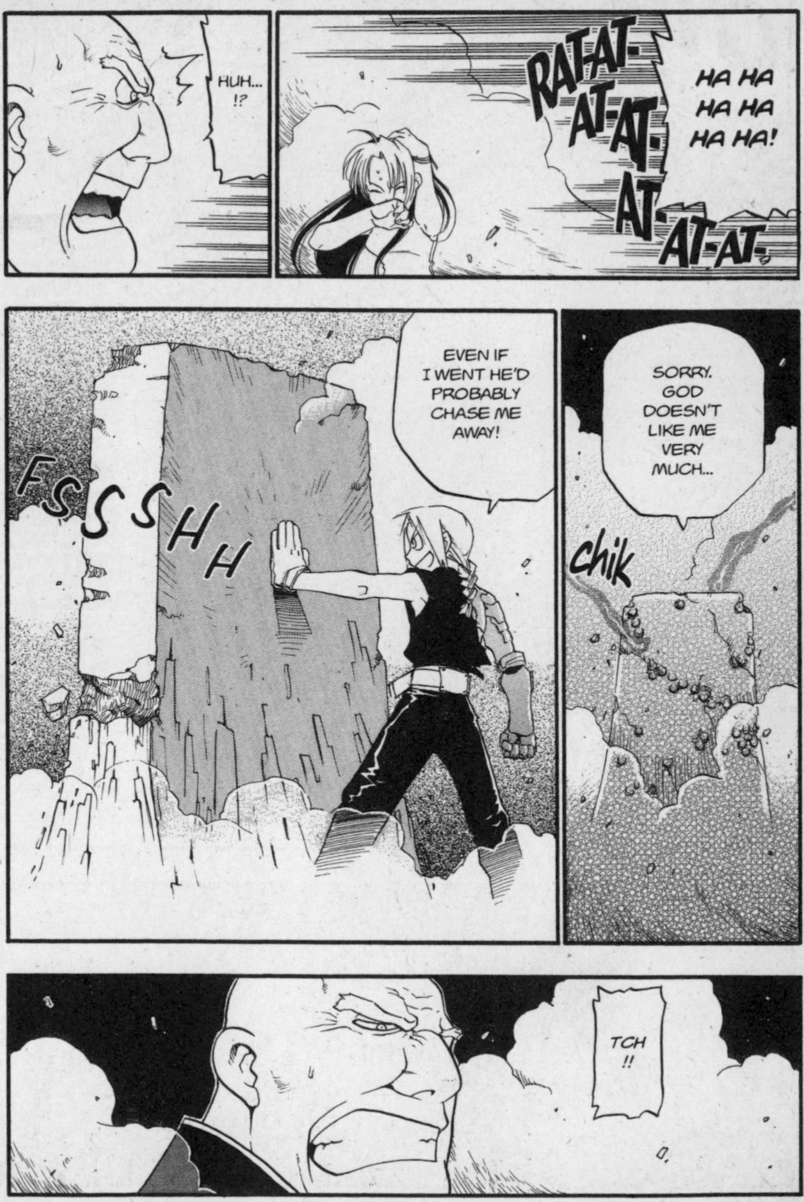
HA HA
HA HA
HA HA!
RAT-AT-AT-AT-AT-AT-AT-AT-
HUH... !?
SORRY. GOD DOESN'T LIKE ME VERY MUCH...
chik
EVEN IF I WENT HE'D PROBABLY CHASE ME AWAY!
FSSHH
TCH !!

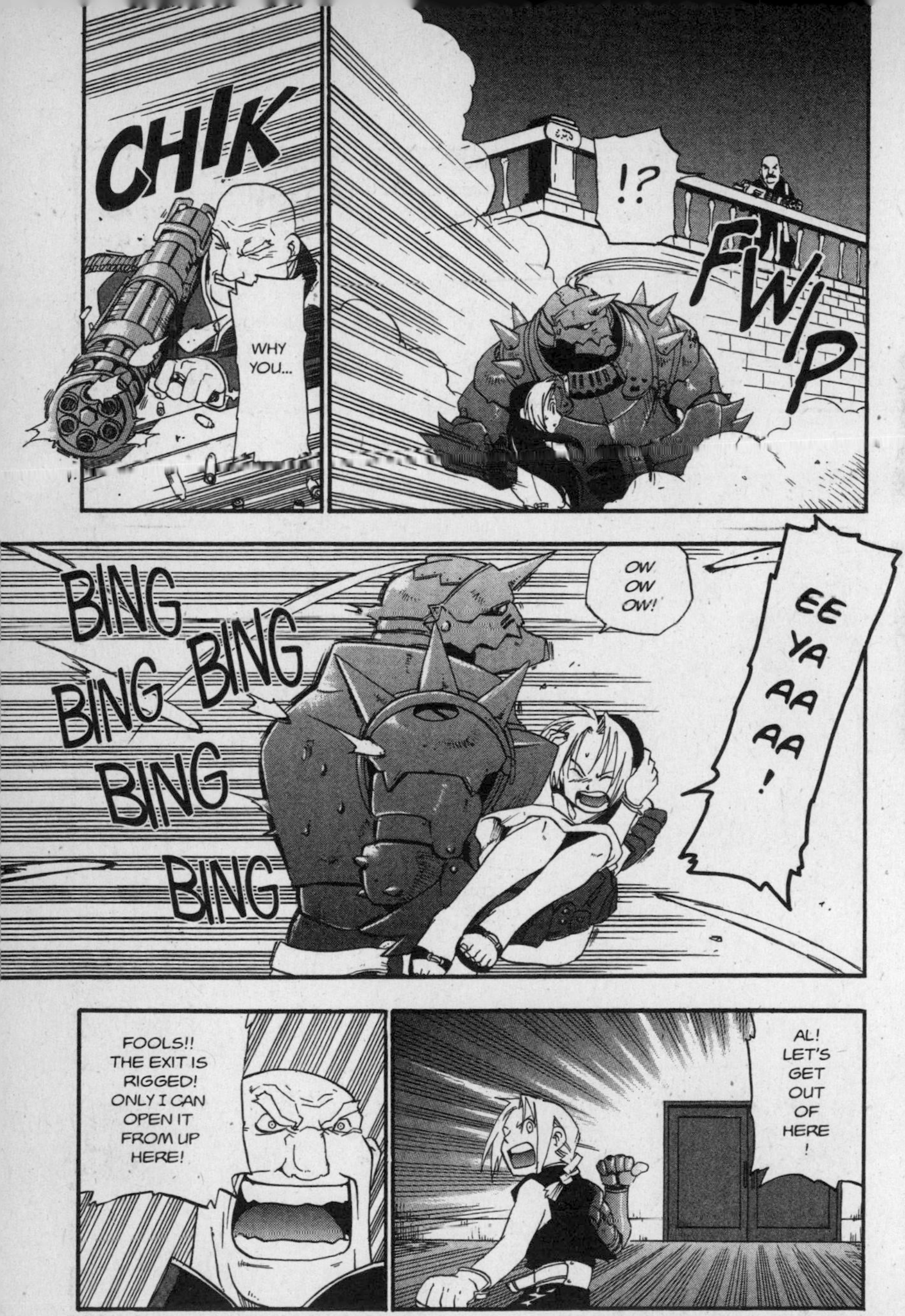
!?
FWIP
CHIK
WHY YOU...
EE YA AA AA!
OW OW OW!
BING
BING BING
BING
BING
AL! LET'S GET OUT OF HERE!
FOOLS!! THE EXIT IS RIGGED! ONLY I CAN OPEN IT FROM UP HERE!

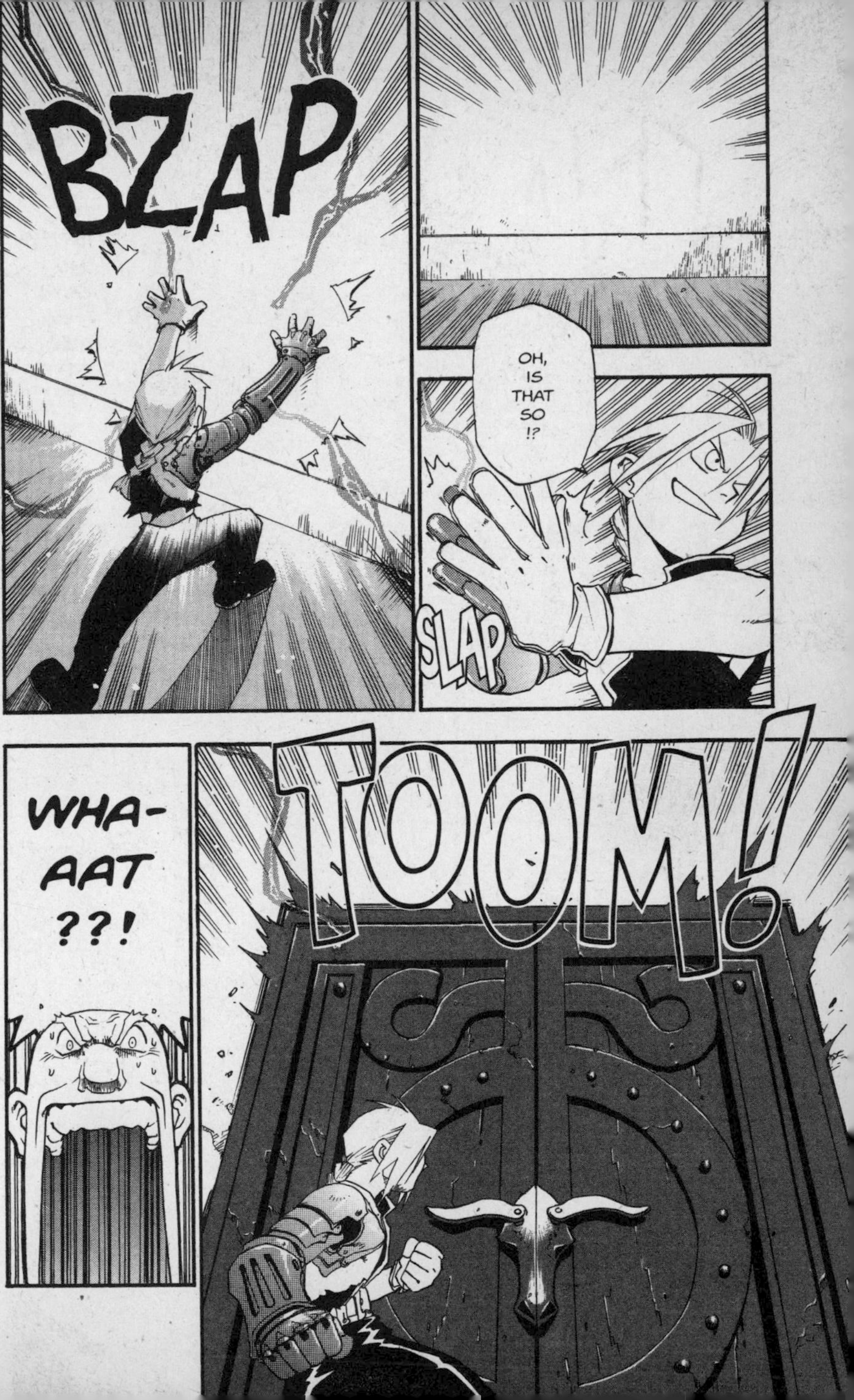
OH, IS THAT SO !?
SLAP
BZAP
TOOM!
WHA-AAT ??!

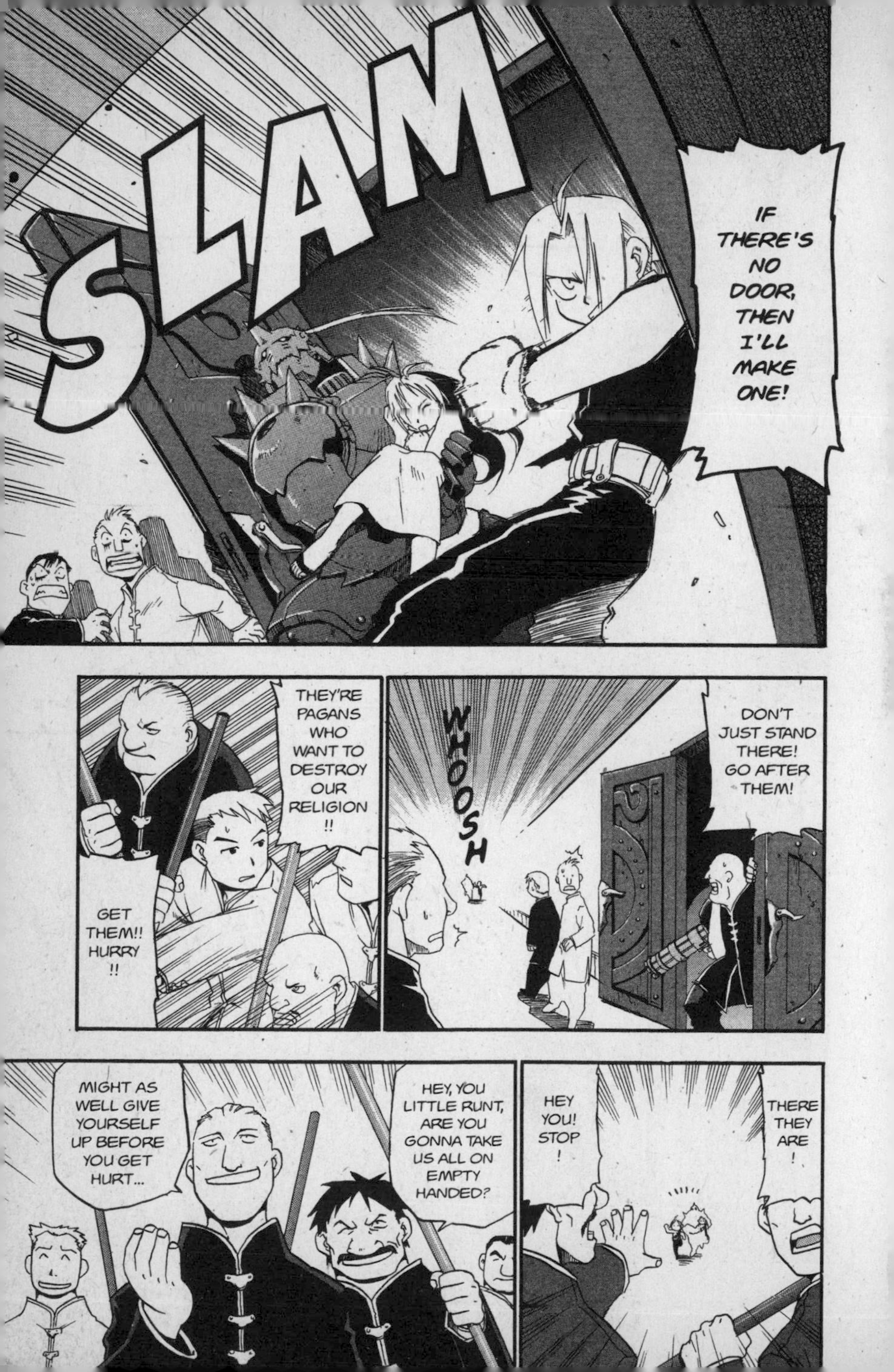
IF THERE'S NO DOOR, THEN I'LL MAKE ONE!
SLAM
DON'T JUST STAND THERE! GO AFTER THEM!
WHOOSH
THEY'RE PAGANS WHO WANT TO DESTROY OUR RELIGION!!
GET THEM!! HURRY!!
THERE THEY ARE!
HEY YOU! STOP!
HEY, YOU LITTLE RUNT, ARE YOU GONNA TAKE US ALL ON EMPTY HANDED?
MIGHT AS WELL GIVE YOURSELF UP BEFORE YOU GET HURT...

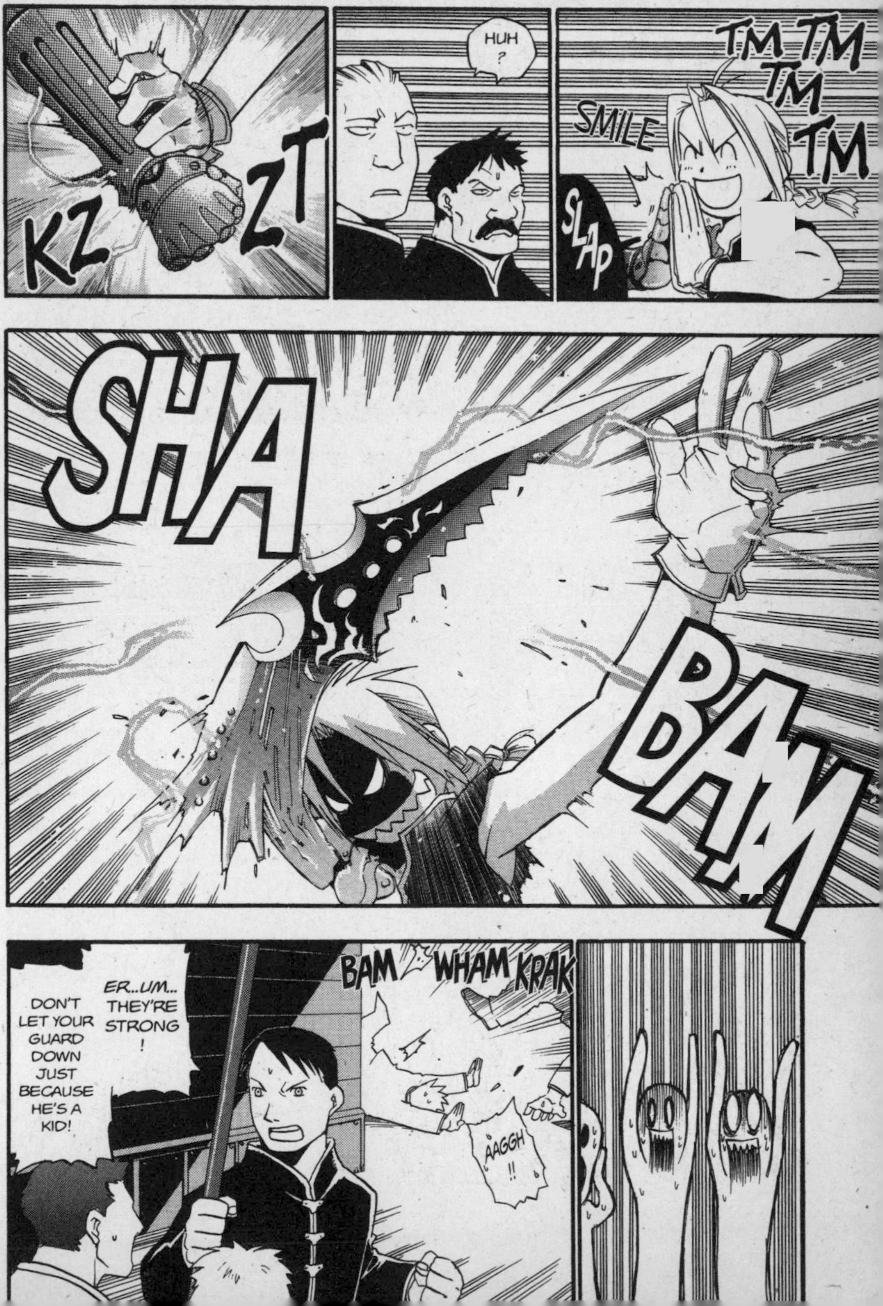
TM TM TM TM TM
SMILE
SLAP
HUH ?
KZ ZT
SHA
BAM
BAM WHAM KRAK
AAGGH !!
ER...UM... THEY'RE STRONG !
DON'T LET YOUR GUARD DOWN JUST BECAUSE HE'S A KID!

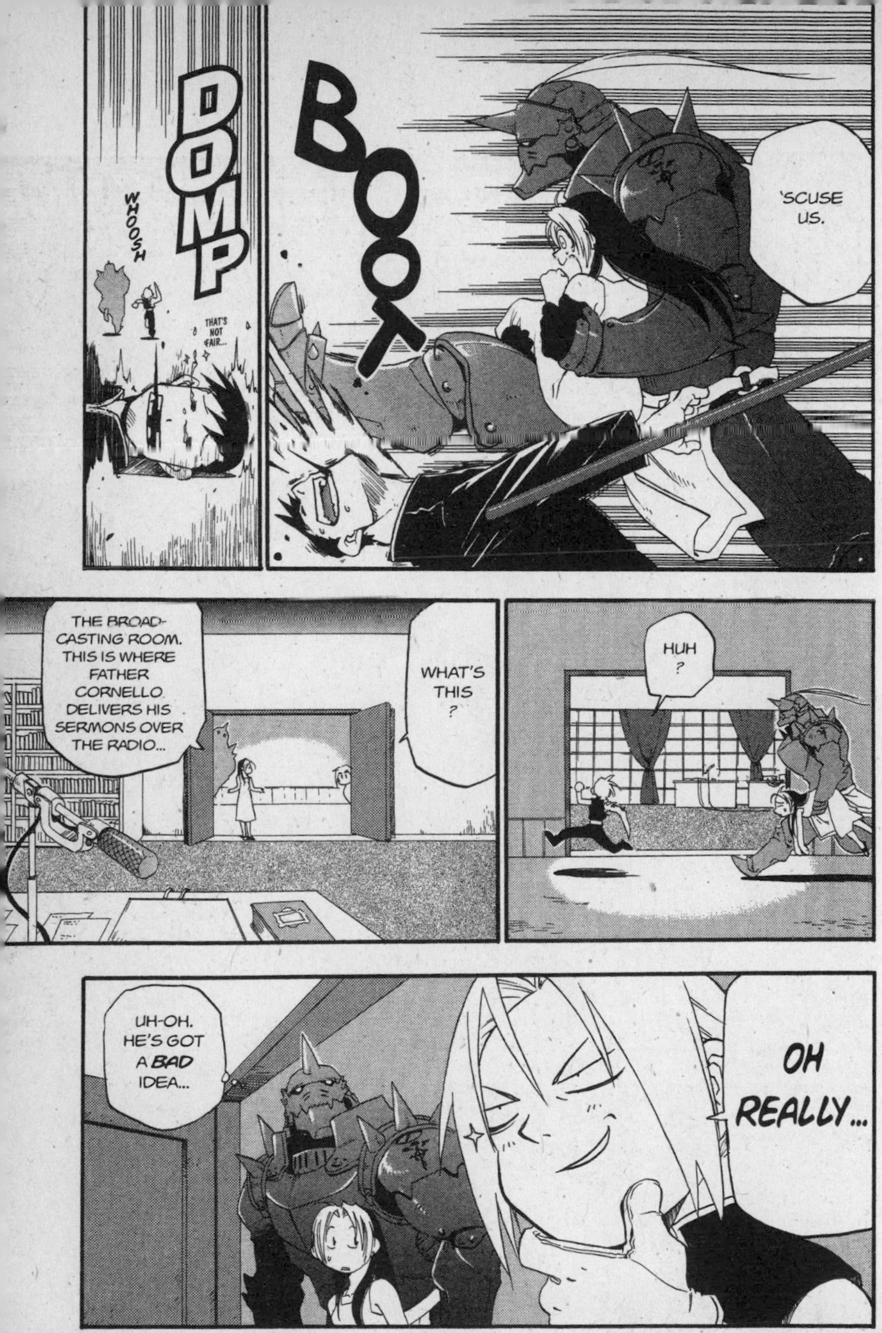
'SCUSE US.
BOOT
DOMP
WHOOSH
THAT'S NOT FAIR...
HUH ?
WHAT'S THIS ?
THE BROAD-CASTING ROOM. THIS IS WHERE FATHER CORNELLO DELIVERS HIS SERMONS OVER THE RADIO...
OH REALLY...
UH-OH. HE'S GOT A *BAD* IDEA...

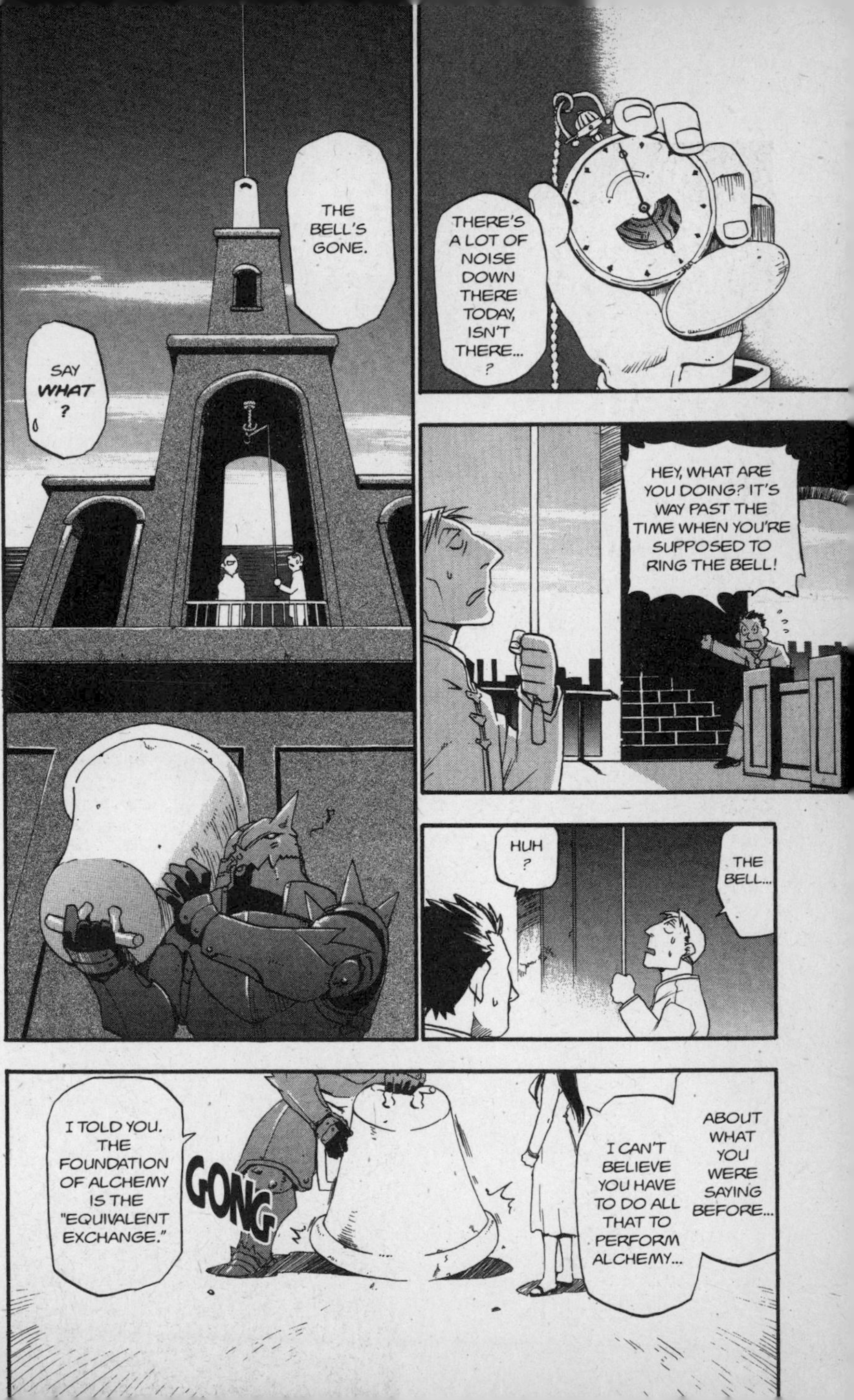
THERE'S A LOT OF NOISE DOWN THERE TODAY, ISN'T THERE...?
HEY, WHAT ARE YOU DOING? IT'S WAY PAST THE TIME WHEN YOU'RE SUPPOSED TO RING THE BELL!
THE BELL...
HUH?
THE BELL'S GONE.
SAY **WHAT**?
ABOUT WHAT YOU WERE SAYING BEFORE...
I CAN'T BELIEVE YOU HAVE TO DO ALL THAT TO PERFORM ALCHEMY...
GONG
I TOLD YOU. THE FOUNDATION OF ALCHEMY IS THE "EQUIVALENT EXCHANGE."

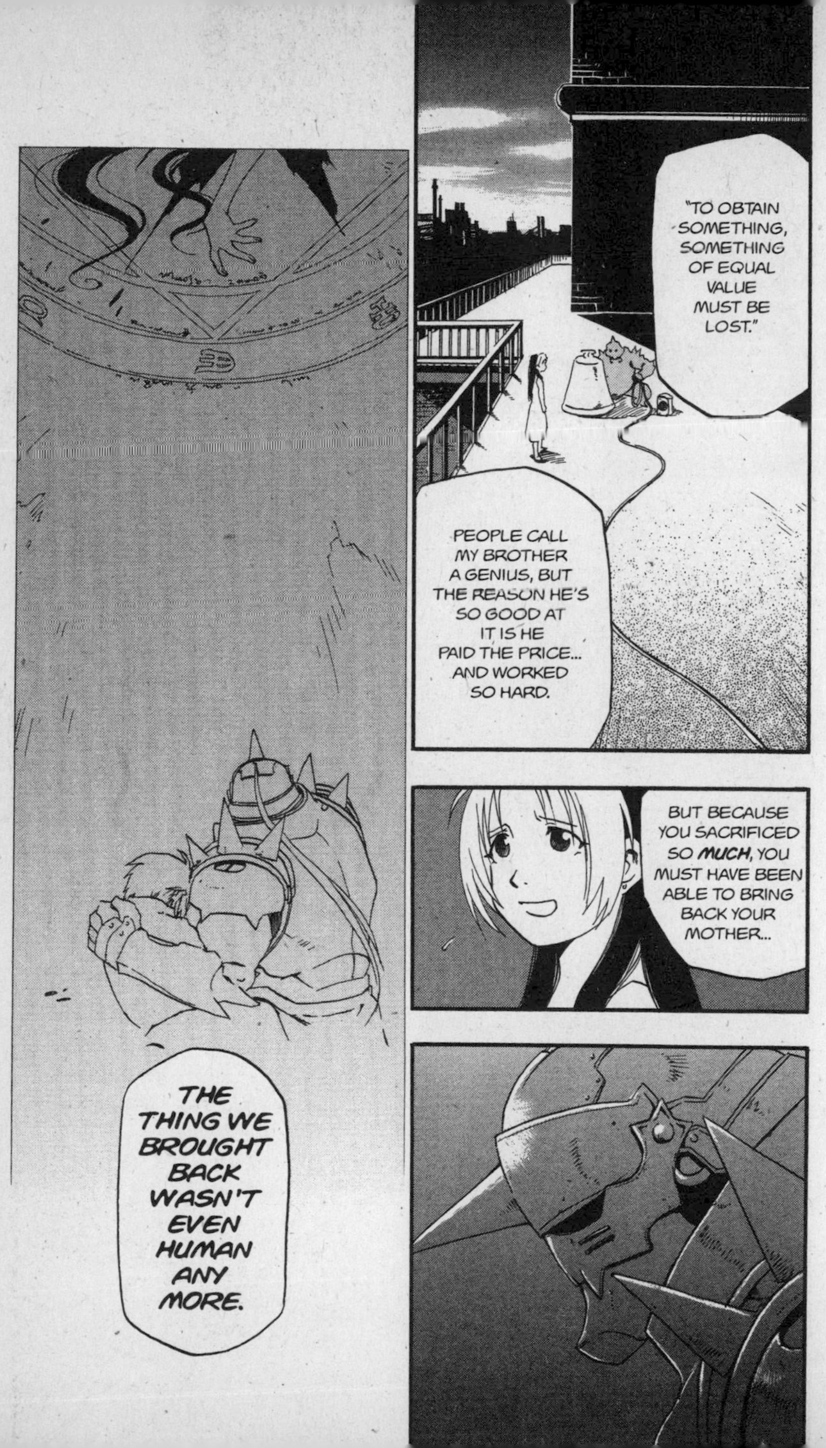
"TO OBTAIN SOMETHING, SOMETHING OF EQUAL VALUE MUST BE LOST."
PEOPLE CALL MY BROTHER A GENIUS, BUT THE REASON HE'S SO GOOD AT IT IS HE PAID THE PRICE... AND WORKED SO HARD.
BUT BECAUSE YOU SACRIFICED SO *MUCH*, YOU MUST HAVE BEEN ABLE TO BRING BACK YOUR MOTHER...
THE THING WE BROUGHT BACK WASN'T EVEN HUMAN ANY MORE.

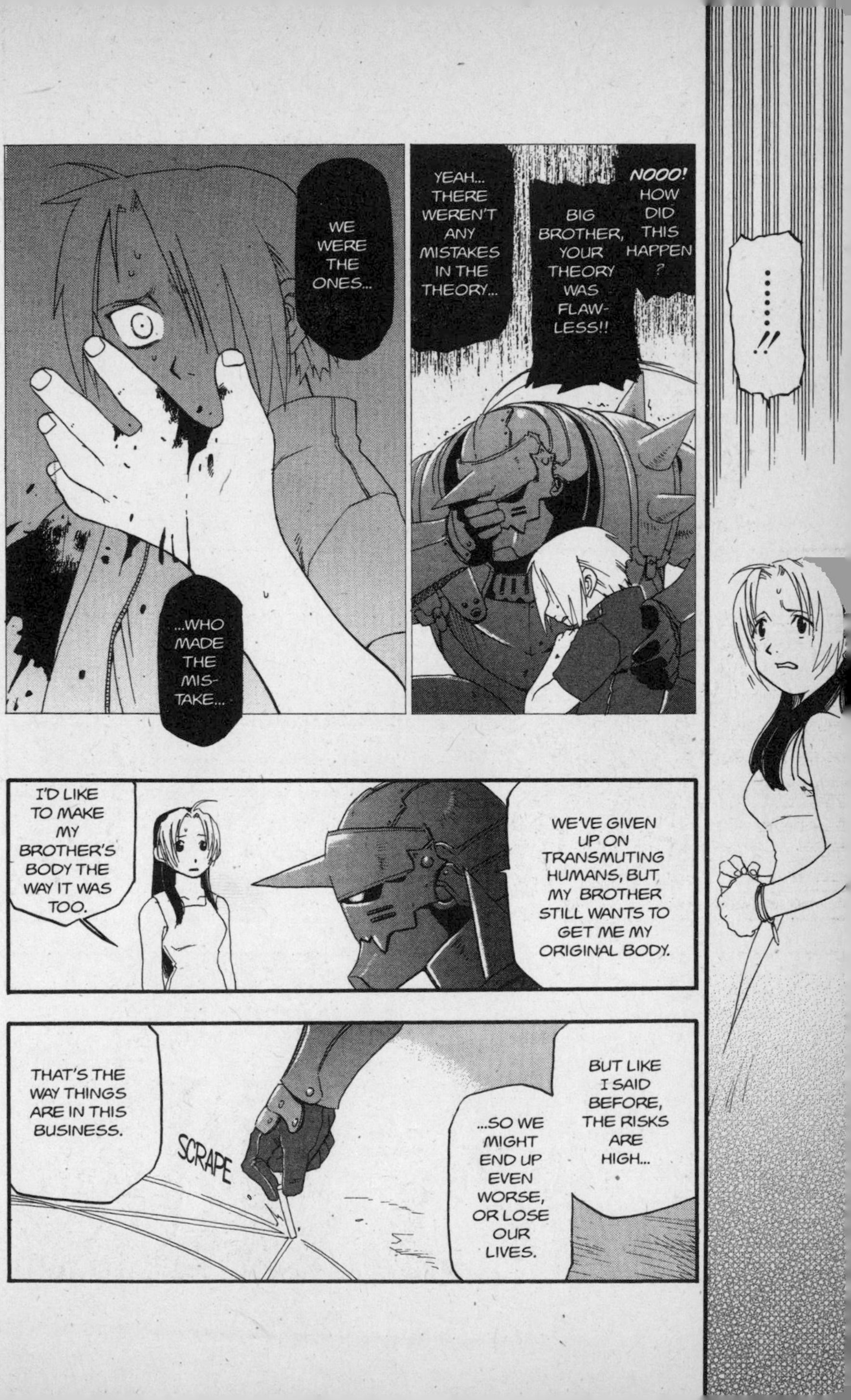
......!!
NOOO! HOW DID THIS HAPPEN?
BIG BROTHER, YOUR THEORY WAS FLAWLESS!!
YEAH... THERE WEREN'T ANY MISTAKES IN THE THEORY...
WE WERE THE ONES...
...WHO MADE THE MISTAKE...
WE'VE GIVEN UP ON TRANSMUTING HUMANS, BUT, MY BROTHER STILL WANTS TO GET ME MY ORIGINAL BODY.
I'D LIKE TO MAKE MY BROTHER'S BODY THE WAY IT WAS TOO.
BUT LIKE I SAID BEFORE, THE RISKS ARE HIGH...
...SO WE MIGHT END UP EVEN WORSE, OR LOSE OUR LIVES.
SCRAPE
THAT'S THE WAY THINGS ARE IN THIS BUSINESS.

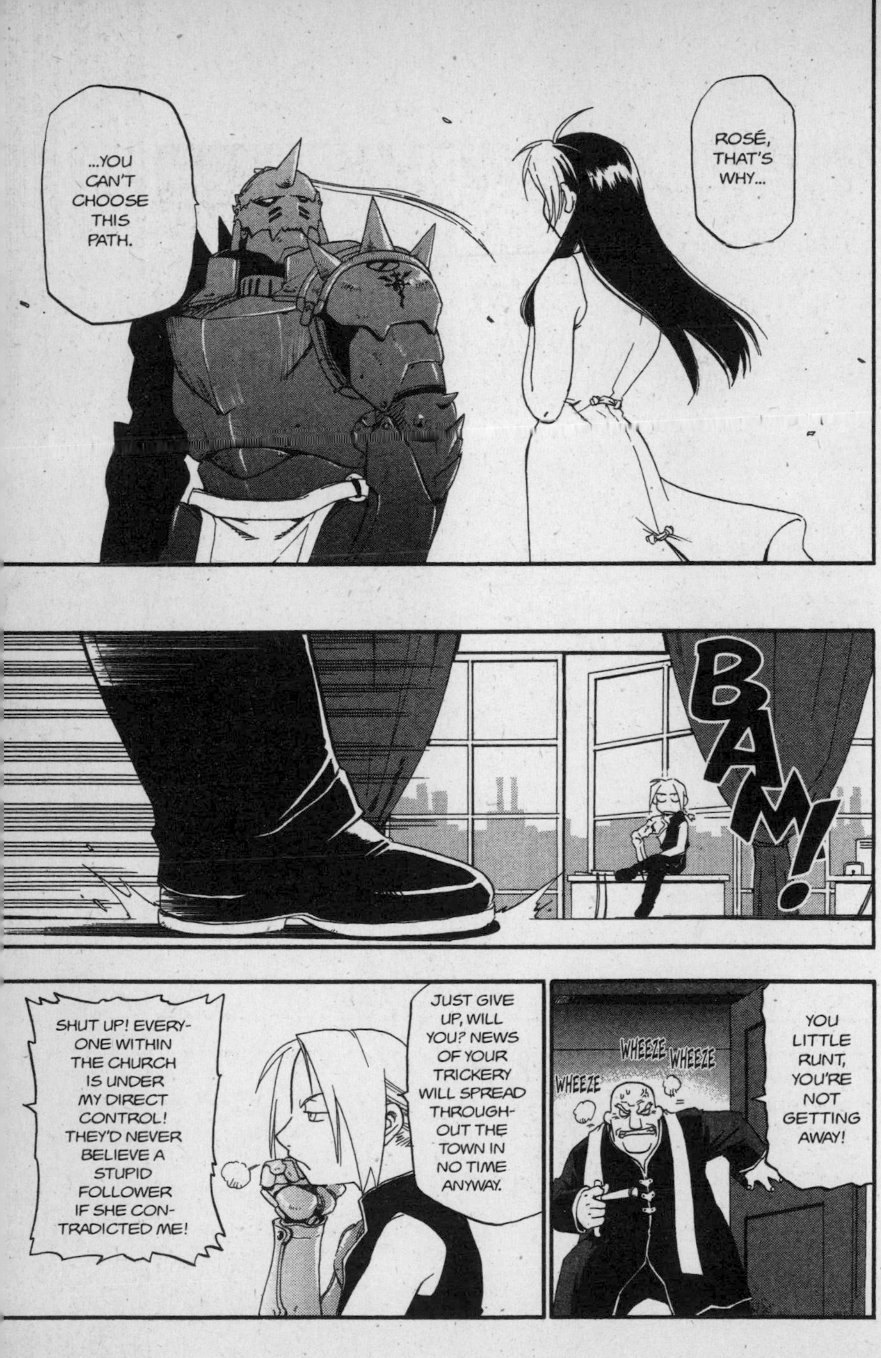
ROSÉ, THAT'S WHY...
...YOU CAN'T CHOOSE THIS PATH.
BAM!
WHEEZE WHEEZE
WHEEZE
YOU LITTLE RUNT, YOU'RE NOT GETTING AWAY!
JUST GIVE UP, WILL YOU? NEWS OF YOUR TRICKERY WILL SPREAD THROUGH-OUT THE TOWN IN NO TIME ANYWAY.
SHUT UP! EVERY-ONE WITHIN THE CHURCH IS UNDER MY DIRECT CONTROL! THEY'D NEVER BELIEVE A STUPID FOLLOWER IF SHE CON-TRADICTED ME!

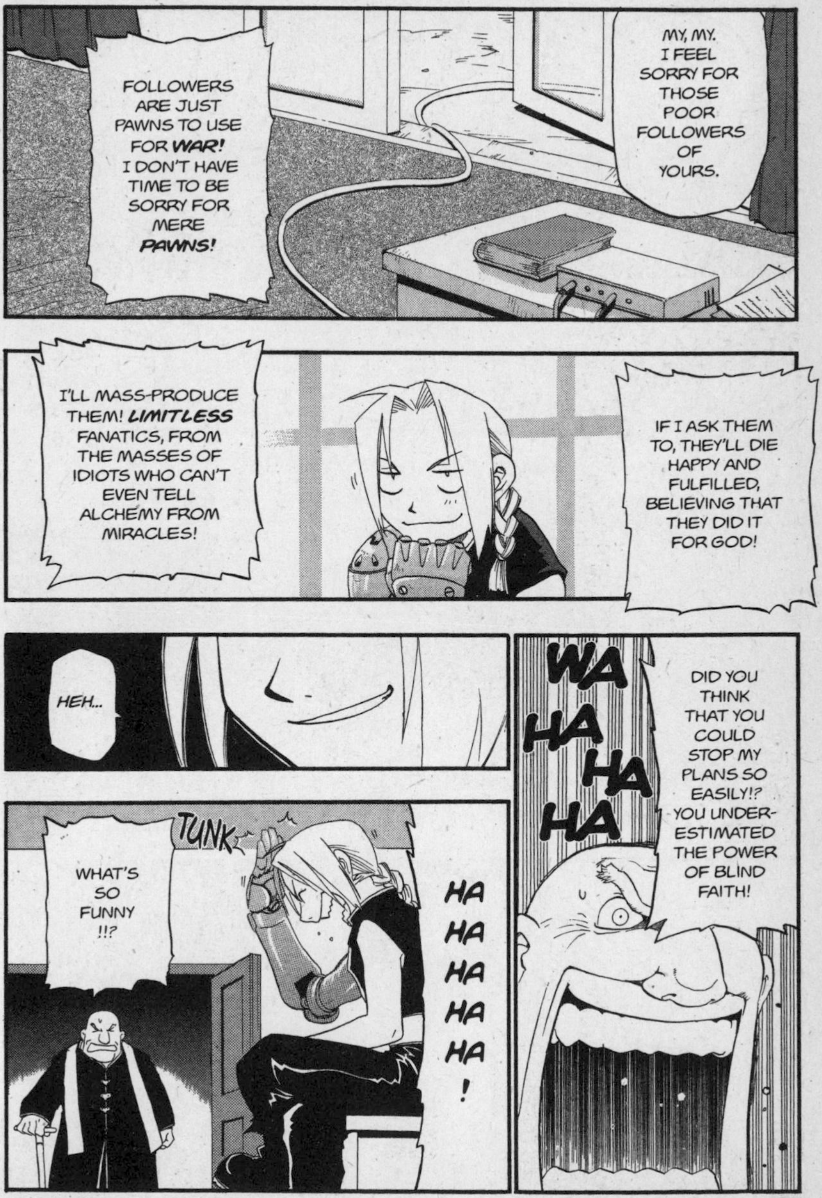

MY, MY. I FEEL SORRY FOR THOSE POOR FOLLOWERS OF YOURS.
FOLLOWERS ARE JUST PAWNS TO USE FOR **WAR!** I DON'T HAVE TIME TO BE SORRY FOR MERE **PAWNS!**
IF I ASK THEM TO, THEY'LL DIE HAPPY AND FULFILLED, BELIEVING THAT THEY DID IT FOR GOD!
I'LL MASS-PRODUCE THEM! ***LIMITLESS*** FANATICS, FROM THE MASSES OF IDIOTS WHO CAN'T EVEN TELL ALCHEMY FROM MIRACLES!
WA HA HA HA
DID YOU THINK THAT YOU COULD STOP MY PLANS SO EASILY!? YOU UNDER-ESTIMATED THE POWER OF BLIND FAITH!
HEH...
TUNK
HA HA HA HA HA!
WHAT'S SO FUNNY !!?

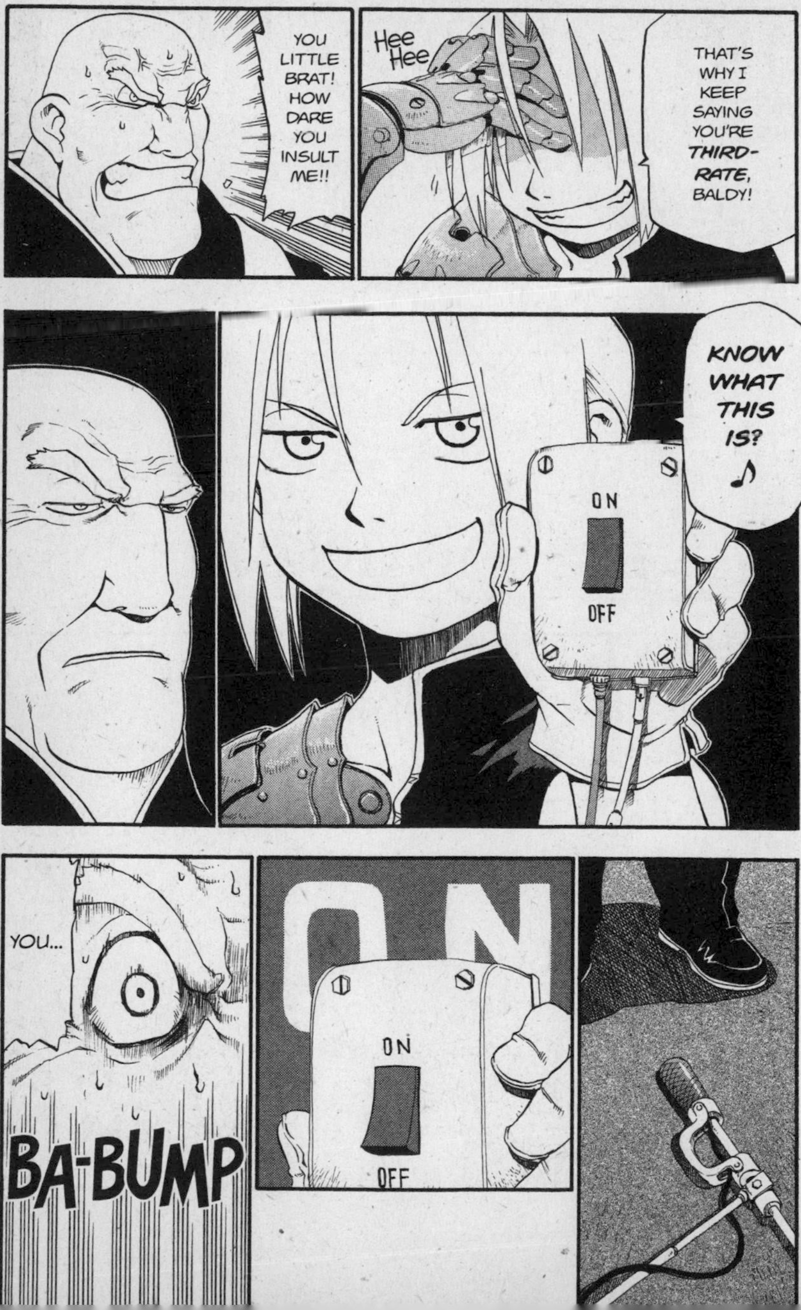
THAT'S WHY I KEEP SAYING YOU'RE THIRD-RATE, BALDY!
Hee Hee
YOU LITTLE BRAT! HOW DARE YOU INSULT ME!!
KNOW WHAT THIS IS? ♪
ON
OFF
ON
ON
OFF
YOU...
BA-BUMP

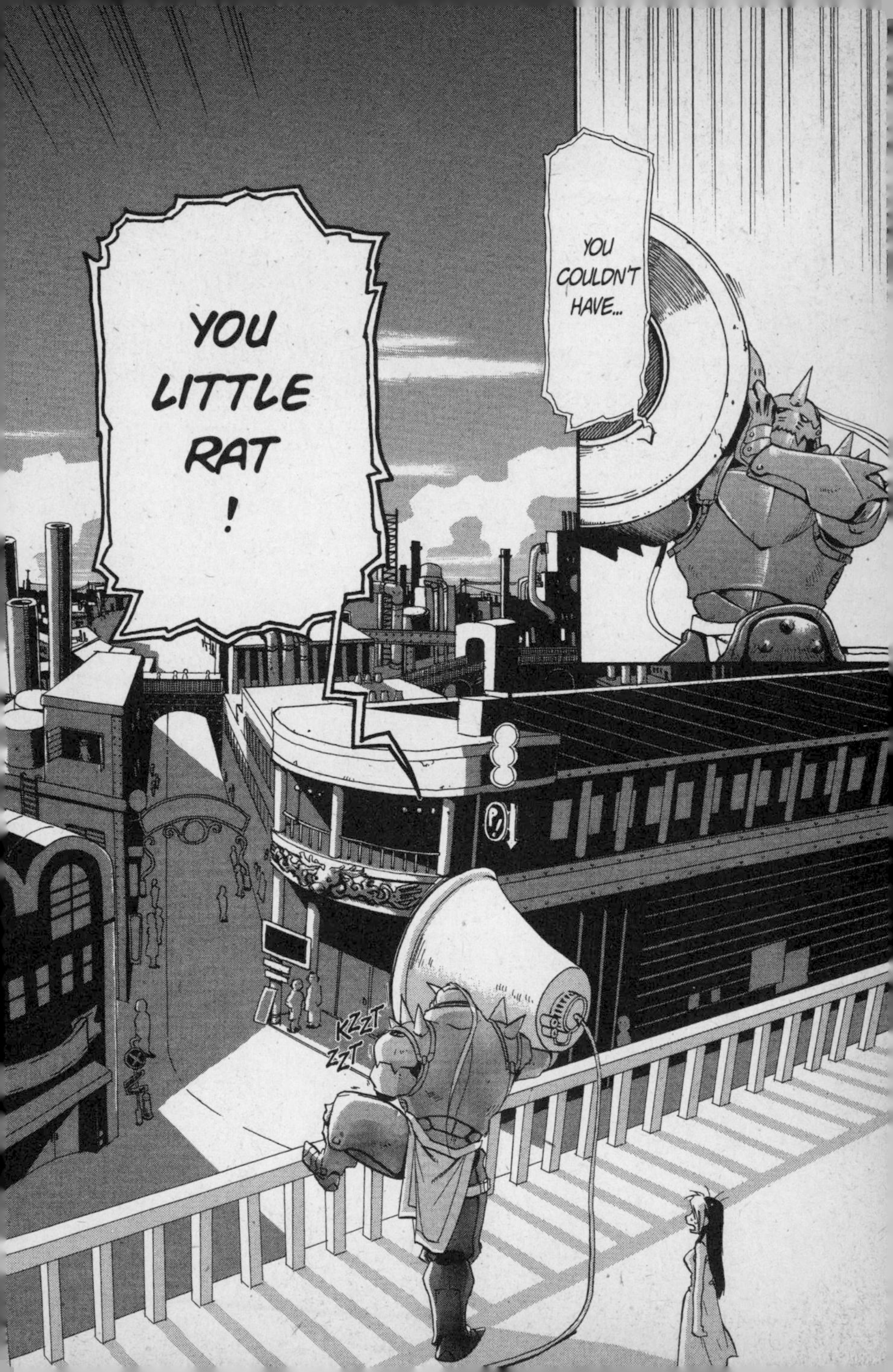
YOU COULDN'T HAVE...
YOU LITTLE RAT!
KZZT ZZT

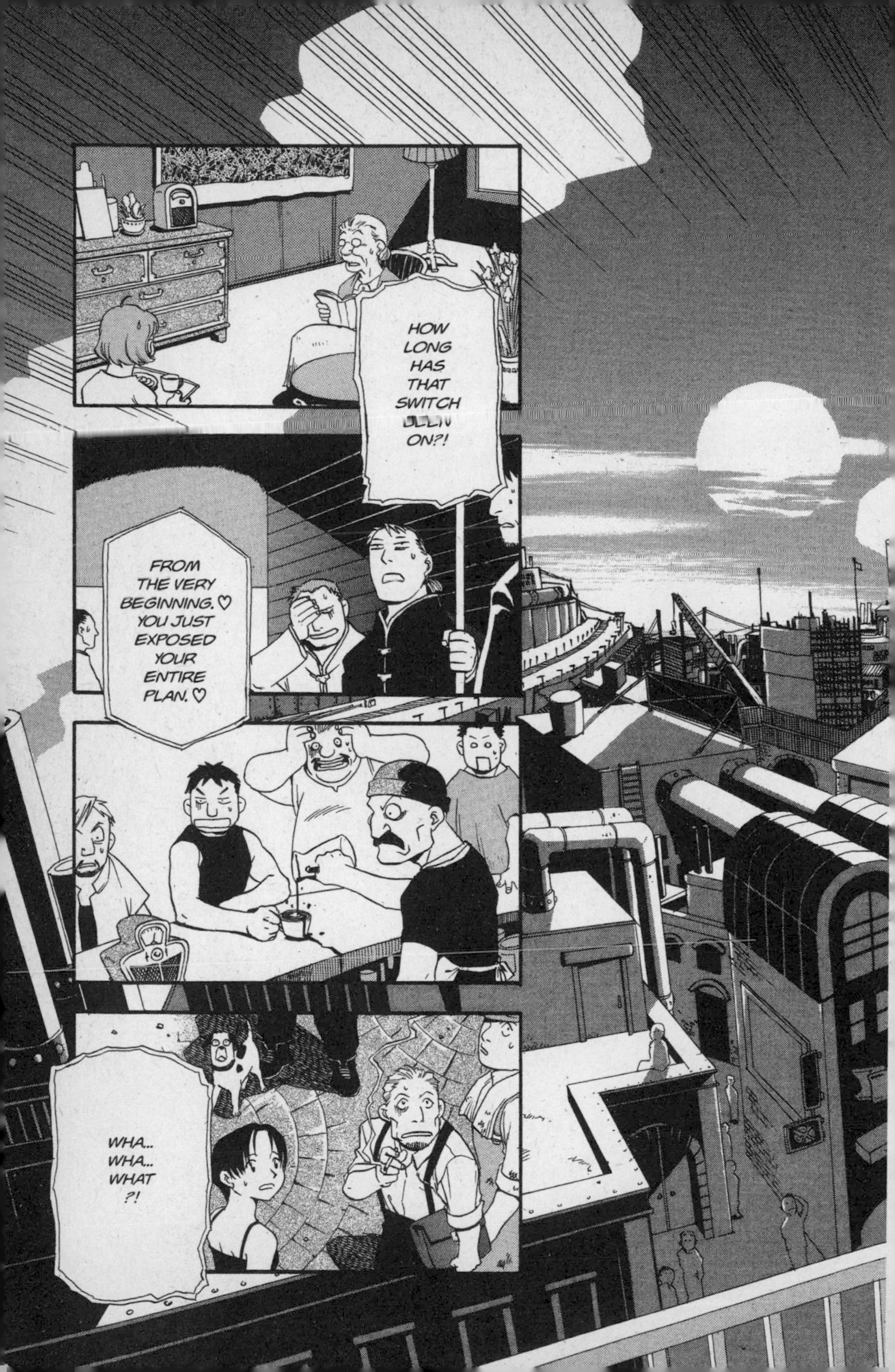
HOW LONG HAS THAT SWITCH BEEN ON?!
FROM THE VERY BEGINNING. ♡ YOU JUST EXPOSED YOUR ENTIRE PLAN. ♡
WHA... WHA... WHAT ?!

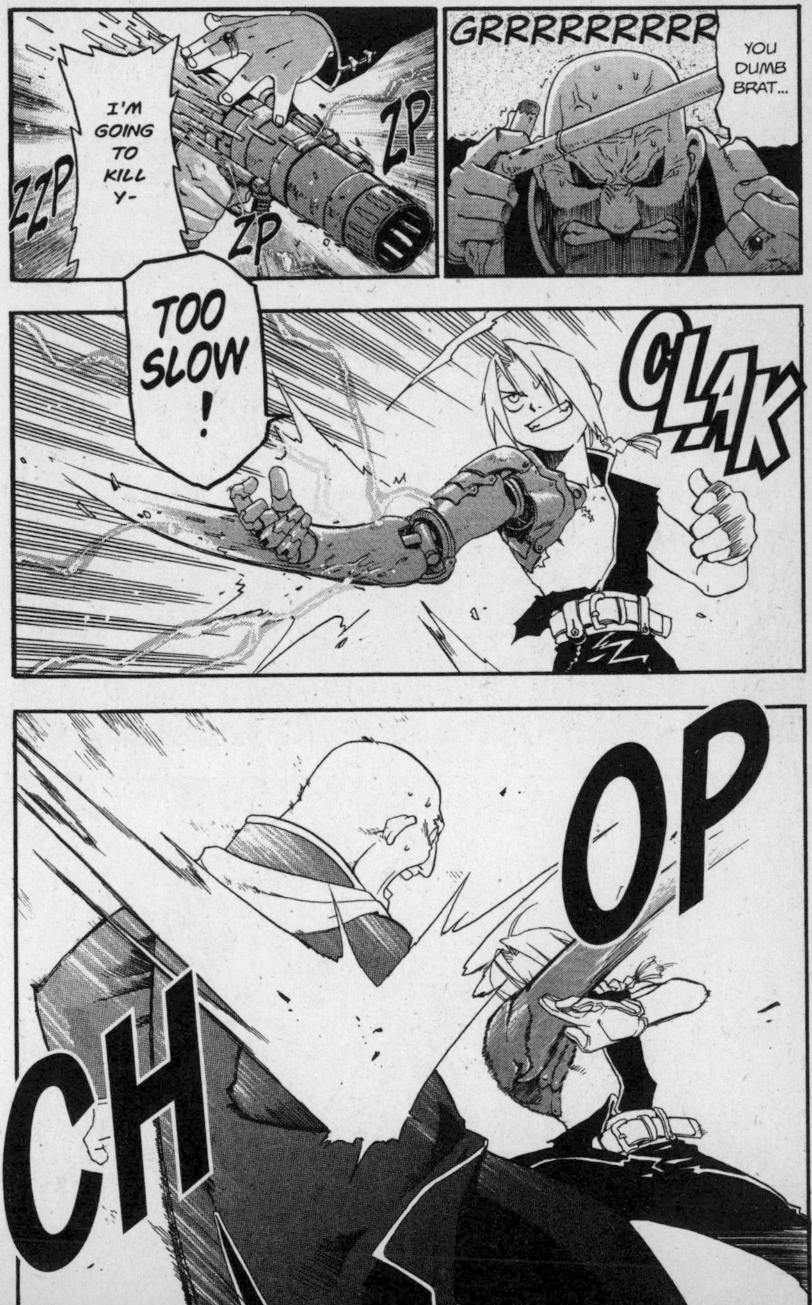
GRRRRRRRRR
YOU DUMB BRAT...
ZP
I'M GOING TO KILL Y-
ZZP
ZP
CLAK
TOO SLOW!
OP
CH

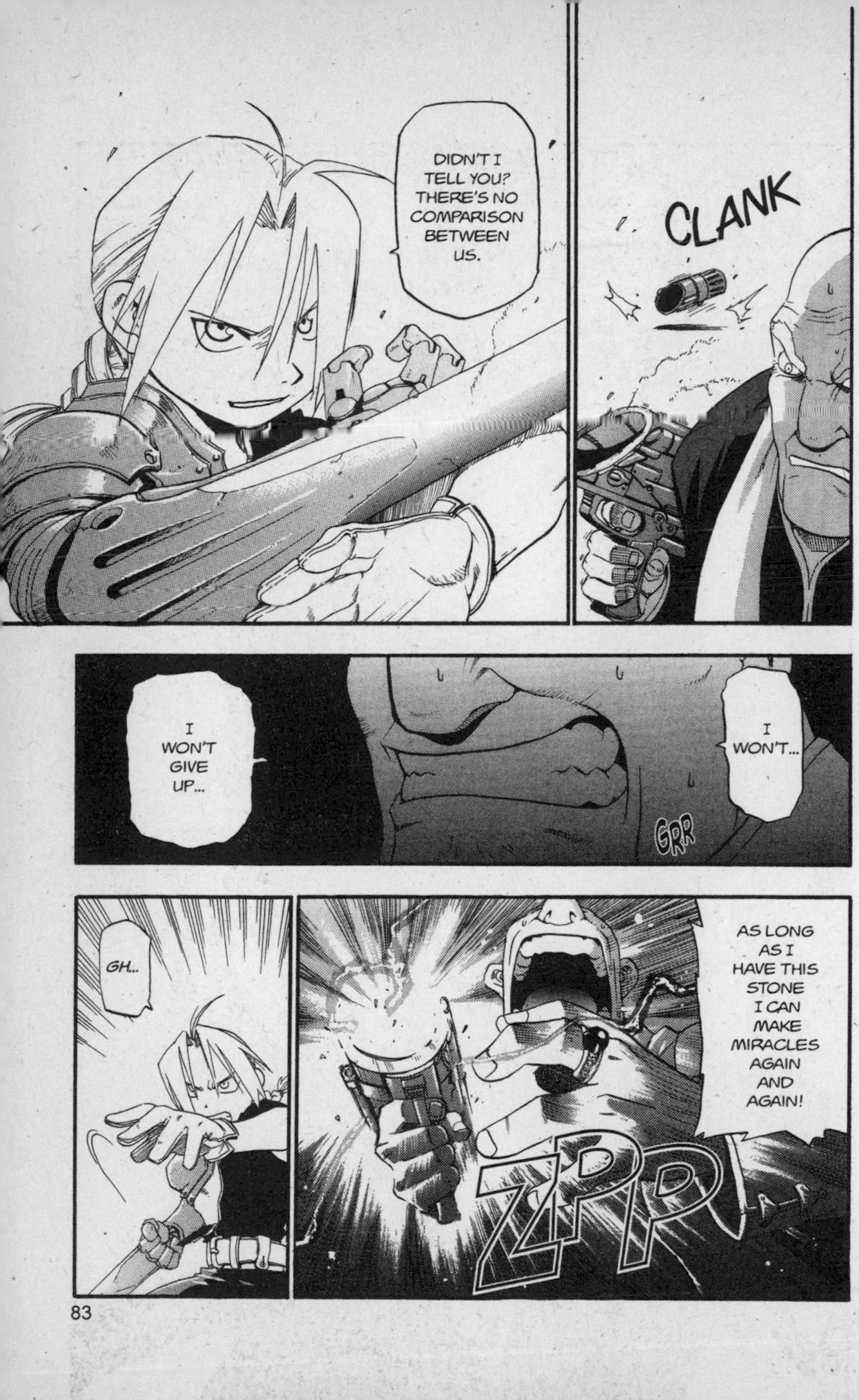
CLANK
DIDN'T I TELL YOU? THERE'S NO COMPARISON BETWEEN US.
I WON'T...
GRR
I WON'T GIVE UP...
AS LONG AS I HAVE THIS STONE I CAN MAKE MIRACLES AGAIN AND AGAIN!
ZPP
GH...

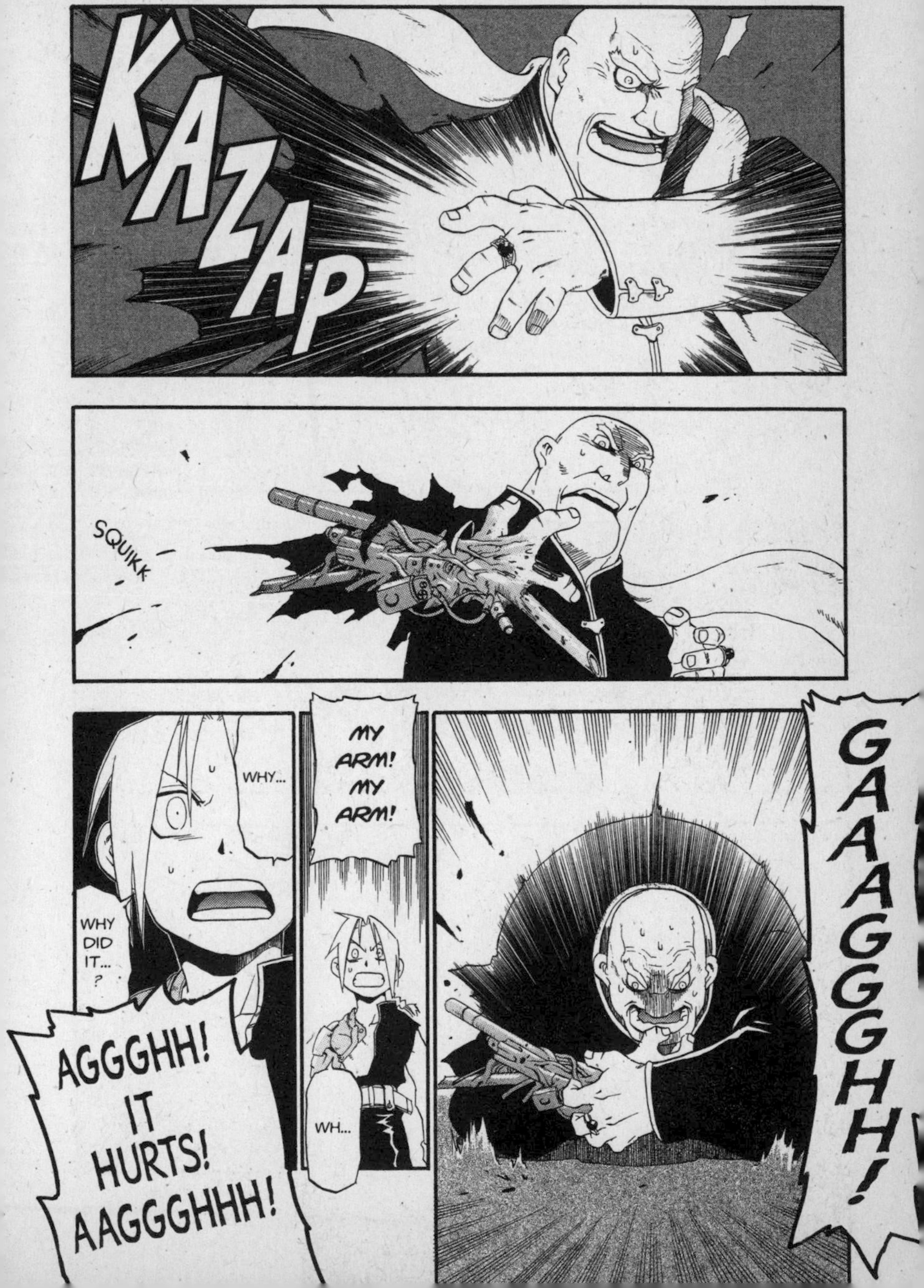
KAZAP
SQUIKK
GAAAGGGGH!
MY ARM! MY ARM!
WH...
WHY...
WHY DID IT...?
AGGGHH! IT HURTS! AAGGGHHH!

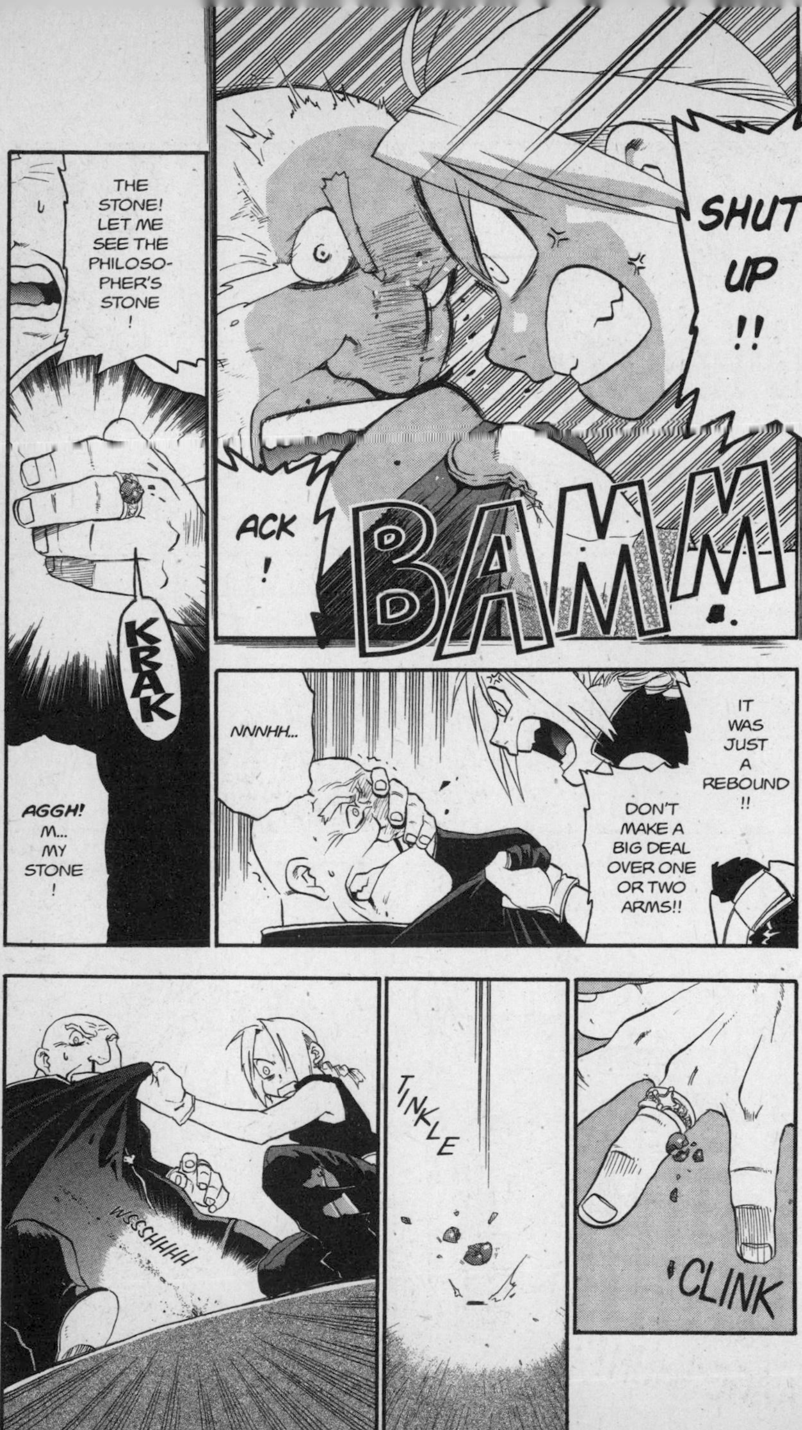
SHUT UP!!
ACK!
BAMM
IT WAS JUST A REBOUND!!
DON'T MAKE A BIG DEAL OVER ONE OR TWO ARMS!!
NNNHH...
THE STONE! LET ME SEE THE PHILOSOPHER'S STONE!
KRAK
AGGH! M... MY STONE!
CLINK
TINKLE
WSSSHHHH

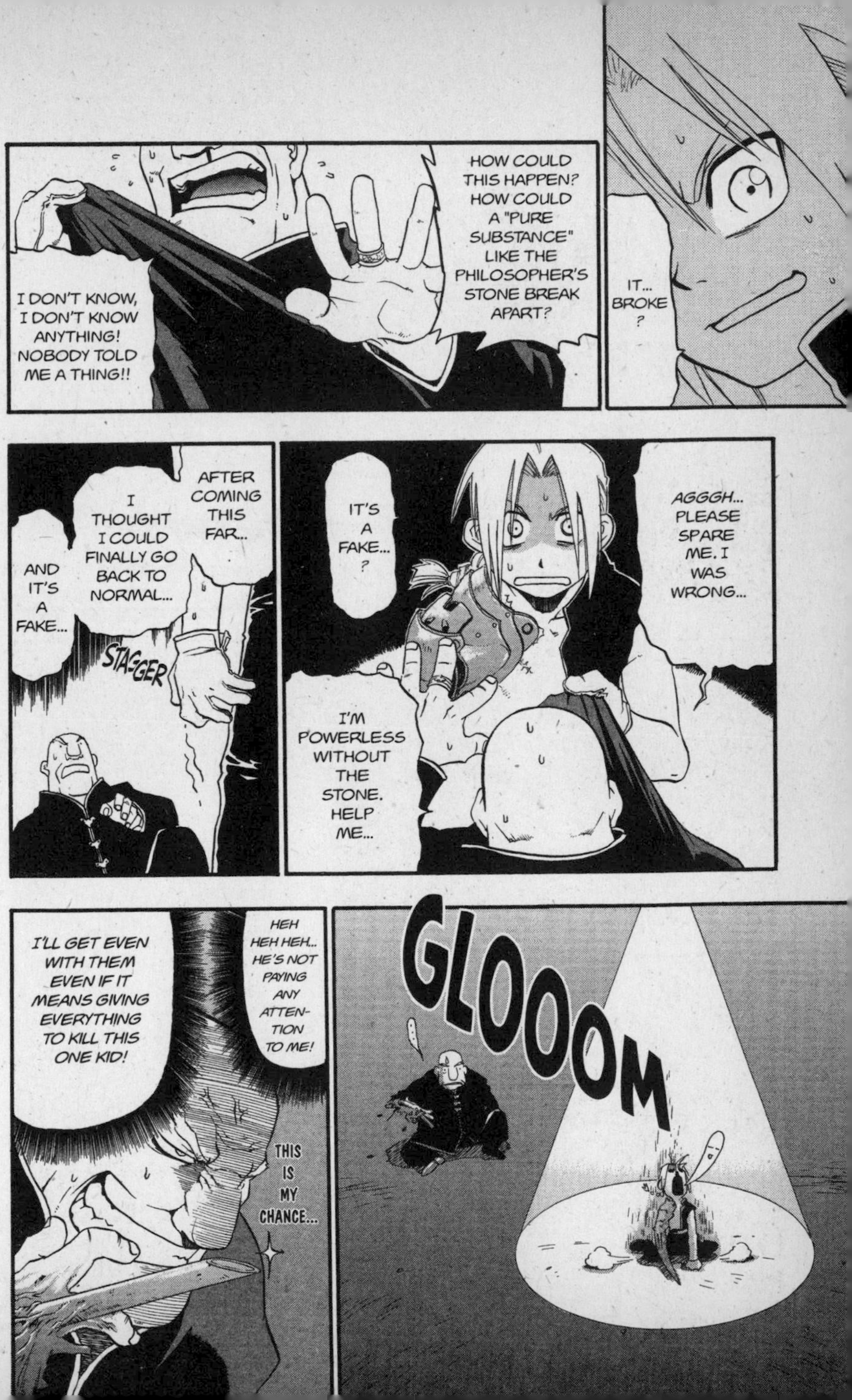
IT... BROKE?
HOW COULD THIS HAPPEN? HOW COULD A "PURE SUBSTANCE" LIKE THE PHILOSOPHER'S STONE BREAK APART?
I DON'T KNOW, I DON'T KNOW ANYTHING! NOBODY TOLD ME A THING!!
AGGGH... PLEASE SPARE ME. I WAS WRONG...
IT'S A FAKE...?
I'M POWERLESS WITHOUT THE STONE. HELP ME...
AFTER COMING THIS FAR...
I THOUGHT I COULD FINALLY GO BACK TO NORMAL...
AND IT'S A FAKE...
STAGGER
GLOOOM
HEH HEH HEH... HE'S NOT PAYING ANY ATTENTION TO ME!
I'LL GET EVEN WITH THEM EVEN IF IT MEANS GIVING EVERYTHING TO KILL THIS ONE KID!
THIS IS MY CHANCE...

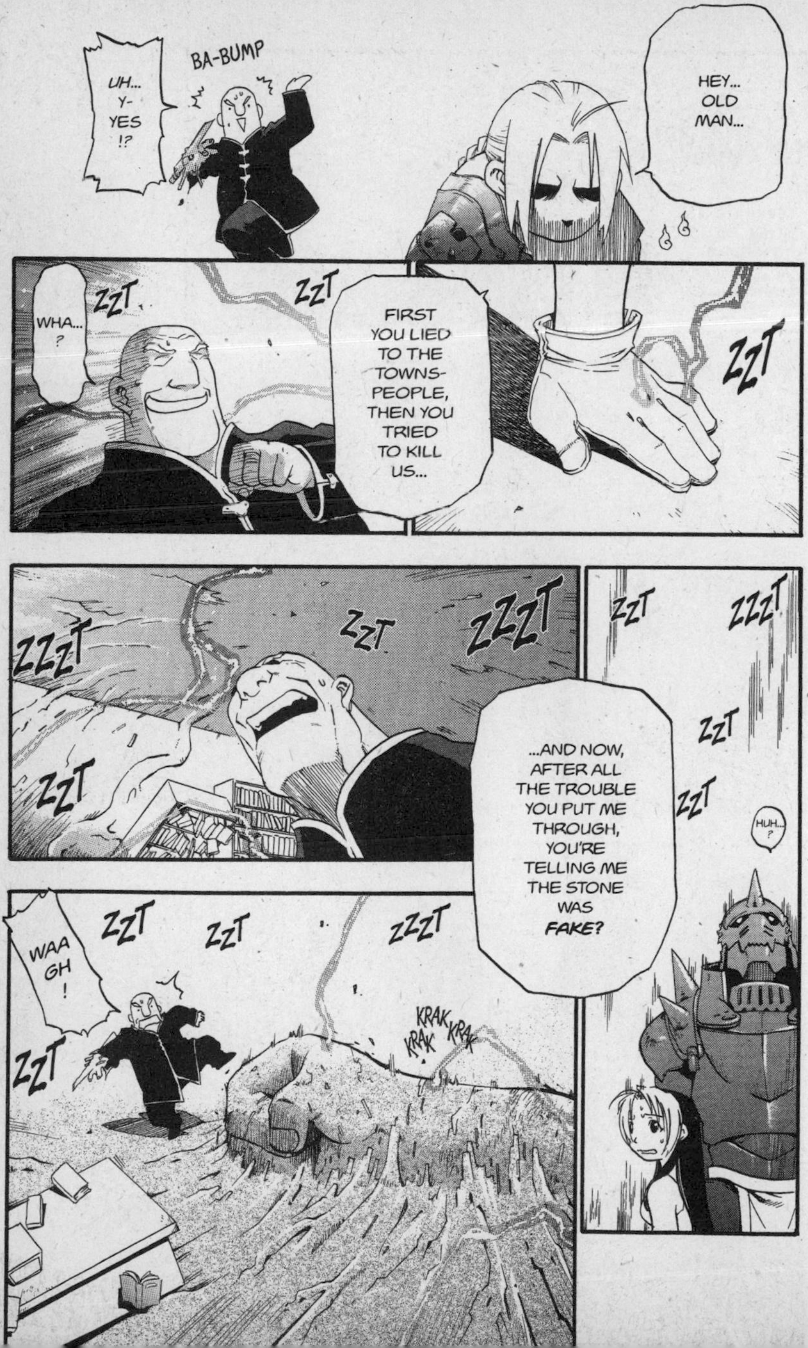
HEY... OLD MAN...
BA-BUMP
UH... Y-YES!?
ZZT
FIRST YOU LIED TO THE TOWNS-PEOPLE, THEN YOU TRIED TO KILL US...
ZZT
ZZT
WHA...?
ZZT
ZZZT
ZZT
ZZT
...AND NOW, AFTER ALL THE TROUBLE YOU PUT ME THROUGH, YOU'RE TELLING ME THE STONE WAS **FAKE?**
HUH...?
ZZZT
ZZT
ZZZT
ZZT
ZZZT
ZZT
ZZT
WAAGH!
ZZT
KRAK KRAK KRAK

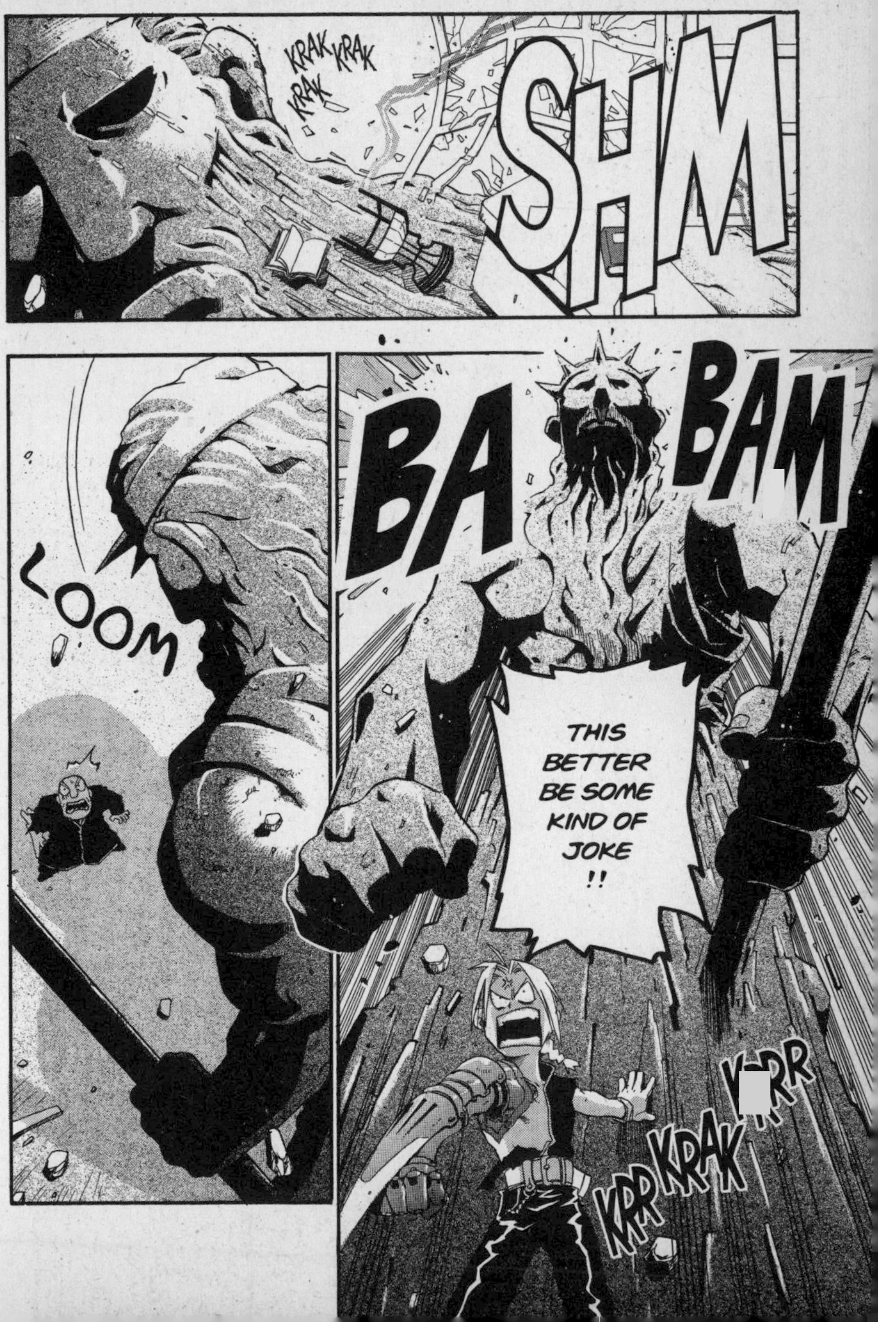
KRAK KRAK KRAK
SHM
BA BAM
THIS BETTER BE SOME KIND OF JOKE !!
KRR KRAK KRR
LOOM

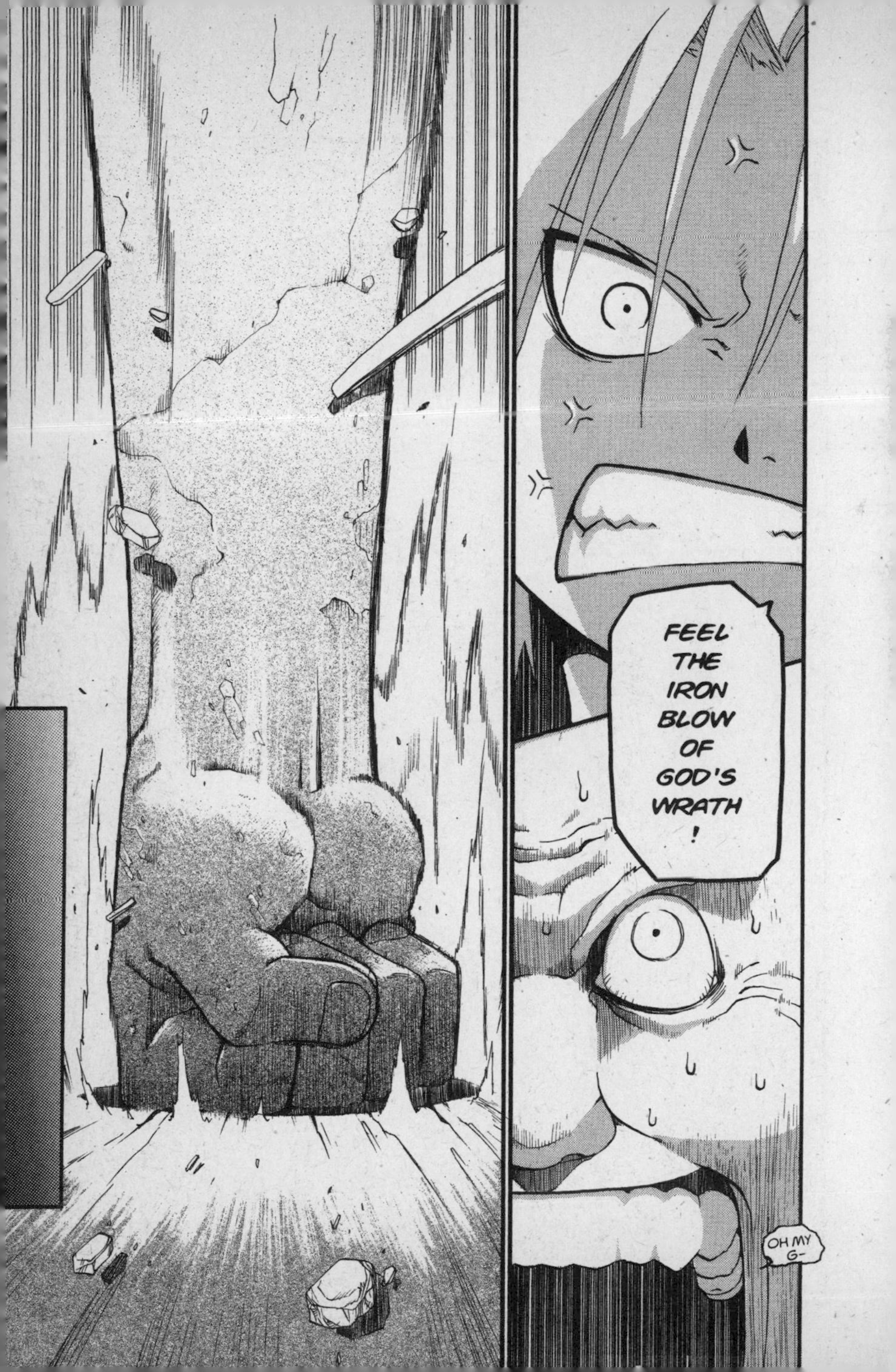
FEEL THE IRON BLOW OF GOD'S WRATH !
OH MY G-

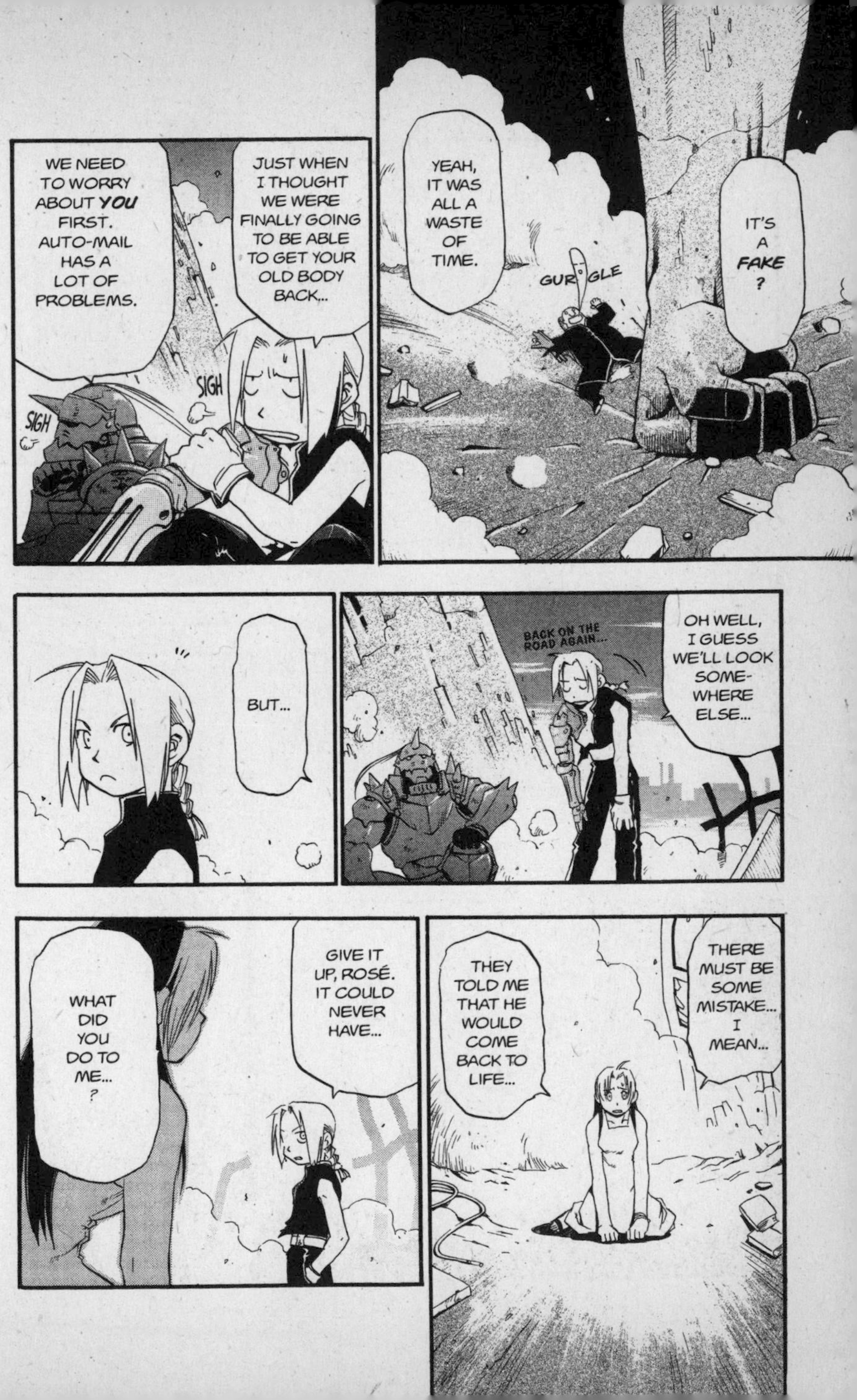
IT'S A *FAKE* ?
YEAH, IT WAS ALL A WASTE OF TIME.
GURGLE
JUST WHEN I THOUGHT WE WERE FINALLY GOING TO BE ABLE TO GET YOUR OLD BODY BACK...
WE NEED TO WORRY ABOUT *YOU* FIRST. AUTO-MAIL HAS A LOT OF PROBLEMS.
SIGH
SIGH
OH WELL, I GUESS WE'LL LOOK SOME-WHERE ELSE...
BACK ON THE ROAD AGAIN...
BUT...
THERE MUST BE SOME MISTAKE... I MEAN...
THEY TOLD ME THAT HE WOULD COME BACK TO LIFE...
GIVE IT UP, ROSÉ. IT COULD NEVER HAVE...
WHAT DID YOU DO TO ME... ?

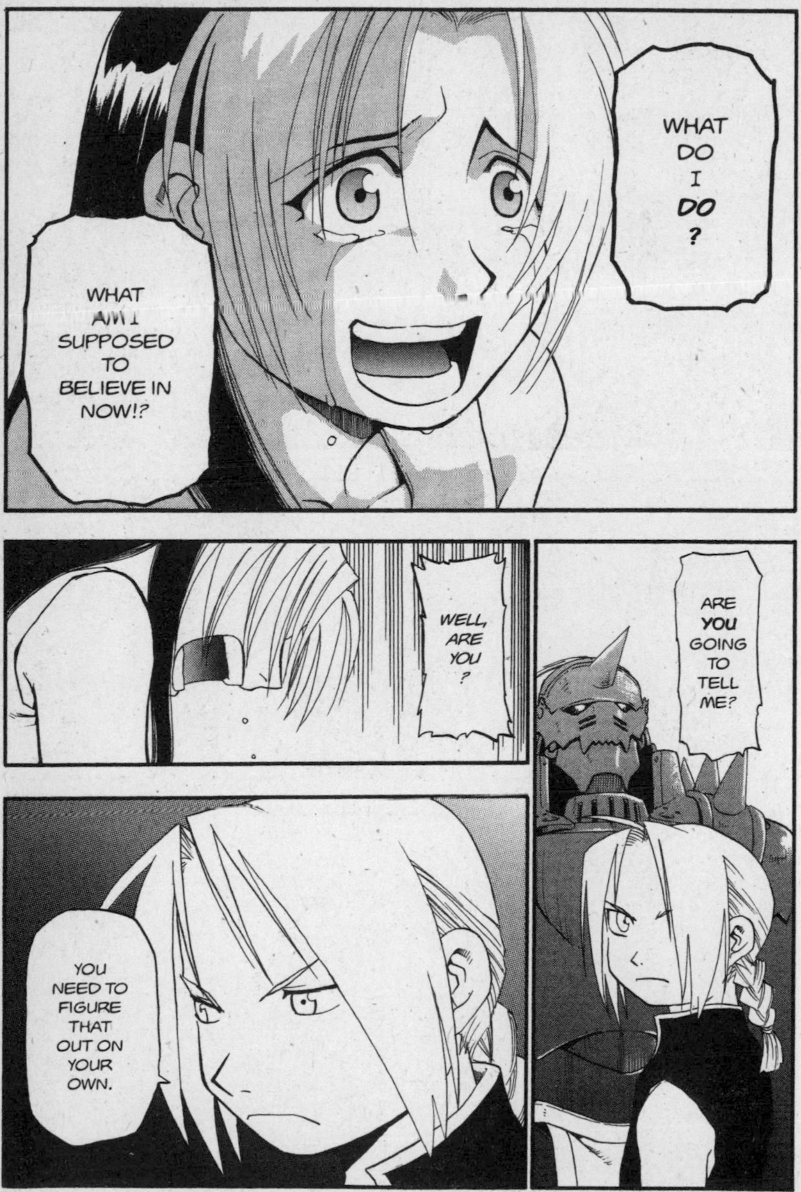
WHAT DO I DO?
WHAT AM I SUPPOSED TO BELIEVE IN NOW!?
ARE YOU GOING TO TELL ME?
WELL, ARE YOU?
YOU NEED TO FIGURE THAT OUT ON YOUR OWN.

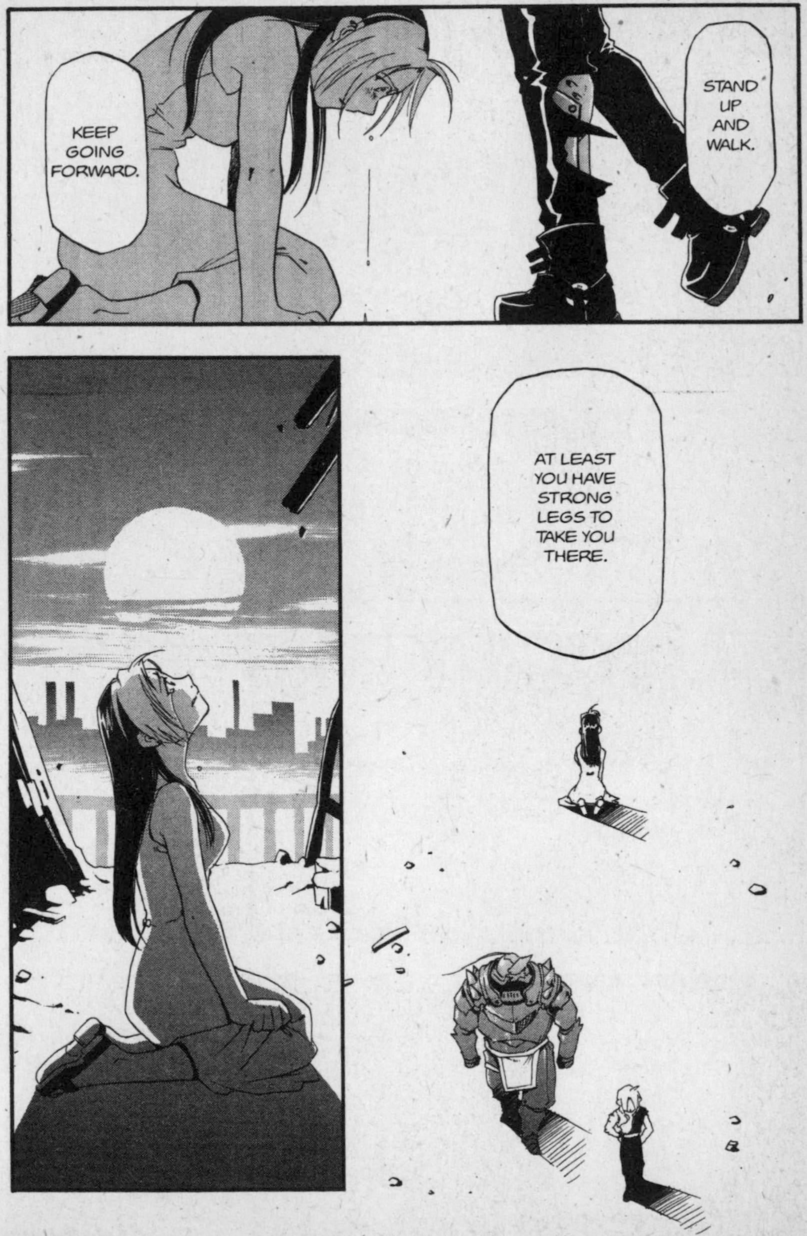
STAND UP AND WALK.
KEEP GOING FORWARD.
AT LEAST YOU HAVE STRONG LEGS TO TAKE YOU THERE.

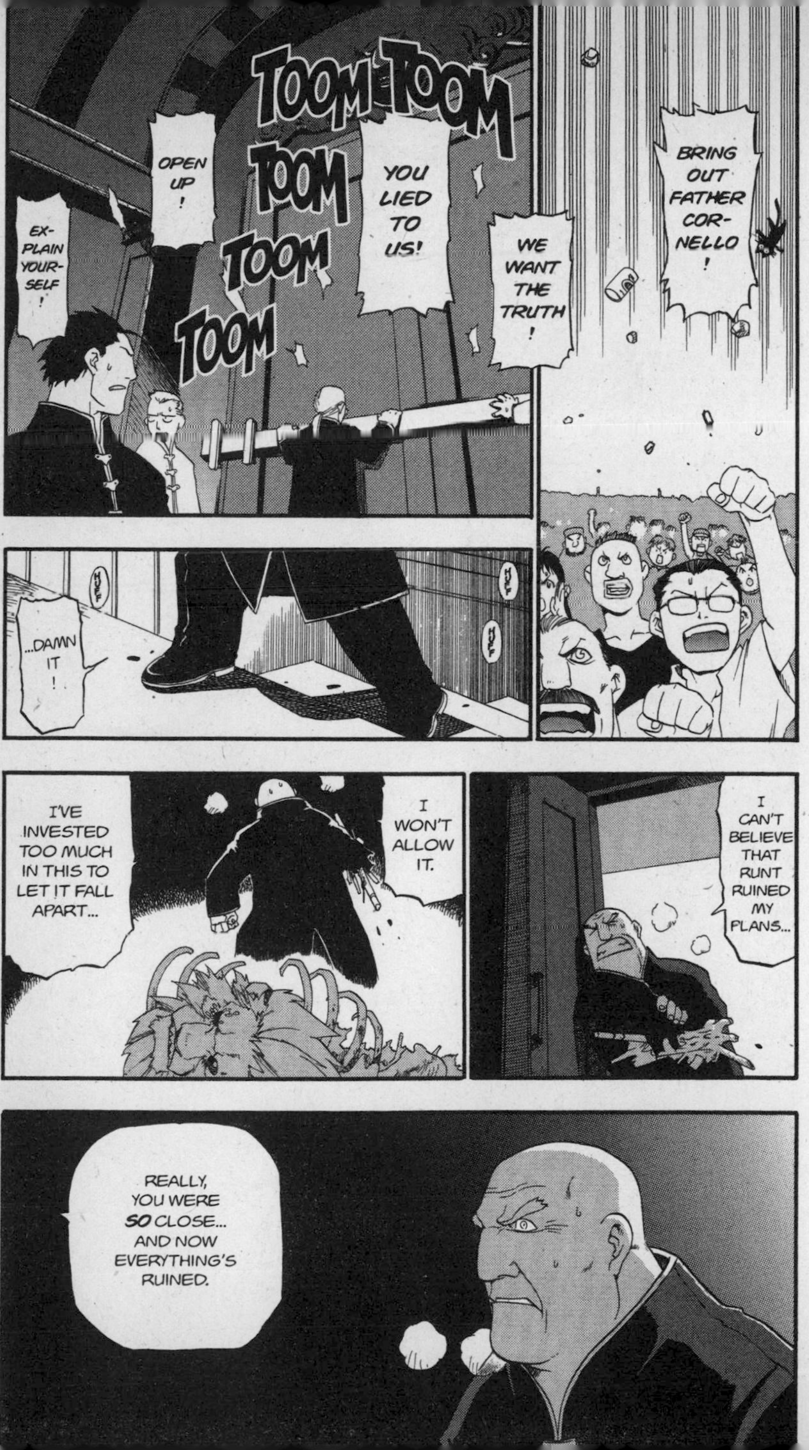
BRING OUT FATHER COR-NELLO!
WE WANT THE TRUTH!
TOOM TOOM
YOU LIED TO US!
TOOM TOOM TOOM
OPEN UP!
EX-PLAIN YOUR-SELF!
HUFF
HUFF
HUFF
...DAMN IT!
I CAN'T BELIEVE THAT RUNT RUINED MY PLANS...
I WON'T ALLOW IT.
I'VE INVESTED TOO MUCH IN THIS TO LET IT FALL APART...
REALLY, YOU WERE SO CLOSE... AND NOW EVERYTHING'S RUINED.

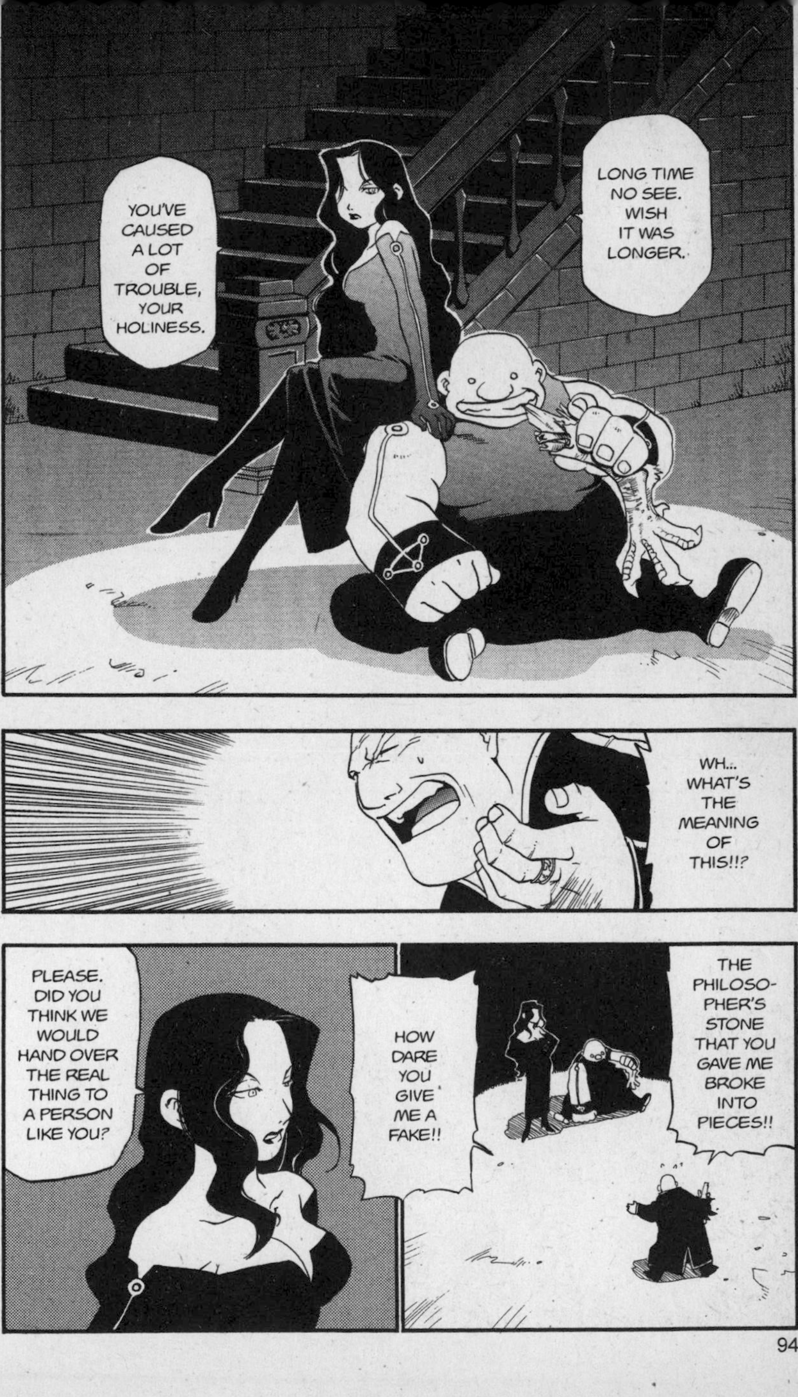
LONG TIME NO SEE. WISH IT WAS LONGER.
YOU'VE CAUSED A LOT OF TROUBLE, YOUR HOLINESS.
WH... WHAT'S THE MEANING OF THIS!!?
THE PHILOSO-PHER'S STONE THAT YOU GAVE ME BROKE INTO PIECES!!
HOW DARE YOU GIVE ME A FAKE!!
PLEASE. DID YOU THINK WE WOULD HAND OVER THE REAL THING TO A PERSON LIKE YOU?

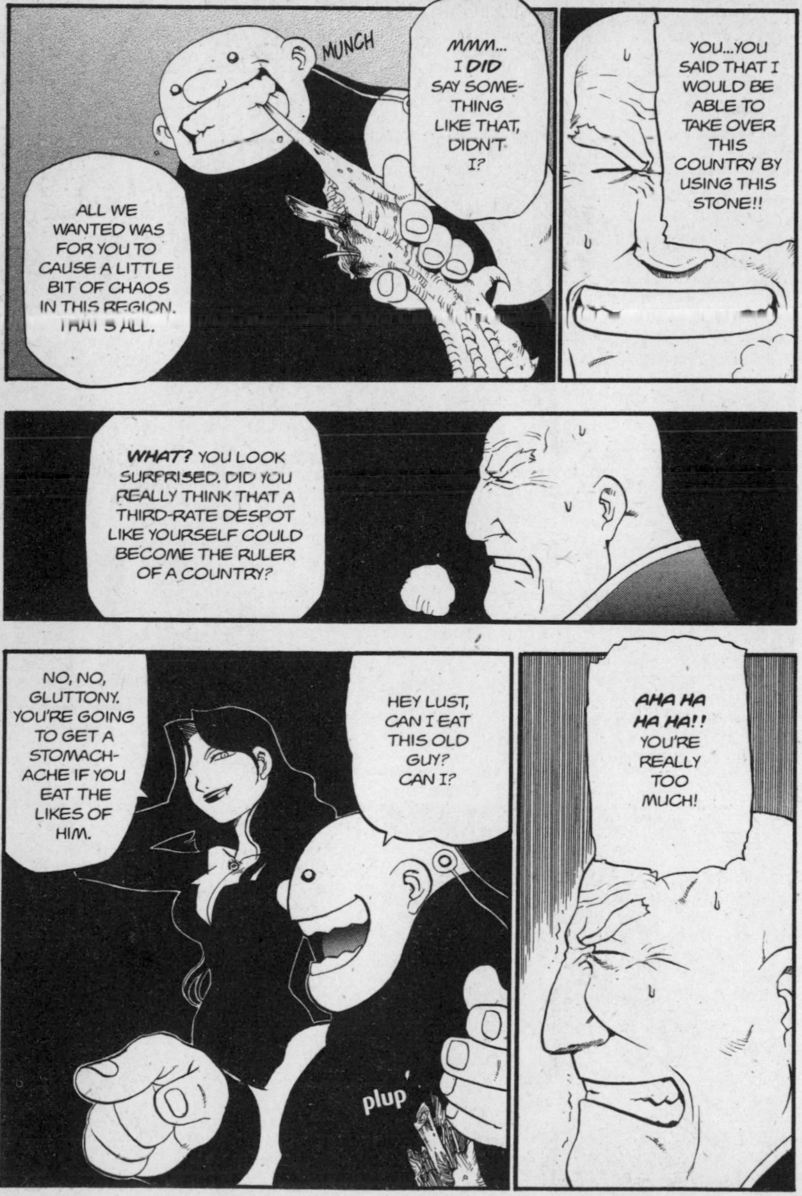
YOU...YOU SAID THAT I WOULD BE ABLE TO TAKE OVER THIS COUNTRY BY USING THIS STONE!!
MUNCH
MMM... I DID SAY SOME-THING LIKE THAT, DIDN'T I?
ALL WE WANTED WAS FOR YOU TO CAUSE A LITTLE BIT OF CHAOS IN THIS REGION. THAT'S ALL.
WHAT? YOU LOOK SURPRISED. DID YOU REALLY THINK THAT A THIRD-RATE DESPOT LIKE YOURSELF COULD BECOME THE RULER OF A COUNTRY?
AHA HA HA HA!! YOU'RE REALLY TOO MUCH!
HEY LUST, CAN I EAT THIS OLD GUY? CAN I?
NO, NO, GLUTTONY. YOU'RE GOING TO GET A STOMACH-ACHE IF YOU EAT THE LIKES OF HIM.
plup

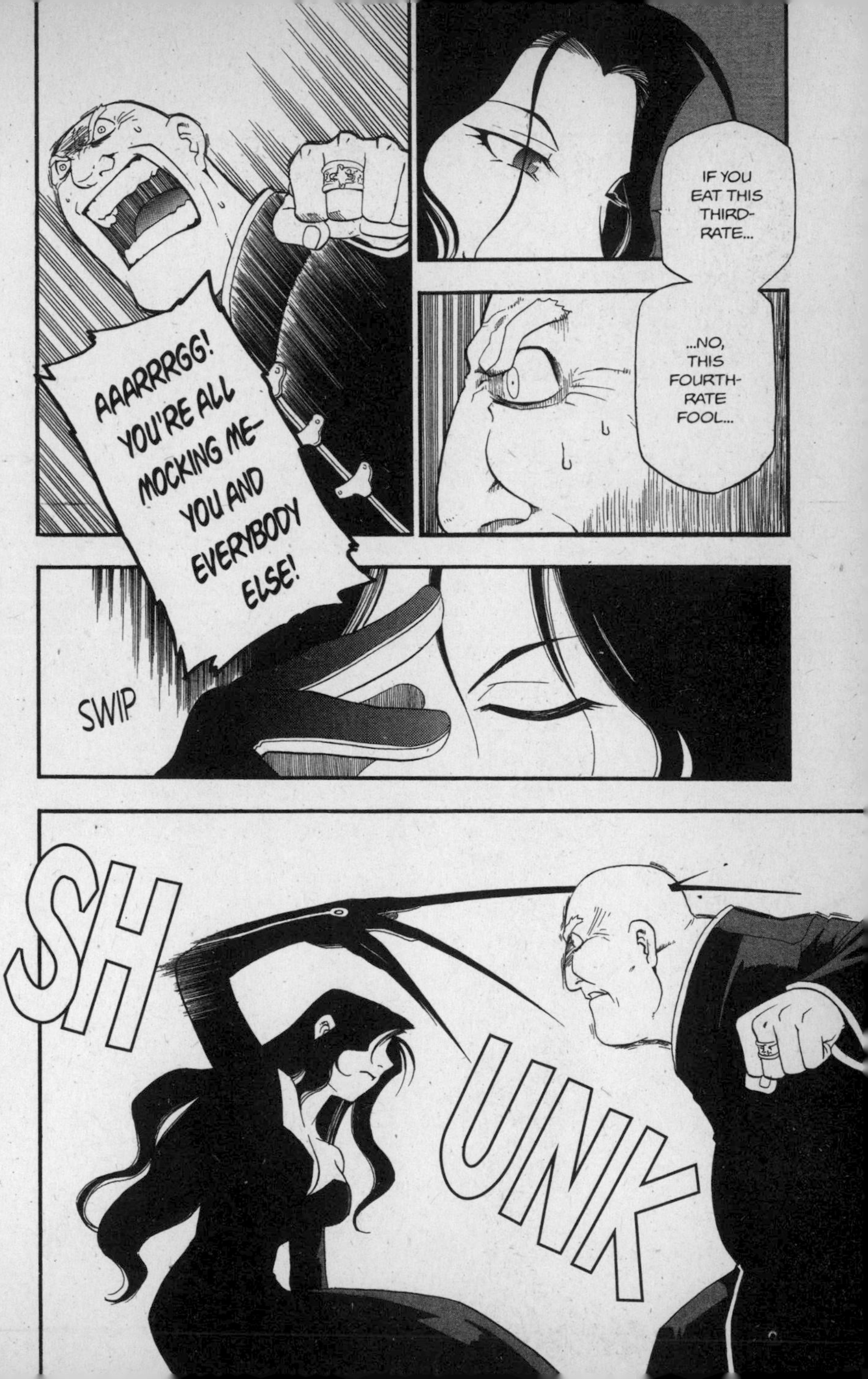
IF YOU EAT THIS THIRD-RATE...
...NO, THIS FOURTH-RATE FOOL...
AAARRRGG! YOU'RE ALL MOCKING ME—YOU AND EVERYBODY ELSE!
SWIP
SHUNK

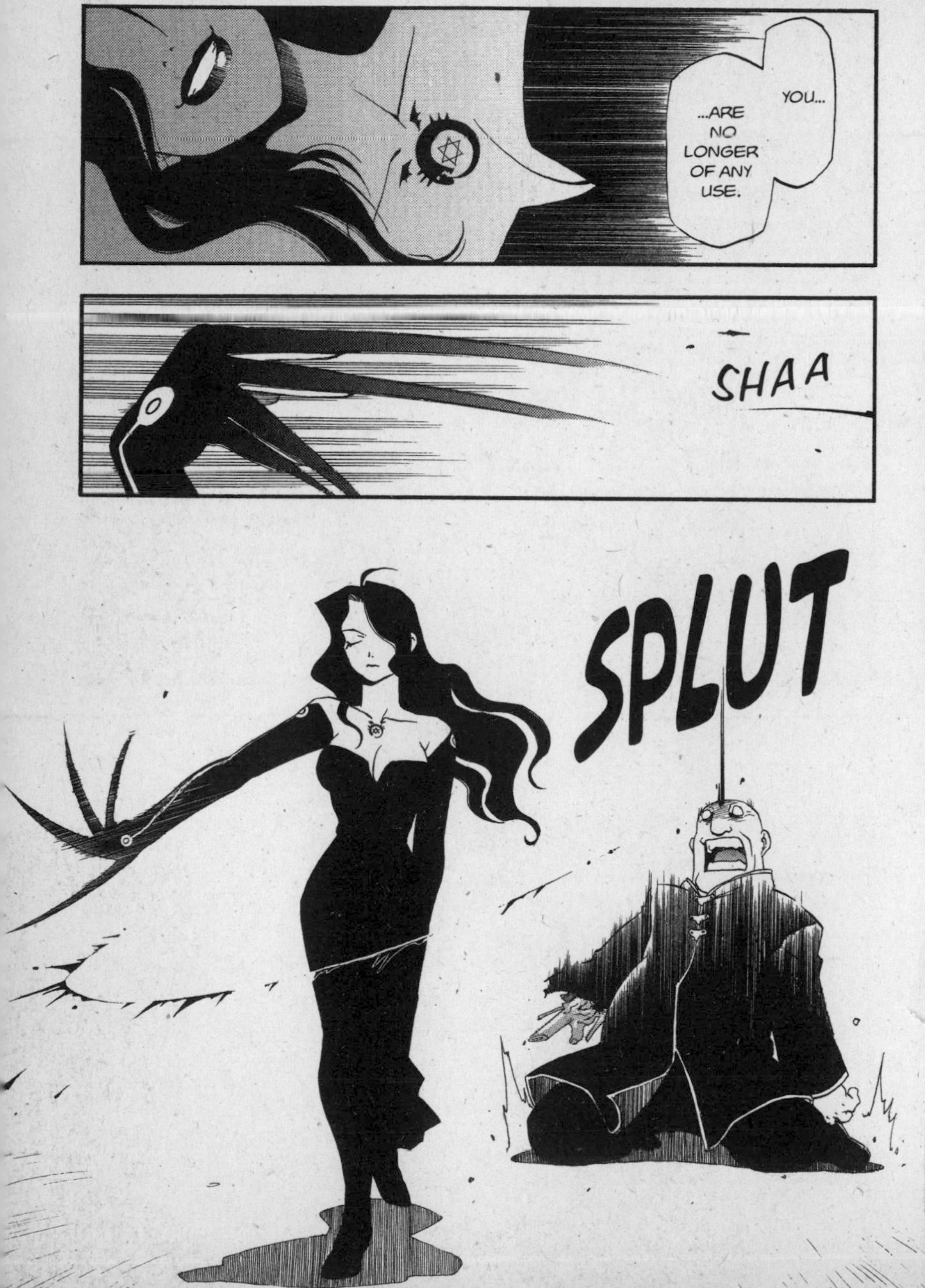
YOU...
...ARE NO LONGER OF ANY USE.
SHAA
SPLUT

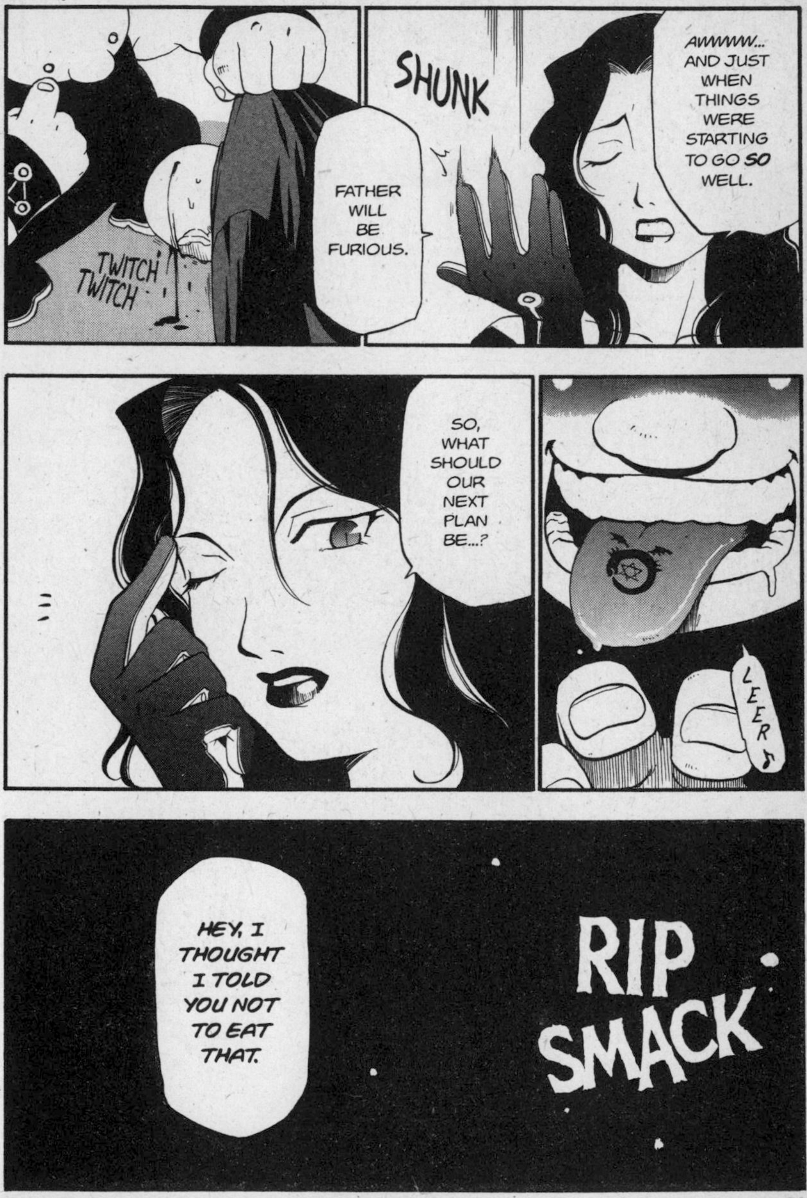
AWWWW... AND JUST WHEN THINGS WERE STARTING TO GO SO WELL.
SHUNK
FATHER WILL BE FURIOUS.
TWITCH TWITCH
LEER♪
SO, WHAT SHOULD OUR NEXT PLAN BE...?
RIP SMACK
HEY, I THOUGHT I TOLD YOU NOT TO EAT THAT.

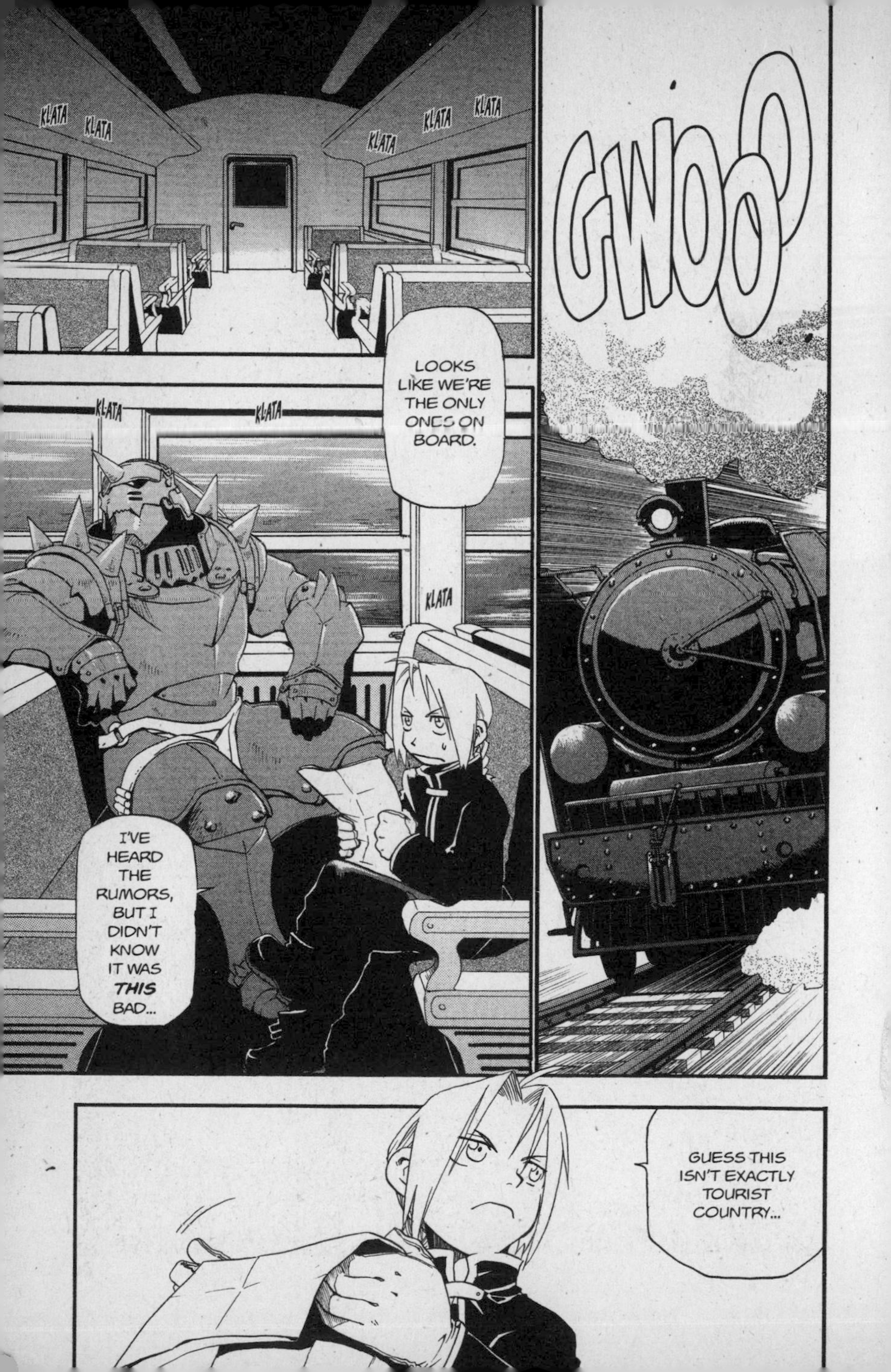
GWOOO
KLATA KLATA KLATA KLATA KLATA
KLATA KLATA
LOOKS LIKE WE'RE THE ONLY ONES ON BOARD.
KLATA
I'VE HEARD THE RUMORS, BUT I DIDN'T KNOW IT WAS **THIS** BAD...
GUESS THIS ISN'T EXACTLY TOURIST COUNTRY...

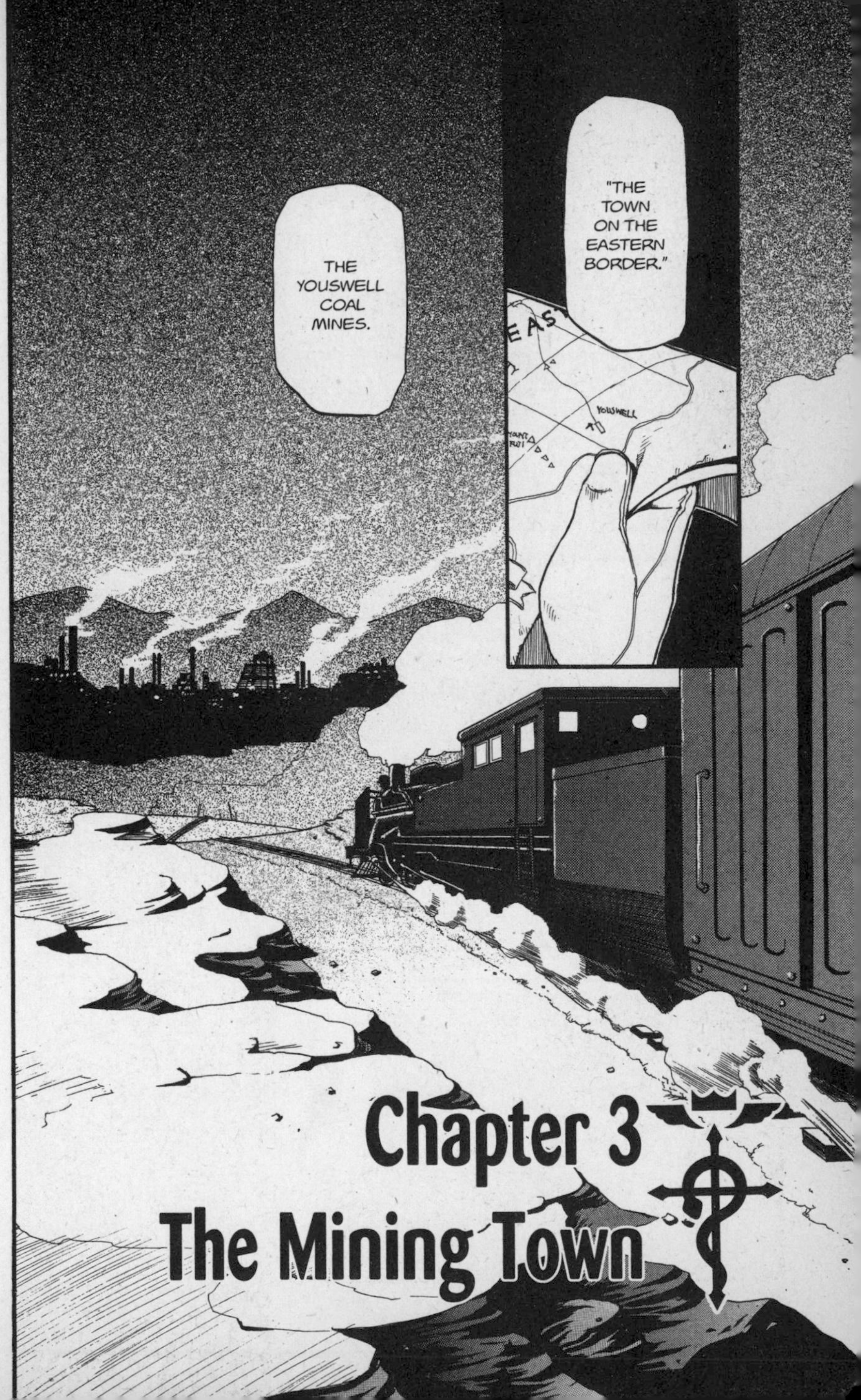
"THE TOWN ON THE EASTERN BORDER."
EAST
YOUSWELL
THE YOUSWELL COAL MINES.

Chapter 3 The Mining Town

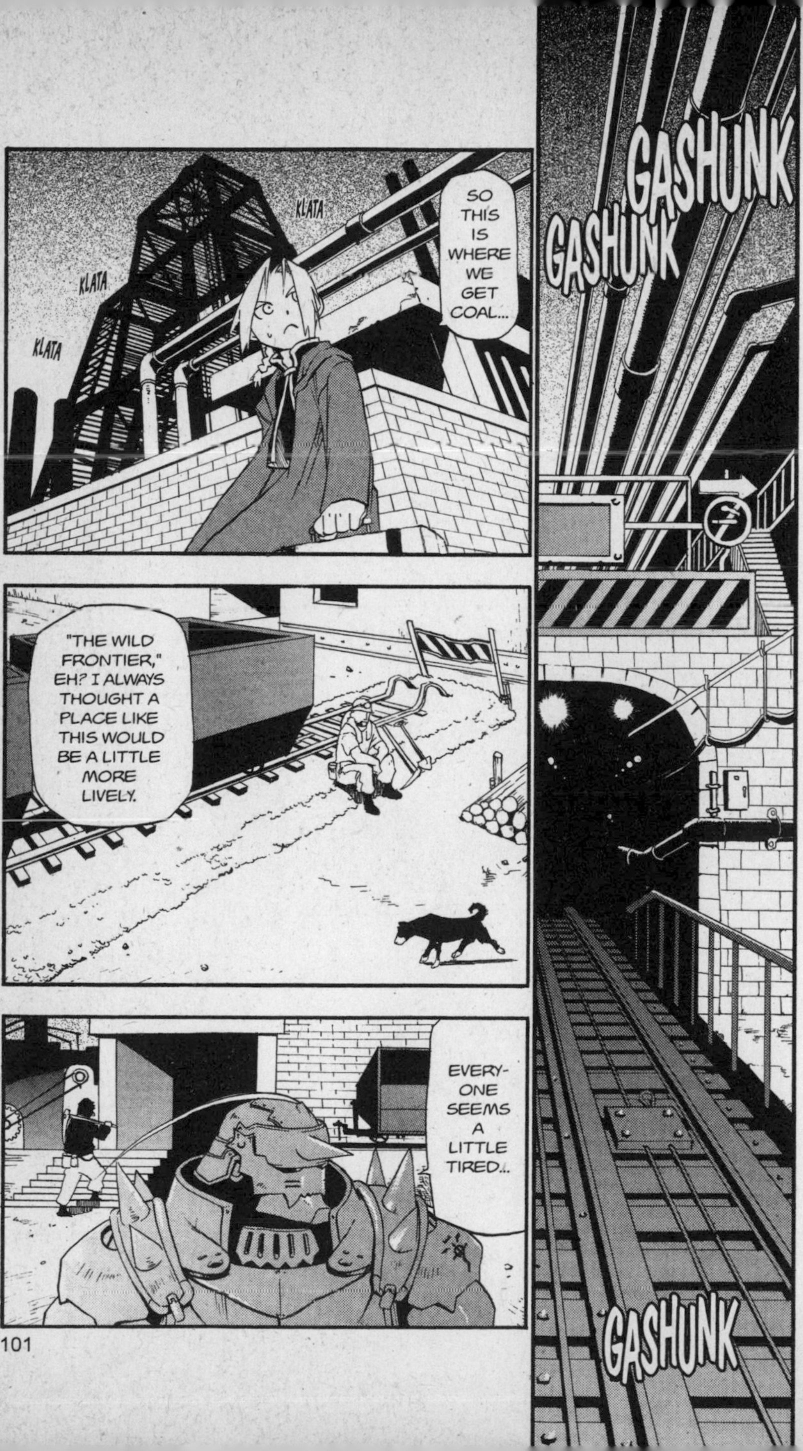
GASHUNK
GASHUNK
GASHUNK
SO THIS IS WHERE WE GET COAL...
KLATA
KLATA
KLATA
"THE WILD FRONTIER," EH? I ALWAYS THOUGHT A PLACE LIKE THIS WOULD BE A LITTLE MORE LIVELY.
EVERY-ONE SEEMS A LITTLE TIRED...

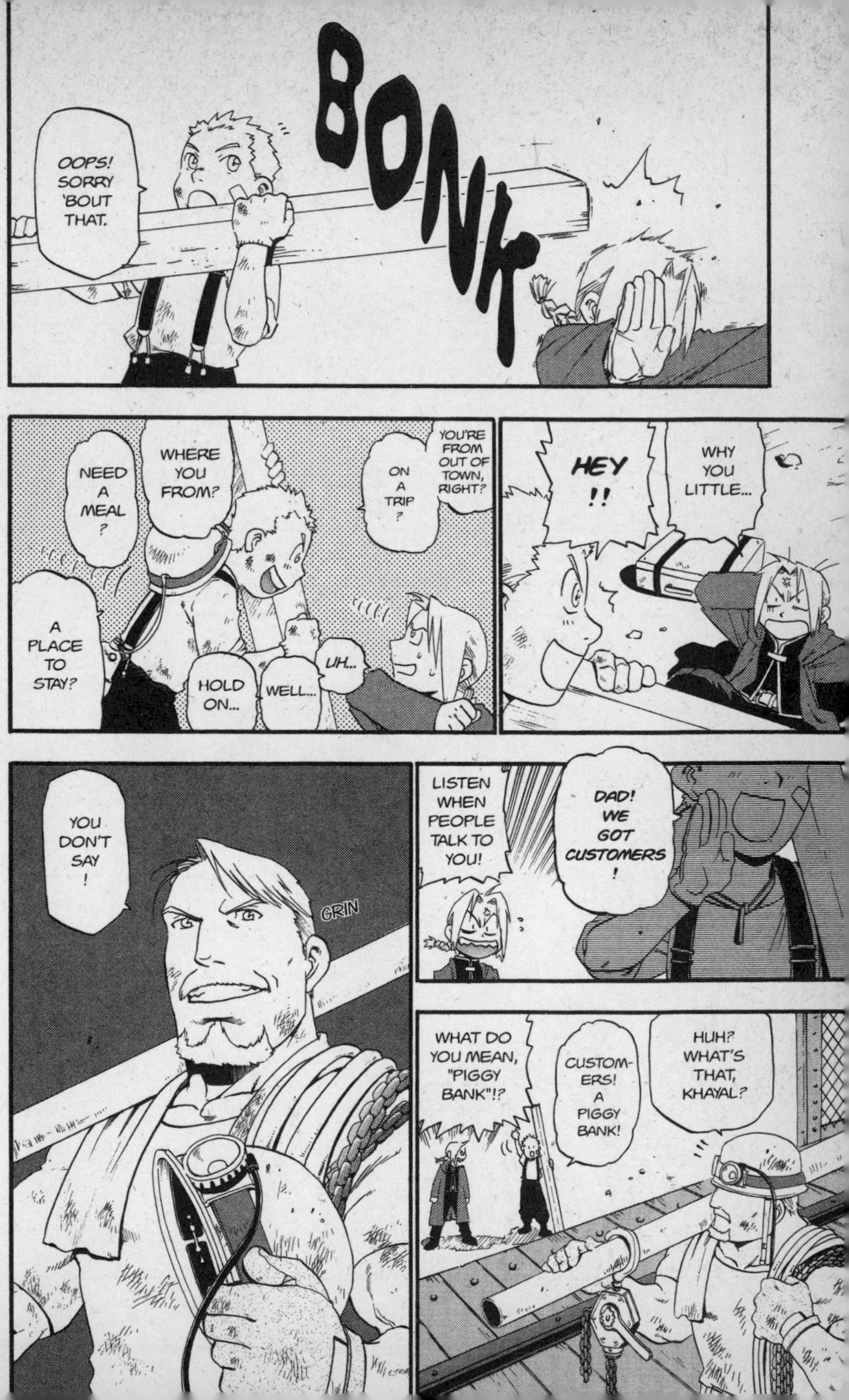
BONK
OOPS! SORRY 'BOUT THAT.
WHY YOU LITTLE...
HEY!!
YOU'RE FROM OUT OF TOWN, RIGHT?
ON A TRIP?
WHERE YOU FROM?
NEED A MEAL?
A PLACE TO STAY?
UH...
WELL...
HOLD ON...
DAD! WE GOT CUSTOMERS!
LISTEN WHEN PEOPLE TALK TO YOU!
HUH? WHAT'S THAT, KHAYAL?
CUSTOMERS! A PIGGY BANK!
WHAT DO YOU MEAN, "PIGGY BANK"!?
YOU DON'T SAY!
GRIN

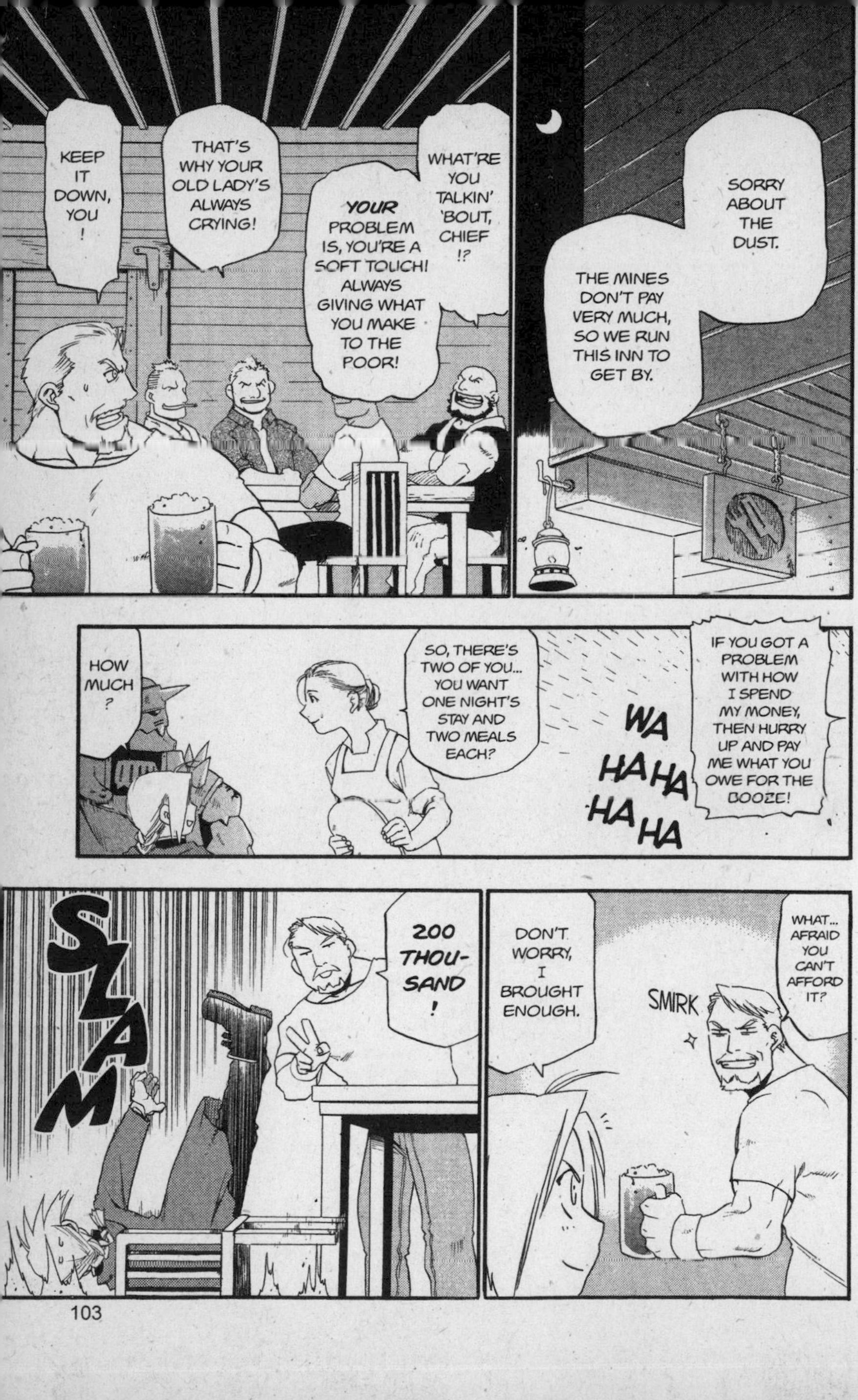
SORRY ABOUT THE DUST.
THE MINES DON'T PAY VERY MUCH, SO WE RUN THIS INN TO GET BY.
WHAT'RE YOU TALKIN' 'BOUT, CHIEF!?
YOUR PROBLEM IS, YOU'RE A SOFT TOUCH! ALWAYS GIVING WHAT YOU MAKE TO THE POOR!
THAT'S WHY YOUR OLD LADY'S ALWAYS CRYING!
KEEP IT DOWN, YOU!
IF YOU GOT A PROBLEM WITH HOW I SPEND MY MONEY, THEN HURRY UP AND PAY ME WHAT YOU OWE FOR THE BOOZE!
WA HAHA HAHA
SO, THERE'S TWO OF YOU... YOU WANT ONE NIGHT'S STAY AND TWO MEALS EACH?
HOW MUCH?
WHAT... AFRAID YOU CAN'T AFFORD IT?
SMIRK
DON'T WORRY, I BROUGHT ENOUGH.
200 THOUSAND!
SLAM

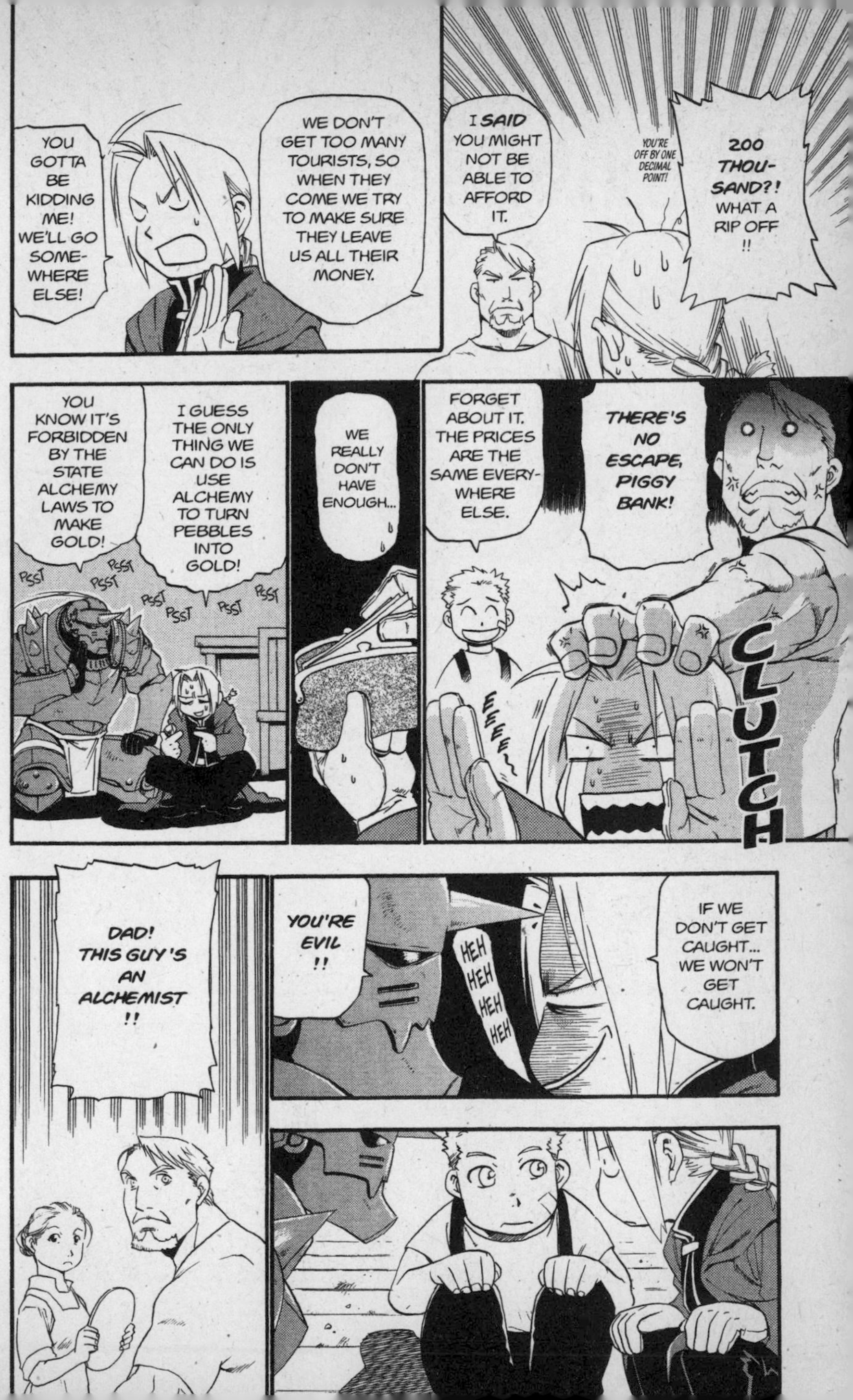
200 THOU-SAND?! WHAT A RIP OFF !!
YOU'RE OFF BY ONE DECIMAL POINT!
I SAID YOU MIGHT NOT BE ABLE TO AFFORD IT.
WE DON'T GET TOO MANY TOURISTS, SO WHEN THEY COME WE TRY TO MAKE SURE THEY LEAVE US ALL THEIR MONEY.
YOU GOTTA BE KIDDING ME! WE'LL GO SOME-WHERE ELSE!
THERE'S NO ESCAPE, PIGGY BANK!
CLUTCH
FORGET ABOUT IT. THE PRICES ARE THE SAME EVERY-WHERE ELSE.
EEEE~
WE REALLY DON'T HAVE ENOUGH...
I GUESS THE ONLY THING WE CAN DO IS USE ALCHEMY TO TURN PEBBLES INTO GOLD!
YOU KNOW IT'S FORBIDDEN BY THE STATE ALCHEMY LAWS TO MAKE GOLD!
PSST PSST PSST PSST PSST PSST PSST
IF WE DON'T GET CAUGHT... WE WON'T GET CAUGHT.
HEH HEH HEH HEH
YOU'RE EVIL !!
DAD! THIS GUY'S AN ALCHEMIST !!

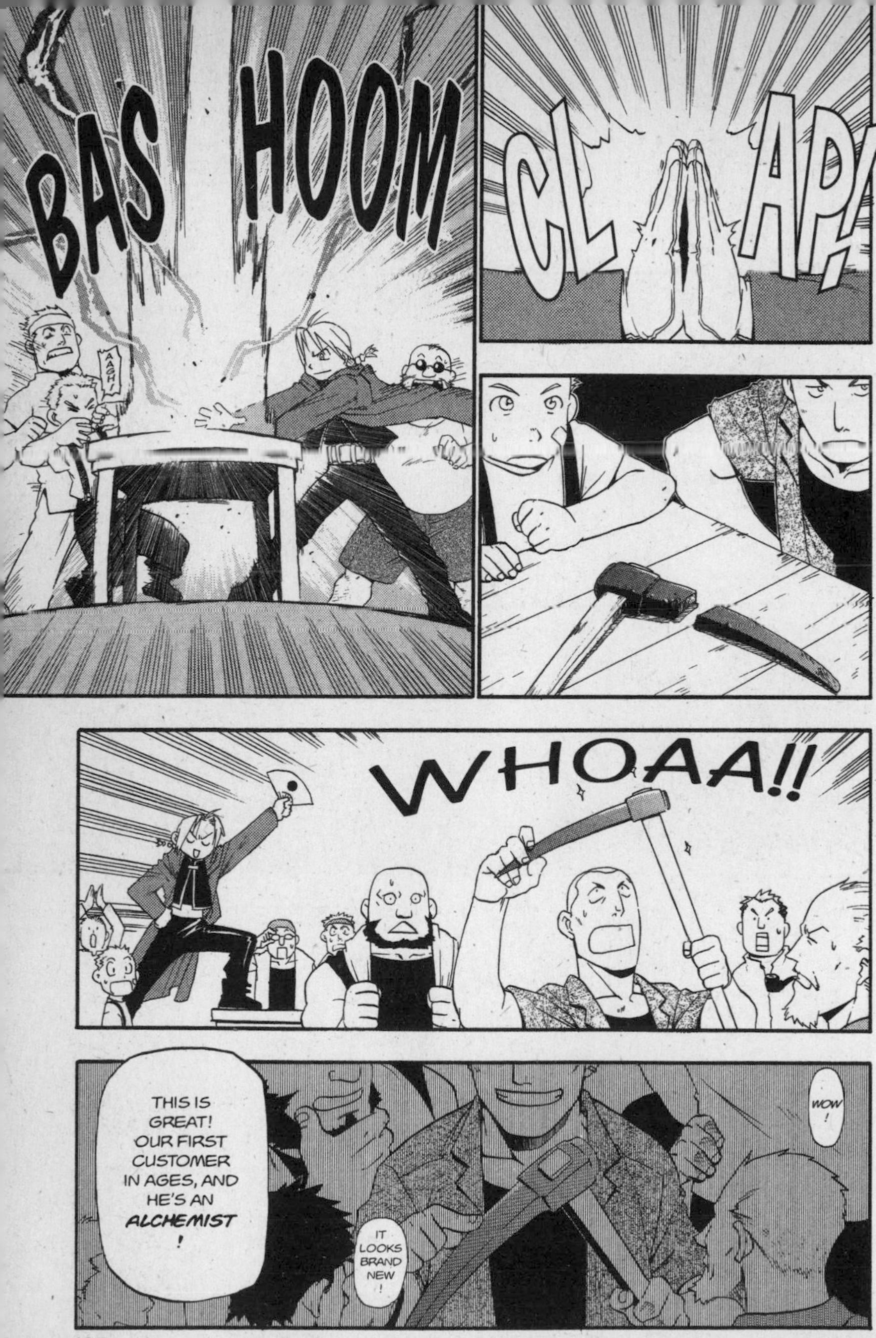
CLAP!
BAS HOOM
AASH!
WHOAA!!
WOW!
IT LOOKS BRAND NEW!
THIS IS GREAT! OUR FIRST CUSTOMER IN AGES, AND HE'S AN ***ALCHEMIST***!

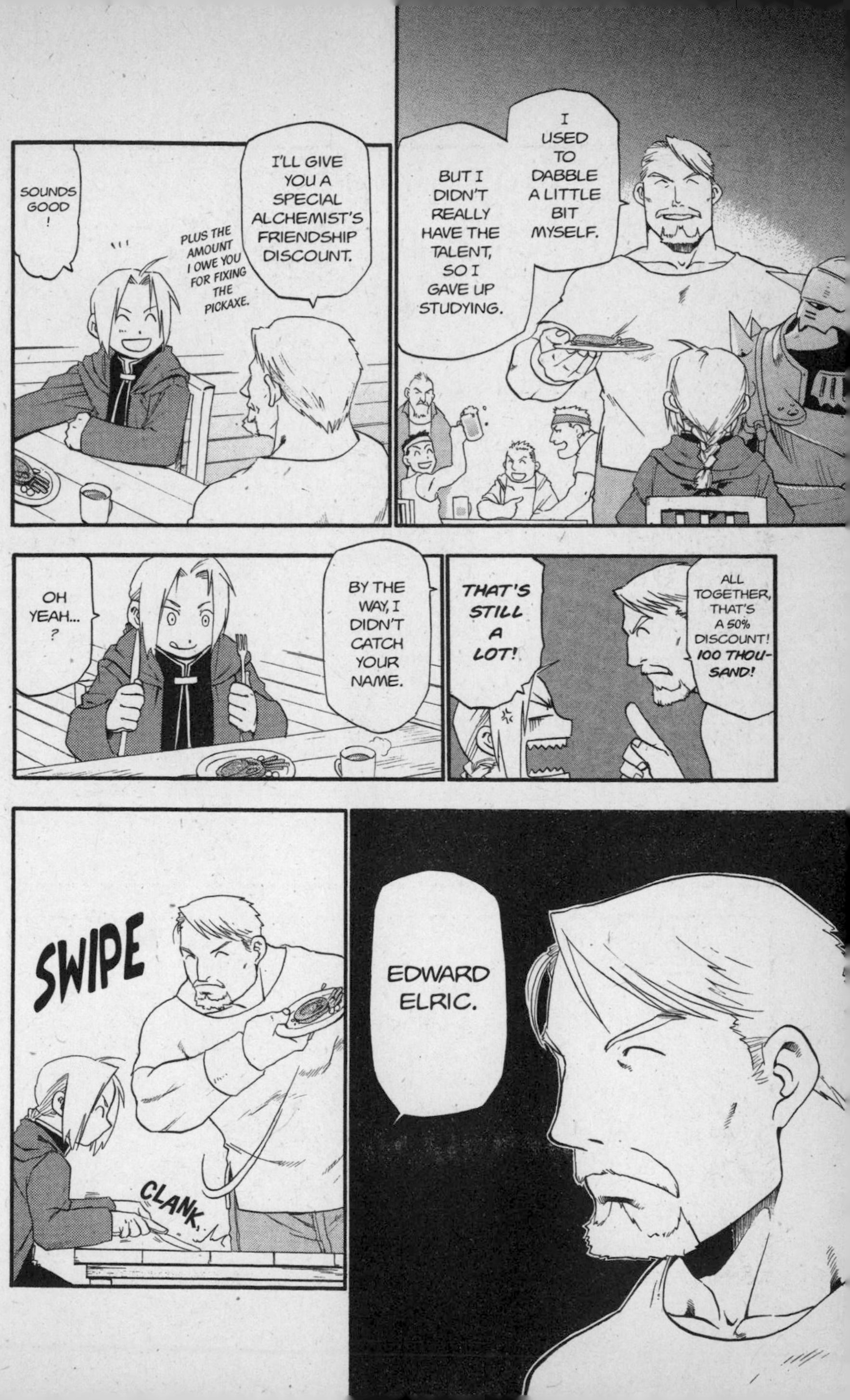
I USED TO DABBLE A LITTLE BIT MYSELF.
BUT I DIDN'T REALLY HAVE THE TALENT, SO I GAVE UP STUDYING.
I'LL GIVE YOU A SPECIAL ALCHEMIST'S FRIENDSHIP DISCOUNT.
PLUS THE AMOUNT I OWE YOU FOR FIXING THE PICKAXE.
SOUNDS GOOD!
ALL TOGETHER, THAT'S A 50% DISCOUNT! 100 THOUSAND!
THAT'S STILL A LOT!
BY THE WAY, I DIDN'T CATCH YOUR NAME.
OH YEAH...?
EDWARD ELRIC.
SWIPE
CLANK

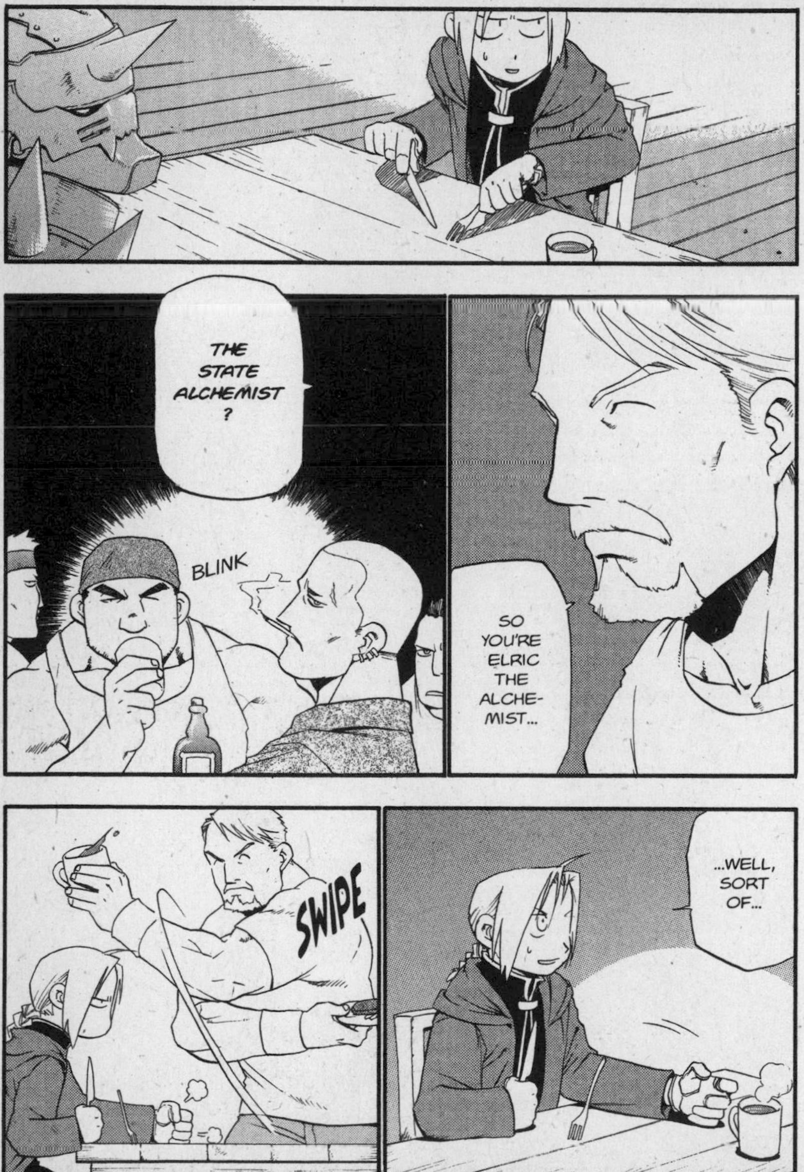
SO YOU'RE ELRIC THE ALCHEMIST...
THE STATE ALCHEMIST?
BLINK
...WELL, SORT OF...
SWIPE

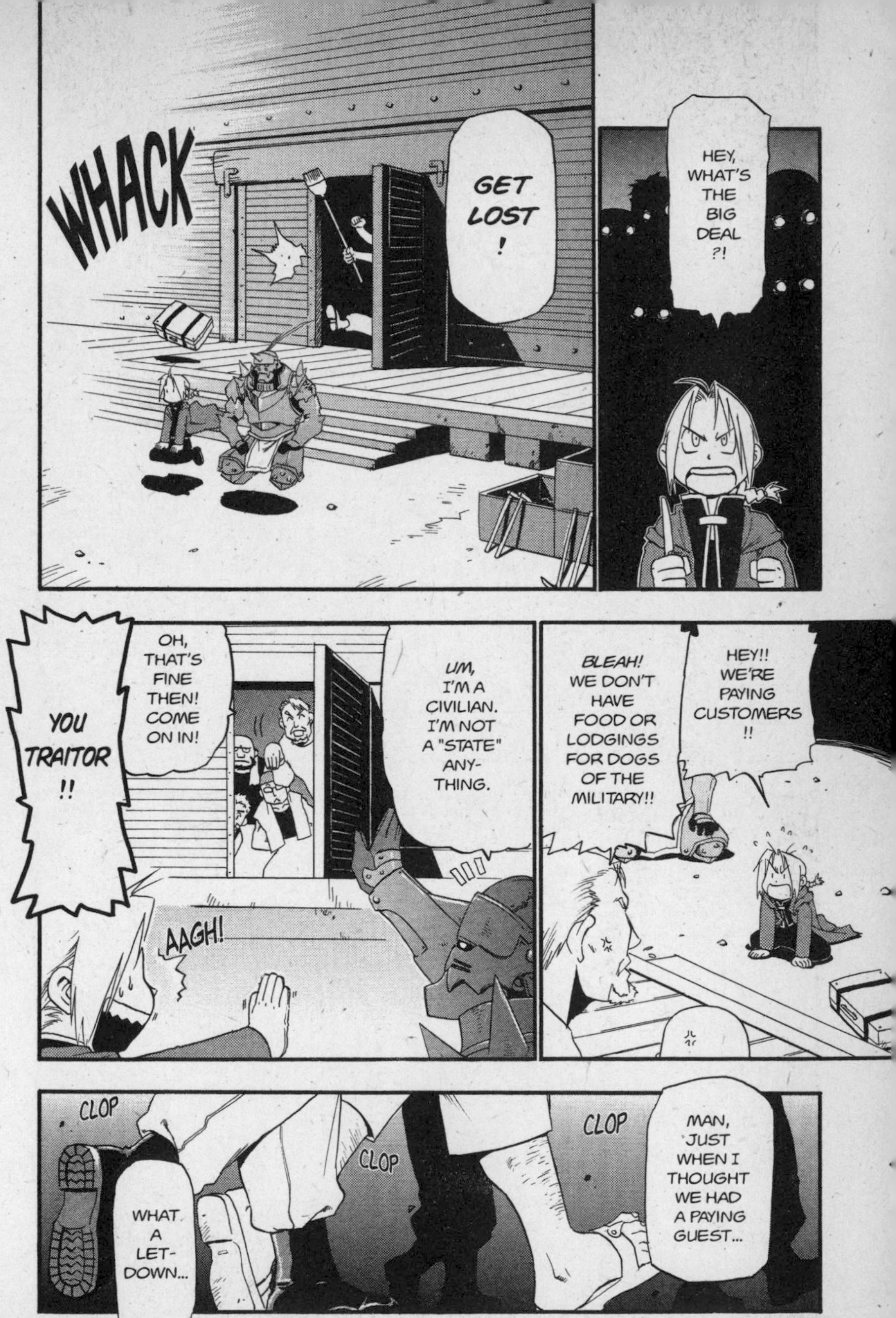
HEY, WHAT'S THE BIG DEAL ?!
WHACK
GET LOST !
HEY!! WE'RE PAYING CUSTOMERS !!
BLEAH! WE DON'T HAVE FOOD OR LODGINGS FOR DOGS OF THE MILITARY!!
UM, I'M A CIVILIAN. I'M NOT A "STATE" ANY-THING.
OH, THAT'S FINE THEN! COME ON IN!
YOU TRAITOR !!
AAGH!
CLOP
MAN, JUST WHEN I THOUGHT WE HAD A PAYING GUEST...
CLOP
WHAT A LET-DOWN...
CLOP

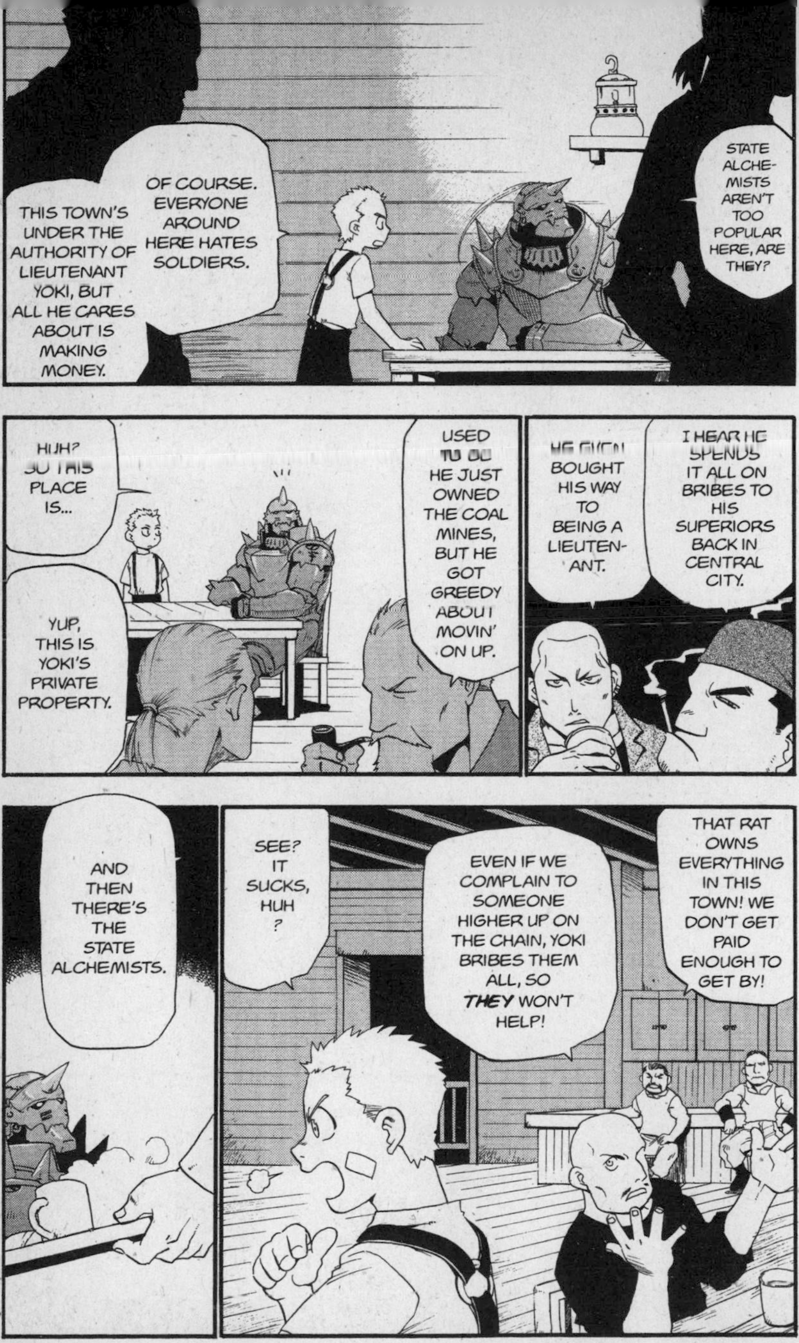
STATE ALCHEMISTS AREN'T TOO POPULAR HERE, ARE THEY?
OF COURSE. EVERYONE AROUND HERE HATES SOLDIERS.
THIS TOWN'S UNDER THE AUTHORITY OF LIEUTENANT YOKI, BUT ALL HE CARES ABOUT IS MAKING MONEY.
I HEAR HE SPENDS IT ALL ON BRIBES TO HIS SUPERIORS BACK IN CENTRAL CITY.
HE EVEN BOUGHT HIS WAY TO BEING A LIEUTEN-ANT.
USED TO BE HE JUST OWNED THE COAL MINES, BUT HE GOT GREEDY ABOUT MOVIN' ON UP.
HUH? SO THIS PLACE IS...
YUP, THIS IS YOKI'S PRIVATE PROPERTY.
THAT RAT OWNS EVERYTHING IN THIS TOWN! WE DON'T GET PAID ENOUGH TO GET BY!
EVEN IF WE COMPLAIN TO SOMEONE HIGHER UP ON THE CHAIN, YOKI BRIBES THEM ALL, SO *THEY* WON'T HELP!
SEE? IT SUCKS, HUH?
AND THEN THERE'S THE STATE ALCHEMISTS.

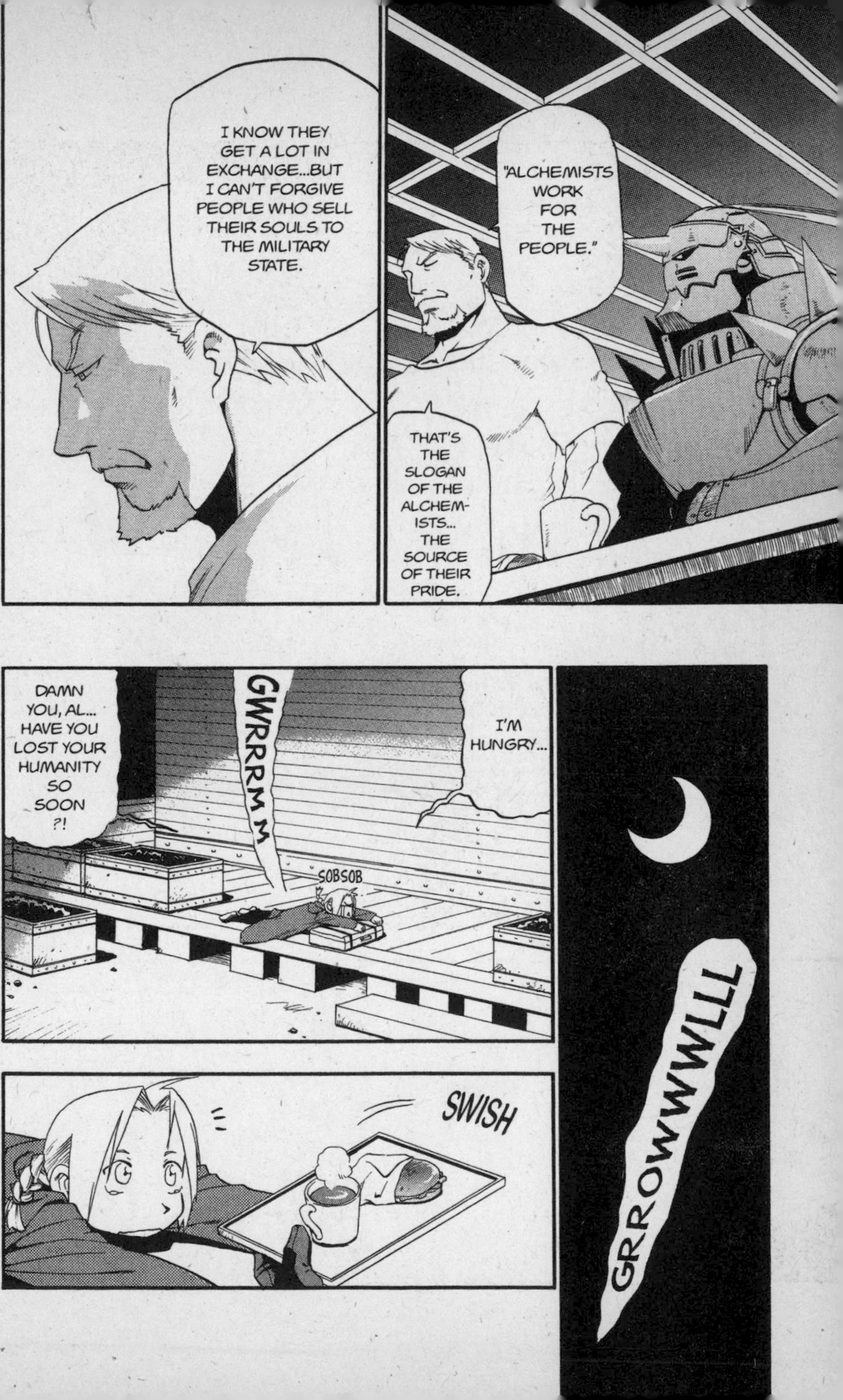
"ALCHEMISTS WORK FOR THE PEOPLE."
THAT'S THE SLOGAN OF THE ALCHEMISTS... THE SOURCE OF THEIR PRIDE.
I KNOW THEY GET A LOT IN EXCHANGE...BUT I CAN'T FORGIVE PEOPLE WHO SELL THEIR SOULS TO THE MILITARY STATE.
GRROWWWLLL
I'M HUNGRY...
GWRRRMM
SOBSOB
DAMN YOU, AL... HAVE YOU LOST YOUR HUMANITY SO SOON?!
SWISH

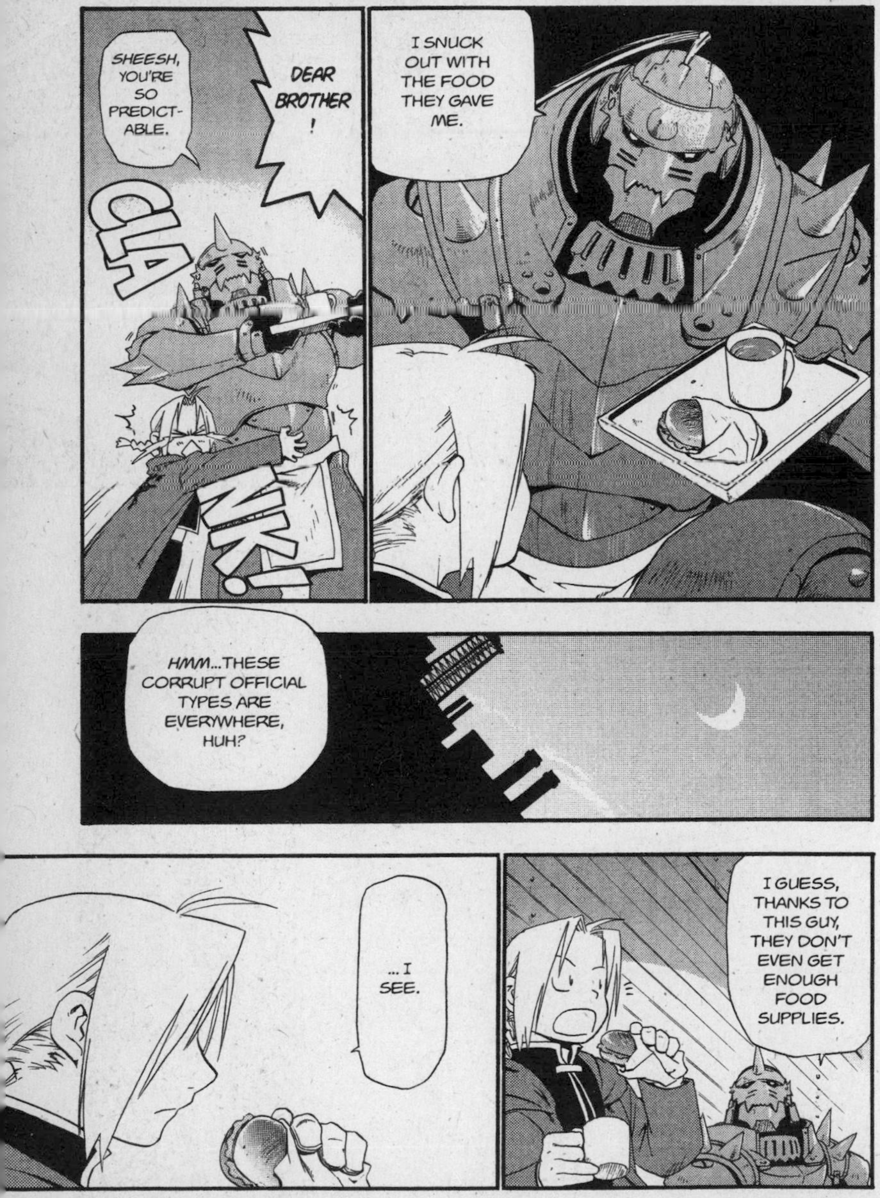
I SNUCK OUT WITH THE FOOD THEY GAVE ME.
DEAR BROTHER!
SHEESH, YOU'RE SO PREDICTABLE.
CLANK!
HMM...THESE CORRUPT OFFICIAL TYPES ARE EVERYWHERE, HUH?
I GUESS, THANKS TO THIS GUY, THEY DON'T EVEN GET ENOUGH FOOD SUPPLIES.
...I SEE.

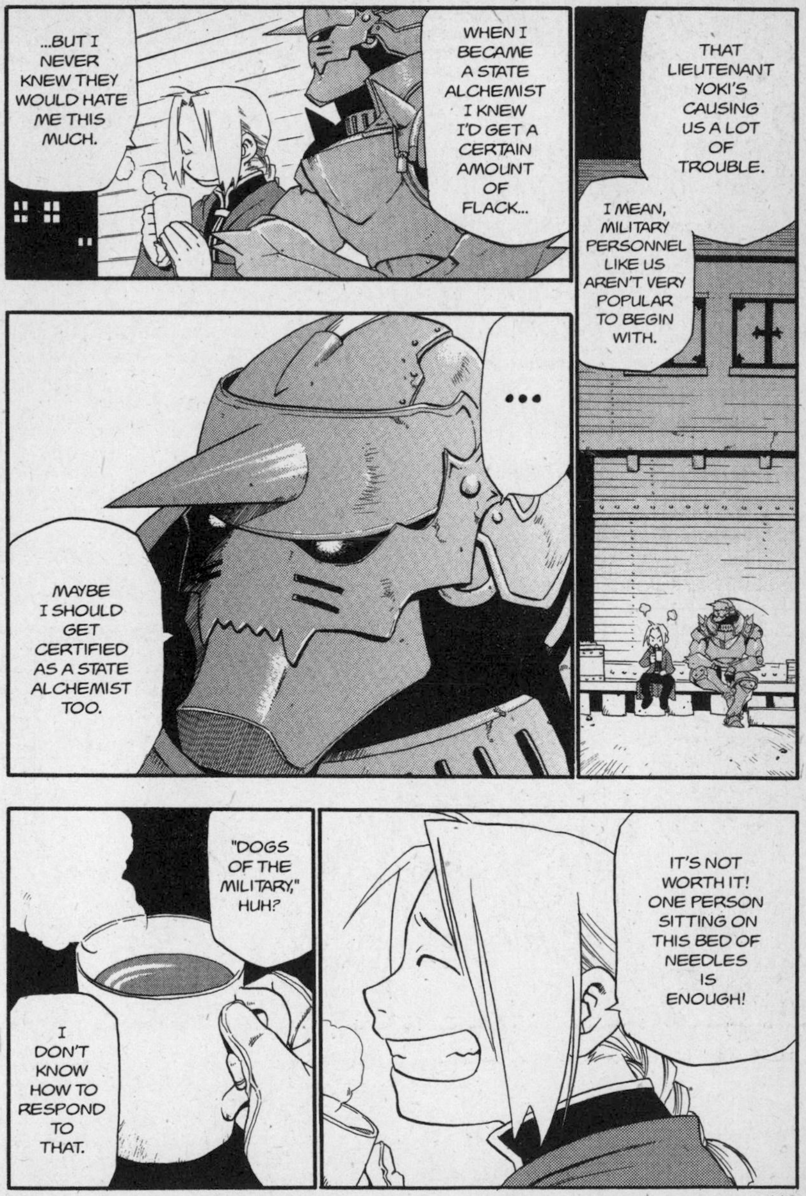
THAT LIEUTENANT YOKI'S CAUSING US A LOT OF TROUBLE.
I MEAN, MILITARY PERSONNEL LIKE US AREN'T VERY POPULAR TO BEGIN WITH.
WHEN I BECAME A STATE ALCHEMIST I KNEW I'D GET A CERTAIN AMOUNT OF FLACK...
...BUT I NEVER KNEW THEY WOULD HATE ME THIS MUCH.
...
MAYBE I SHOULD GET CERTIFIED AS A STATE ALCHEMIST TOO.
IT'S NOT WORTH IT! ONE PERSON SITTING ON THIS BED OF NEEDLES IS ENOUGH!
"DOGS OF THE MILITARY," HUH?
I DON'T KNOW HOW TO RESPOND TO THAT.

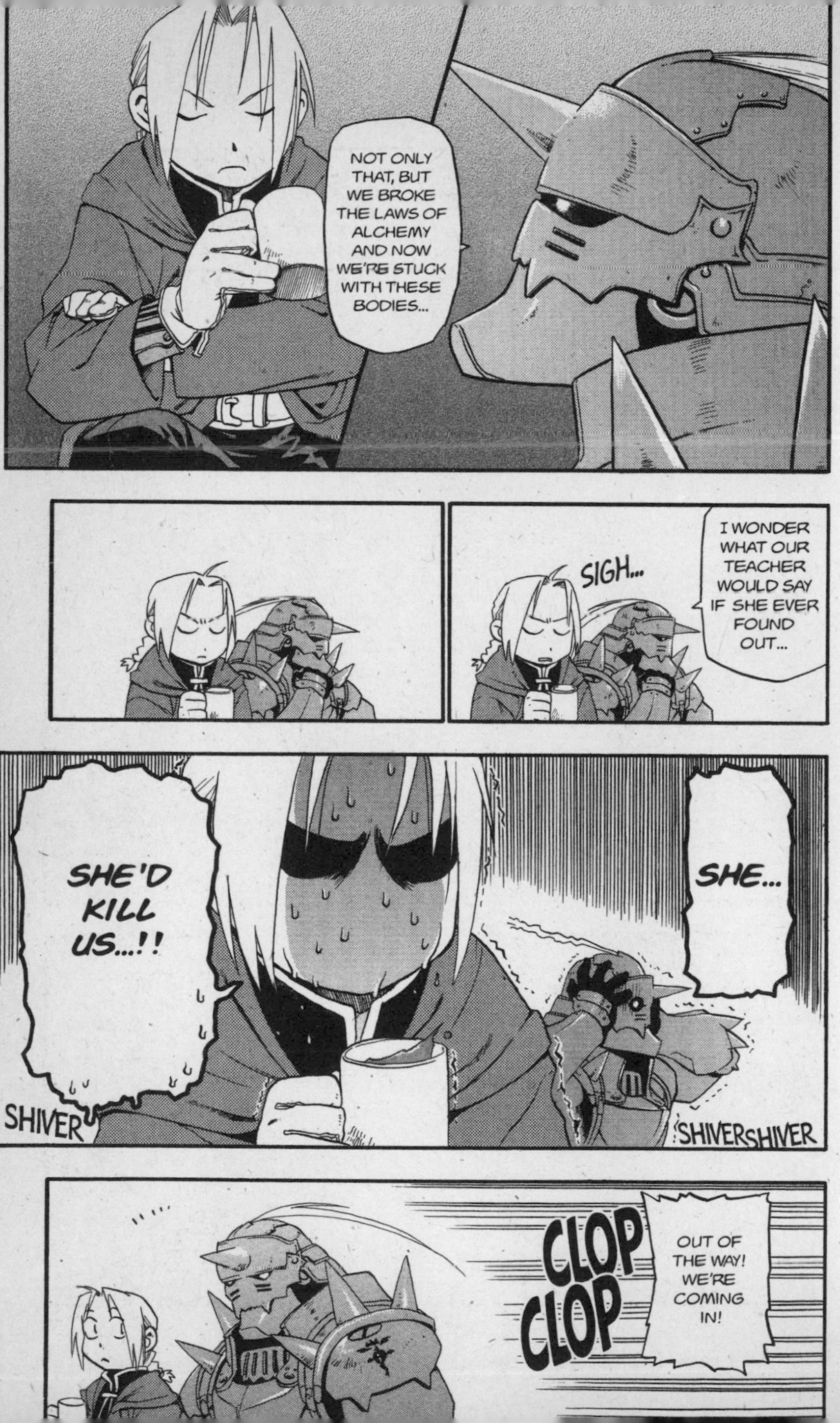
NOT ONLY THAT, BUT WE BROKE THE LAWS OF ALCHEMY AND NOW WE'RE STUCK WITH THESE BODIES...
SIGH...
I WONDER WHAT OUR TEACHER WOULD SAY IF SHE EVER FOUND OUT...
SHE...
SHE'D KILL US...!!
SHIVERSHIVER
SHIVER
OUT OF THE WAY! WE'RE COMING IN!
CLOP CLOP

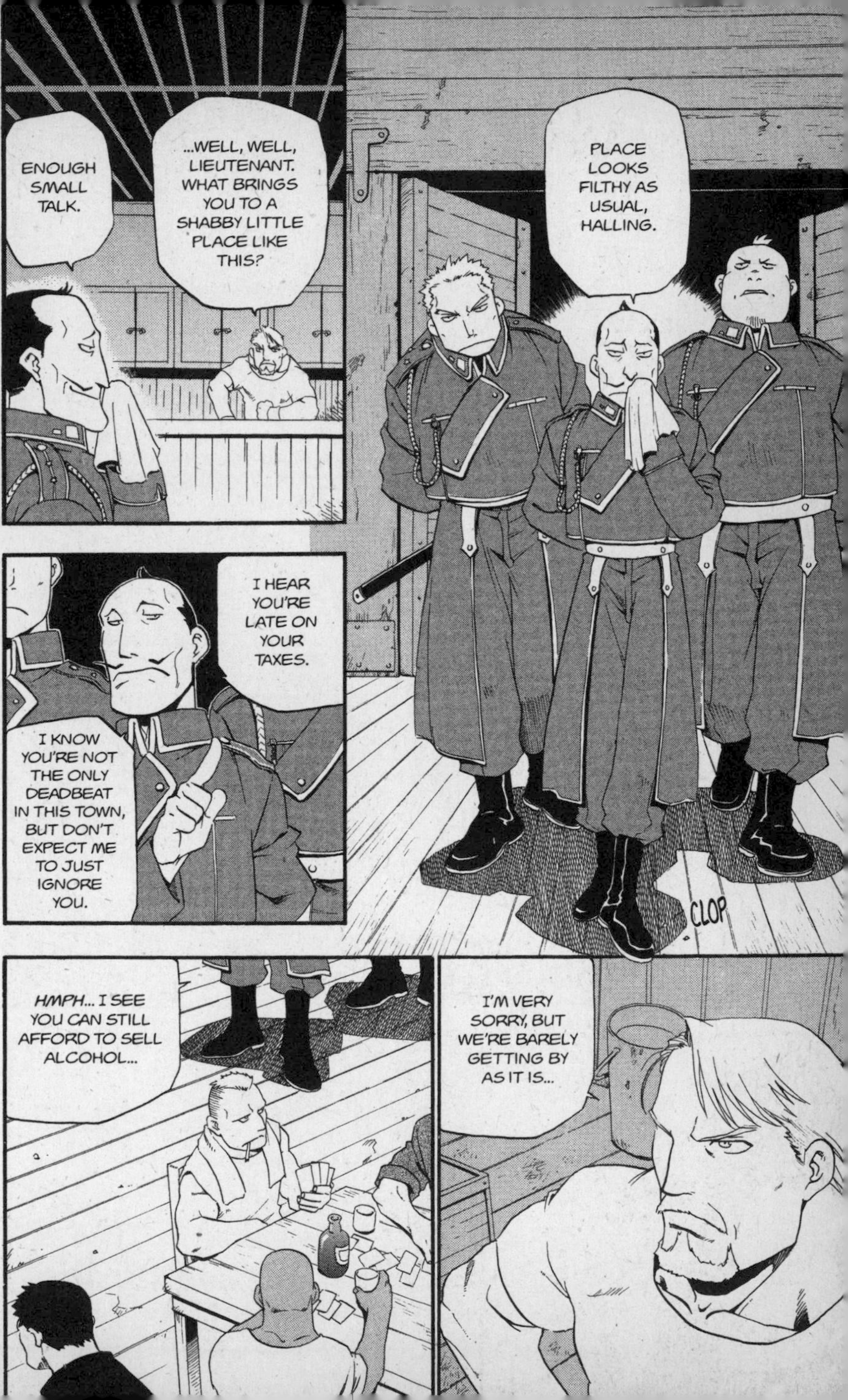
PLACE LOOKS FILTHY AS USUAL, HALLING.
CLOP
...WELL, WELL, LIEUTENANT. WHAT BRINGS YOU TO A SHABBY LITTLE PLACE LIKE THIS?
ENOUGH SMALL TALK.
I HEAR YOU'RE LATE ON YOUR TAXES.
I KNOW YOU'RE NOT THE ONLY DEADBEAT IN THIS TOWN, BUT DON'T EXPECT ME TO JUST IGNORE YOU.
I'M VERY SORRY, BUT WE'RE BARELY GETTING BY AS IT IS...
HMPH... I SEE YOU CAN STILL AFFORD TO SELL ALCOHOL...

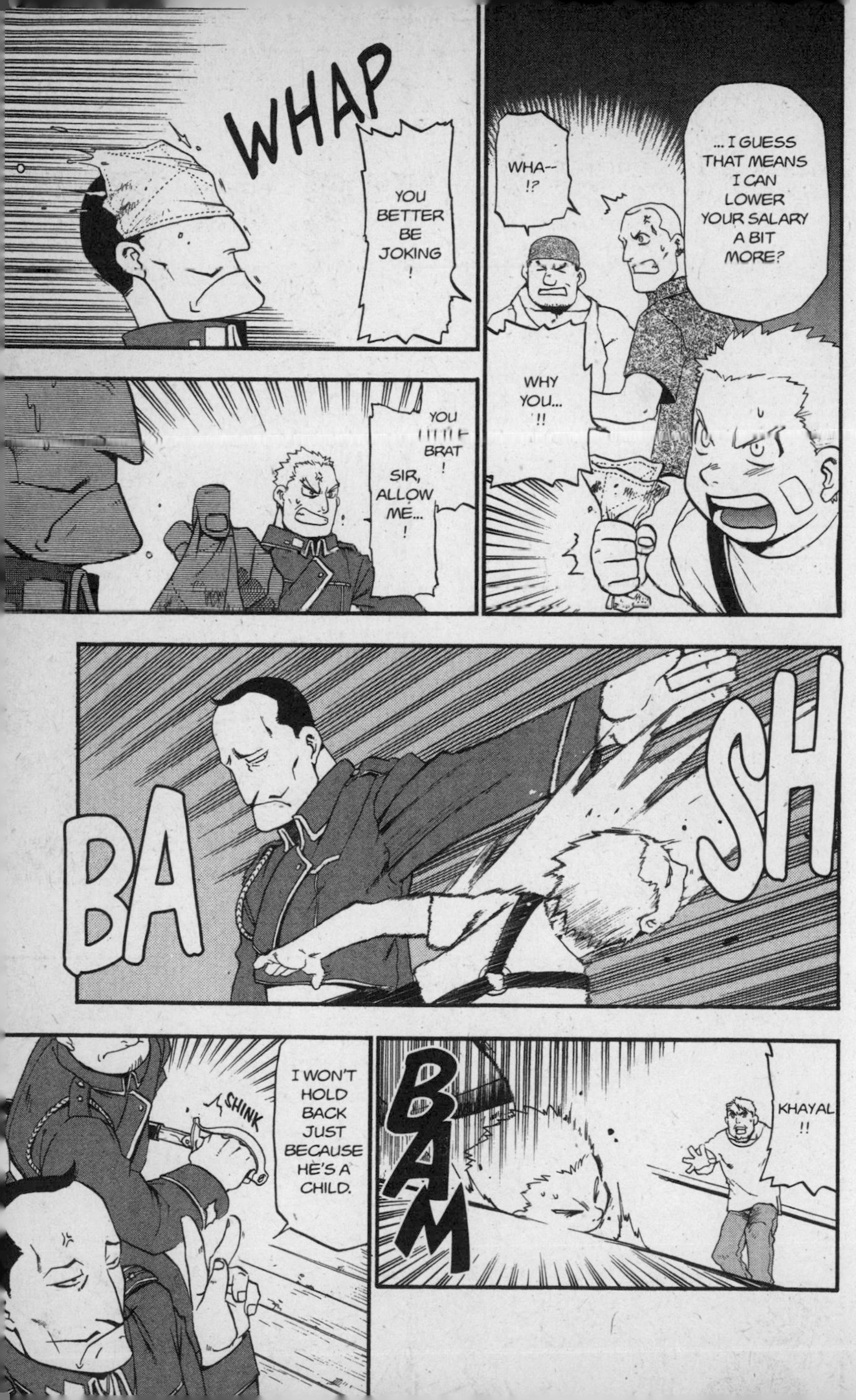
...I GUESS THAT MEANS I CAN LOWER YOUR SALARY A BIT MORE?
WHA-- !?
WHY YOU... !!
WHAP
YOU BETTER BE JOKING!
YOU BRAT!
SIR, ALLOW ME...!
BASH
BAM
KHAYAL!!
SHINK
I WON'T HOLD BACK JUST BECAUSE HE'S A CHILD.

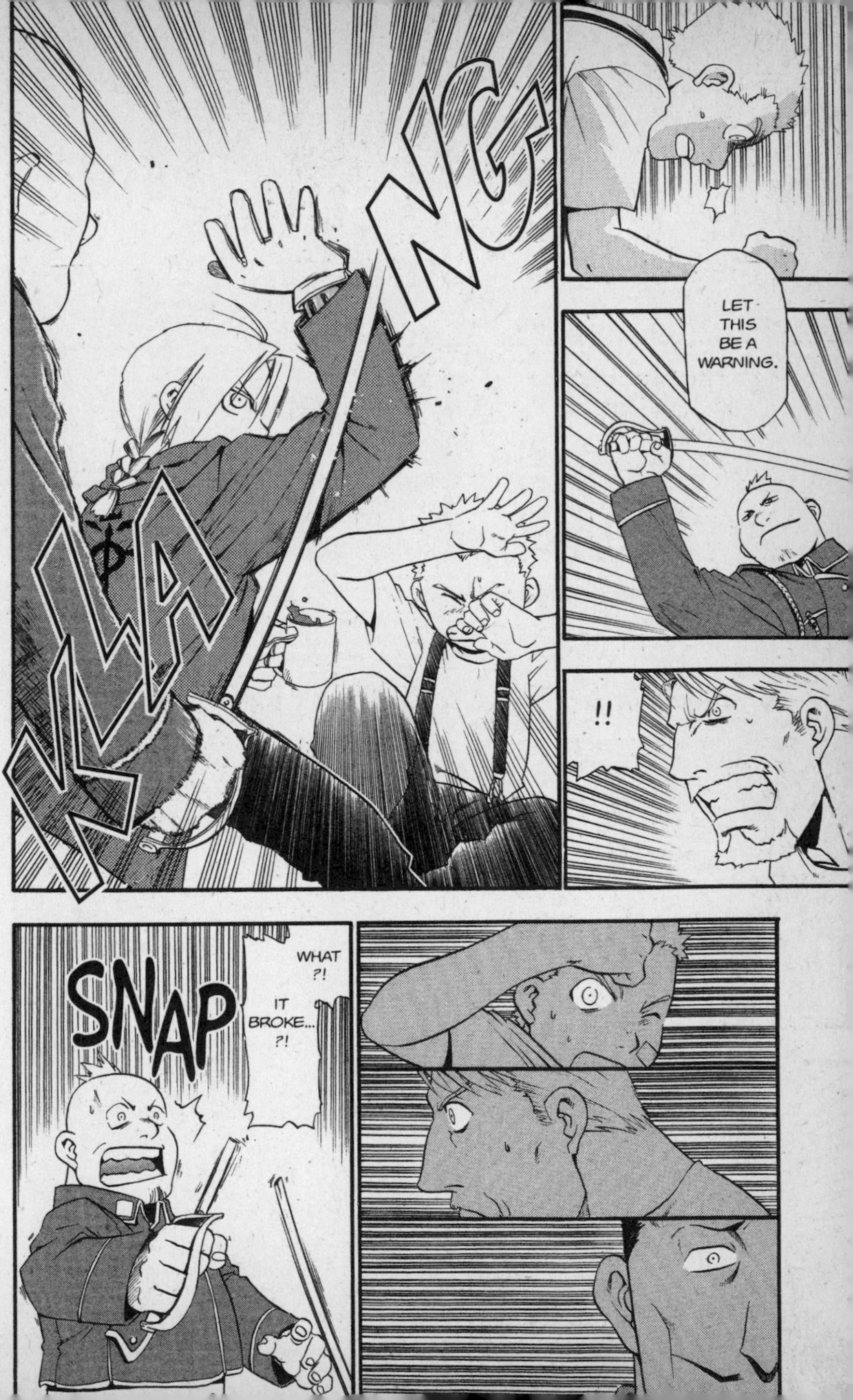
LET THIS BE A WARNING.
!!
KLANG
SNAP
WHAT ?!
IT BROKE... ?!

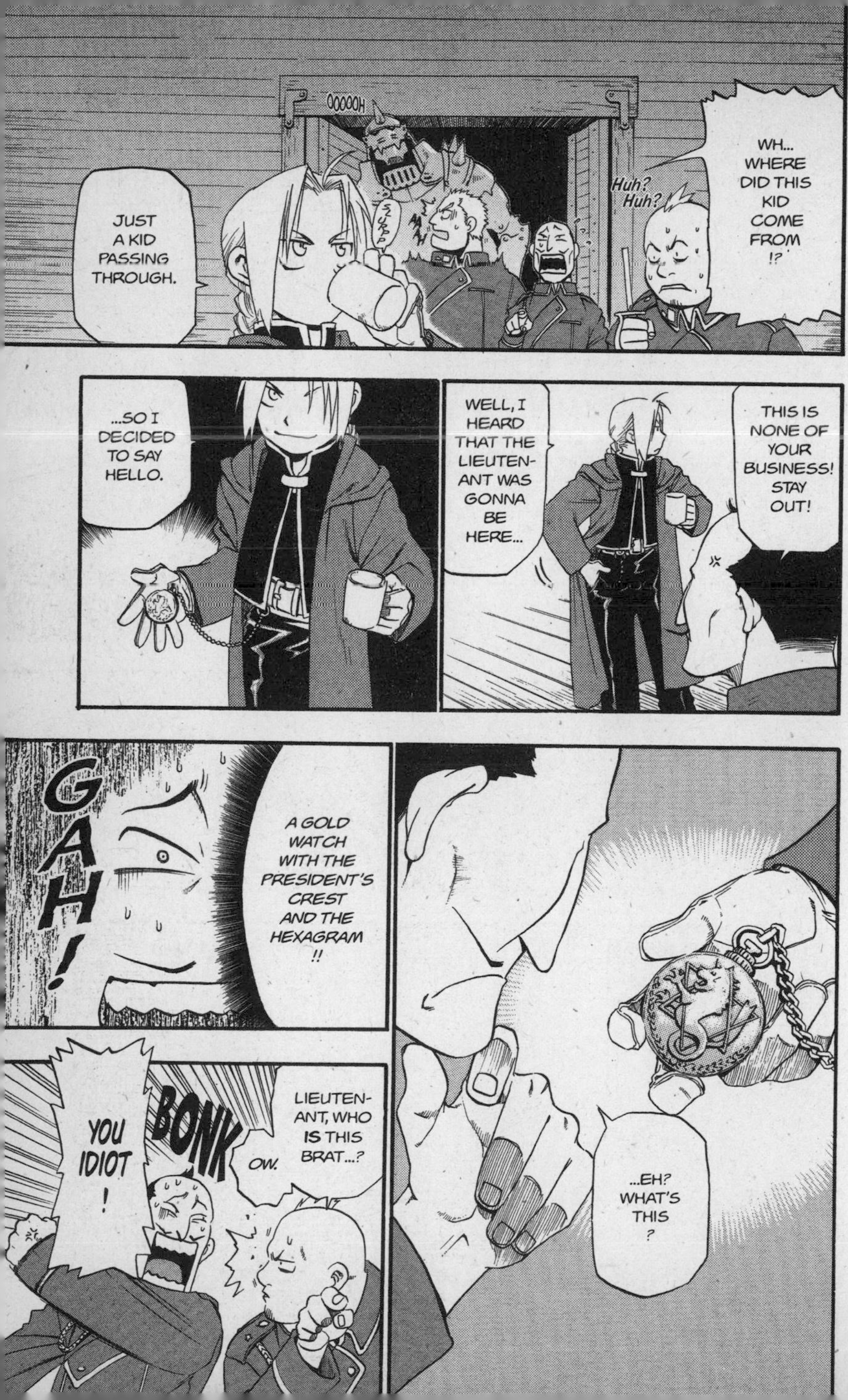

WH... WHERE DID THIS KID COME FROM !?
Huh? Huh?
SLURP
JUST A KID PASSING THROUGH.
THIS IS NONE OF YOUR BUSINESS! STAY OUT!
WELL, I HEARD THAT THE LIEUTEN-ANT WAS GONNA BE HERE...
...SO I DECIDED TO SAY HELLO.
...EH? WHAT'S THIS ?
A GOLD WATCH WITH THE PRESIDENT'S CREST AND THE HEXAGRAM !!
GAH!
LIEUTEN-ANT, WHO IS THIS BRAT...?
OW.
BONK
YOU IDIOT !

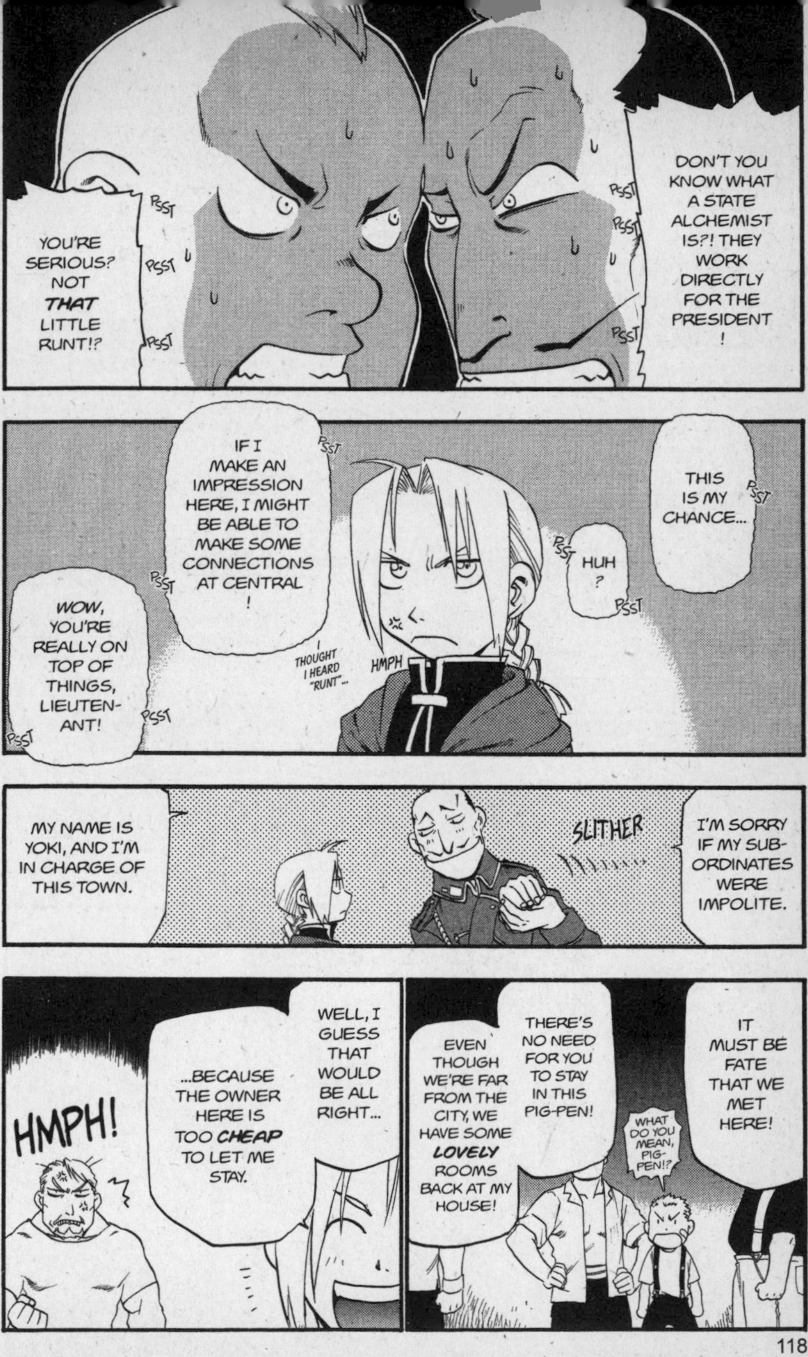
DON'T YOU KNOW WHAT A STATE ALCHEMIST IS?! THEY WORK DIRECTLY FOR THE PRESIDENT!
PSST
PSST
PSST
PSST
PSST
PSST
YOU'RE SERIOUS? NOT *THAT* LITTLE RUNT!?
THIS IS MY CHANCE...
PSST
HUH?
PSST
PSST
IF I MAKE AN IMPRESSION HERE, I MIGHT BE ABLE TO MAKE SOME CONNECTIONS AT CENTRAL!
PSST
HMPH
I THOUGHT I HEARD "RUNT"...
PSST
WOW, YOU'RE REALLY ON TOP OF THINGS, LIEUTENANT!
PSST
PSST
I'M SORRY IF MY SUBORDINATES WERE IMPOLITE.
SLITHER
MY NAME IS YOKI, AND I'M IN CHARGE OF THIS TOWN.
IT MUST BE FATE THAT WE MET HERE!
WHAT DO YOU MEAN, PIG-PEN!?
THERE'S NO NEED FOR YOU TO STAY IN THIS PIG-PEN!
EVEN THOUGH WE'RE FAR FROM THE CITY, WE HAVE SOME *LOVELY* ROOMS BACK AT MY HOUSE!
WELL, I GUESS THAT WOULD BE ALL RIGHT...
...BECAUSE THE OWNER HERE IS TOO *CHEAP* TO LET ME STAY.
HMPH!

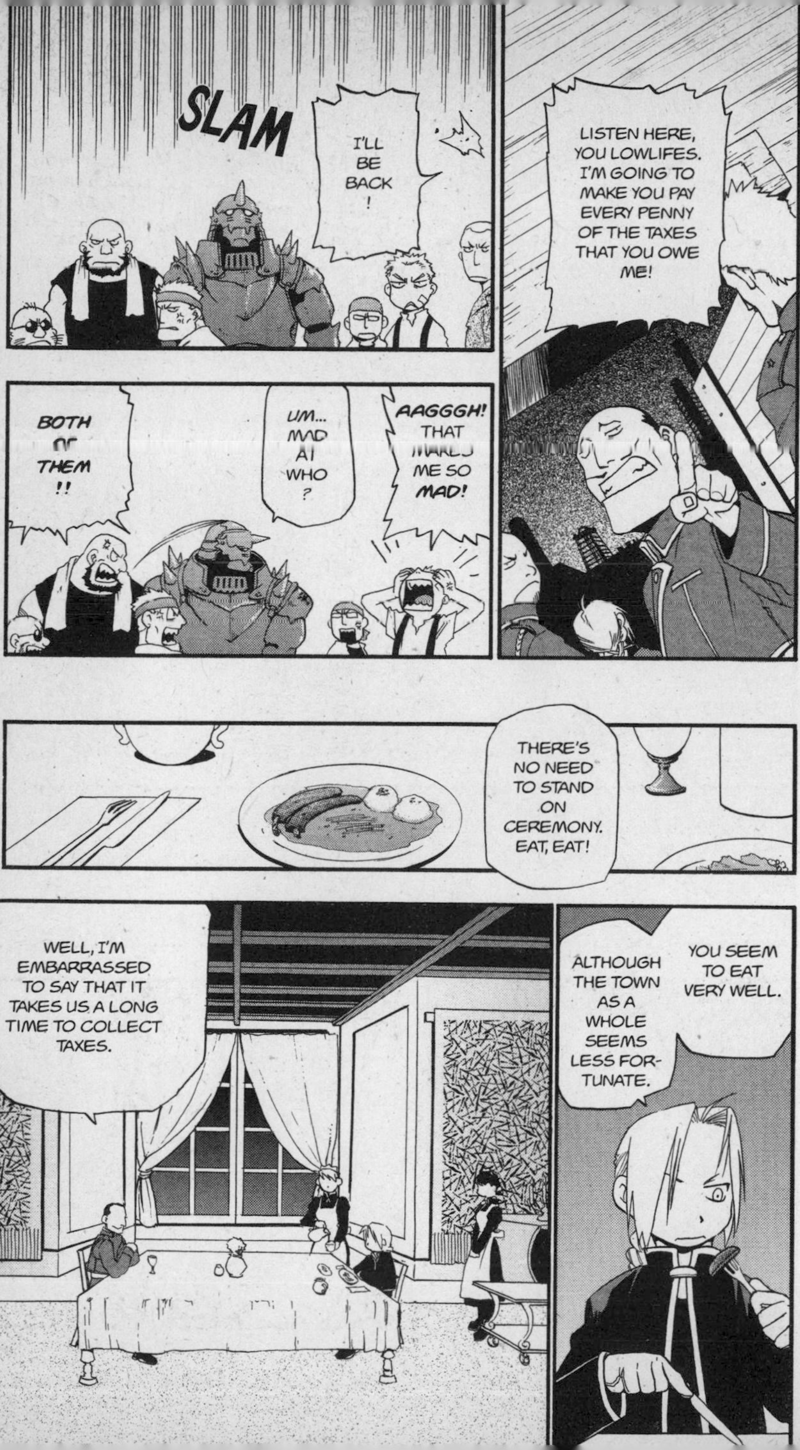
LISTEN HERE, YOU LOWLIFES. I'M GOING TO MAKE YOU PAY EVERY PENNY OF THE TAXES THAT YOU OWE ME!
SLAM
I'LL BE BACK!
AAGGGH! THAT MAKES ME SO MAD!
UM... MAD AT WHO?
BOTH OF THEM!!
THERE'S NO NEED TO STAND ON CEREMONY. EAT, EAT!
YOU SEEM TO EAT VERY WELL.
ALTHOUGH THE TOWN AS A WHOLE SEEMS LESS FORTUNATE.
WELL, I'M EMBARRASSED TO SAY THAT IT TAKES US A LONG TIME TO COLLECT TAXES.

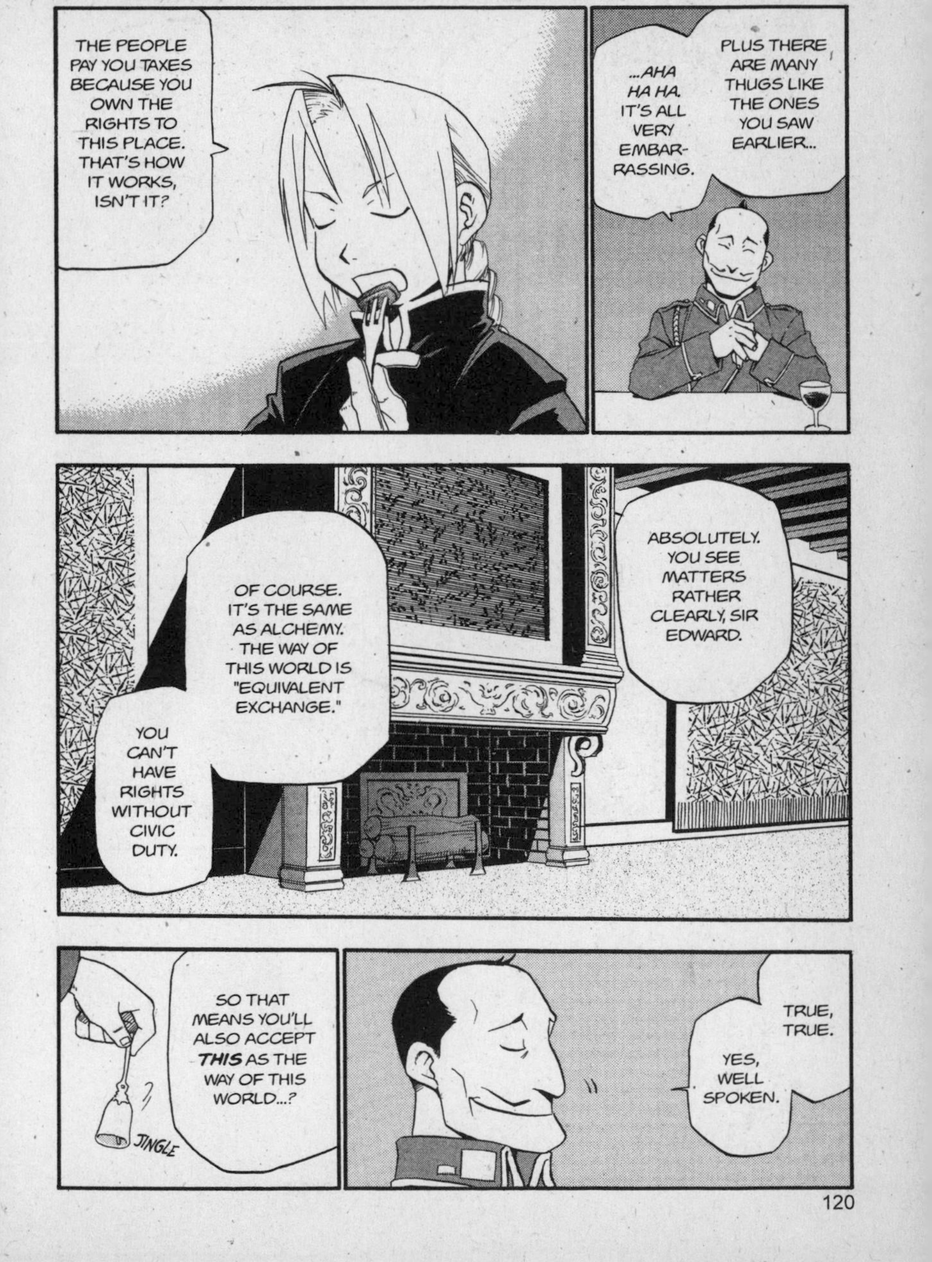
...AHA HA HA. IT'S ALL VERY EMBARRASSING.
PLUS THERE ARE MANY THUGS LIKE THE ONES YOU SAW EARLIER...
THE PEOPLE PAY YOU TAXES BECAUSE YOU OWN THE RIGHTS TO THIS PLACE. THAT'S HOW IT WORKS, ISN'T IT?
ABSOLUTELY. YOU SEE MATTERS RATHER CLEARLY, SIR EDWARD.
OF COURSE. IT'S THE SAME AS ALCHEMY. THE WAY OF THIS WORLD IS "EQUIVALENT EXCHANGE."
YOU CAN'T HAVE RIGHTS WITHOUT CIVIC DUTY.
TRUE, TRUE.
YES, WELL SPOKEN.
SO THAT MEANS YOU'LL ALSO ACCEPT ***THIS*** AS THE WAY OF THIS WORLD...?
JINGLE

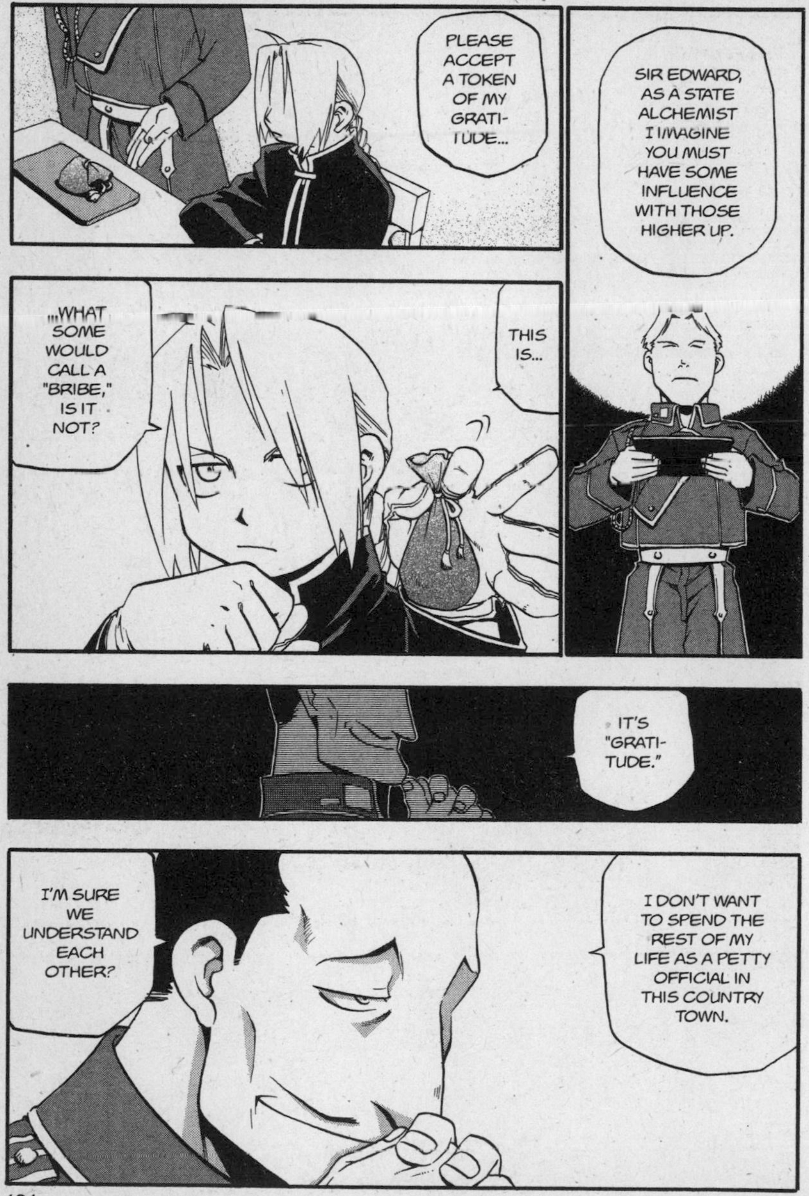
SIR EDWARD, AS A STATE ALCHEMIST I IMAGINE YOU MUST HAVE SOME INFLUENCE WITH THOSE HIGHER UP.
PLEASE ACCEPT A TOKEN OF MY GRATI-TUDE...
THIS IS...
...WHAT SOME WOULD CALL A "BRIBE," IS IT NOT?
IT'S "GRATI-TUDE."
I DON'T WANT TO SPEND THE REST OF MY LIFE AS A PETTY OFFICIAL IN THIS COUNTRY TOWN.
I'M SURE WE UNDERSTAND EACH OTHER?

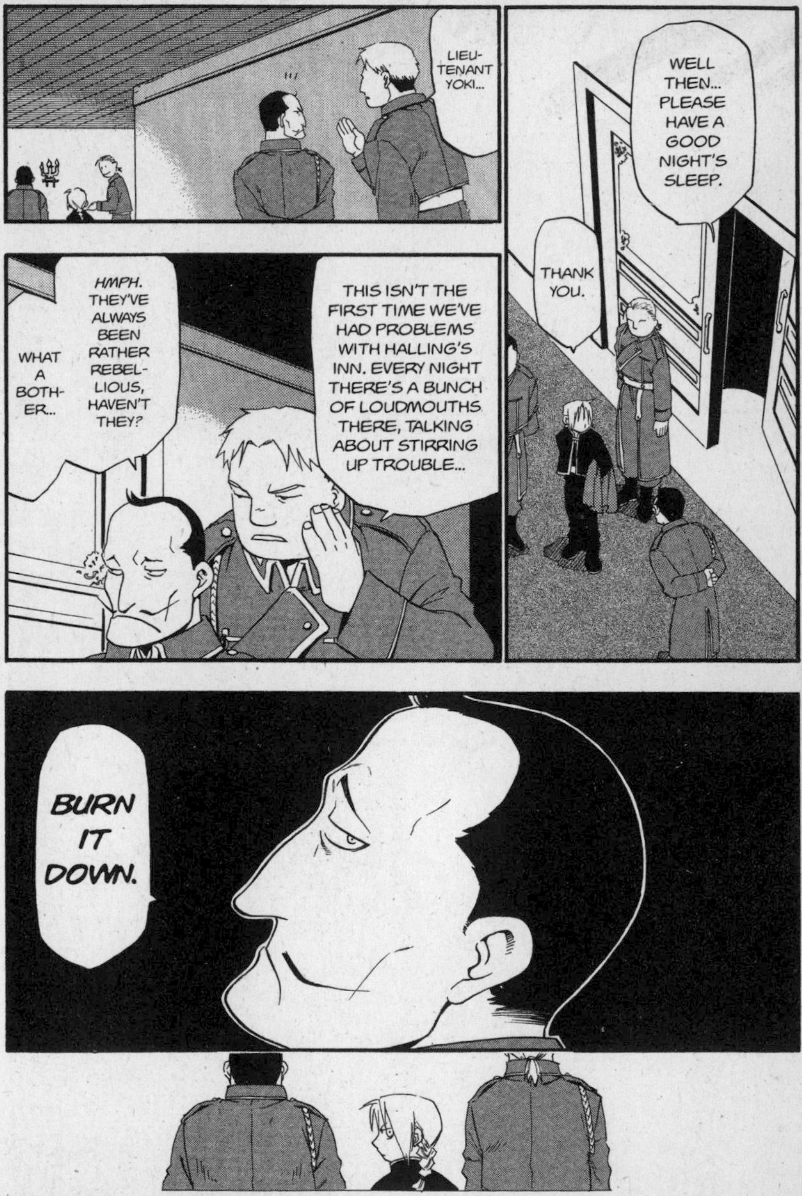
WELL THEN... PLEASE HAVE A GOOD NIGHT'S SLEEP.
THANK YOU.
LIEU-TENANT YOKI...
THIS ISN'T THE FIRST TIME WE'VE HAD PROBLEMS WITH HALLING'S INN. EVERY NIGHT THERE'S A BUNCH OF LOUDMOUTHS THERE, TALKING ABOUT STIRRING UP TROUBLE...
HMPH. THEY'VE ALWAYS BEEN RATHER REBEL-LIOUS, HAVEN'T THEY?
WHAT A BOTH-ER...
BURN IT DOWN.

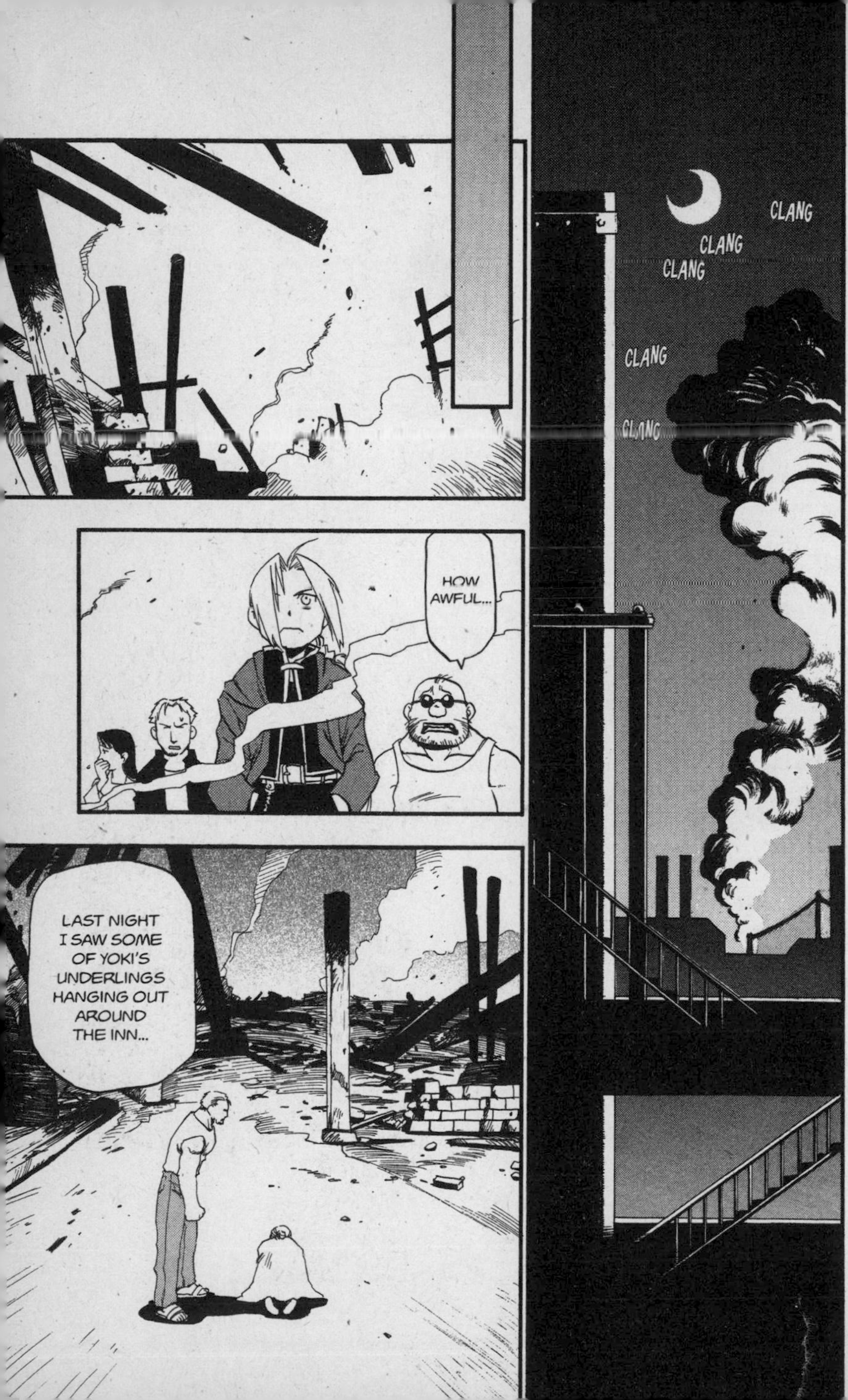
CLANG
CLANG
CLANG
CLANG
CLANG
HOW AWFUL...
LAST NIGHT I SAW SOME OF YOKI'S UNDERLINGS HANGING OUT AROUND THE INN...

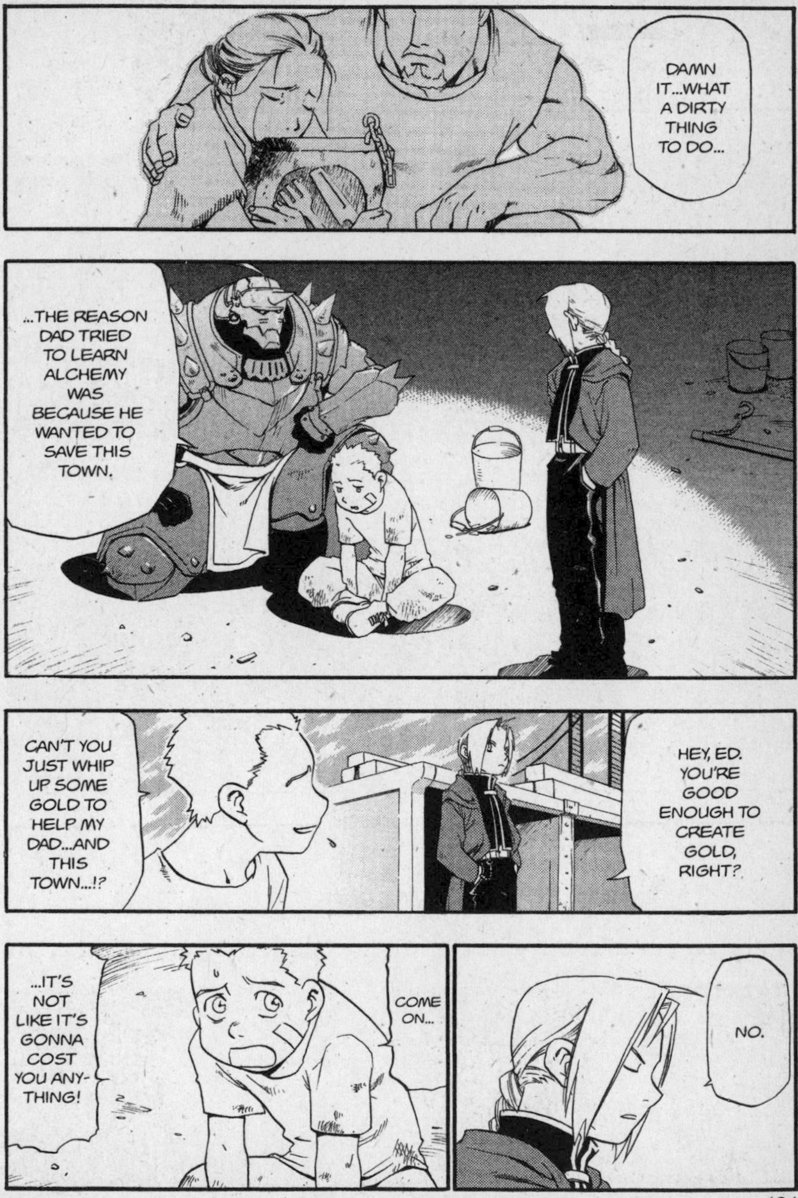
DAMN IT...WHAT A DIRTY THING TO DO...
...THE REASON DAD TRIED TO LEARN ALCHEMY WAS BECAUSE HE WANTED TO SAVE THIS TOWN.
HEY, ED. YOU'RE GOOD ENOUGH TO CREATE GOLD, RIGHT?
CAN'T YOU JUST WHIP UP SOME GOLD TO HELP MY DAD...AND THIS TOWN...!?
NO.
COME ON...
...IT'S NOT LIKE IT'S GONNA COST YOU ANY-THING!

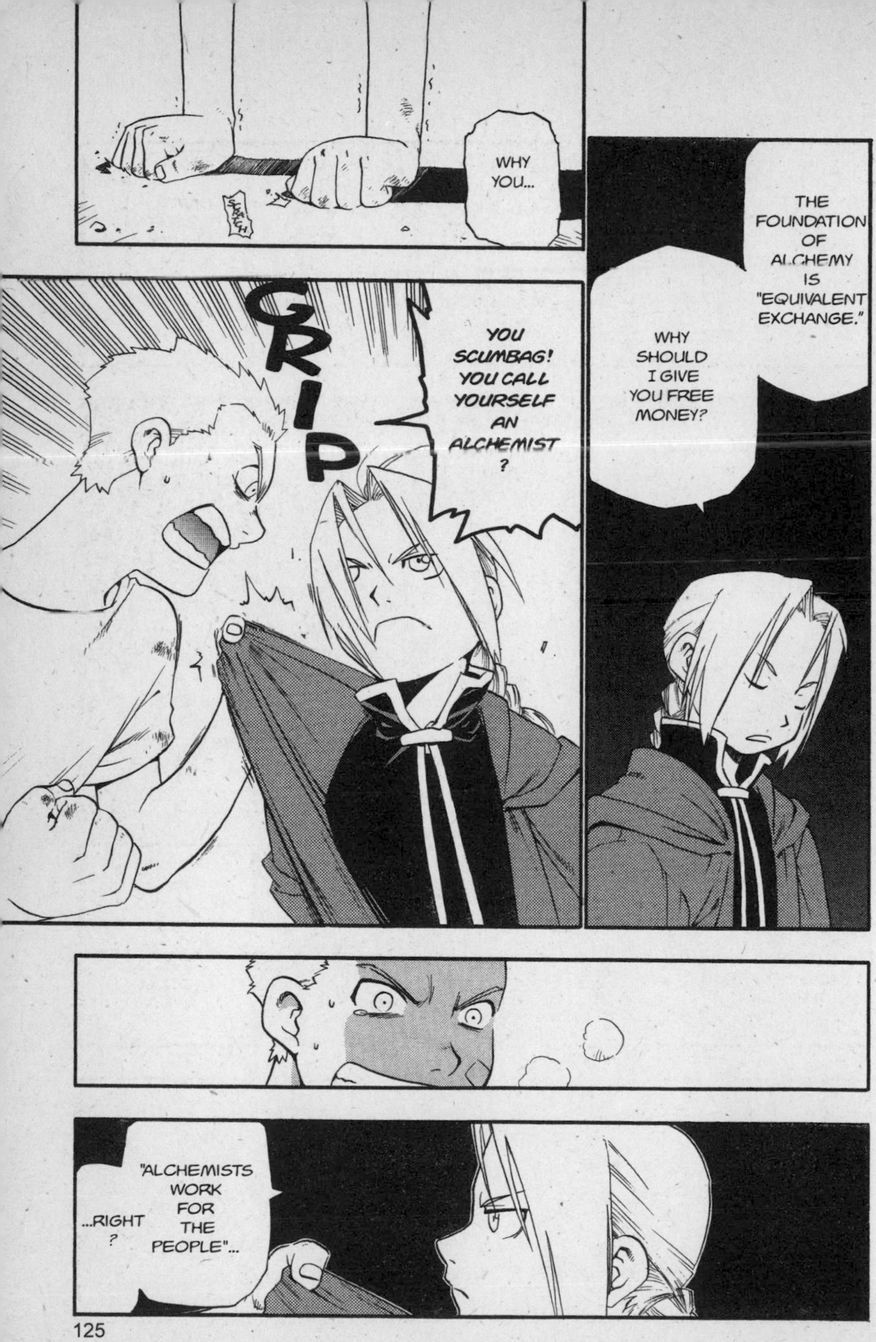
THE FOUNDATION OF ALCHEMY IS "EQUIVALENT EXCHANGE."
WHY SHOULD I GIVE YOU FREE MONEY?
SCRATCH
WHY YOU...
GRIP
YOU SCUMBAG! YOU CALL YOURSELF AN ALCHEMIST?
"ALCHEMISTS WORK FOR THE PEOPLE"...
...RIGHT?

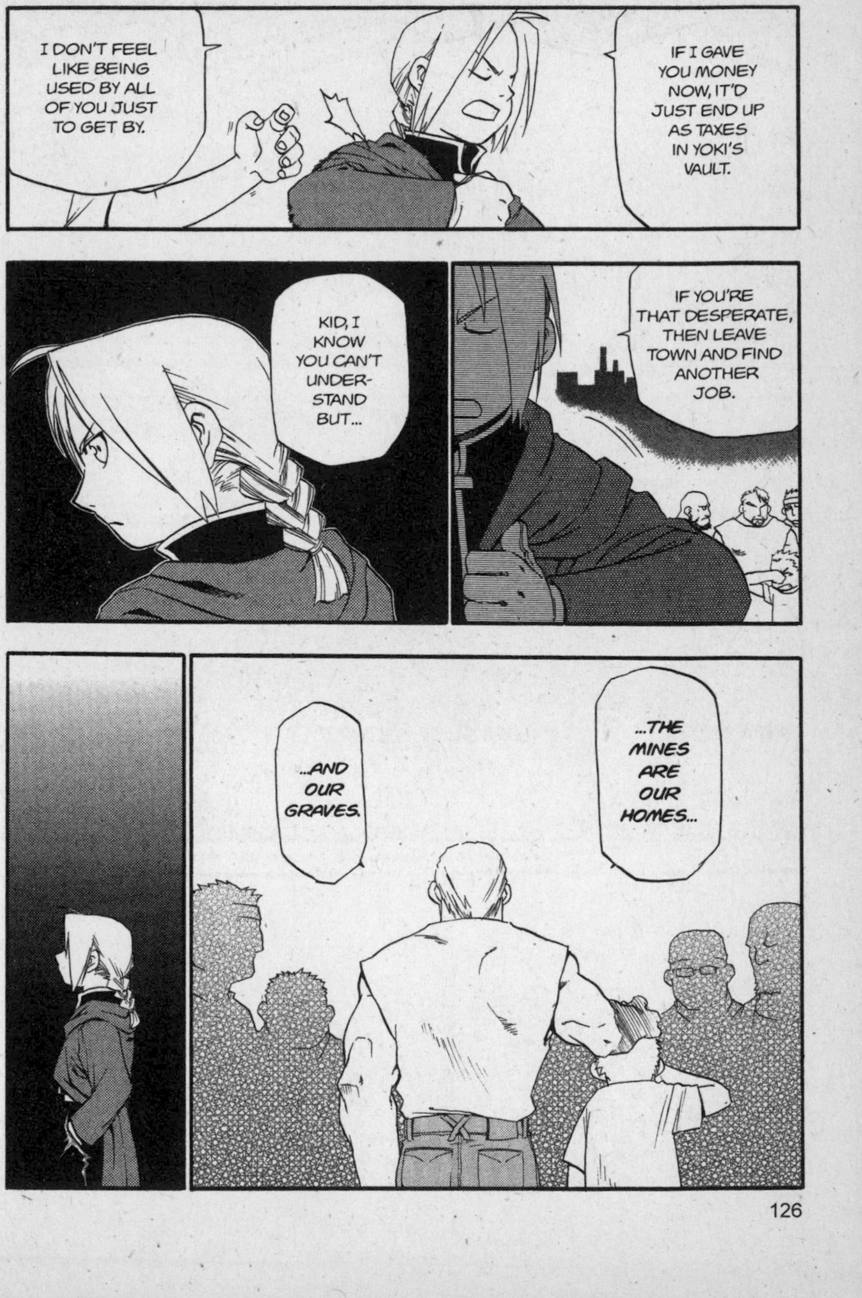
IF I GAVE YOU MONEY NOW, IT'D JUST END UP AS TAXES IN YOKI'S VAULT.
I DON'T FEEL LIKE BEING USED BY ALL OF YOU JUST TO GET BY.
IF YOU'RE THAT DESPERATE, THEN LEAVE TOWN AND FIND ANOTHER JOB.
KID, I KNOW YOU CAN'T UNDER-STAND BUT...
...THE MINES ARE OUR HOMES...
...AND OUR GRAVES.

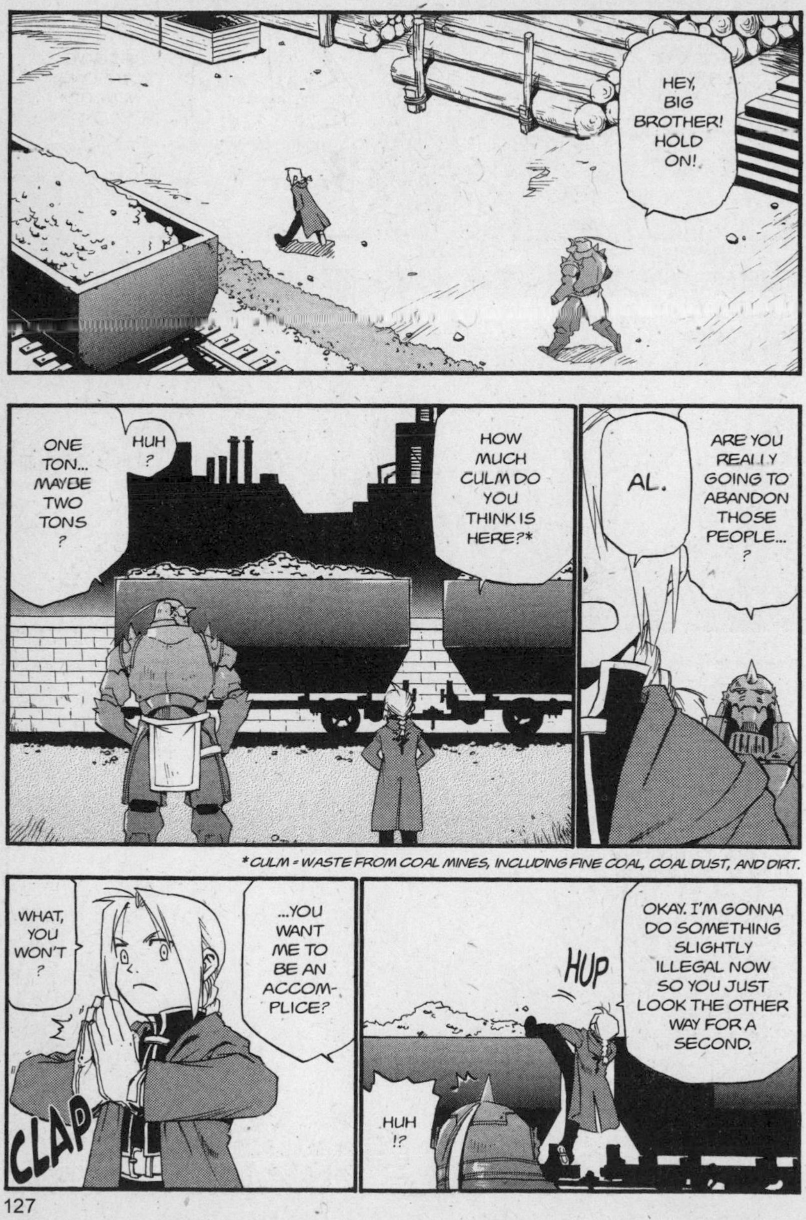
HEY, BIG BROTHER! HOLD ON!
ARE YOU REALLY GOING TO ABANDON THOSE PEOPLE...?
AL.
HOW MUCH CULM DO YOU THINK IS HERE?*
HUH?
ONE TON... MAYBE TWO TONS?
OKAY. I'M GONNA DO SOMETHING SLIGHTLY ILLEGAL NOW SO YOU JUST LOOK THE OTHER WAY FOR A SECOND.
HUP
HUH!?
...YOU WANT ME TO BE AN ACCOMPLICE?
WHAT, YOU WON'T?
CLAP

*CULM = WASTE FROM COAL MINES, INCLUDING FINE COAL, COAL DUST, AND DIRT.

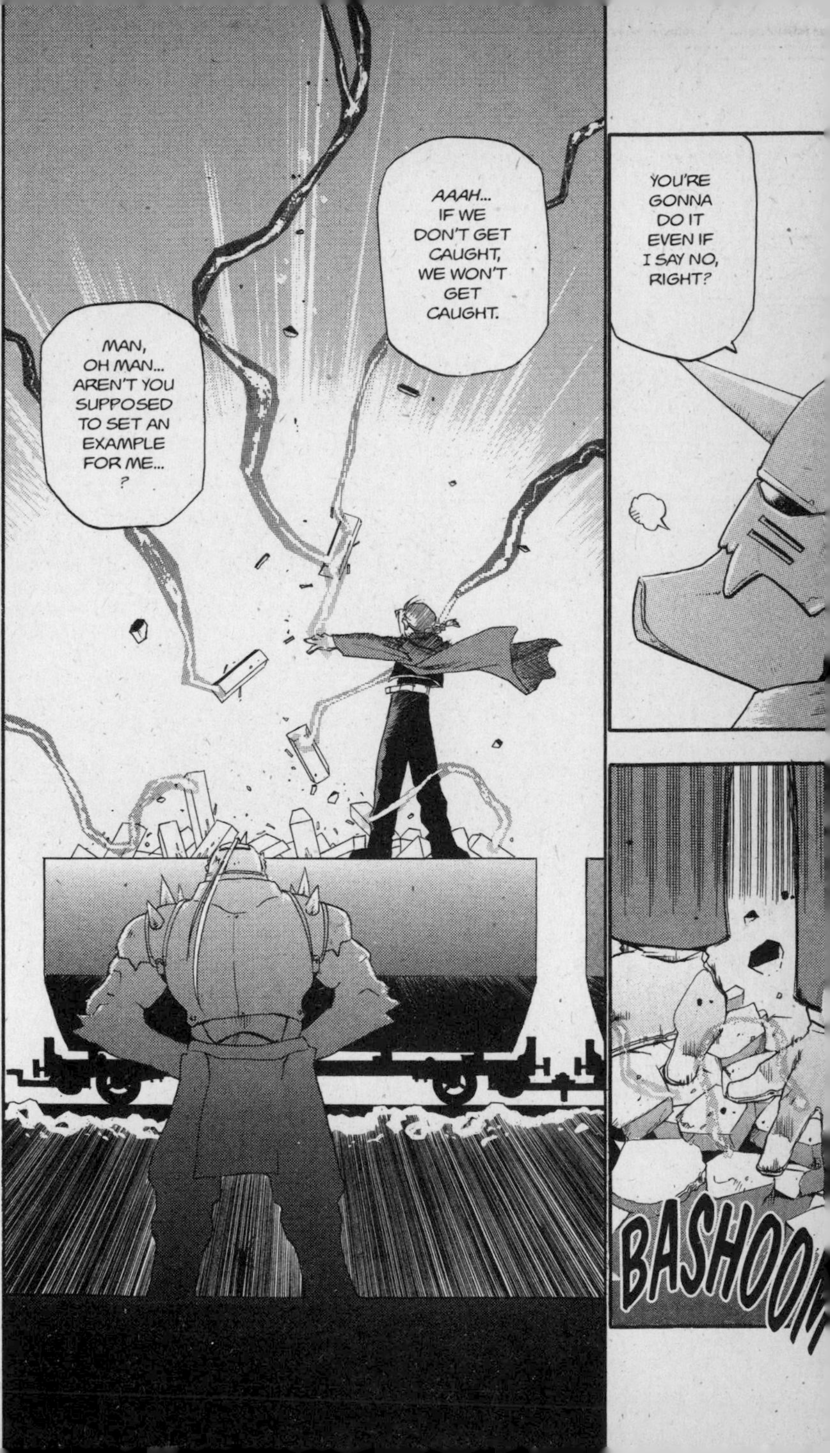

YOU'RE GONNA DO IT EVEN IF I SAY NO, RIGHT?
BASHOOM
AAAH... IF WE DON'T GET CAUGHT, WE WON'T GET CAUGHT.
MAN, OH MAN... AREN'T YOU SUPPOSED TO SET AN EXAMPLE FOR ME... ?

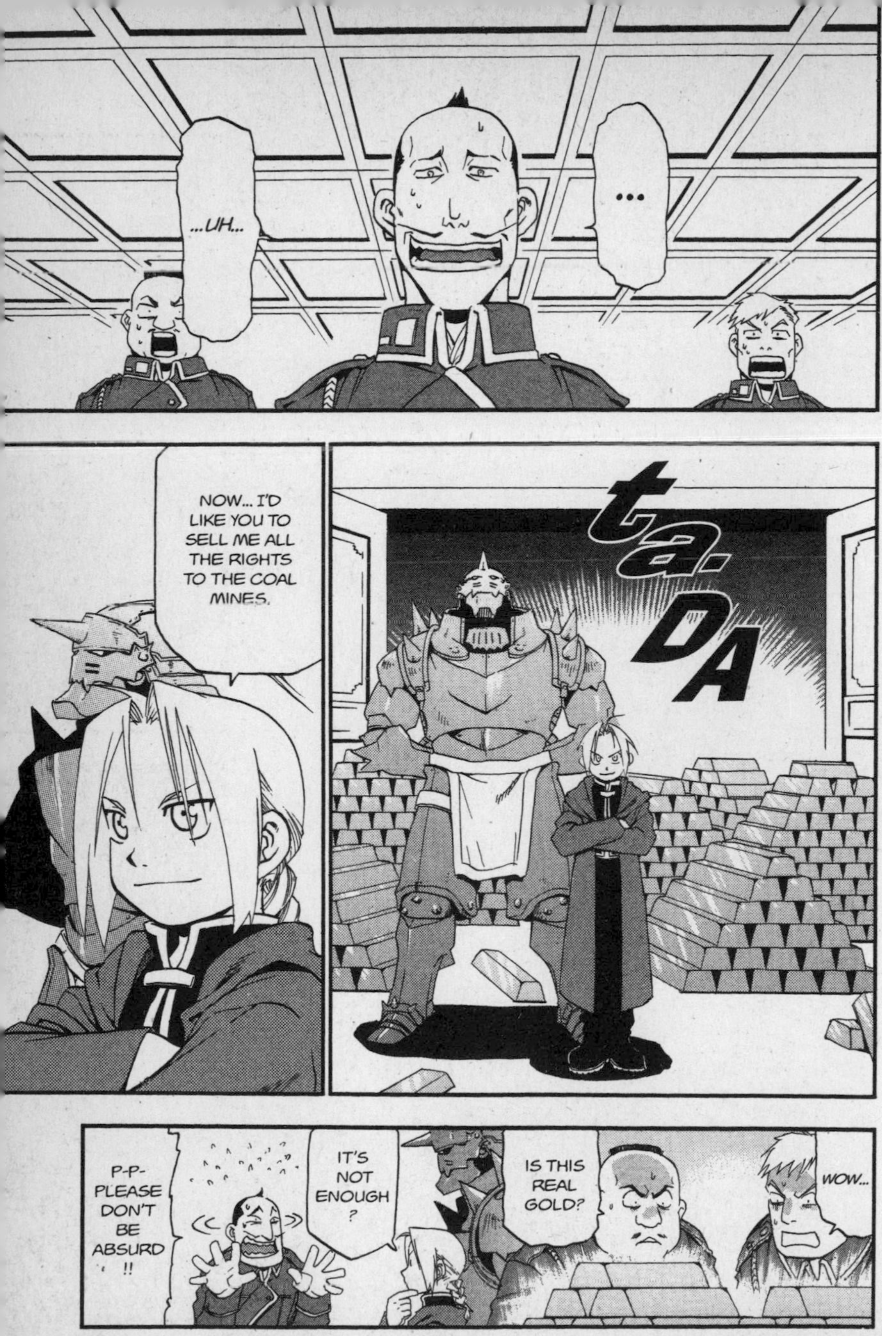
...
...UH...
ta. DA
NOW... I'D LIKE YOU TO SELL ME ALL THE RIGHTS TO THE COAL MINES.
WOW...
IS THIS REAL GOLD?
IT'S NOT ENOUGH?
P-P-PLEASE DON'T BE ABSURD!!

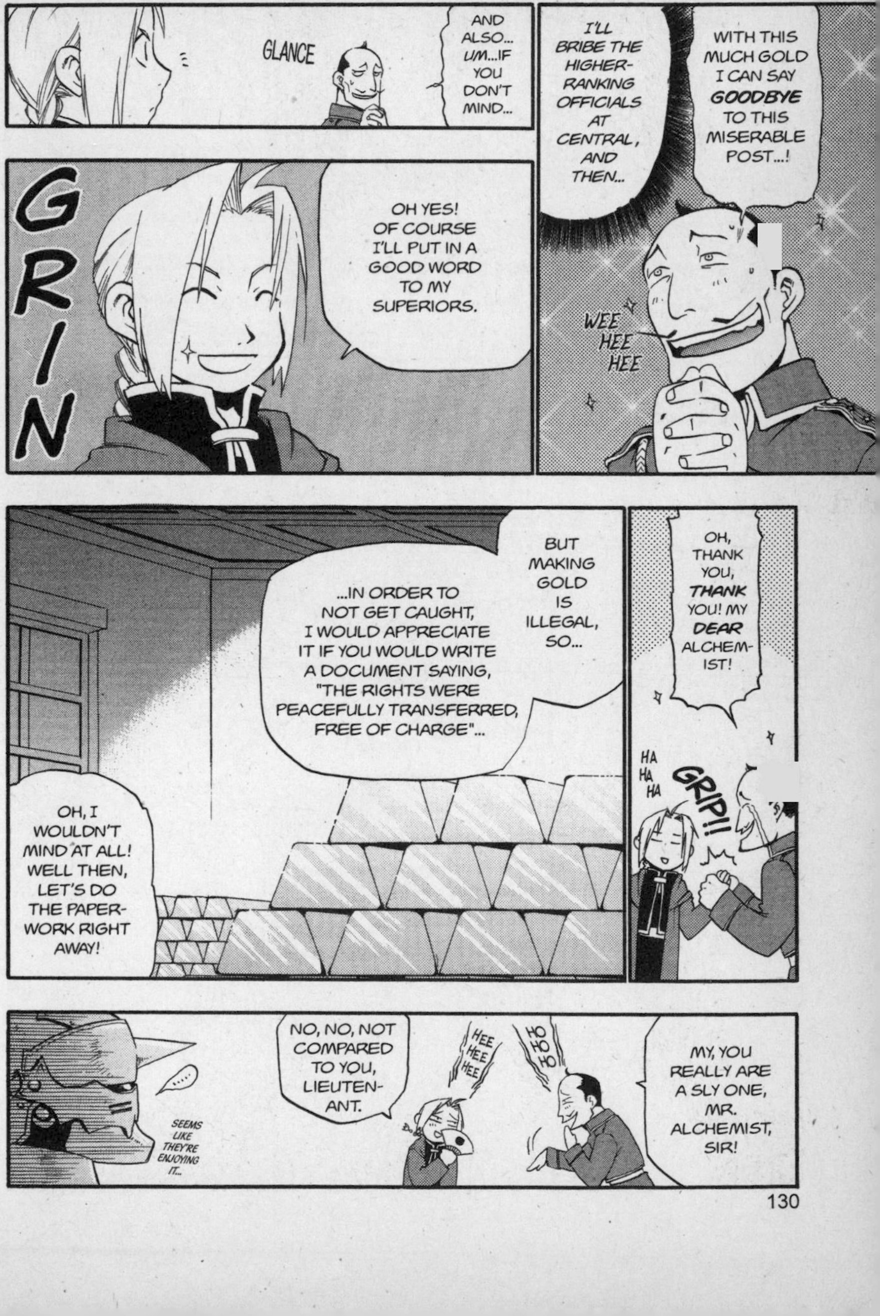
WITH THIS MUCH GOLD I CAN SAY GOODBYE TO THIS MISERABLE POST...!
I'LL BRIBE THE HIGHER-RANKING OFFICIALS AT CENTRAL, AND THEN...
WEE HEE HEE
AND ALSO... UM...IF YOU DON'T MIND...
GLANCE
OH YES! OF COURSE I'LL PUT IN A GOOD WORD TO MY SUPERIORS.
GRIN
OH, THANK YOU, THANK YOU! MY DEAR ALCHEMIST!
GRIP!!
HA HA HA
BUT MAKING GOLD IS ILLEGAL, SO...
...IN ORDER TO NOT GET CAUGHT, I WOULD APPRECIATE IT IF YOU WOULD WRITE A DOCUMENT SAYING, "THE RIGHTS WERE PEACEFULLY TRANSFERRED, FREE OF CHARGE"...
OH, I WOULDN'T MIND AT ALL! WELL THEN, LET'S DO THE PAPER-WORK RIGHT AWAY!
MY, YOU REALLY ARE A SLY ONE, MR. ALCHEMIST, SIR!
HO HO HO
HEE HEE HEE
NO, NO, NOT COMPARED TO YOU, LIEUTEN-ANT.
SEEMS LIKE THEY'RE ENJOYING IT...
...

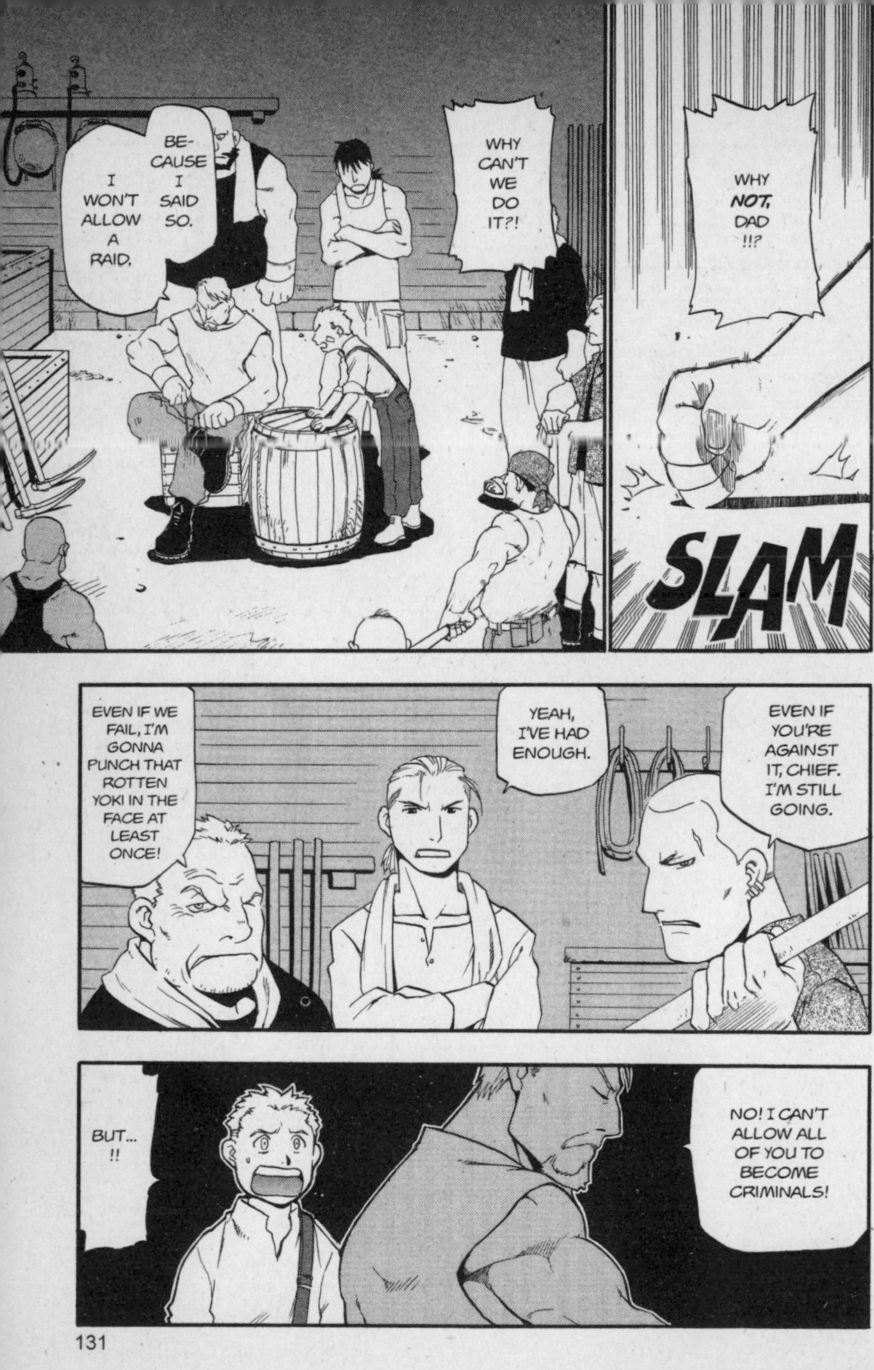
WHY NOT, DAD !!?
SLAM
WHY CAN'T WE DO IT?!
BECAUSE I SAID SO.
I WON'T ALLOW A RAID.
EVEN IF YOU'RE AGAINST IT, CHIEF. I'M STILL GOING.
YEAH, I'VE HAD ENOUGH.
EVEN IF WE FAIL, I'M GONNA PUNCH THAT ROTTEN YOKI IN THE FACE AT LEAST ONCE!
NO! I CAN'T ALLOW ALL OF YOU TO BECOME CRIMINALS!
BUT... !!

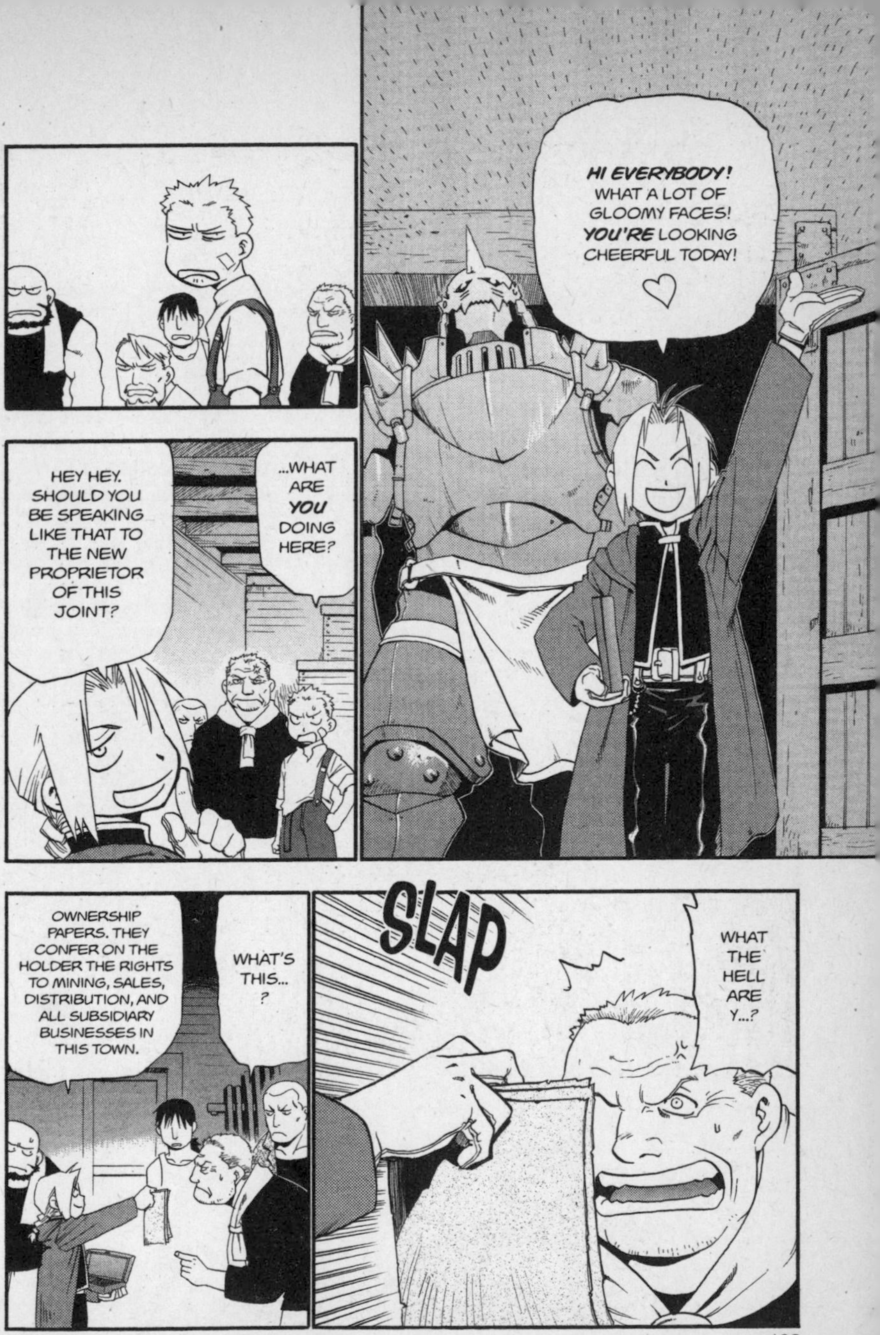
HI EVERYBODY! WHAT A LOT OF GLOOMY FACES! YOU'RE LOOKING CHEERFUL TODAY! ♡
...WHAT ARE YOU DOING HERE?
HEY HEY. SHOULD YOU BE SPEAKING LIKE THAT TO THE NEW PROPRIETOR OF THIS JOINT?
SLAP
WHAT THE HELL ARE Y...?
WHAT'S THIS...?
OWNERSHIP PAPERS. THEY CONFER ON THE HOLDER THE RIGHTS TO MINING, SALES, DISTRIBUTION, AND ALL SUBSIDIARY BUSINESSES IN THIS TOWN.

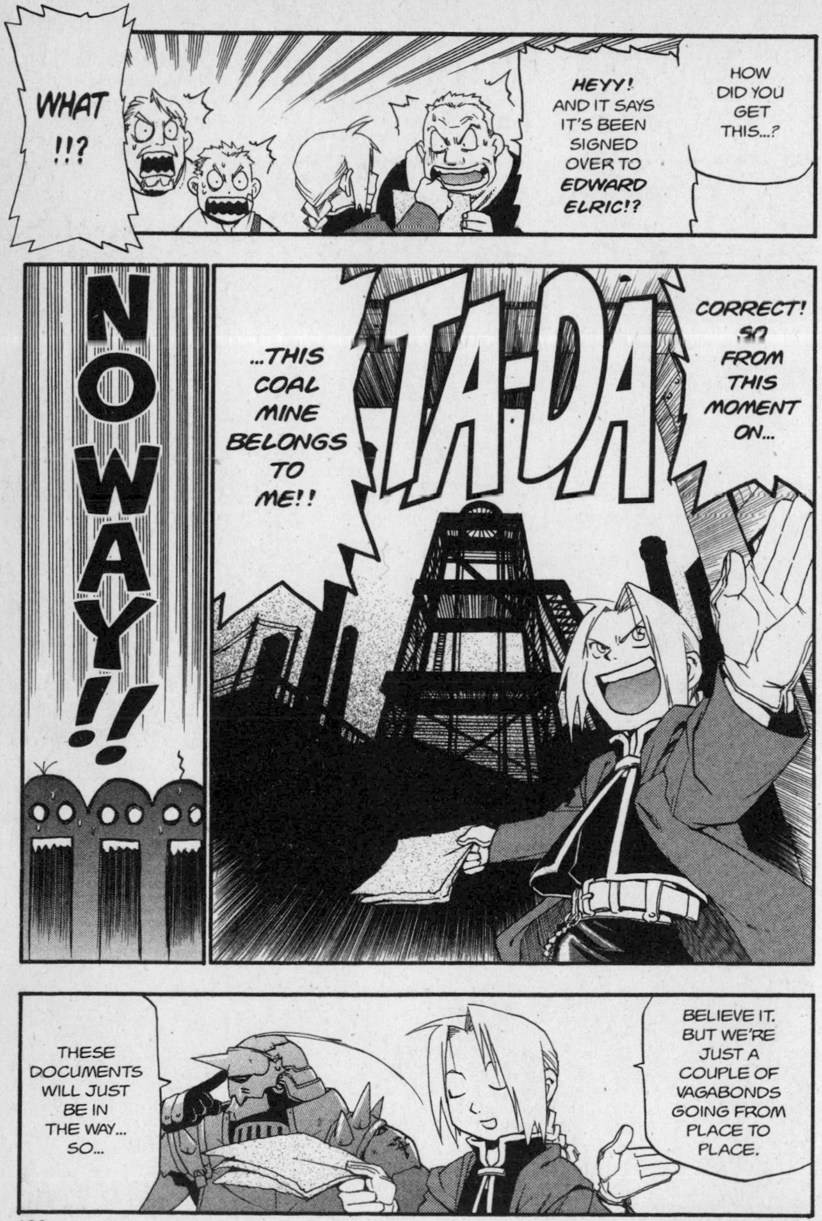
HOW DID YOU GET THIS...?
HEYY! AND IT SAYS IT'S BEEN SIGNED OVER TO EDWARD ELRIC!?
WHAT !!?
CORRECT! SO FROM THIS MOMENT ON...
TA-DA
...THIS COAL MINE BELONGS TO ME!!
NO WAY!!
BELIEVE IT. BUT WE'RE JUST A COUPLE OF VAGABONDS GOING FROM PLACE TO PLACE.
THESE DOCUMENTS WILL JUST BE IN THE WAY... SO...

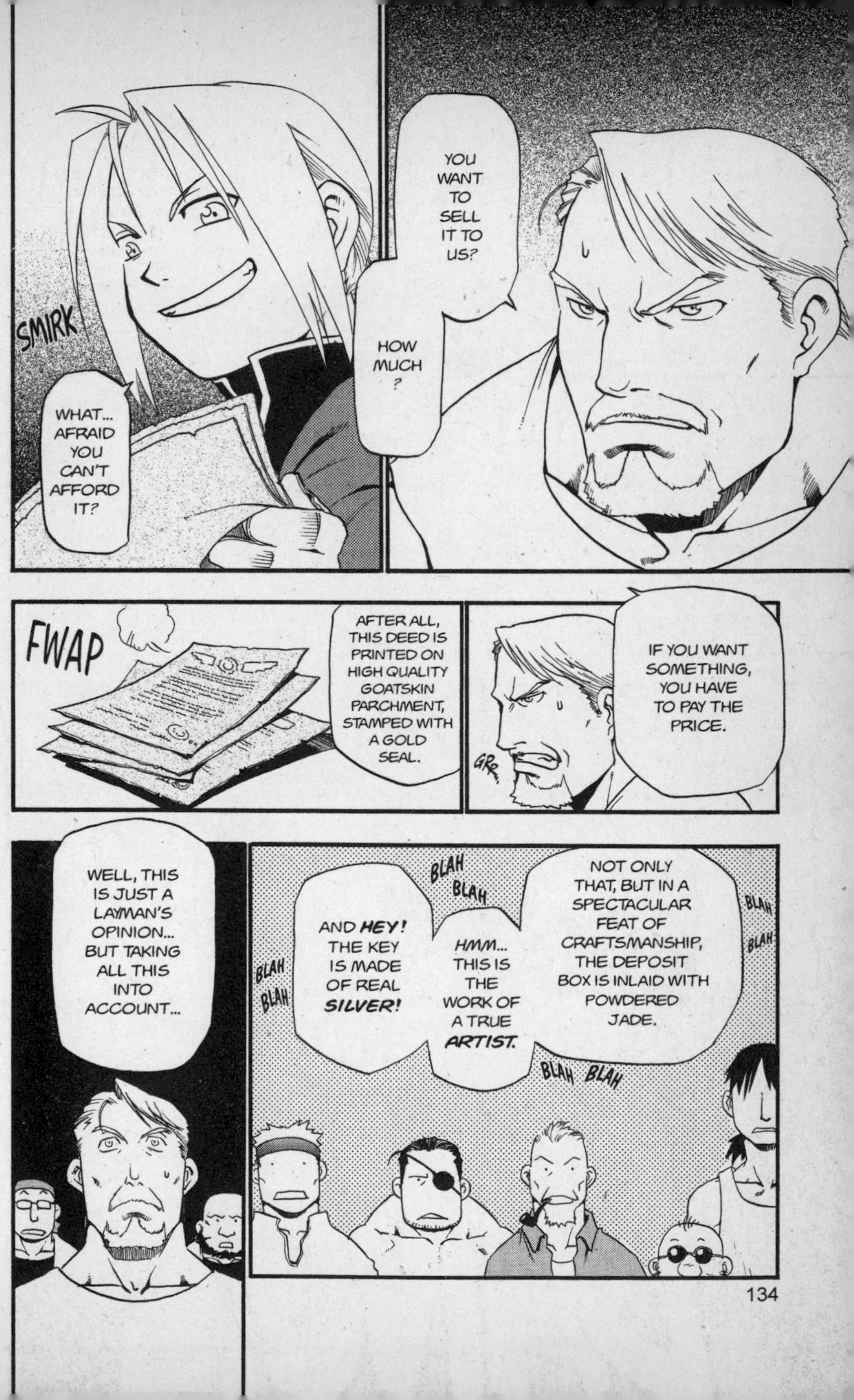
YOU WANT TO SELL IT TO US?
HOW MUCH?
SMIRK
WHAT... AFRAID YOU CAN'T AFFORD IT?
IF YOU WANT SOMETHING, YOU HAVE TO PAY THE PRICE.
GRR
AFTER ALL, THIS DEED IS PRINTED ON HIGH QUALITY GOATSKIN PARCHMENT, STAMPED WITH A GOLD SEAL.
FWAP
BLAH BLAH
NOT ONLY THAT, BUT IN A SPECTACULAR FEAT OF CRAFTSMANSHIP, THE DEPOSIT BOX IS INLAID WITH POWDERED JADE.
BLAH BLAH
HMM... THIS IS THE WORK OF A TRUE ***ARTIST.***
AND ***HEY!*** THE KEY IS MADE OF REAL ***SILVER!***
BLAH BLAH
BLAH BLAH
WELL, THIS IS JUST A LAYMAN'S OPINION... BUT TAKING ALL THIS INTO ACCOUNT...

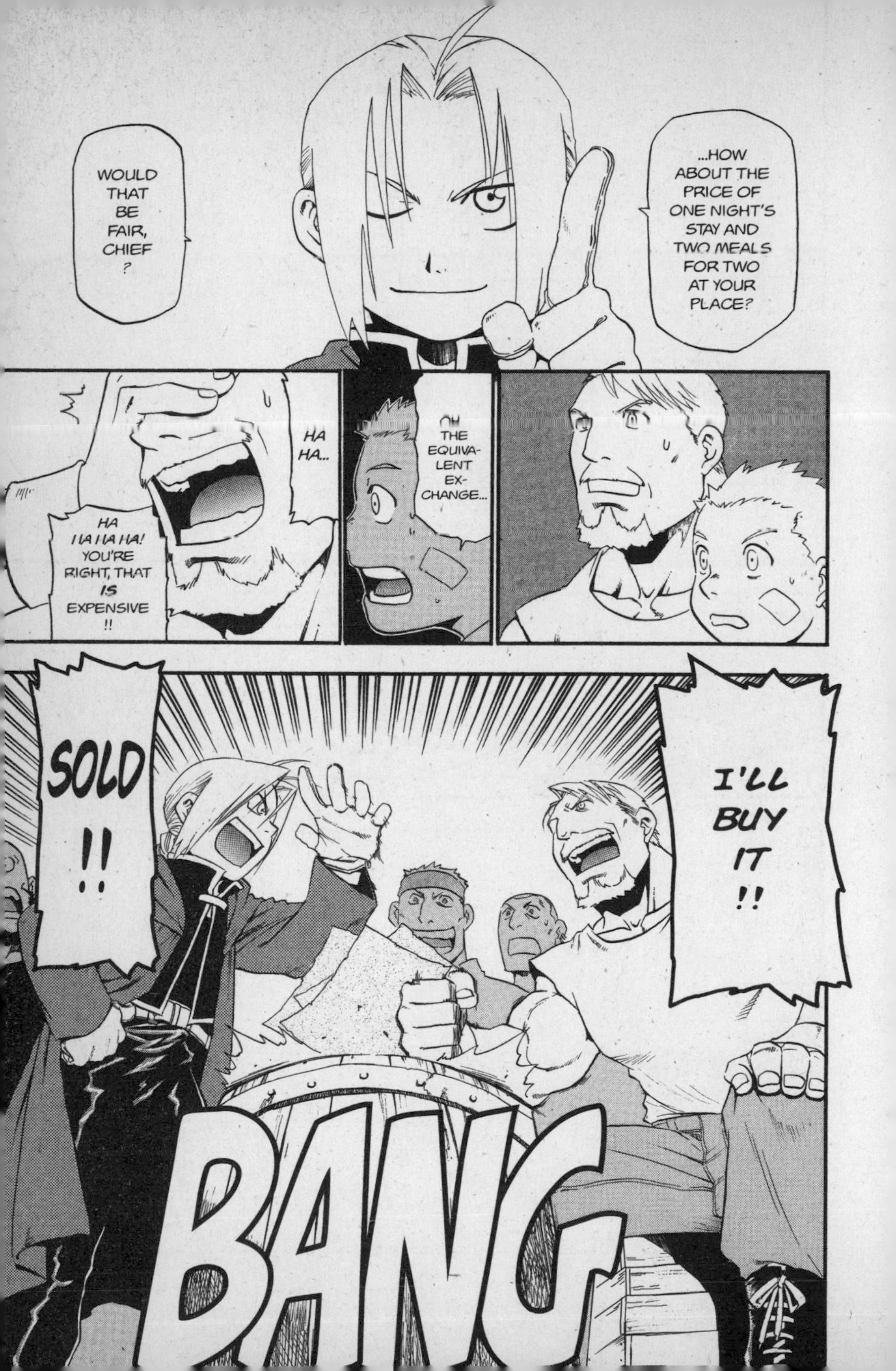
...HOW ABOUT THE PRICE OF ONE NIGHT'S STAY AND TWO MEALS FOR TWO AT YOUR PLACE?
WOULD THAT BE FAIR, CHIEF?
OH THE EQUIVALENT EXCHANGE...
HA HA...
HA HA HA HA HA! YOU'RE RIGHT, THAT *IS* EXPENSIVE!!
I'LL BUY IT!!
SOLD!!
BANG

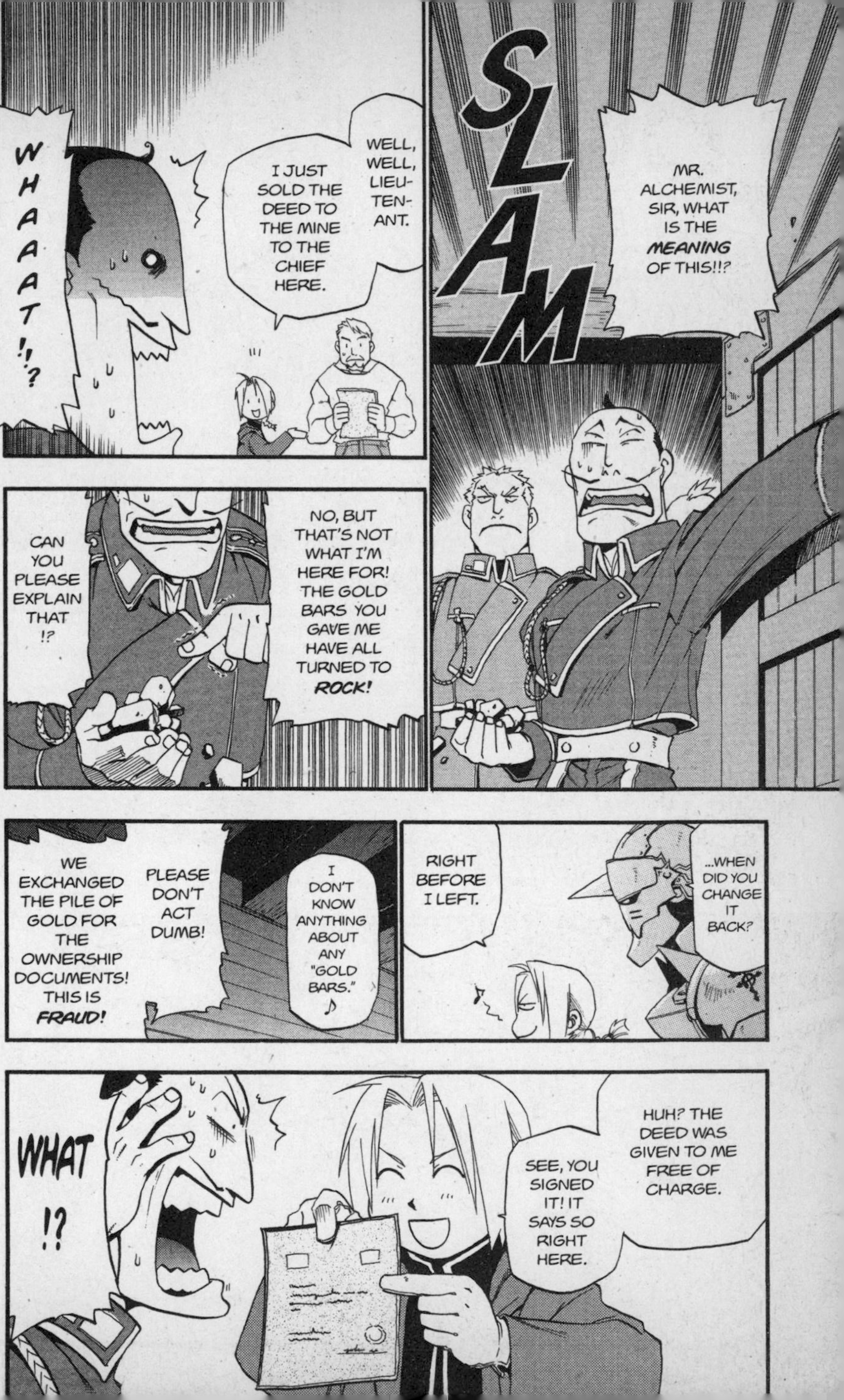
SLAM
MR. ALCHEMIST, SIR, WHAT IS THE ***MEANING*** OF THIS!!?
WELL, WELL, LIEU-TEN-ANT.
I JUST SOLD THE DEED TO THE MINE TO THE CHIEF HERE.
WHAAAAT!!?
NO, BUT THAT'S NOT WHAT I'M HERE FOR! THE GOLD BARS YOU GAVE ME HAVE ALL TURNED TO ***ROCK!***
CAN YOU PLEASE EXPLAIN THAT!?
...WHEN DID YOU CHANGE IT BACK?
RIGHT BEFORE I LEFT.
I DON'T KNOW ANYTHING ABOUT ANY "GOLD BARS." ♪
PLEASE DON'T ACT DUMB!
WE EXCHANGED THE PILE OF GOLD FOR THE OWNERSHIP DOCUMENTS! THIS IS ***FRAUD!***
HUH? THE DEED WAS GIVEN TO ME FREE OF CHARGE.
SEE, YOU SIGNED IT! IT SAYS SO RIGHT HERE.
WHAT!?

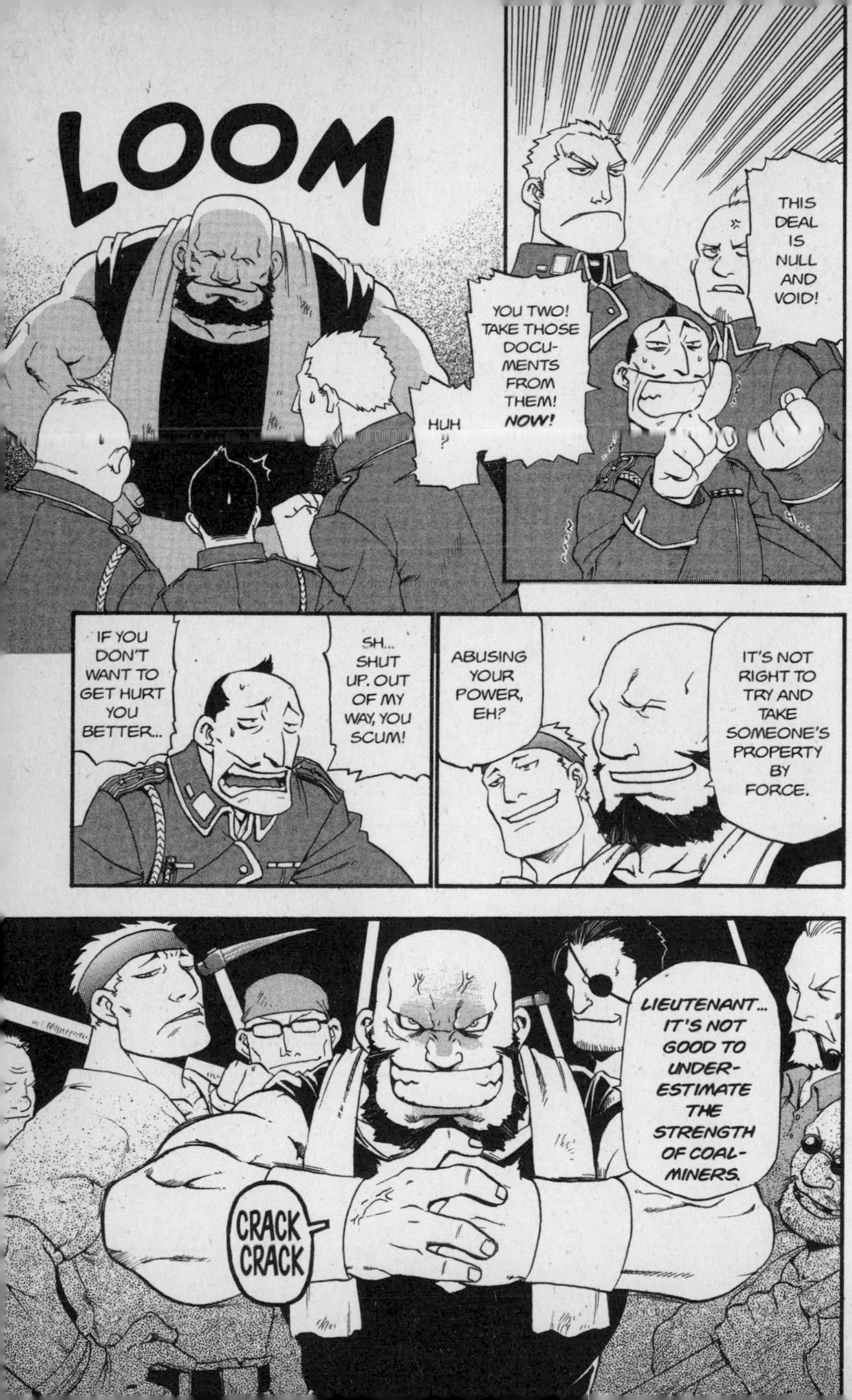
THIS DEAL IS NULL AND VOID!
YOU TWO! TAKE THOSE DOCU-MENTS FROM THEM! NOW!
LOOM
HUH?
IT'S NOT RIGHT TO TRY AND TAKE SOMEONE'S PROPERTY BY FORCE.
ABUSING YOUR POWER, EH?
SH... SHUT UP. OUT OF MY WAY, YOU SCUM!
IF YOU DON'T WANT TO GET HURT YOU BETTER...
LIEUTENANT... IT'S NOT GOOD TO UNDER-ESTIMATE THE STRENGTH OF COAL-MINERS.
CRACK CRACK

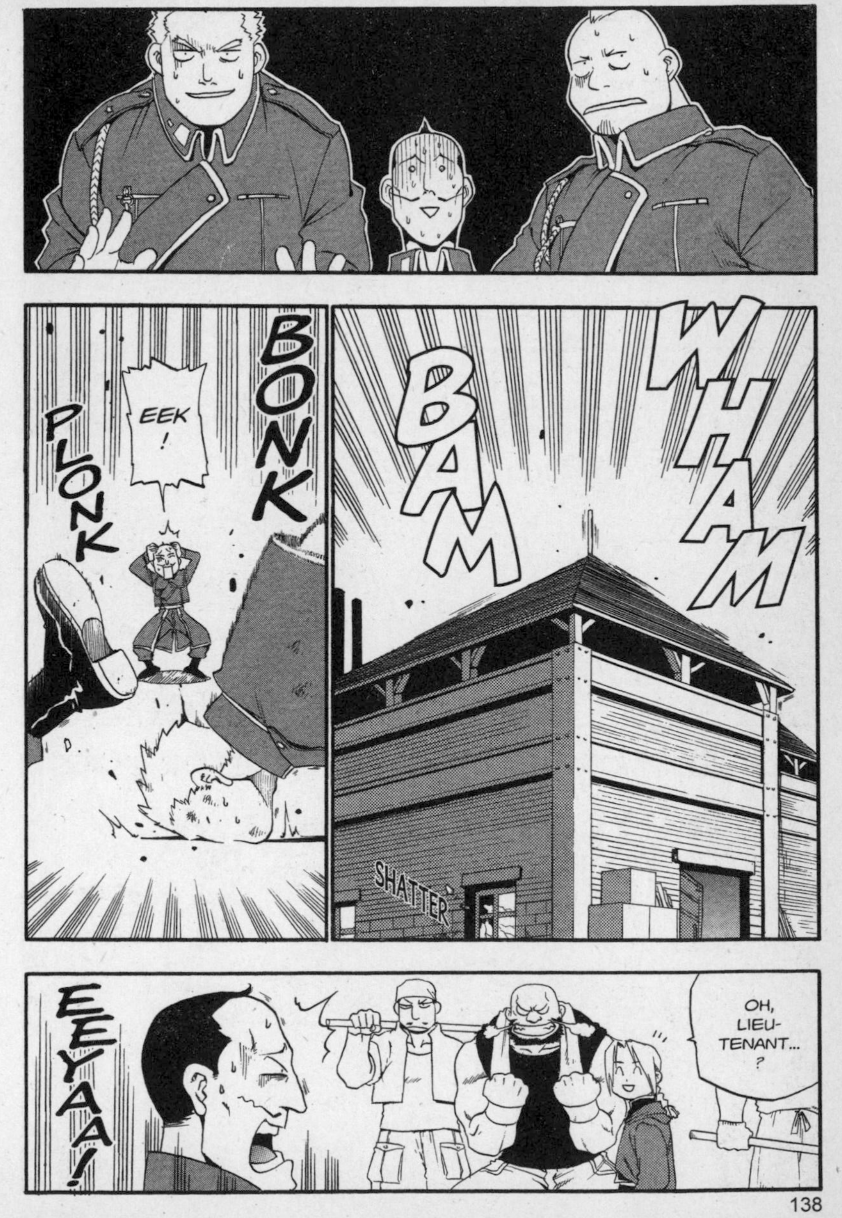
WHAM
BAM
SHATTER
BONK
EEK!
PLONK
OH, LIEU-TENANT...?
EEYAA!

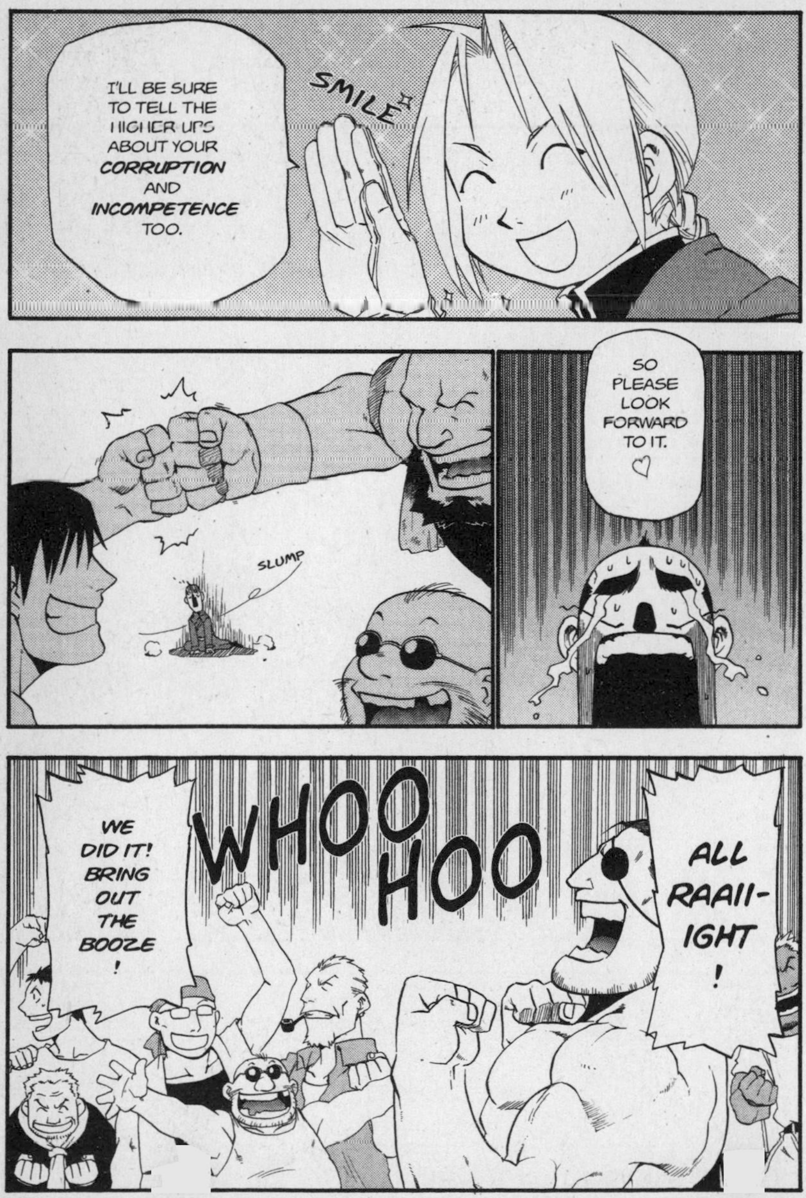
SMILE
I'LL BE SURE TO TELL THE HIGHER UPS ABOUT YOUR CORRUPTION AND INCOMPETENCE TOO.
SO PLEASE LOOK FORWARD TO IT. ♡
SLUMP
ALL RAAII-IGHT!
WHOO HOO
WE DID IT! BRING OUT THE BOOZE!

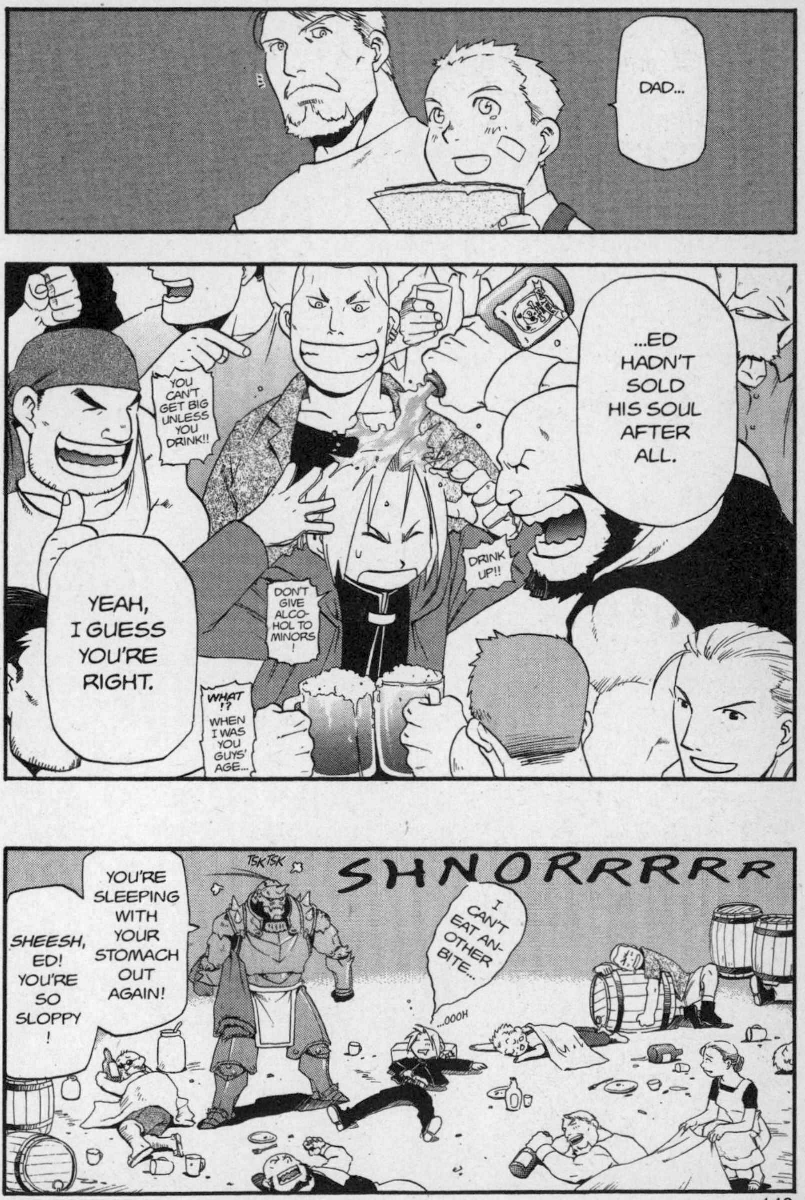
DAD...
...ED HADN'T SOLD HIS SOUL AFTER ALL.
DRINK UP!!
YOU CAN'T GET BIG UNLESS YOU DRINK!!
DON'T GIVE ALCOHOL TO MINORS!
YEAH, I GUESS YOU'RE RIGHT.
WHAT!? WHEN I WAS YOU GUYS' AGE...
SHNORRRRRR
I CAN'T EAT ANOTHER BITE...
TSK TSK
YOU'RE SLEEPING WITH YOUR STOMACH OUT AGAIN!
SHEESH, ED! YOU'RE SO SLOPPY!
...OOOH

Chapter 4
Battle on the Train

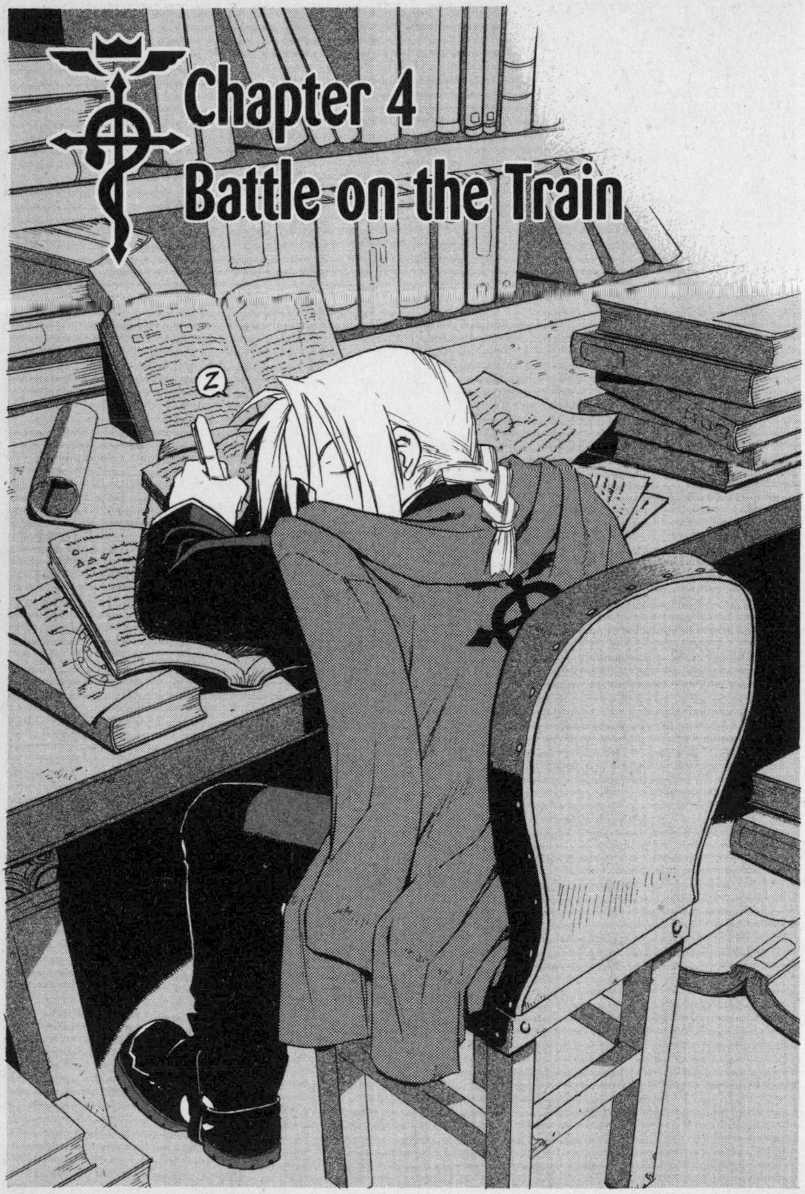

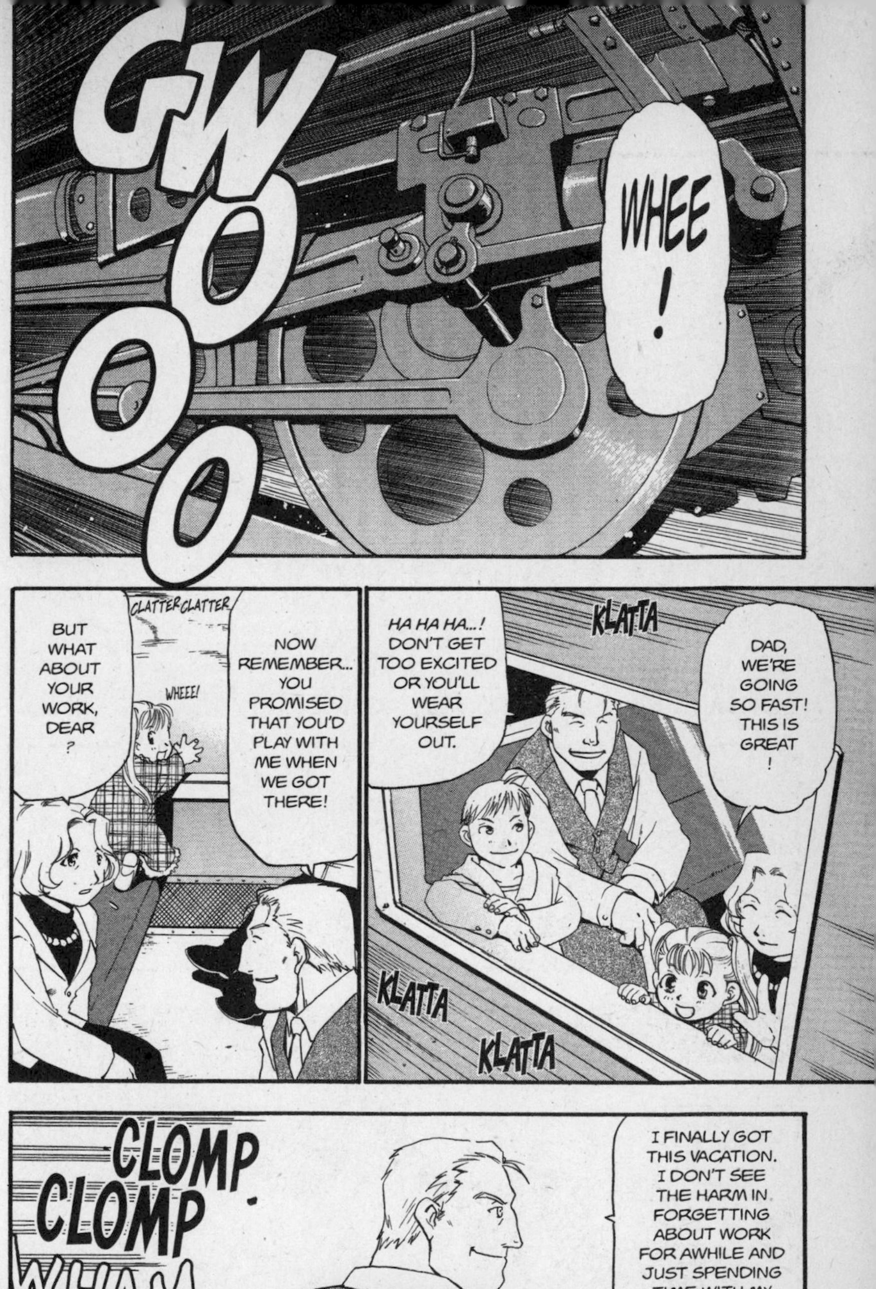
WHEE!
GWOOOO
KLATTA
DAD, WE'RE GOING SO FAST! THIS IS GREAT!
HA HA HA...! DON'T GET TOO EXCITED OR YOU'LL WEAR YOURSELF OUT.
KLATTA
KLATTA
CLATTER CLATTER
NOW REMEMBER... YOU PROMISED THAT YOU'D PLAY WITH ME WHEN WE GOT THERE!
WHEEE!
BUT WHAT ABOUT YOUR WORK, DEAR?
I FINALLY GOT THIS VACATION. I DON'T SEE THE HARM IN FORGETTING ABOUT WORK FOR AWHILE AND JUST SPENDING TIME WITH MY FAMILY.
CLOMP
CLOMP
WHAM

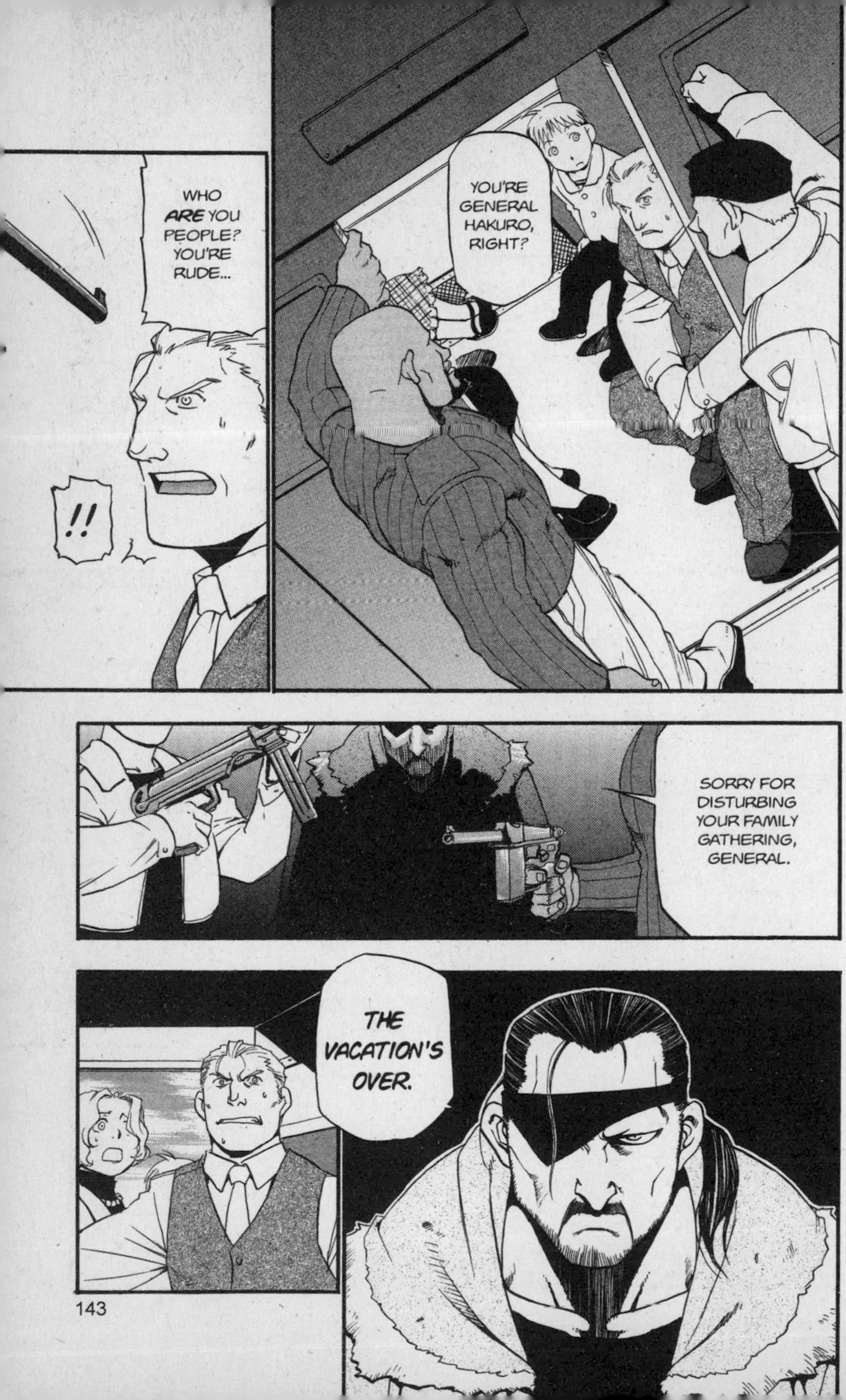
YOU'RE GENERAL HAKURO, RIGHT?
WHO ARE YOU PEOPLE? YOU'RE RUDE...
!!
SORRY FOR DISTURBING YOUR FAMILY GATHERING, GENERAL.
THE VACATION'S OVER.

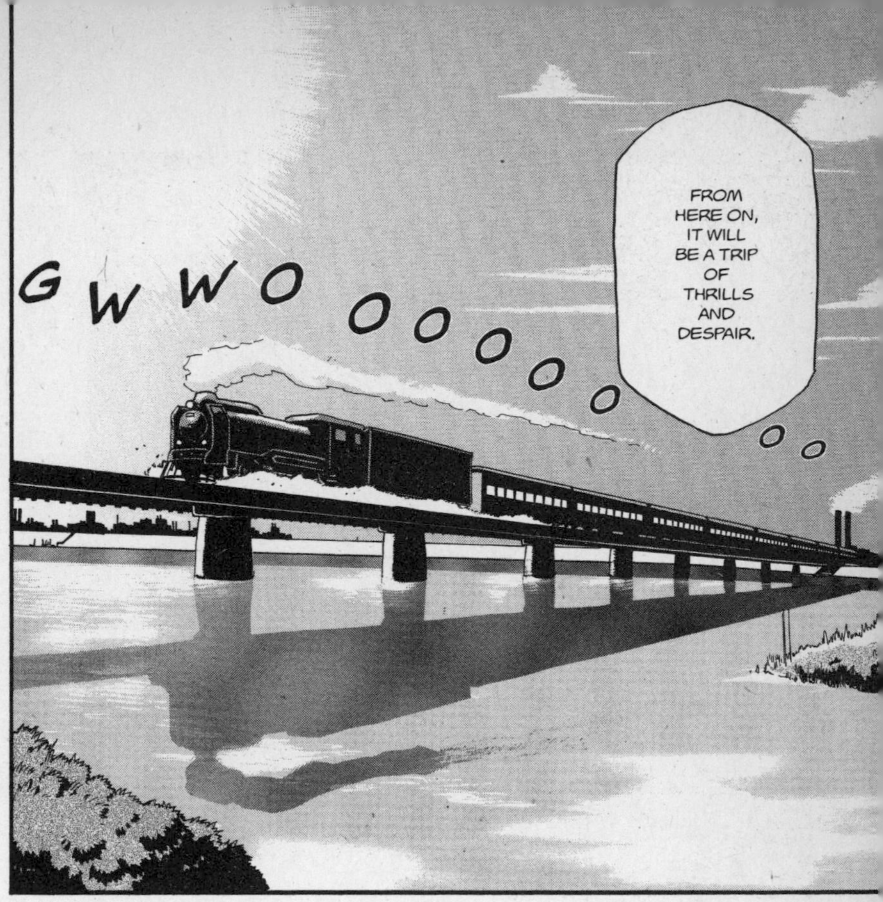
FROM HERE ON, IT WILL BE A TRIP OF THRILLS AND DESPAIR.
GWWOOOOOOOO

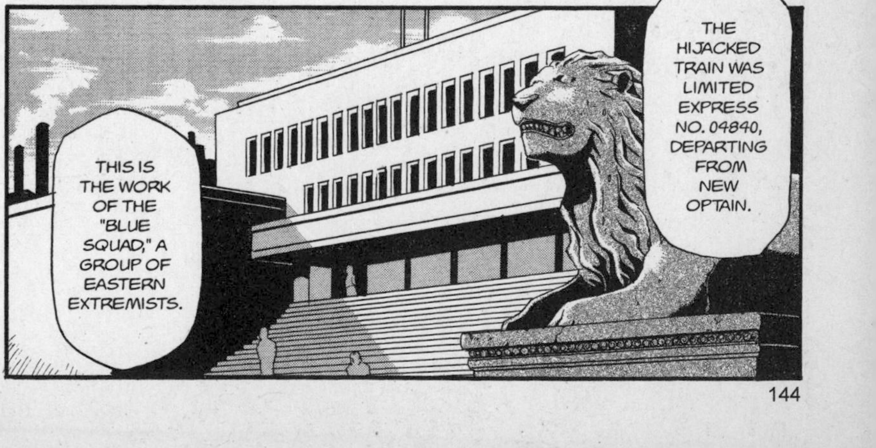
THE HIJACKED TRAIN WAS LIMITED EXPRESS NO. 04840, DEPARTING FROM NEW OPTAIN.
THIS IS THE WORK OF THE "BLUE SQUAD," A GROUP OF EASTERN EXTREMISTS.

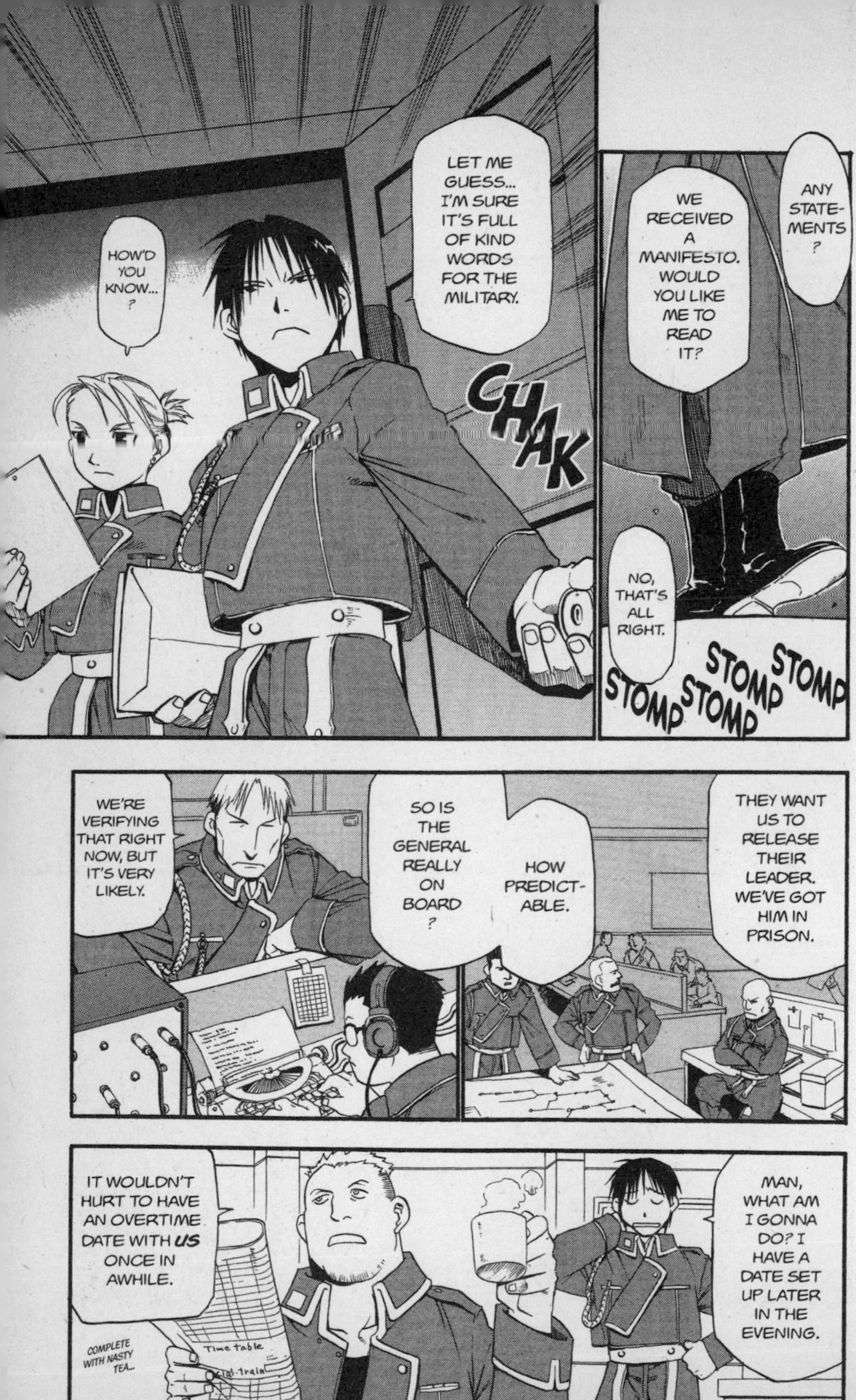
ANY STATEMENTS?
WE RECEIVED A MANIFESTO. WOULD YOU LIKE ME TO READ IT?
NO, THAT'S ALL RIGHT.
STOMP STOMP STOMP STOMP
LET ME GUESS... I'M SURE IT'S FULL OF KIND WORDS FOR THE MILITARY.
HOW'D YOU KNOW...?
CHAK
THEY WANT US TO RELEASE THEIR LEADER. WE'VE GOT HIM IN PRISON.
HOW PREDICTABLE.
SO IS THE GENERAL REALLY ON BOARD?
WE'RE VERIFYING THAT RIGHT NOW, BUT IT'S VERY LIKELY.
MAN, WHAT AM I GONNA DO? I HAVE A DATE SET UP LATER IN THE EVENING.
IT WOULDN'T HURT TO HAVE AN OVERTIME DATE WITH *US* ONCE IN AWHILE.
Time table
COMPLETE WITH NASTY TEA...

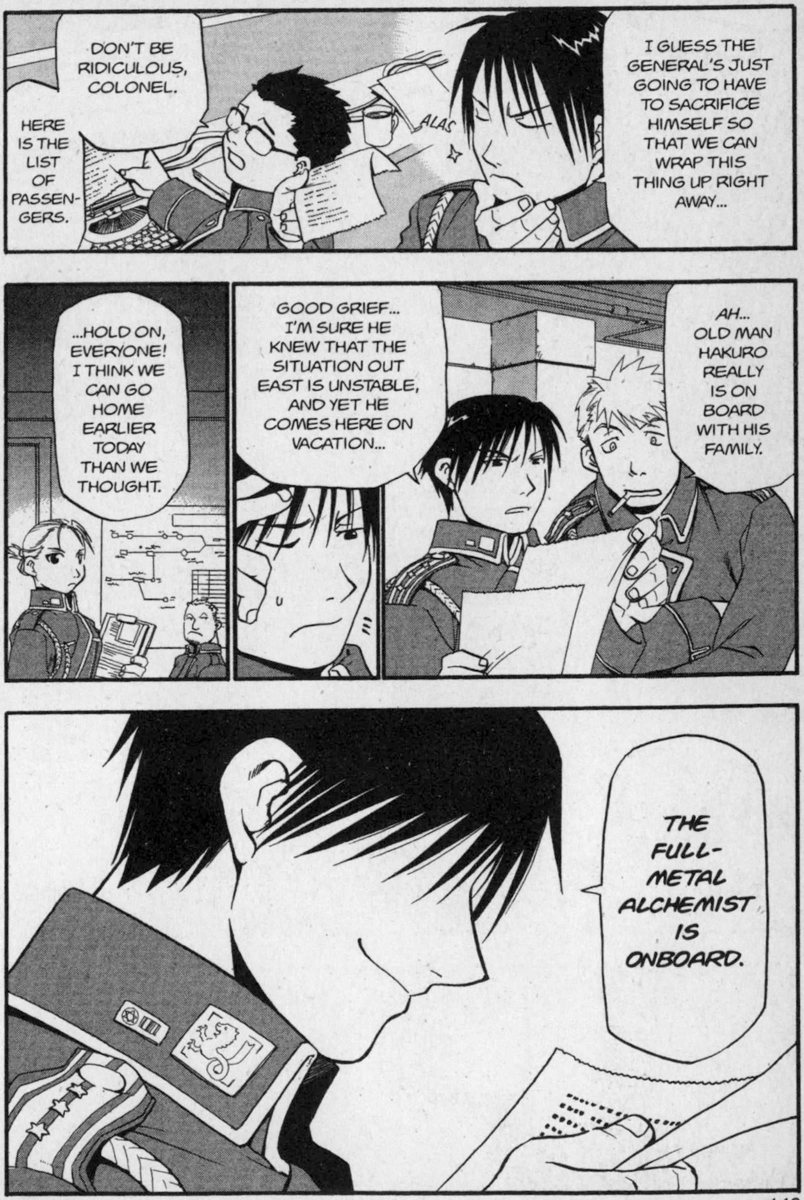
I GUESS THE GENERAL'S JUST GOING TO HAVE TO SACRIFICE HIMSELF SO THAT WE CAN WRAP THIS THING UP RIGHT AWAY...
ALAS
DON'T BE RIDICULOUS, COLONEL.
HERE IS THE LIST OF PASSEN-GERS.
AH... OLD MAN HAKURO REALLY IS ON BOARD WITH HIS FAMILY.
GOOD GRIEF... I'M SURE HE KNEW THAT THE SITUATION OUT EAST IS UNSTABLE, AND YET HE COMES HERE ON VACATION...
...HOLD ON, EVERYONE! I THINK WE CAN GO HOME EARLIER TODAY THAN WE THOUGHT.
THE FULL-METAL ALCHEMIST IS ONBOARD.

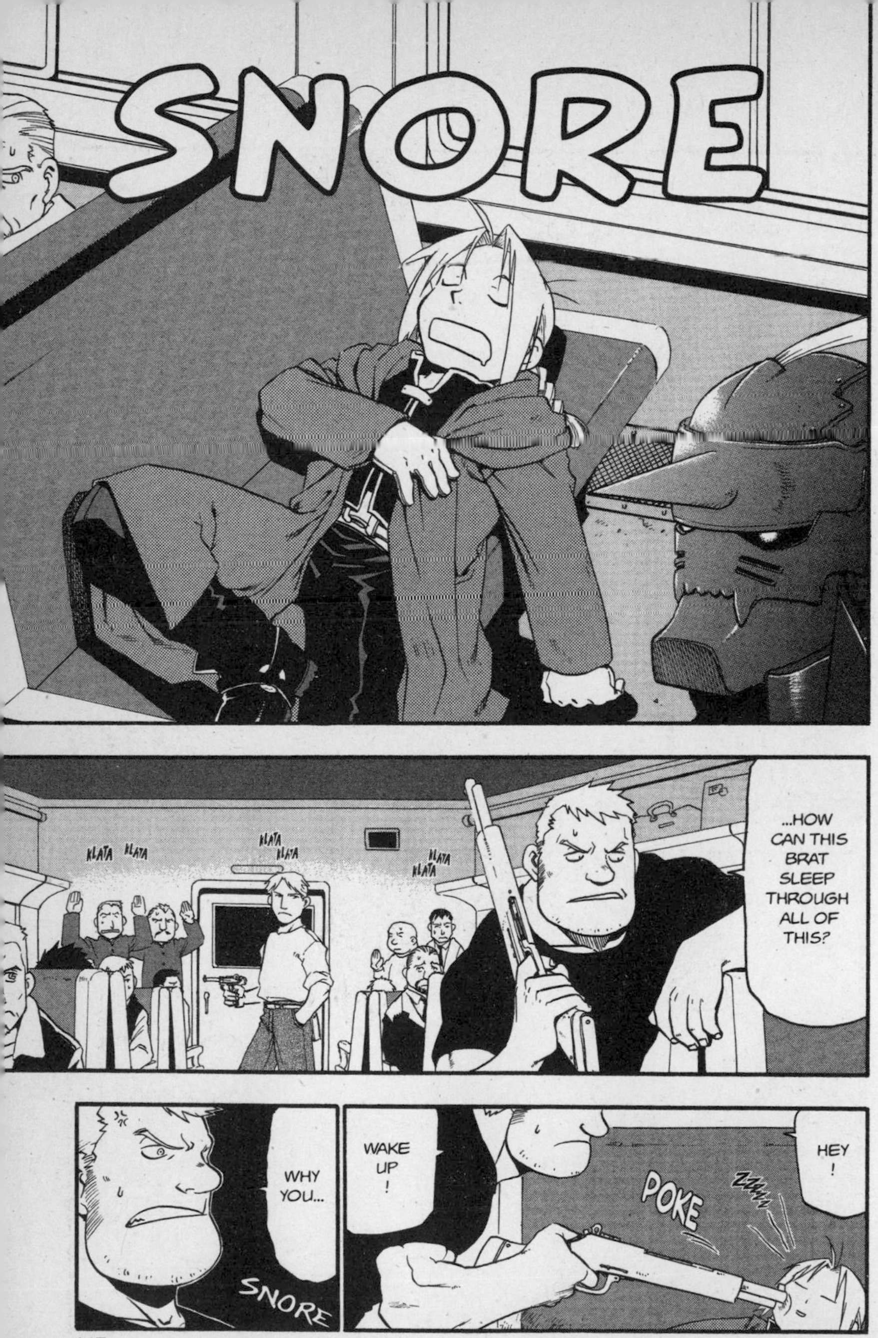
SNORE
KLATA KLATA
KLATA KLATA
KLATA KLATA
...HOW CAN THIS BRAT SLEEP THROUGH ALL OF THIS?
HEY!
POKE
WAKE UP!
WHY YOU...
SNORE

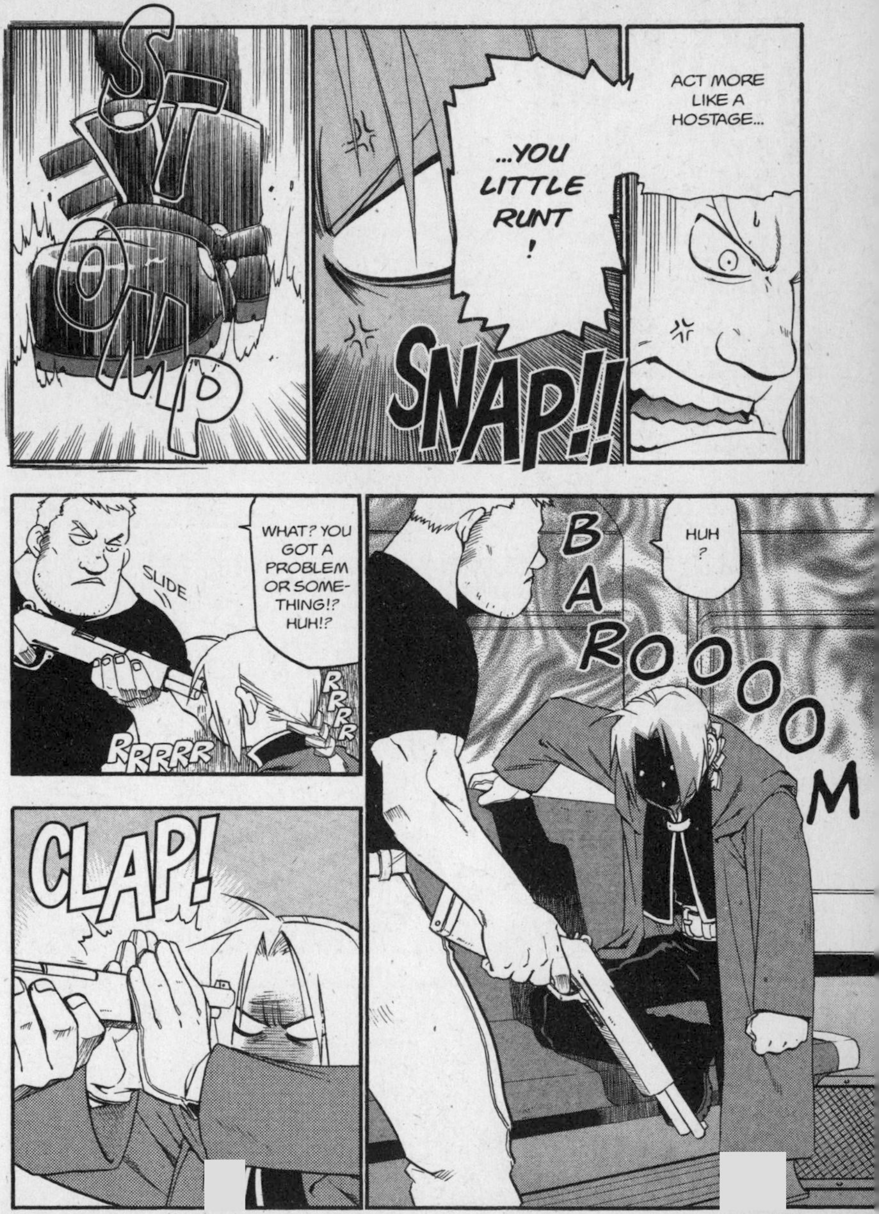
ACT MORE LIKE A HOSTAGE...
...YOU LITTLE RUNT!
SNAP!!
STOMP
BAROOOOOM
HUH?
WHAT? YOU GOT A PROBLEM OR SOME-THING!? HUH!?
SLIDE
RRRR
RRRRR
CLAP!

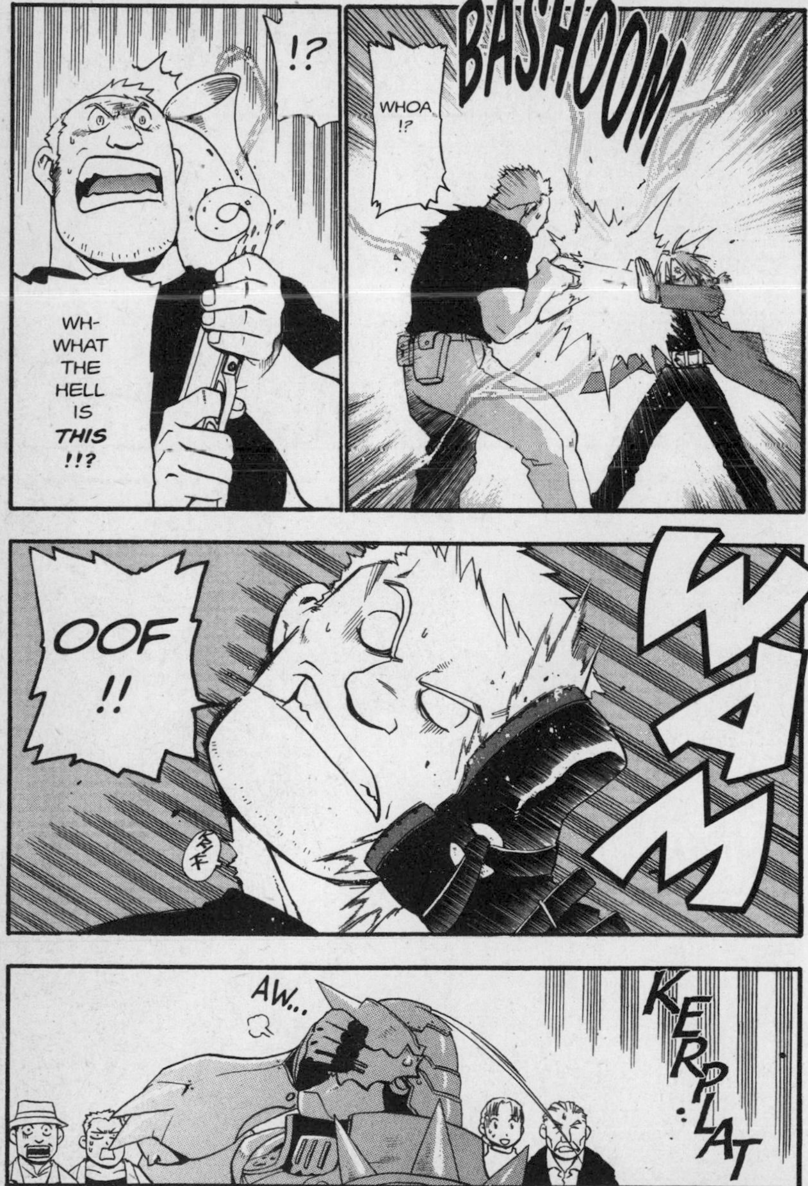
BASHOOM
WHOA !?
!?
WH-WHAT THE HELL IS THIS !!?
WAM
OOF !!
KERPLAT
AW...

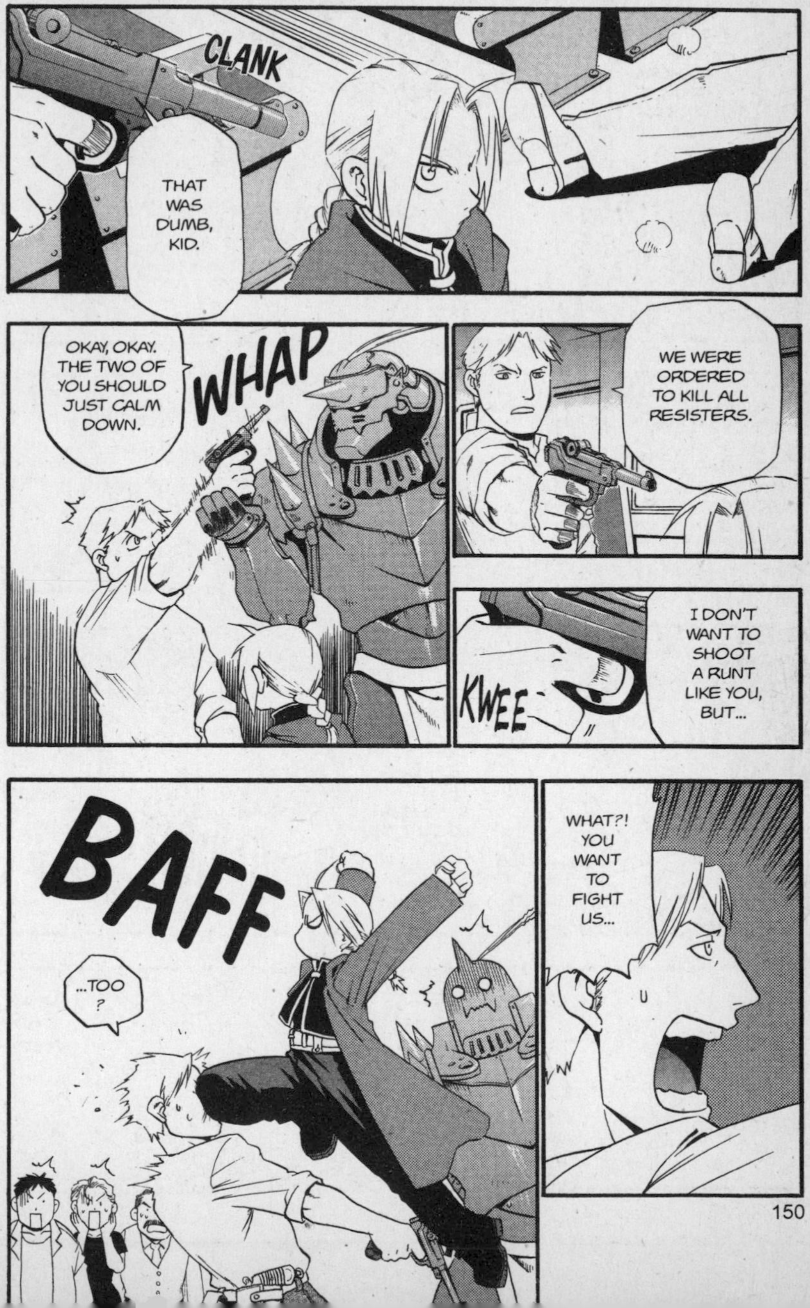
CLANK
THAT WAS DUMB, KID.
WE WERE ORDERED TO KILL ALL RESISTERS.
I DON'T WANT TO SHOOT A RUNT LIKE YOU, BUT...
KWEE
OKAY, OKAY. THE TWO OF YOU SHOULD JUST CALM DOWN.
WHAP
WHAT?! YOU WANT TO FIGHT US...
BAFF
...TOO?

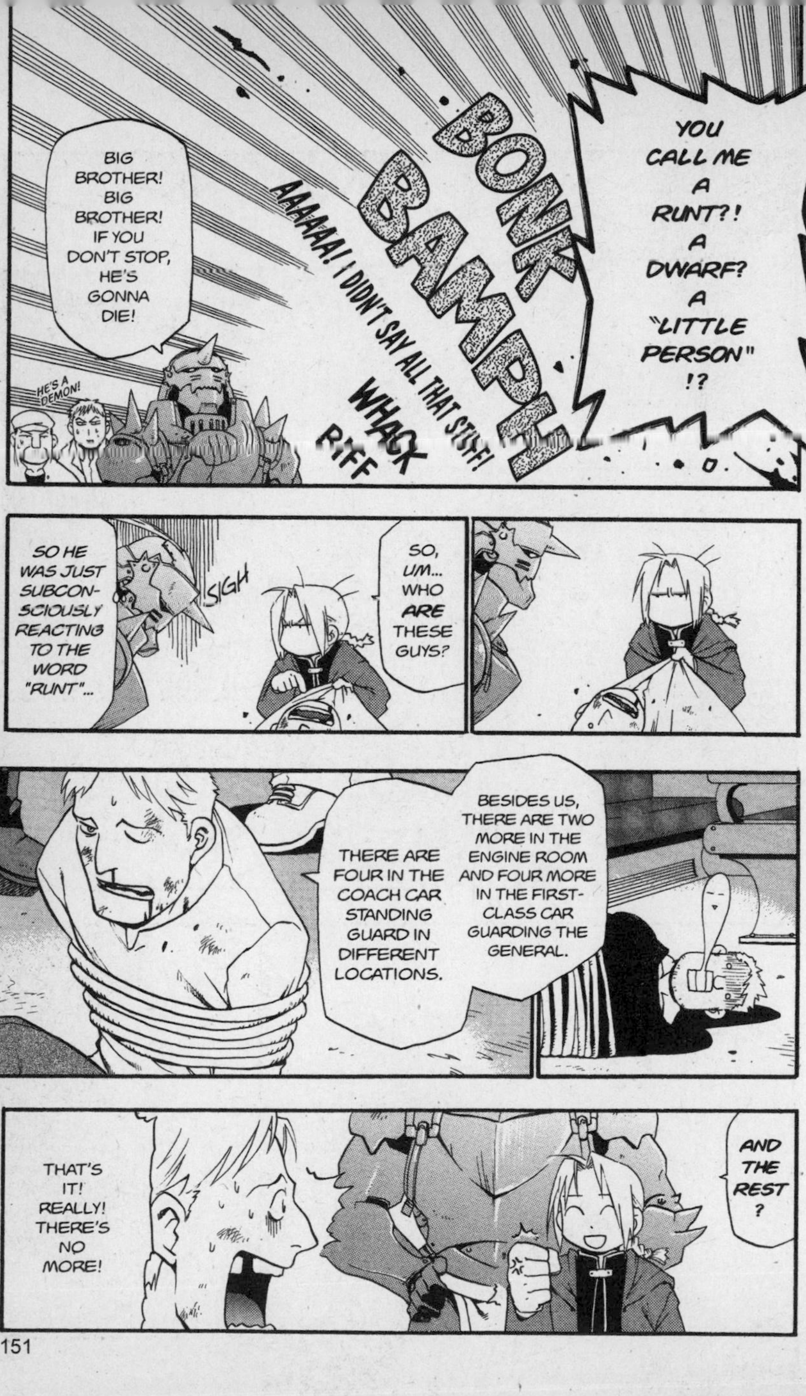
YOU CALL ME A RUNT?! A DWARF? A "LITTLE PERSON"!?
BONK
BAMPH
AAAAAA! I DIDN'T SAY ALL THAT STUFF!
WHACK
RIFF
BIG BROTHER! BIG BROTHER! IF YOU DON'T STOP, HE'S GONNA DIE!
HE'S A DEMON!
SO, UM... WHO ARE THESE GUYS?
SIGH
SO HE WAS JUST SUBCONSCIOUSLY REACTING TO THE WORD "RUNT"...
BESIDES US, THERE ARE TWO MORE IN THE ENGINE ROOM AND FOUR MORE IN THE FIRST-CLASS CAR GUARDING THE GENERAL.
THERE ARE FOUR IN THE COACH CAR STANDING GUARD IN DIFFERENT LOCATIONS.
AND THE REST?
THAT'S IT! REALLY! THERE'S NO MORE!

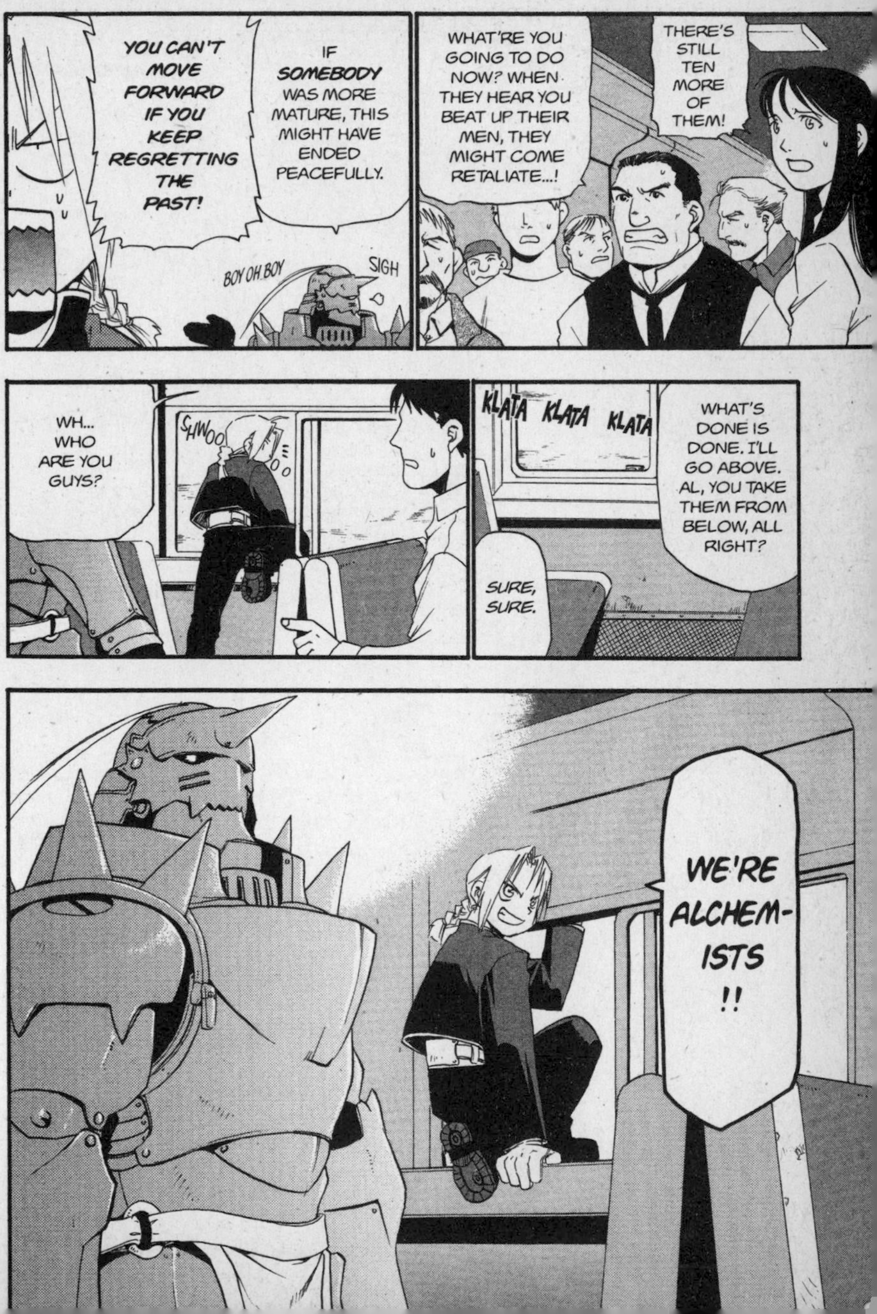
THERE'S STILL TEN MORE OF THEM!
WHAT'RE YOU GOING TO DO NOW? WHEN THEY HEAR YOU BEAT UP THEIR MEN, THEY MIGHT COME RETALIATE...!
IF SOMEBODY WAS MORE MATURE, THIS MIGHT HAVE ENDED PEACEFULLY.
YOU CAN'T MOVE FORWARD IF YOU KEEP REGRETTING THE PAST!
SIGH
BOY OH BOY
KLATA KLATA KLATA
WHAT'S DONE IS DONE. I'LL GO ABOVE. AL, YOU TAKE THEM FROM BELOW, ALL RIGHT?
SURE, SURE.
SHWOOO
WH... WHO ARE YOU GUYS?
WE'RE ALCHEM-ISTS !!

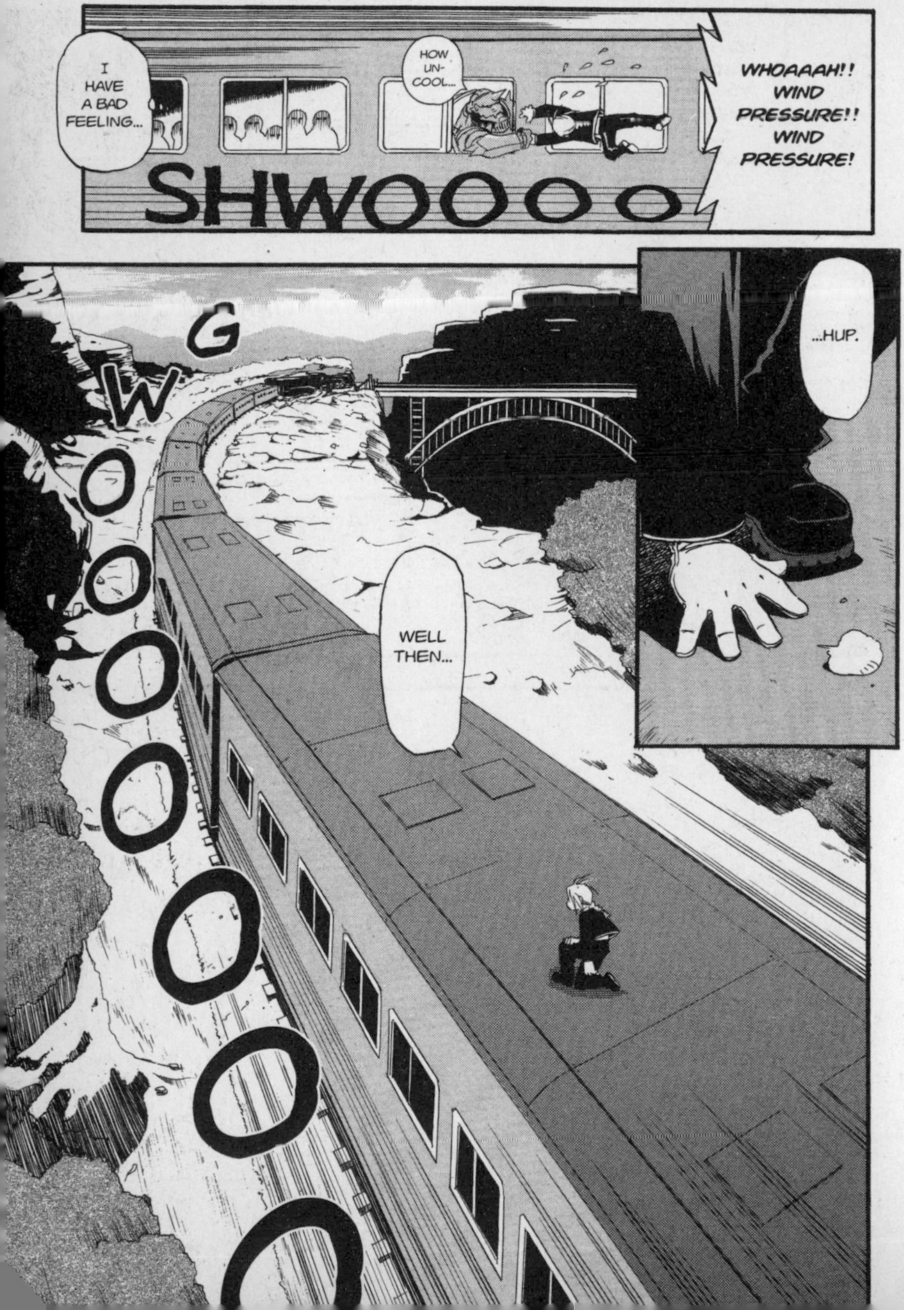

WHOAAAH!! WIND PRESSURE!! WIND PRESSURE!
HOW UN-COOL...
I HAVE A BAD FEELING...
SHWOOOO
...HUP.
WELL THEN...
GWOOOOOOO

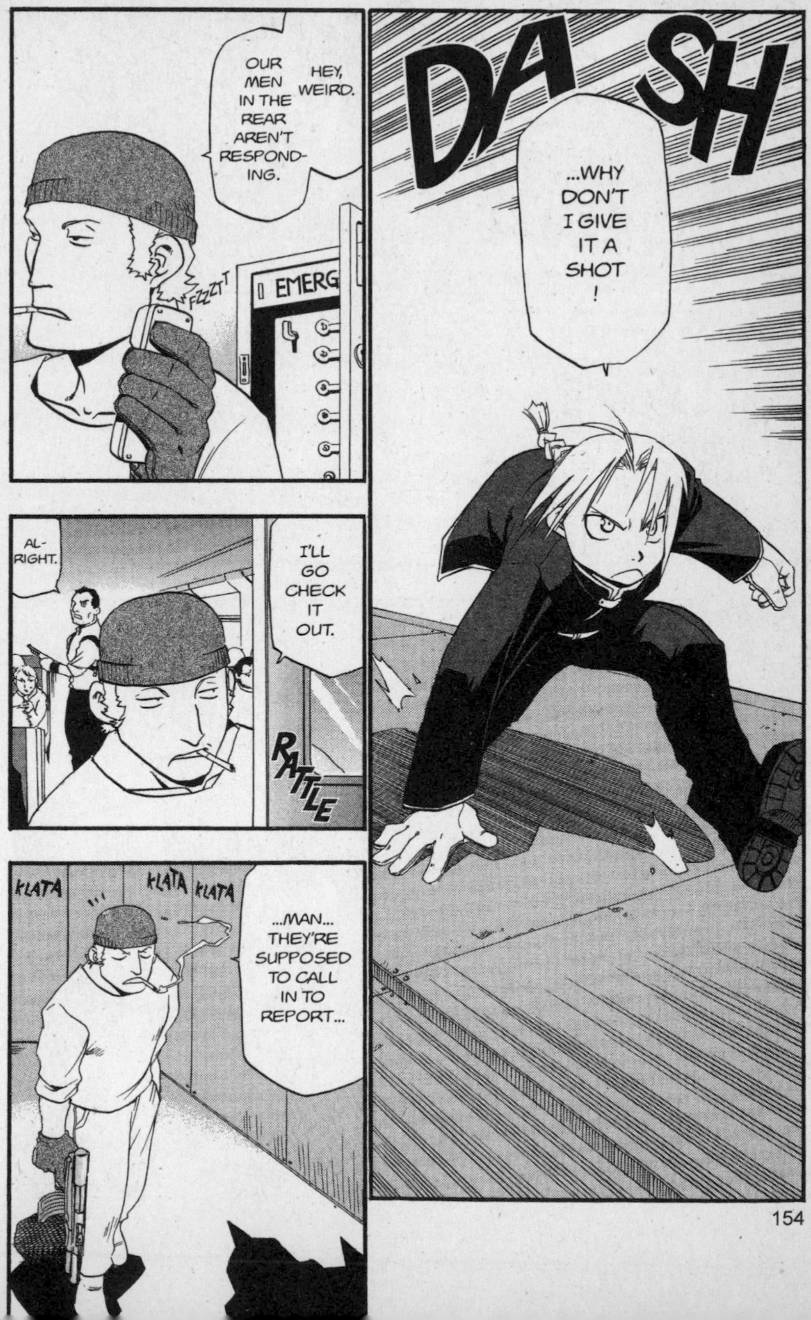
DASH
...WHY DON'T I GIVE IT A SHOT!
HEY, WEIRD.
OUR MEN IN THE REAR AREN'T RESPONDING.
FZZZZT
EMERG
I'LL GO CHECK IT OUT.
RATTLE
ALRIGHT.
...MAN... THEY'RE SUPPOSED TO CALL IN TO REPORT...
KLATA KLATA
KLATA

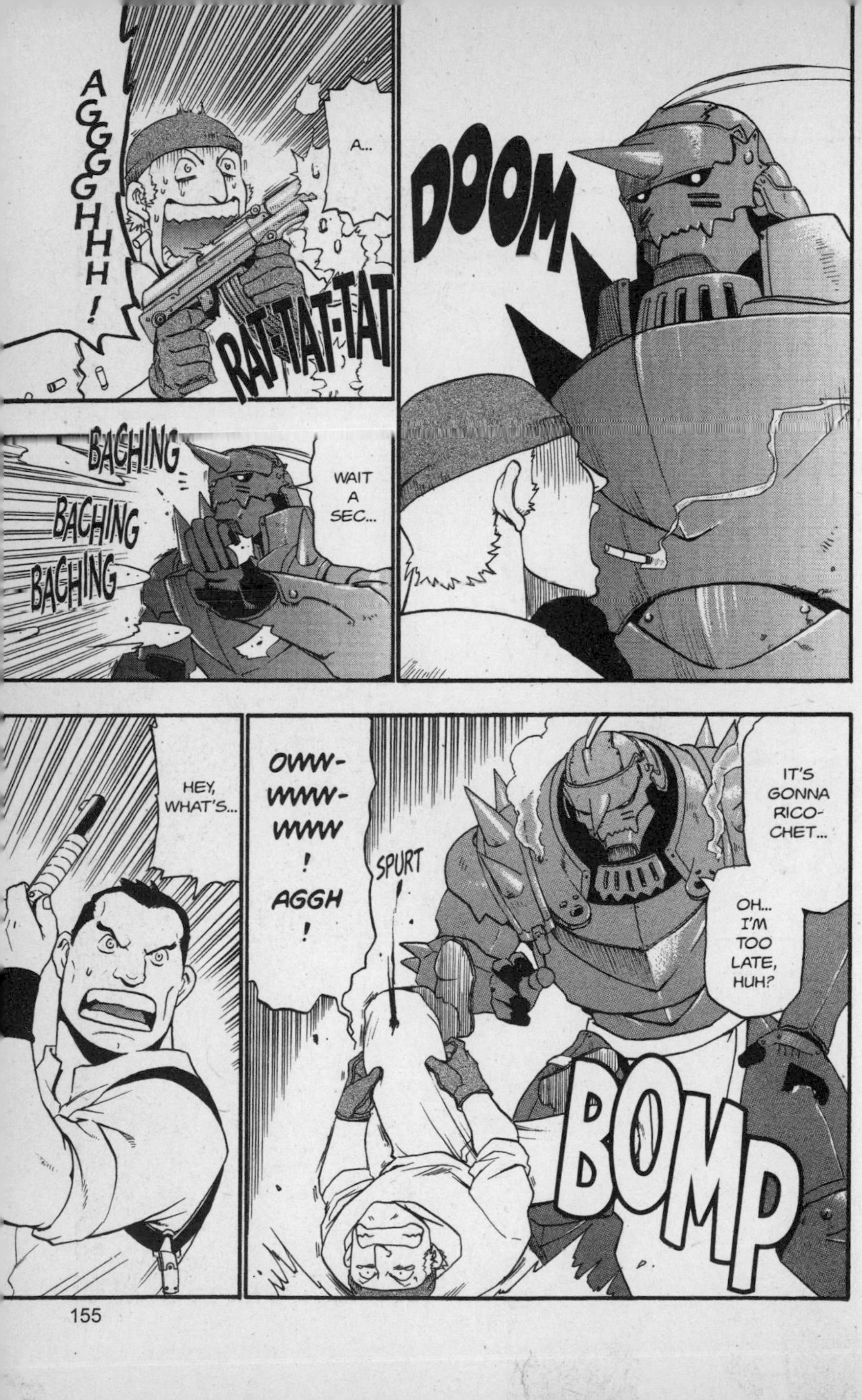
DOOM
A...
AGGGGHHHH!
RAT-TAT-TAT
WAIT A SEC...
BACHING BACHING BACHING
IT'S GONNA RICOCHET...
OH... I'M TOO LATE, HUH?
SPURT!
OWWW-WWW-WWW! AGGH!
BOMP
HEY, WHAT'S...

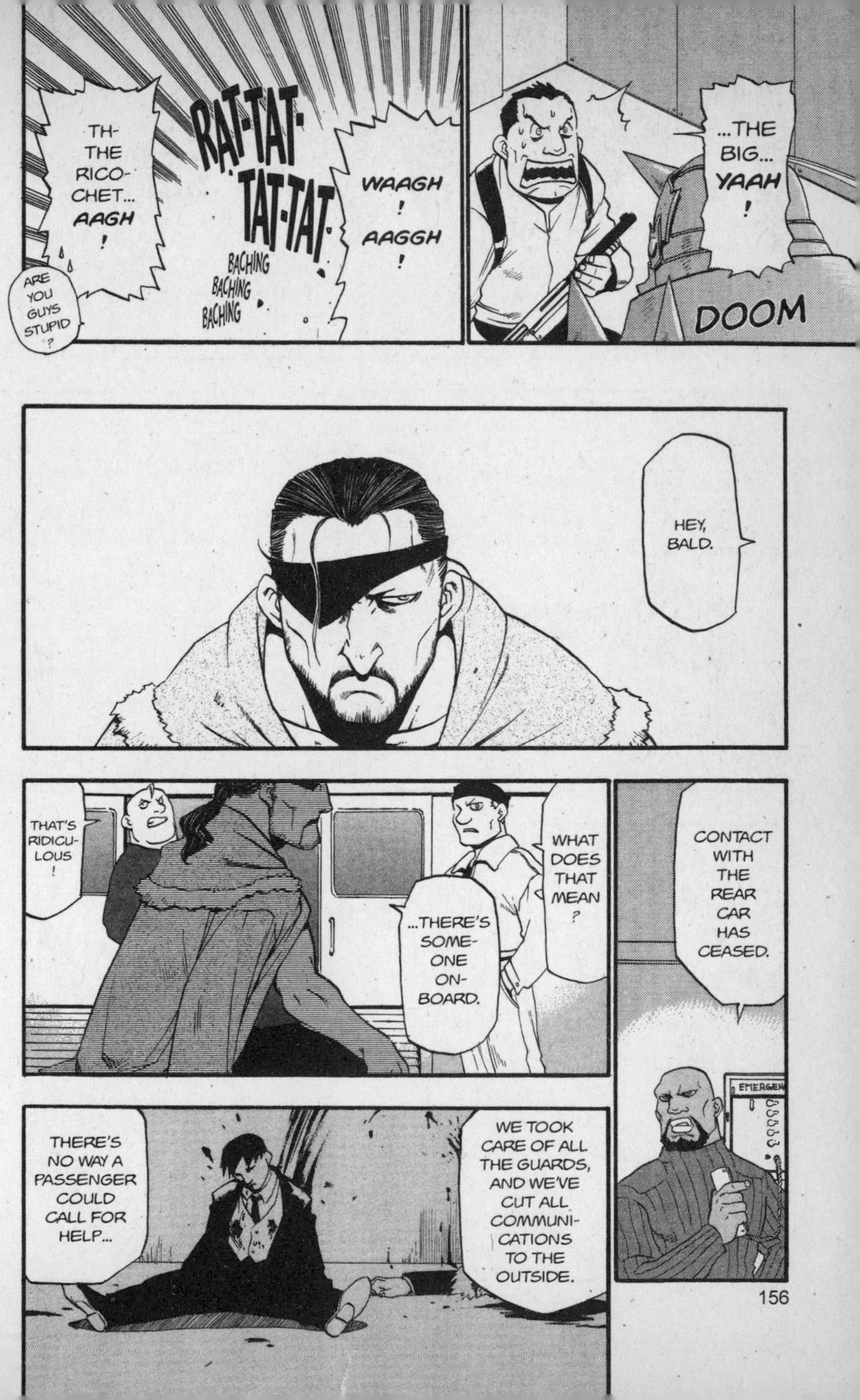
...THE BIG... YAAH!
DOOM
WAAGH! AAGGH!
RAT-TAT-TAT-TAT-TAT
BACHING BACHING BACHING
TH-THE RICOCHET... AAGH!
ARE YOU GUYS STUPID?
HEY, BALD.
CONTACT WITH THE REAR CAR HAS CEASED.
WHAT DOES THAT MEAN?
...THERE'S SOME-ONE ON-BOARD.
THAT'S RIDICU-LOUS!
WE TOOK CARE OF ALL THE GUARDS, AND WE'VE CUT ALL COMMUNI-CATIONS TO THE OUTSIDE.
THERE'S NO WAY A PASSENGER COULD CALL FOR HELP...

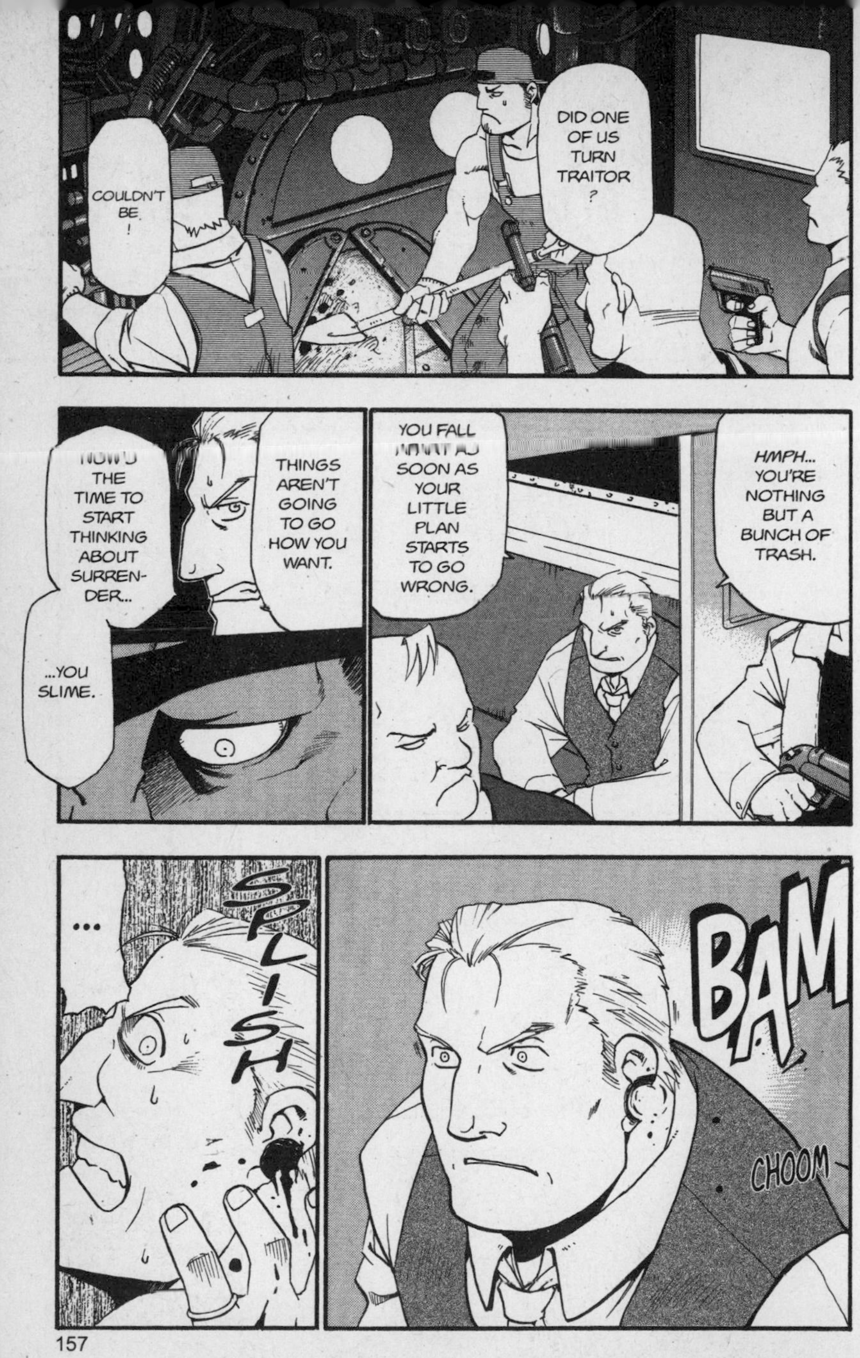
DID ONE OF US TURN TRAITOR?
COULDN'T BE!
HMPH... YOU'RE NOTHING BUT A BUNCH OF TRASH.
YOU FALL AS SOON AS YOUR LITTLE PLAN STARTS TO GO WRONG.
THINGS AREN'T GOING TO GO HOW YOU WANT.
THE TIME TO START THINKING ABOUT SURRENDER...
...YOU SLIME.
BAM
CHOOM
SPLISH
...

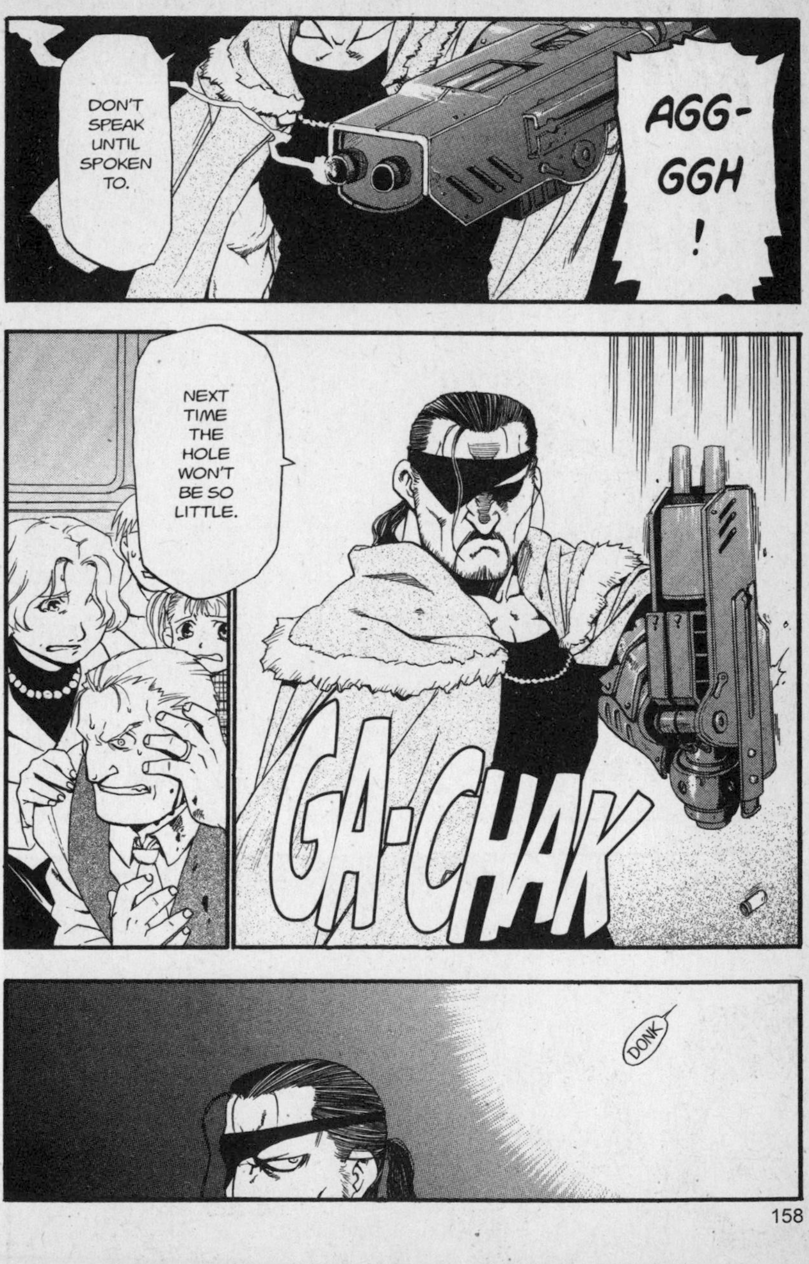

AGG-GGH!
DON'T SPEAK UNTIL SPOKEN TO.
NEXT TIME THE HOLE WON'T BE SO LITTLE.
GA-CHAK
DONK

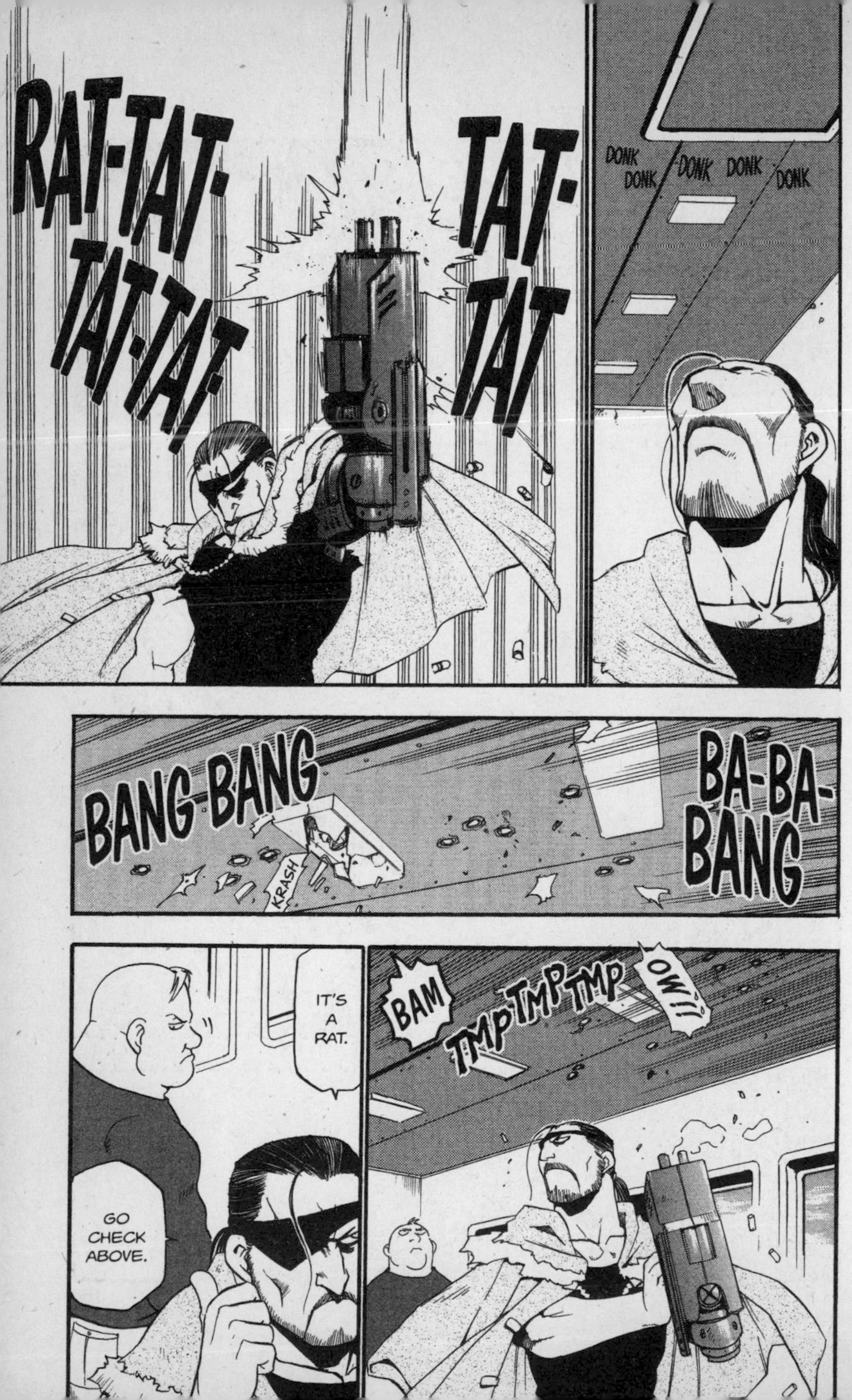
DONK DONK DONK DONK DONK
TAT-TAT-TAT
RAT-TAT-TAT-TAT-TAT
BA-BA-BANG
KRASH
BANG-BANG
OW!!
TMP TMP TMP
BAM
IT'S A RAT.
GO CHECK ABOVE.

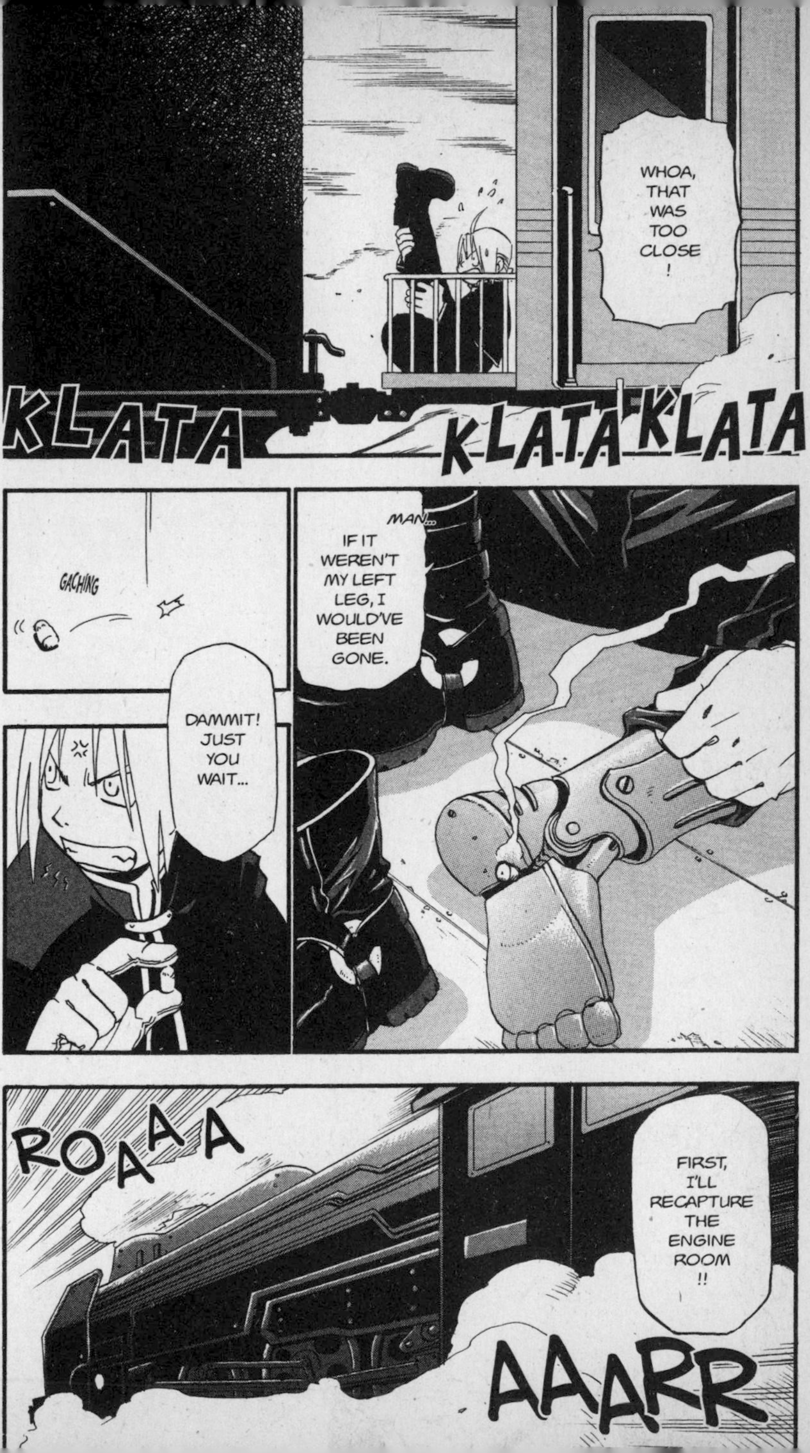
WHOA, THAT WAS TOO CLOSE!
KLATA KLATA
KLATA
MAN...
IF IT WEREN'T MY LEFT LEG, I WOULD'VE BEEN GONE.
GACHING
DAMMIT! JUST YOU WAIT...
FIRST, I'LL RECAPTURE THE ENGINE ROOM!!
ROAAAA
AAARR

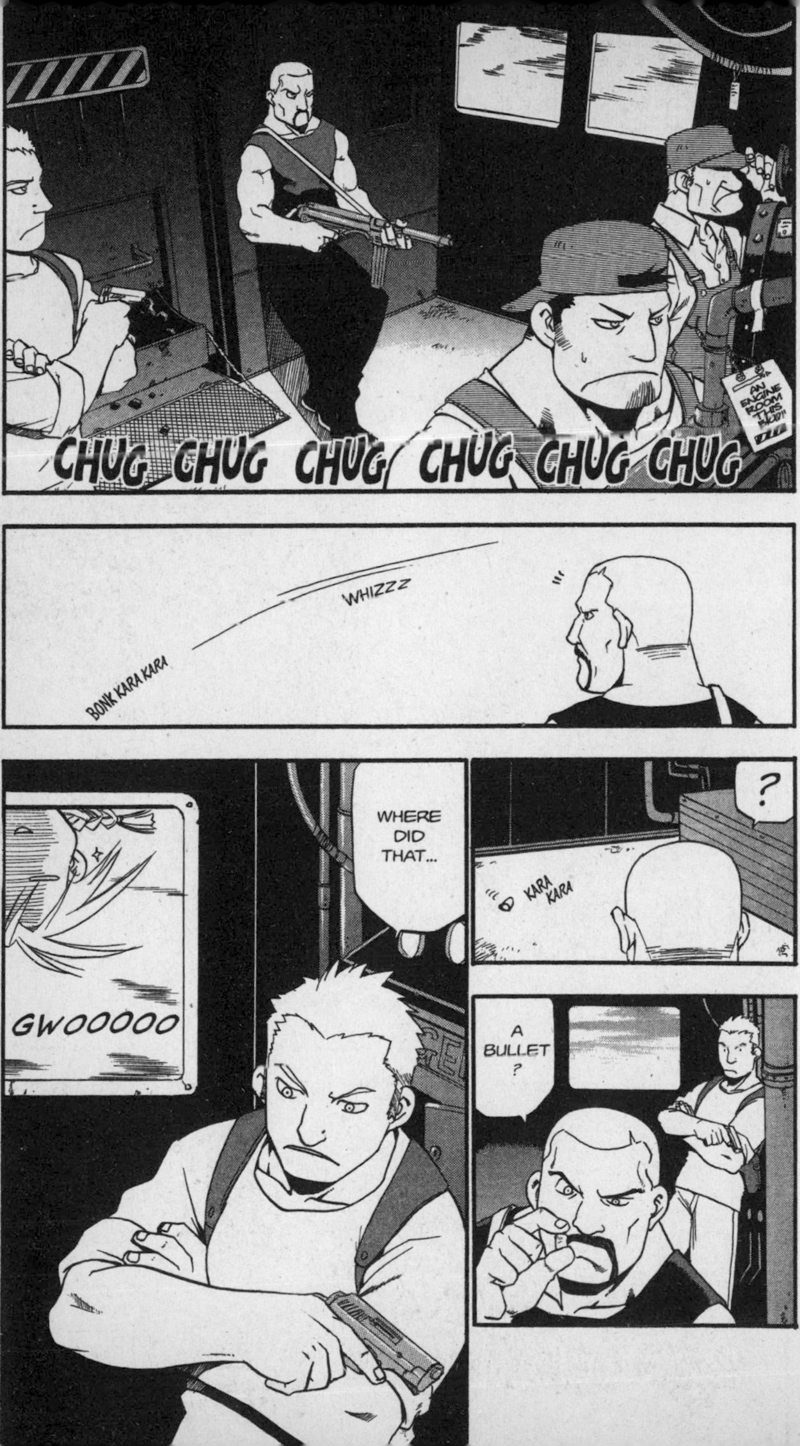
AN ENGINE ROOM THIS
CHUG CHUG CHUG CHUG CHUG CHUG
WHIZZZ
BONK KARA KARA
?
KARA KARA
A BULLET ?
WHERE DID THAT...
GWOOOOO

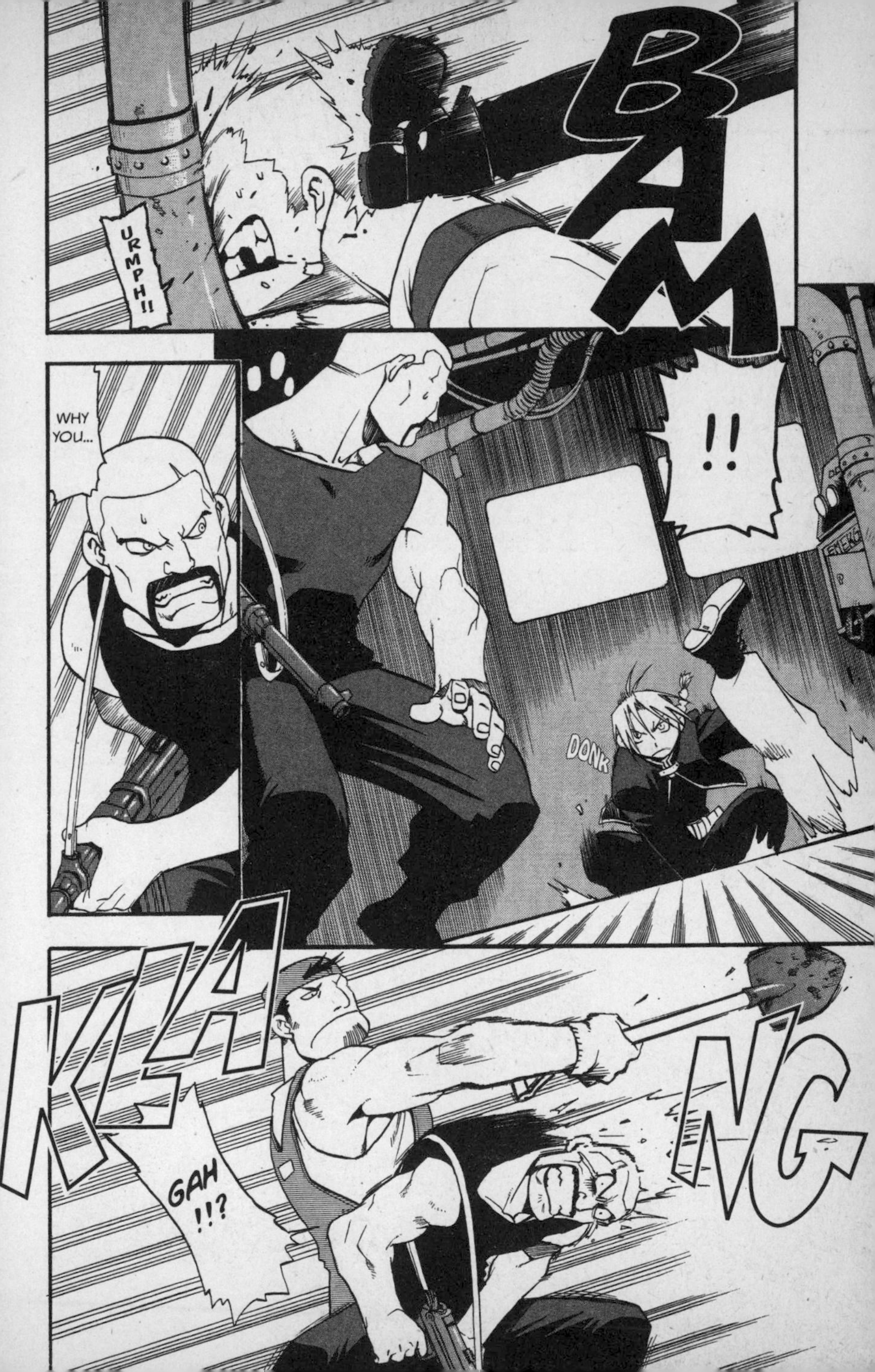
BAM
URMPH!!
!!
DONK
WHY YOU...
KLANG
GAH !!?

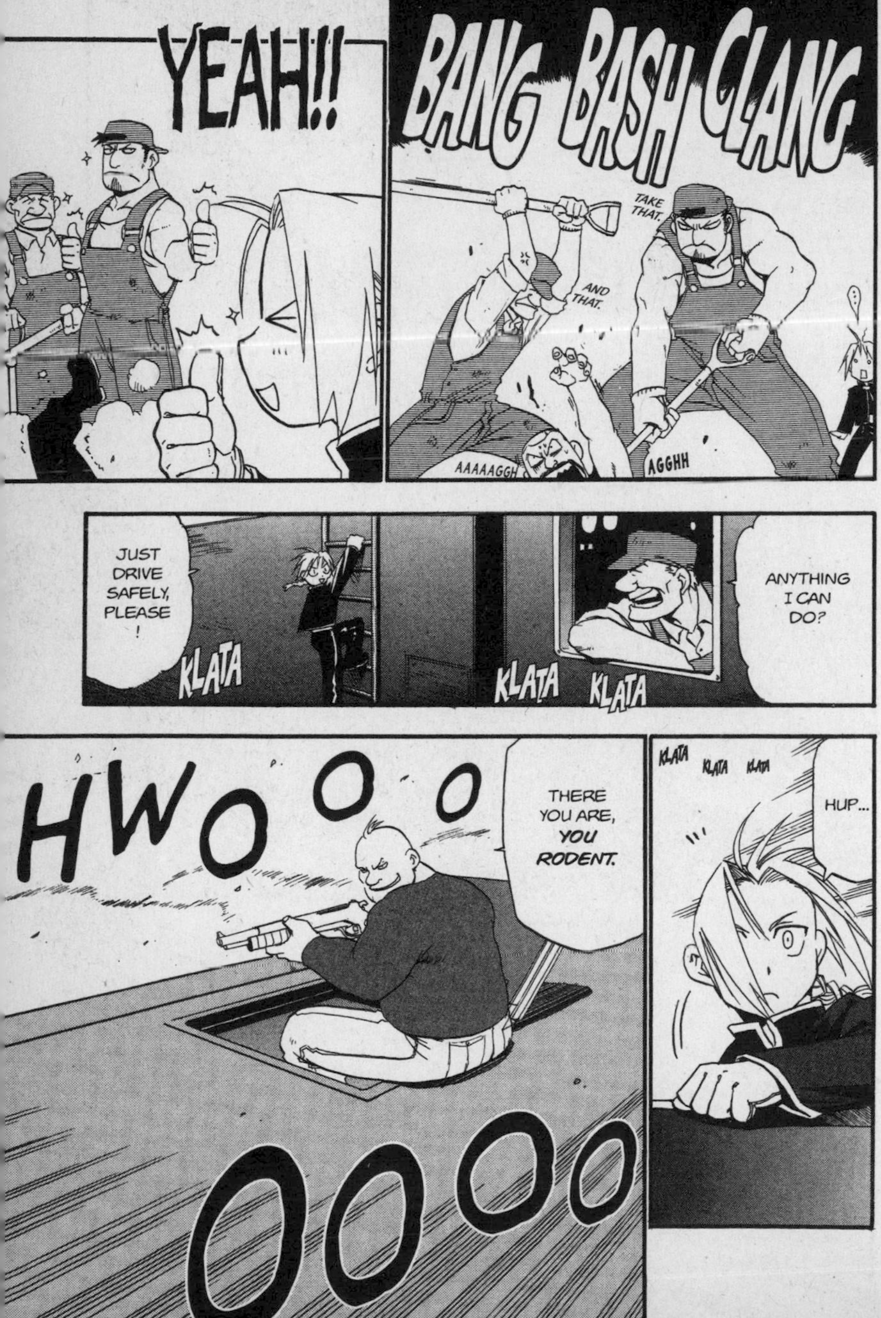
BANG BASH CLANG
TAKE THAT.
AND THAT.
AGGHH
AAAAAGGH
YEAH!!
ANYTHING I CAN DO?
KLATA
KLATA
JUST DRIVE SAFELY, PLEASE!
KLATA
KLATA KLATA KLATA
HUP...
THERE YOU ARE, YOU RODENT.
HWOOO
OOOO

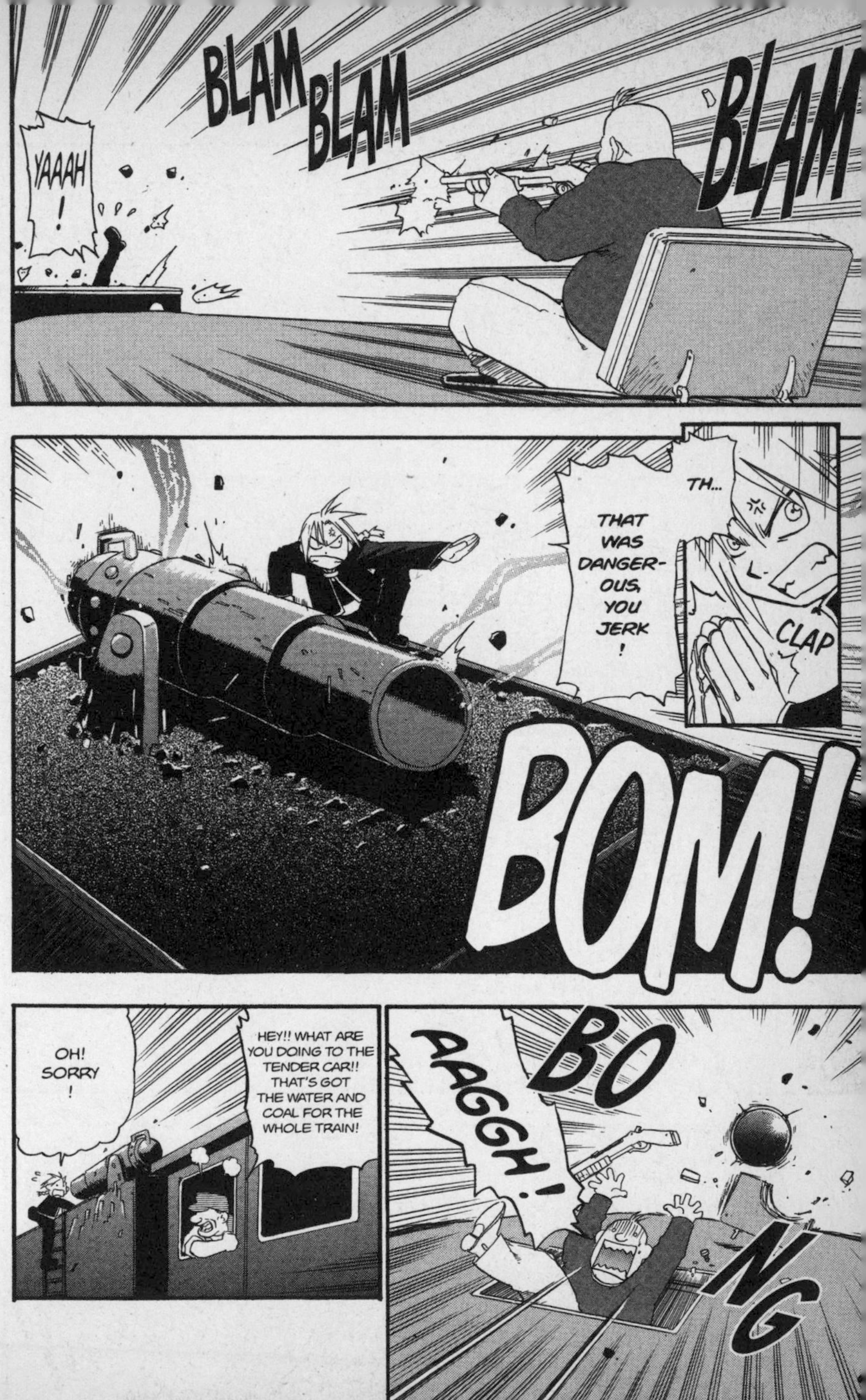
BLAM
BLAM
BLAM
YAAAH!
TH...
THAT WAS DANGEROUS, YOU JERK!
CLAP
BOM!
BO
NG
AAGGH!
HEY!! WHAT ARE YOU DOING TO THE TENDER CAR!! THAT'S GOT THE WATER AND COAL FOR THE WHOLE TRAIN!
OH! SORRY!

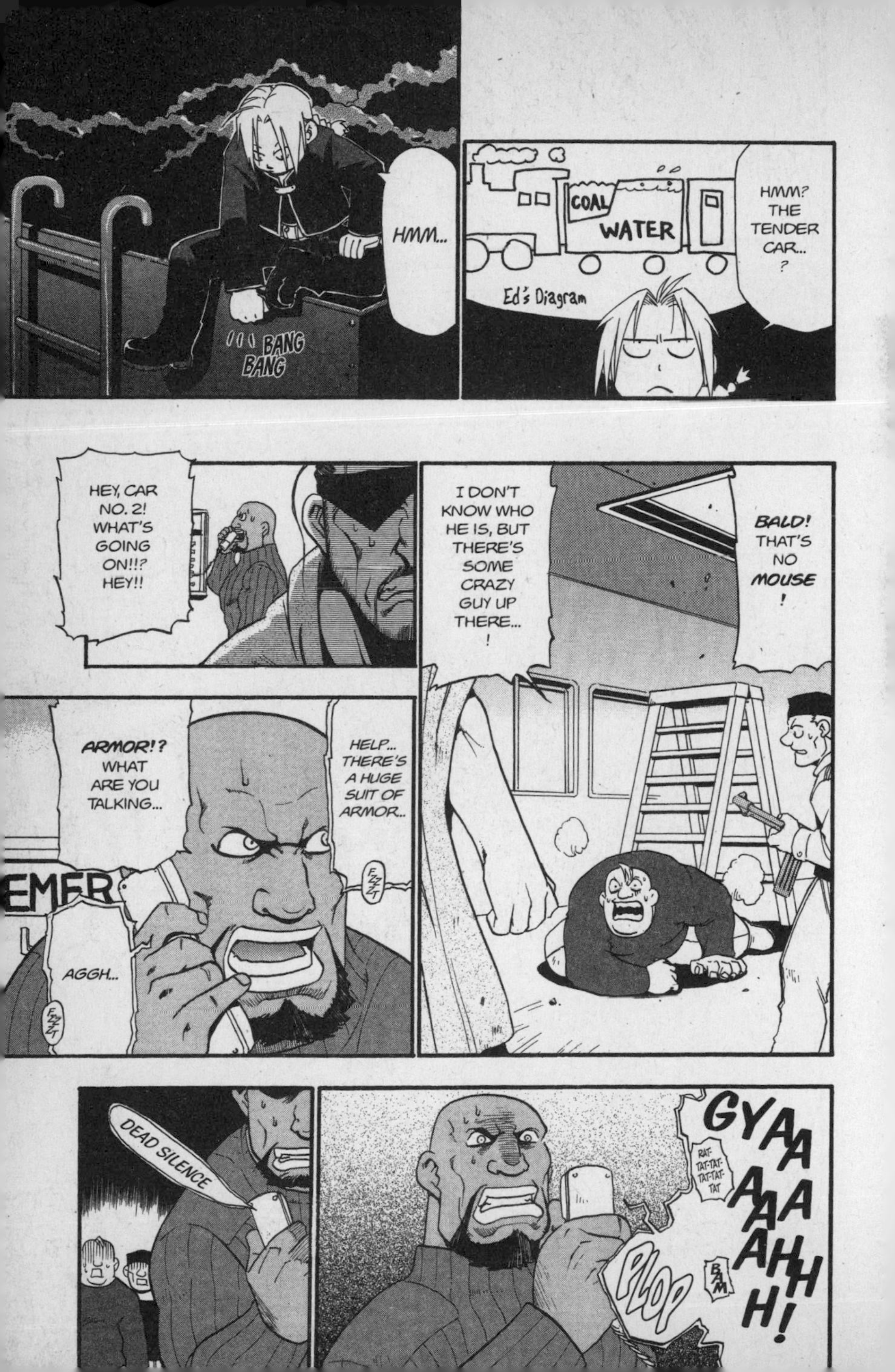

COAL
WATER
Ed's Diagram
HMM? THE TENDER CAR...?
HMM...
BANG BANG
BALD! THAT'S NO MOUSE!
I DON'T KNOW WHO HE IS, BUT THERE'S SOME CRAZY GUY UP THERE...!
HEY, CAR NO. 2! WHAT'S GOING ON!!? HEY!!
HELP... THERE'S A HUGE SUIT OF ARMOR..
ARMOR!? WHAT ARE YOU TALKING...
FZZZT
EMER
AGGH...
FZZZT
GYAAAAAAAHHHH!
RAT-TAT-TAT-TAT-TAT-TAT
BAM
PLOP
DEAD SILENCE

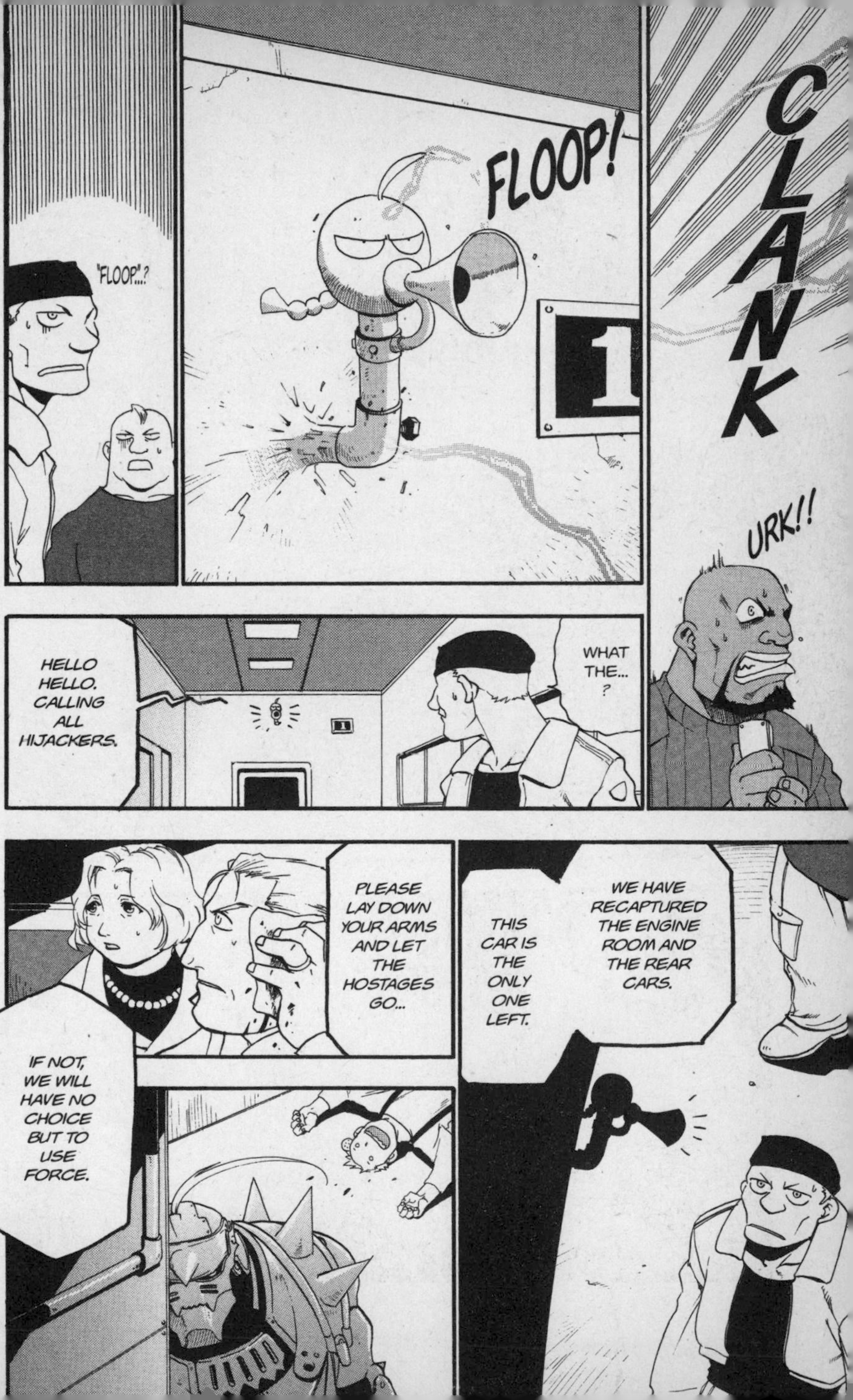

CLANK
URK!!
FLOOP!
"FLOOP"...?
WHAT THE... ?
HELLO HELLO. CALLING ALL HIJACKERS.
WE HAVE RECAPTURED THE ENGINE ROOM AND THE REAR CARS.
THIS CAR IS THE ONLY ONE LEFT.
PLEASE LAY DOWN YOUR ARMS AND LET THE HOSTAGES GO...
IF NOT, WE WILL HAVE NO CHOICE BUT TO USE FORCE.

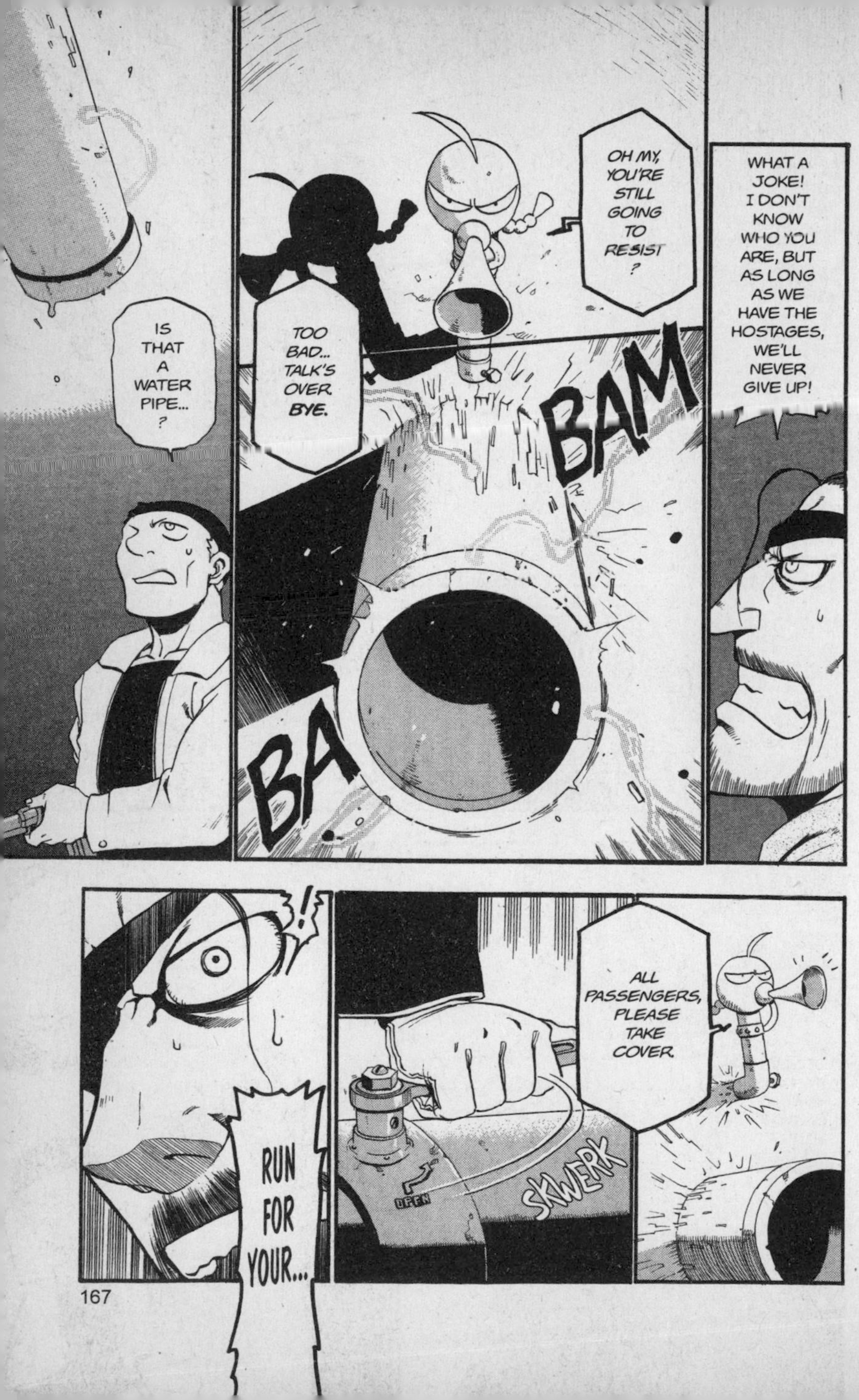
WHAT A JOKE! I DON'T KNOW WHO YOU ARE, BUT AS LONG AS WE HAVE THE HOSTAGES, WE'LL NEVER GIVE UP!
OH MY, YOU'RE STILL GOING TO RESIST?
TOO BAD... TALK'S OVER. BYE.
BAM
BA
IS THAT A WATER PIPE...?
ALL PASSENGERS, PLEASE TAKE COVER.
SKWERK
!
RUN FOR YOUR...

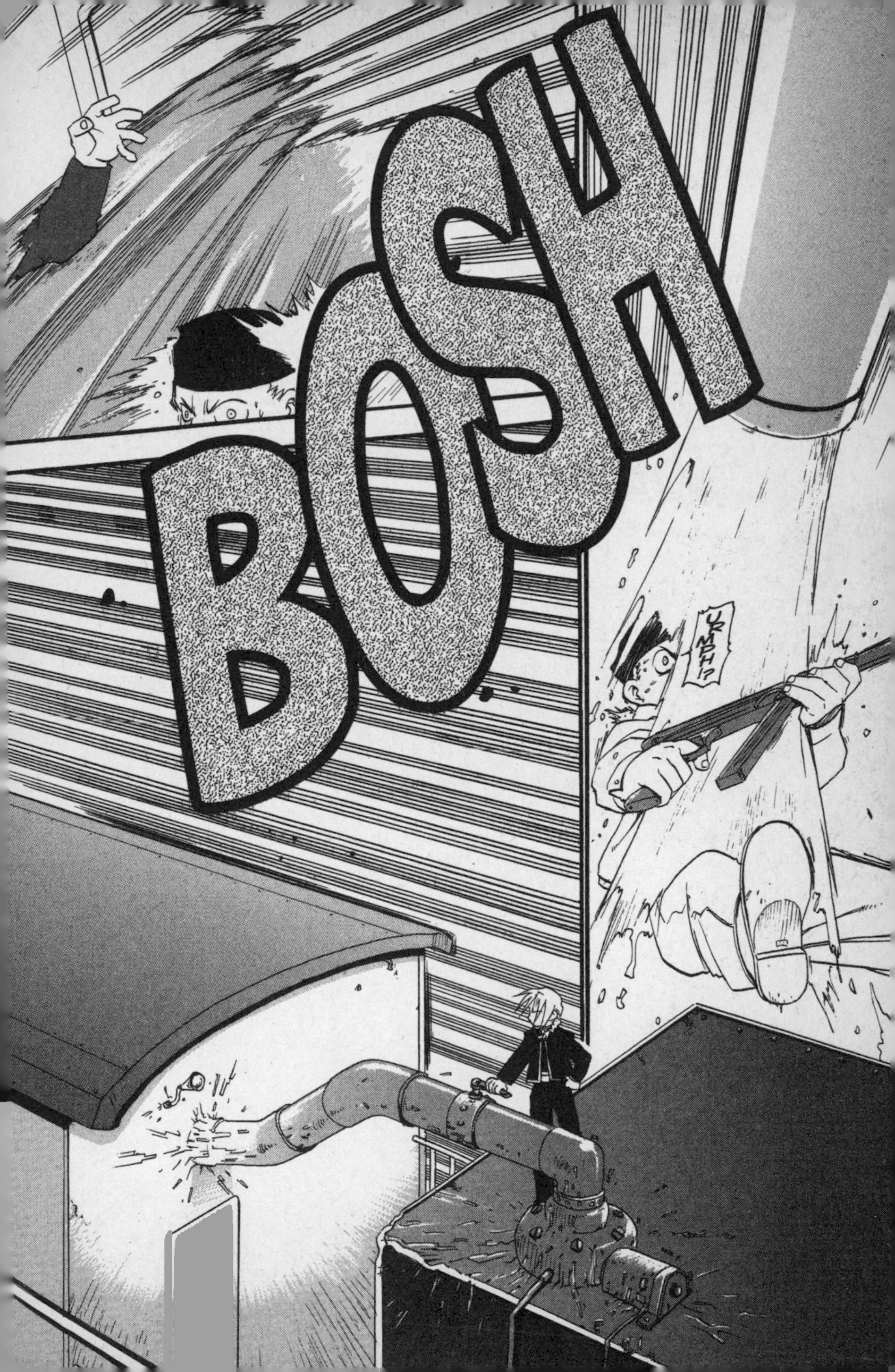

BOSH
URMPH!?

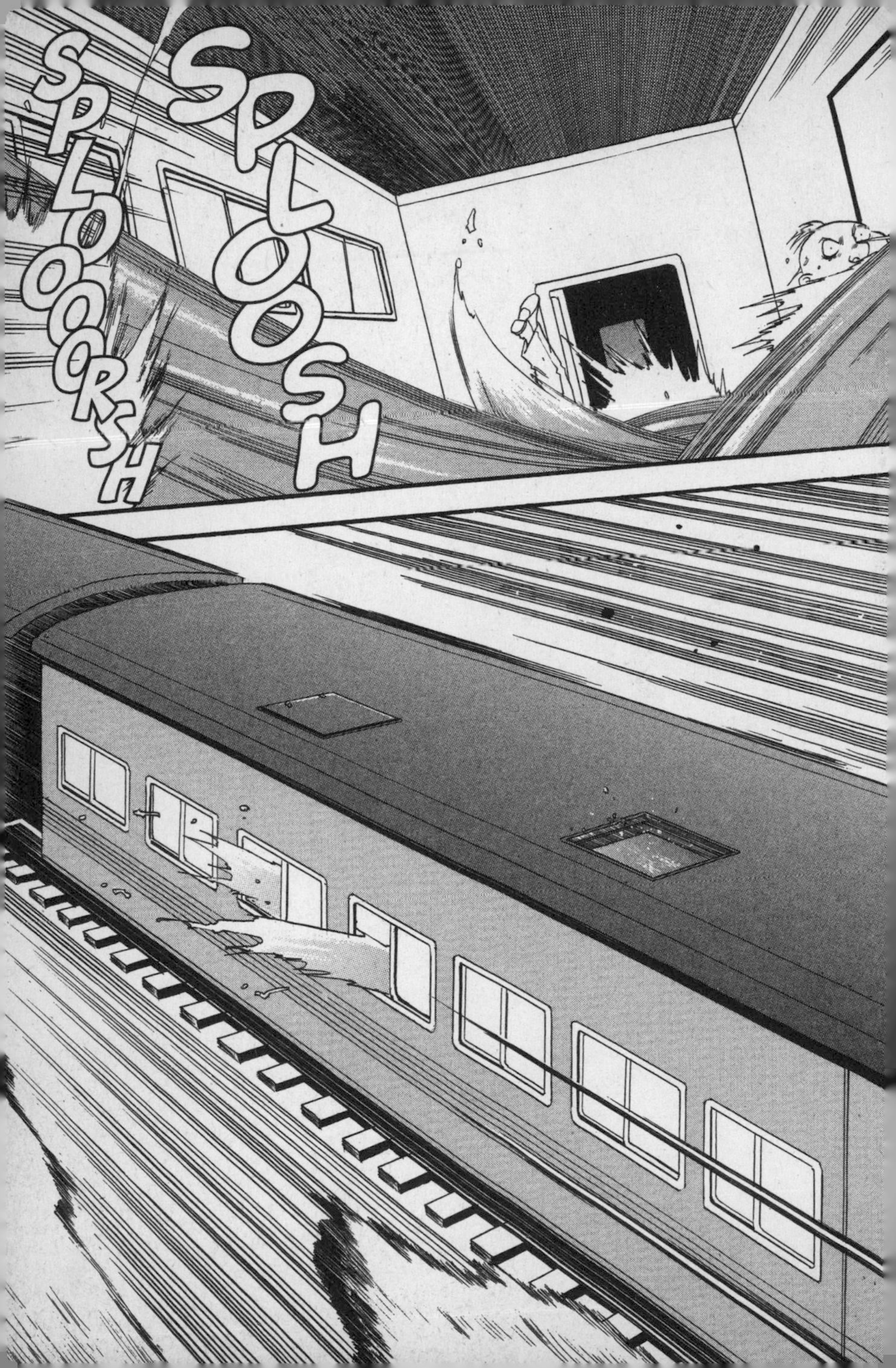
SPLOOSH
SPLOOOORSH

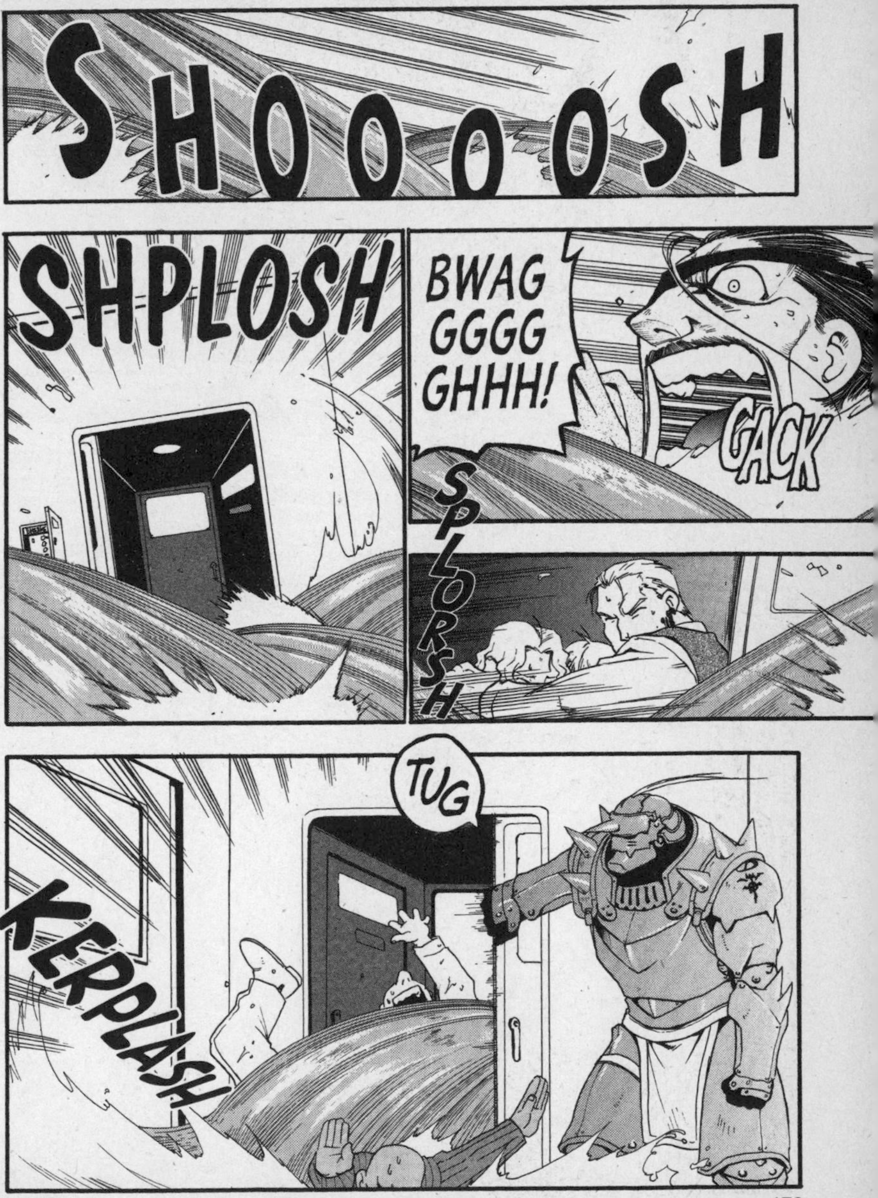
SHOOOOSH
BWAG GGGG GHHH!
GACK
SPLORSH
SHPLOSH
TUG
KERPLASH

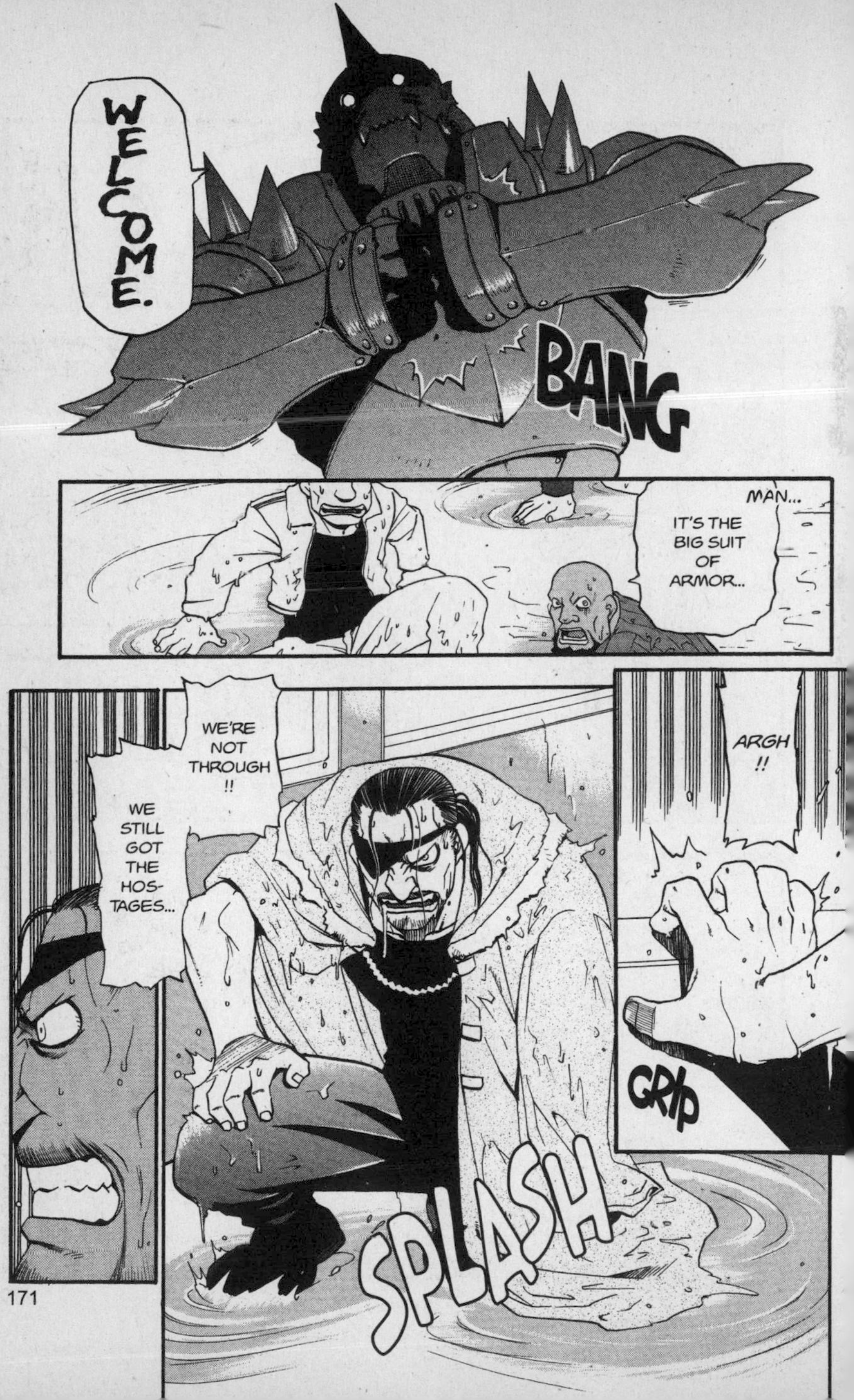
WELCOME.
BANG
MAN... IT'S THE BIG SUIT OF ARMOR...
ARGH !!
GRIP
WE'RE NOT THROUGH !!
WE STILL GOT THE HOS-TAGES...
SPLASH

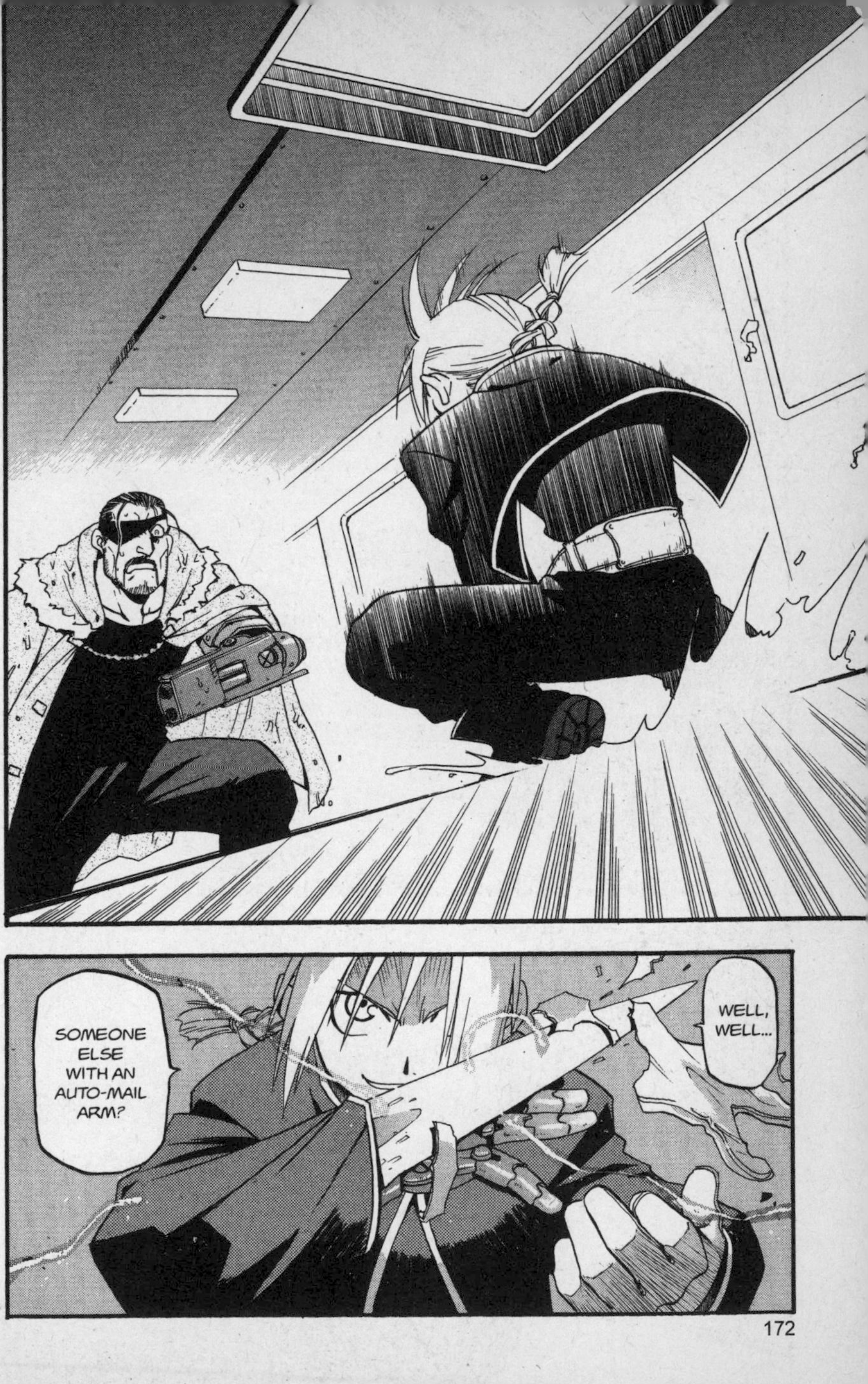
WELL, WELL...
SOMEONE ELSE WITH AN AUTO-MAIL ARM?

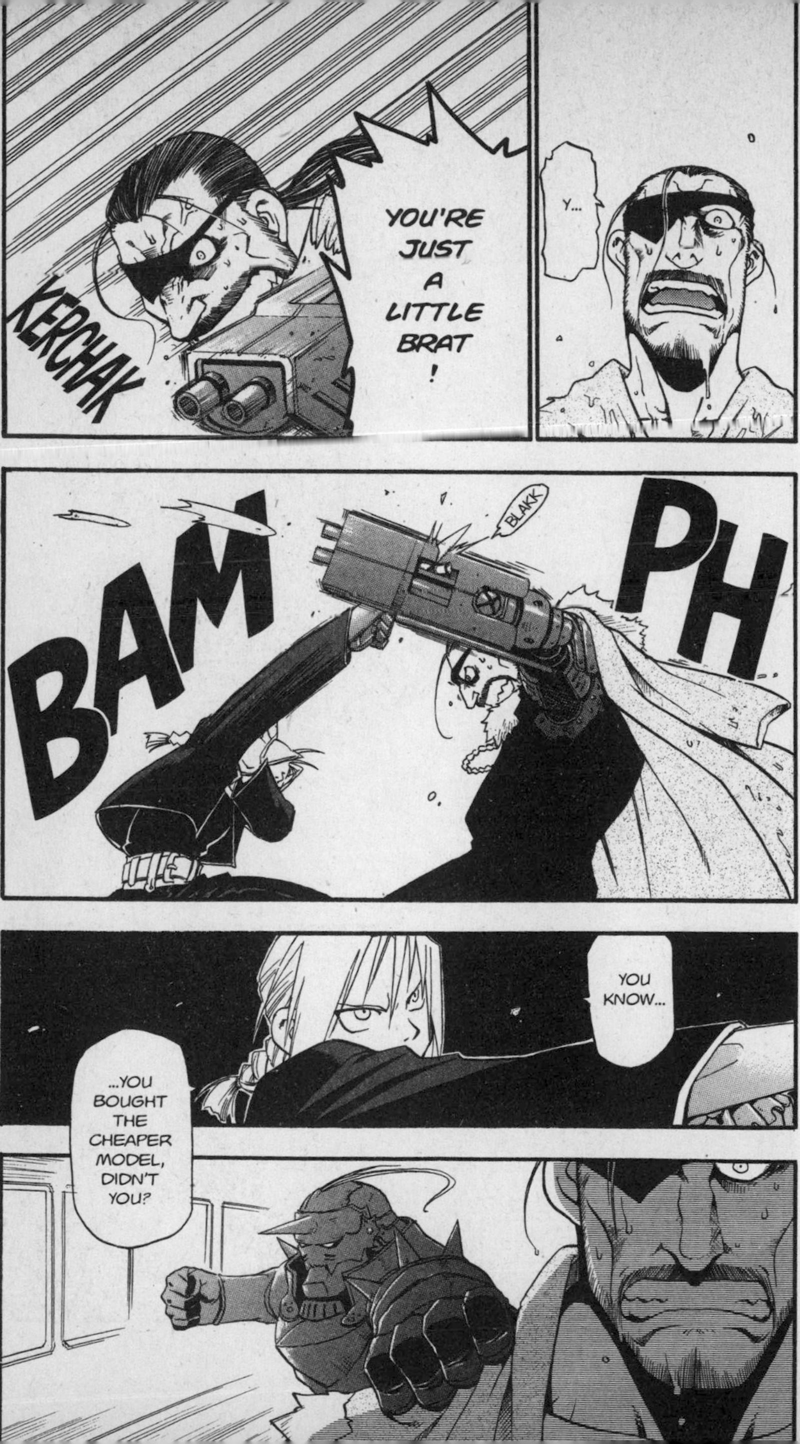
Y...
YOU'RE JUST A LITTLE BRAT!
KERCHAK
PH
BLAKK
BAM
YOU KNOW...
...YOU BOUGHT THE CHEAPER MODEL, DIDN'T YOU?

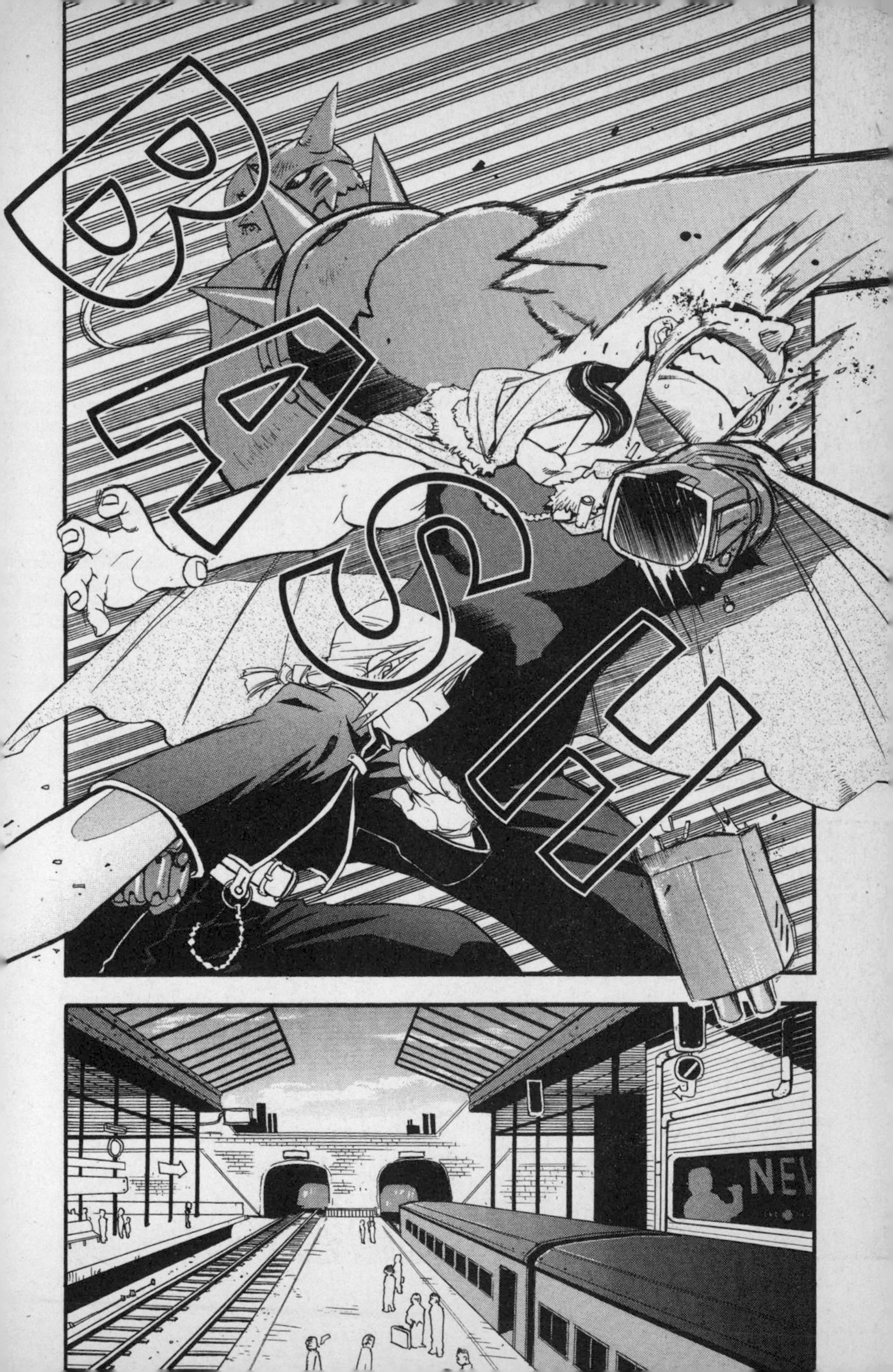
BRASH

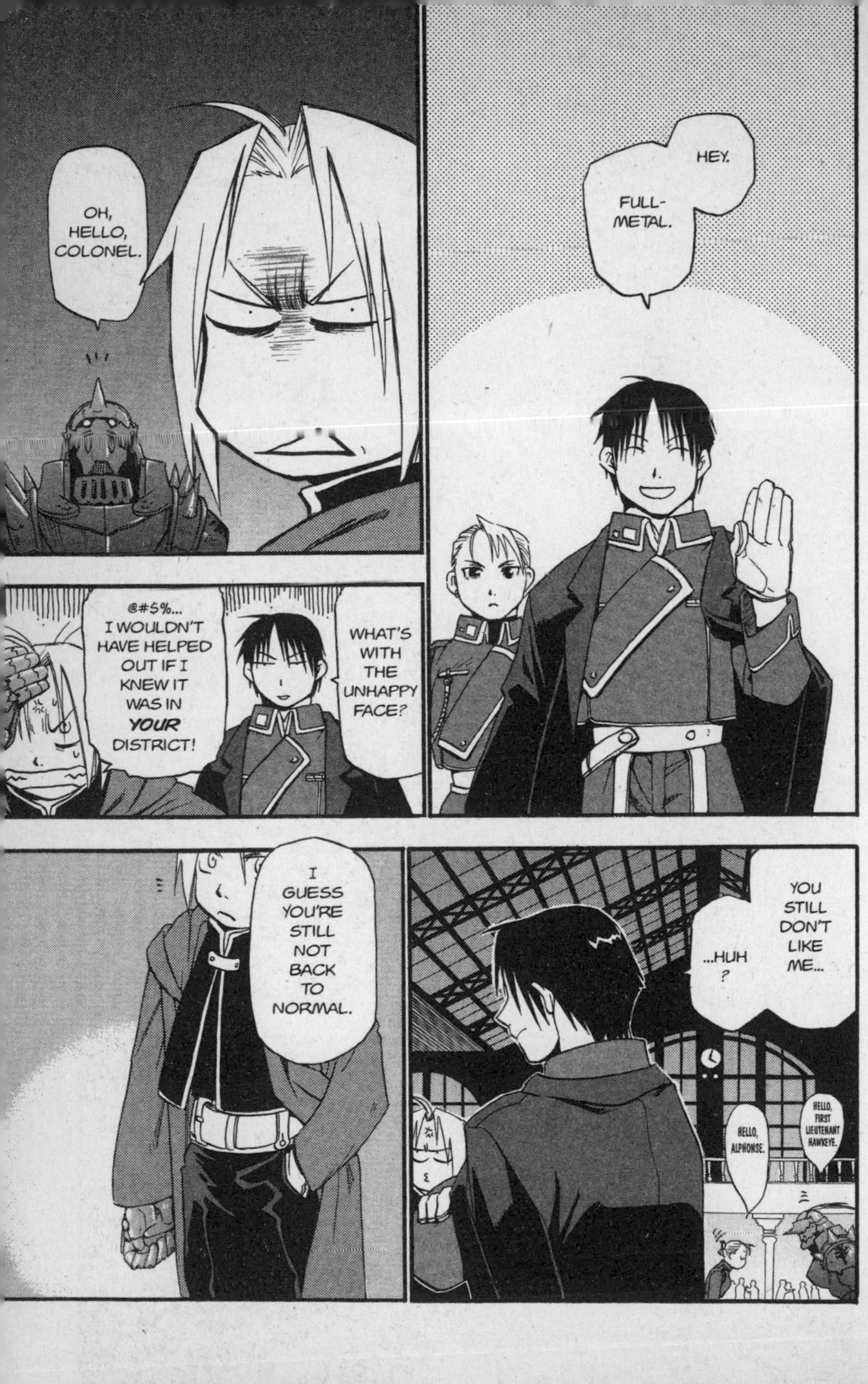

HEY.
FULL-METAL.
OH, HELLO, COLONEL.
WHAT'S WITH THE UNHAPPY FACE?
@#$%... I WOULDN'T HAVE HELPED OUT IF I KNEW IT WAS IN YOUR DISTRICT!
YOU STILL DON'T LIKE ME...
...HUH?
HELLO, FIRST LIEUTENANT HAWKEYE.
HELLO, ALPHONSE.
I GUESS YOU'RE STILL NOT BACK TO NORMAL.

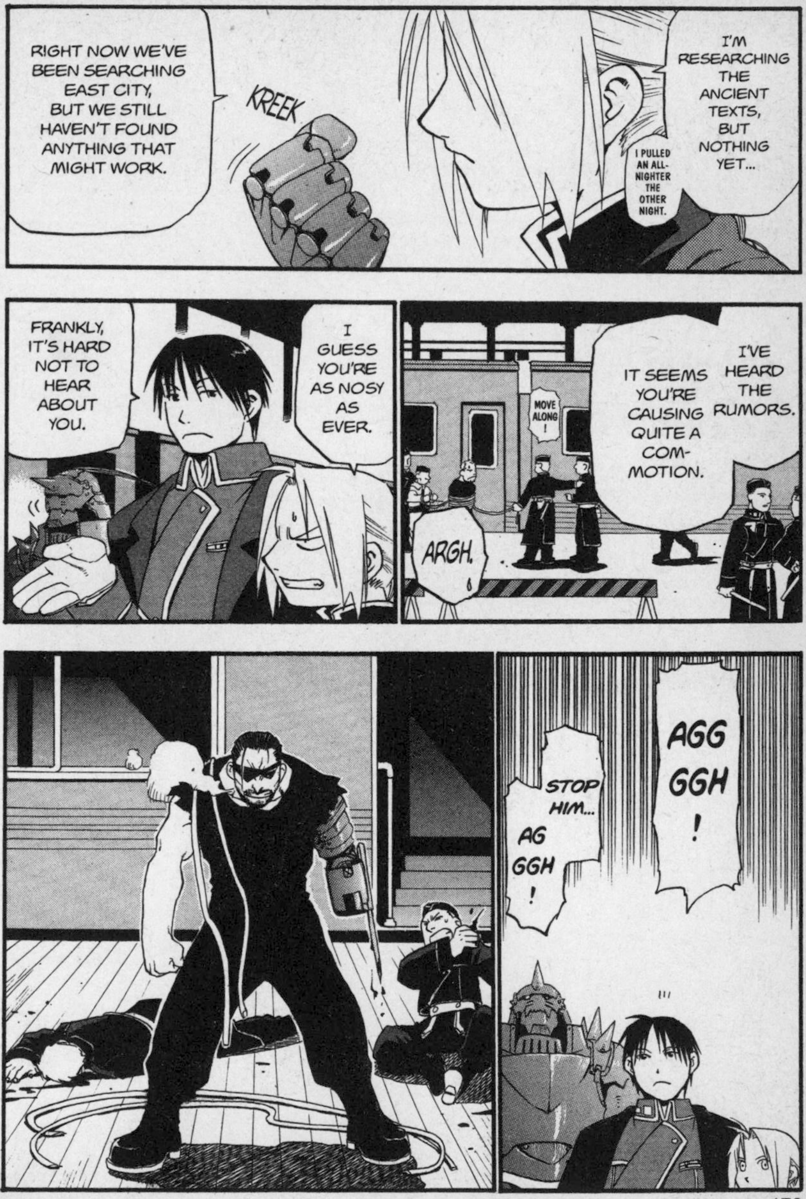
I'M RESEARCHING THE ANCIENT TEXTS, BUT NOTHING YET...
I PULLED AN ALL-NIGHTER THE OTHER NIGHT.
KREEK
RIGHT NOW WE'VE BEEN SEARCHING EAST CITY, BUT WE STILL HAVEN'T FOUND ANYTHING THAT MIGHT WORK.
I'VE HEARD THE RUMORS.
IT SEEMS YOU'RE CAUSING QUITE A COMMOTION.
MOVE ALONG!
ARGH.
I GUESS YOU'RE AS NOSY AS EVER.
FRANKLY, IT'S HARD NOT TO HEAR ABOUT YOU.
AGGGGH!
STOP HIM...
AGGGH!

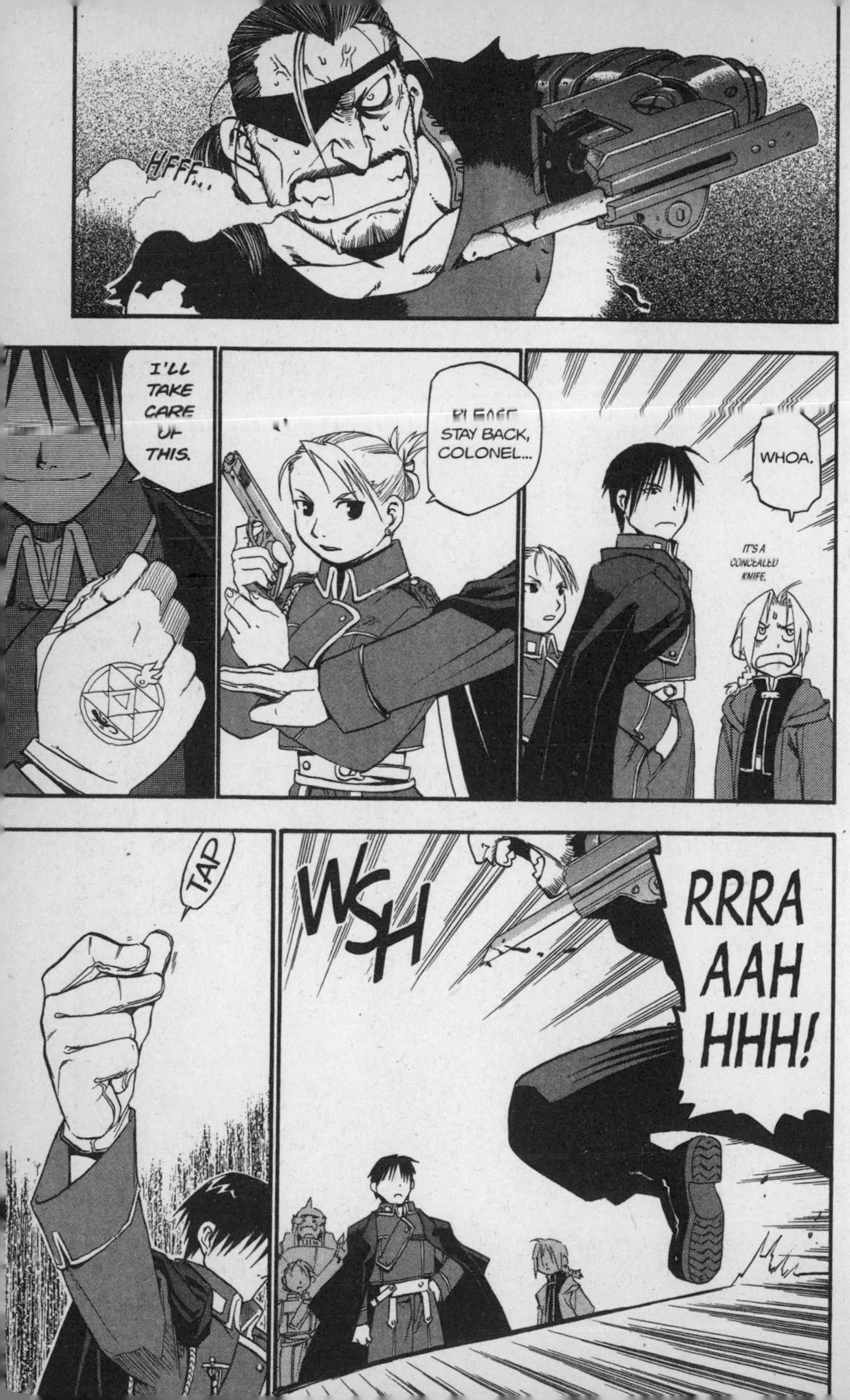
HFFF...
WHOA.
IT'S A CONCEALED KNIFE.
STAY BACK, COLONEL...
I'LL TAKE CARE OF THIS.
WSH
RRRAAAHHHH!
TAP

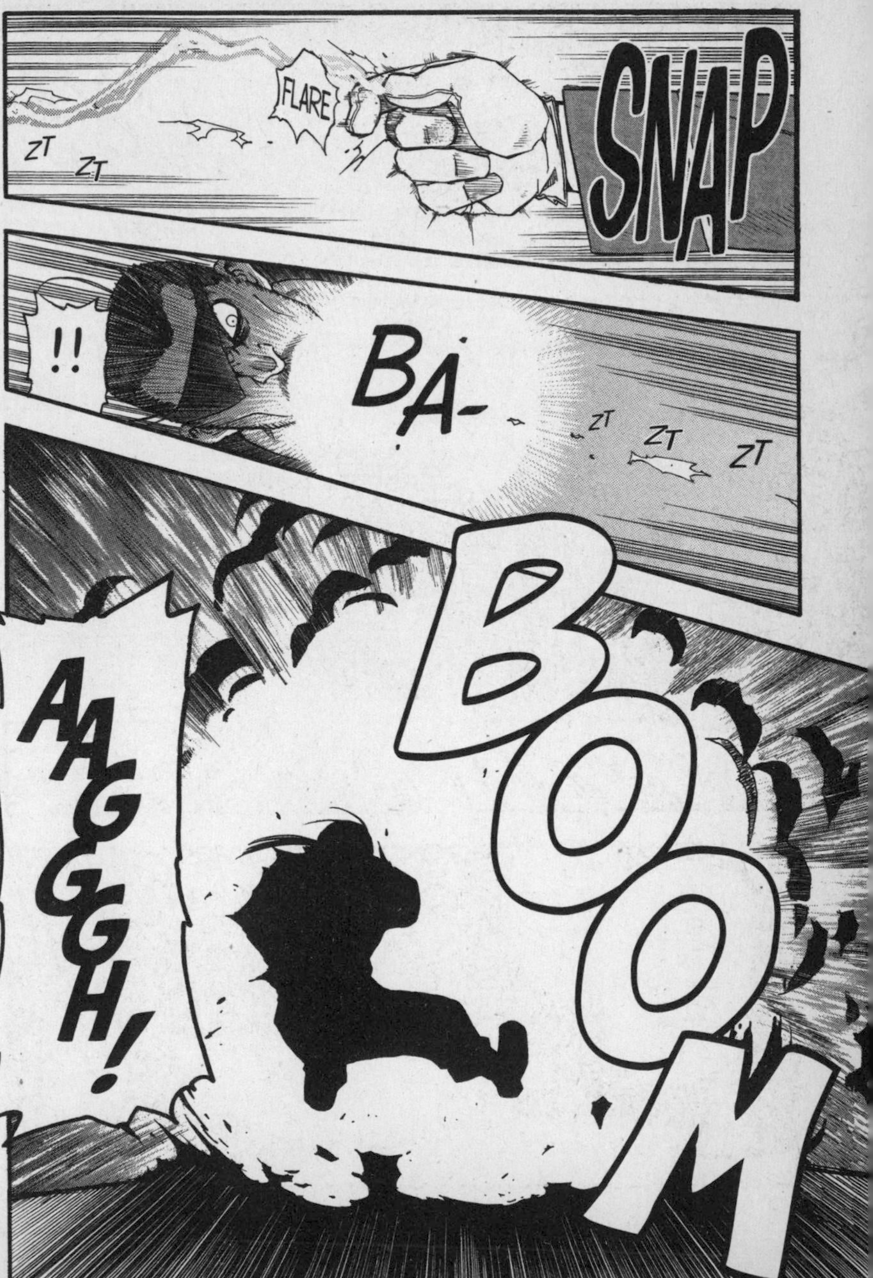
SNAP
FLARE
ZT ZT
ZT ZT ZT
BA-
!!
BOOM
AAGGGH!

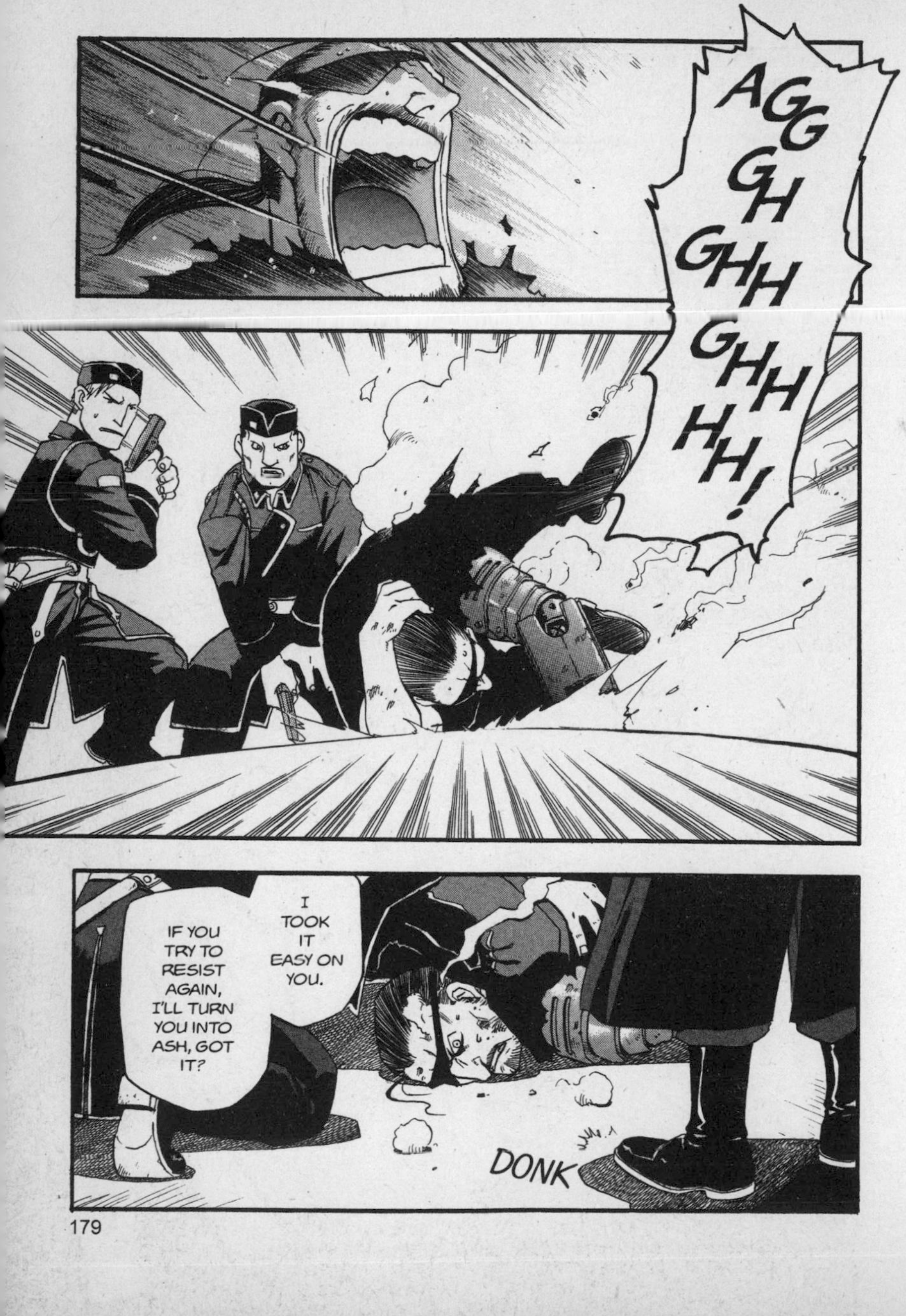
AGGGHGHHGHHHHH!
I TOOK IT EASY ON YOU.
IF YOU TRY TO RESIST AGAIN, I'LL TURN YOU INTO ASH, GOT IT?
DONK

THIS MANGA WAS ORIGINALLY PRINTED IN MONTHLY **SHONEN GANGAN**, AUGUST THROUGH NOVEMBER 2001.

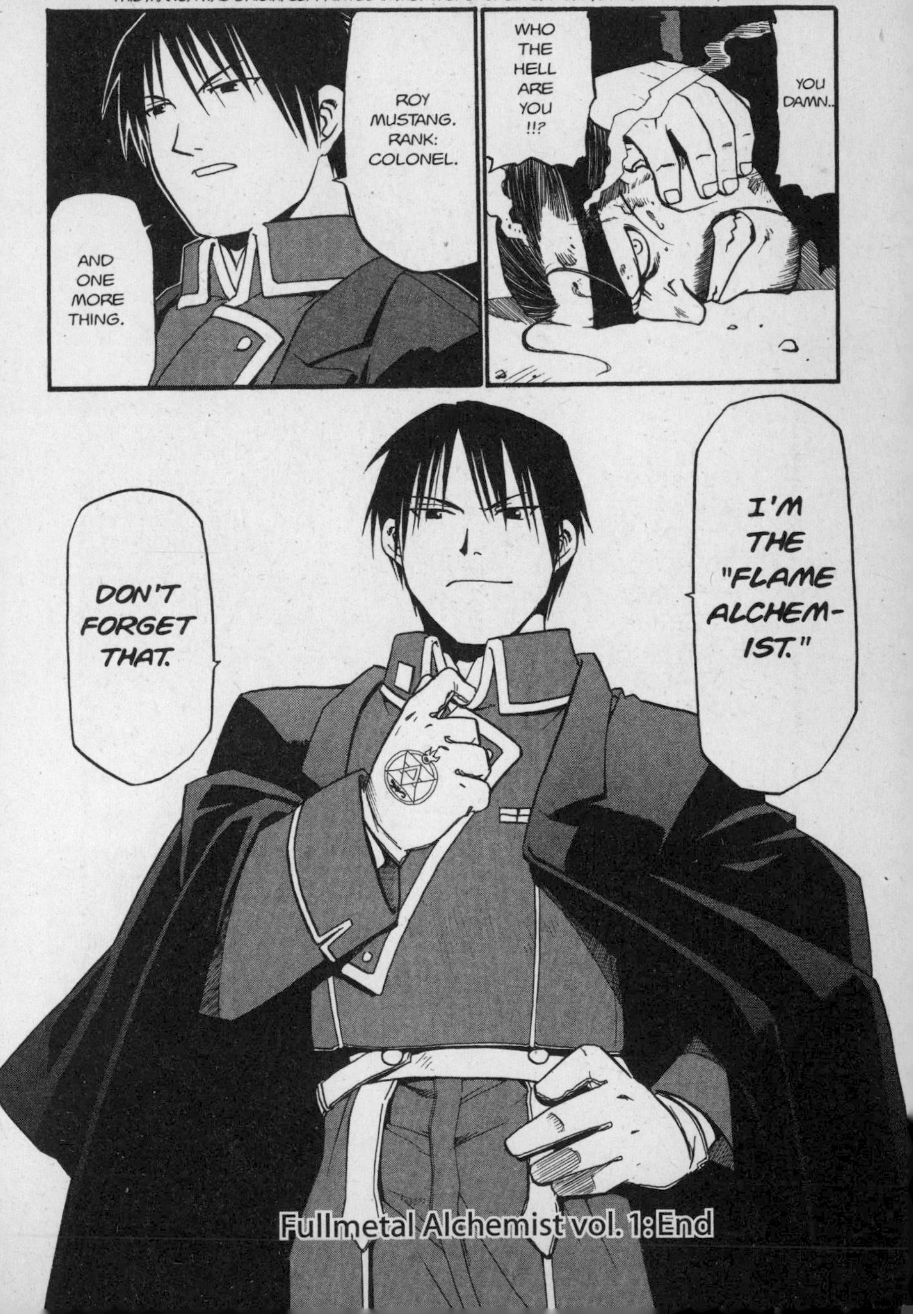
YOU DAMN...
WHO THE HELL ARE YOU !!?
ROY MUSTANG. RANK: COLONEL.
AND ONE MORE THING.
I'M THE "FLAME ALCHEMIST."
DON'T FORGET THAT.
Fullmetal Alchemist vol. 1: End

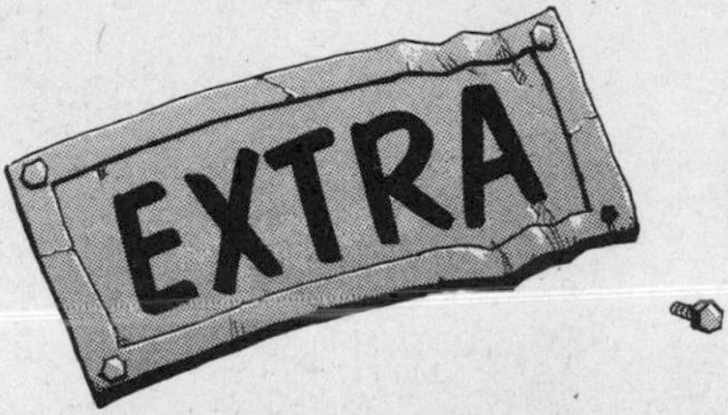
EXTRA

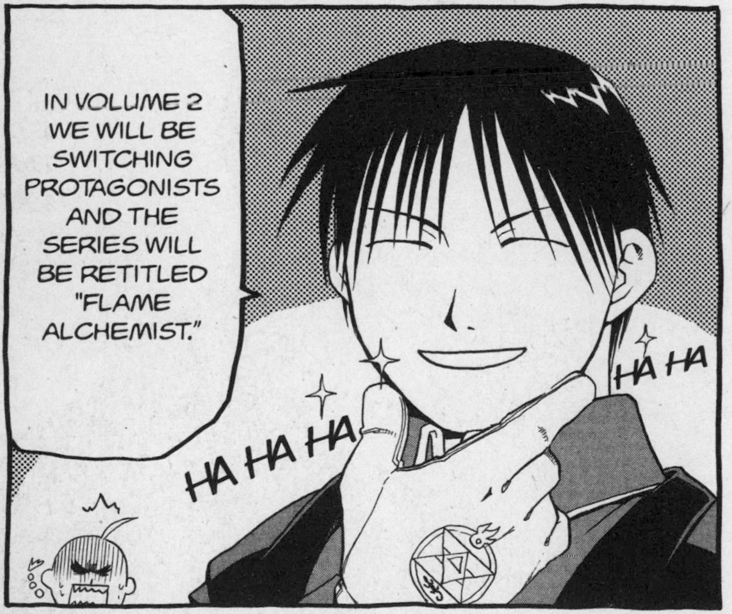
HA HA
IN VOLUME 2 WE WILL BE SWITCHING PROTAGONISTS AND THE SERIES WILL BE RETITLED "FLAME ALCHEMIST."
HA HA HA

That's not true.

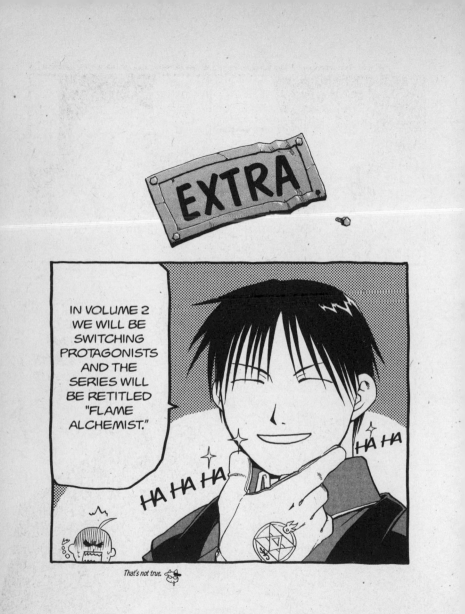

ALCHEMISTS IN FULLMETAL

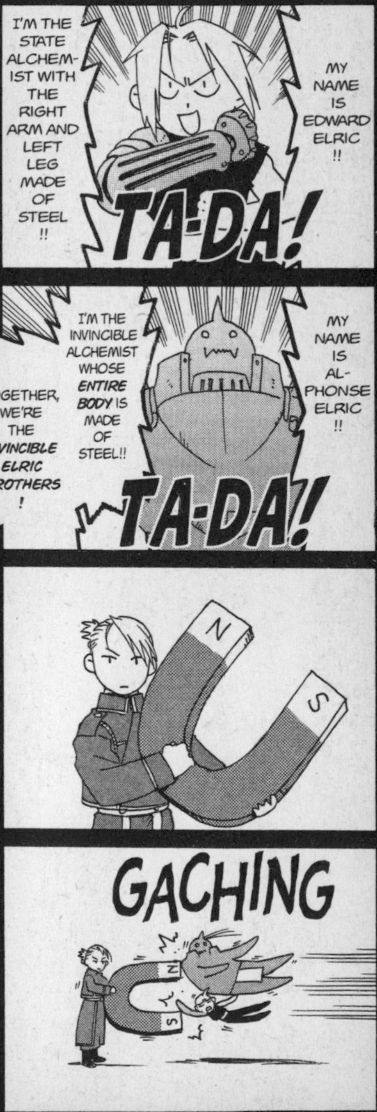
MY NAME IS EDWARD ELRIC!!
I'M THE STATE ALCHEMIST WITH THE RIGHT ARM AND LEFT LEG MADE OF STEEL!!
TA-DA!
MY NAME IS AL-PHONSE ELRIC!!
I'M THE INVINCIBLE ALCHEMIST WHOSE ENTIRE BODY IS MADE OF STEEL!!
TOGETHER, WE'RE THE INVINCIBLE ELRIC BROTHERS!
TA-DA!
N
S
GACHING
N
S

COPPER ALCHEMIST

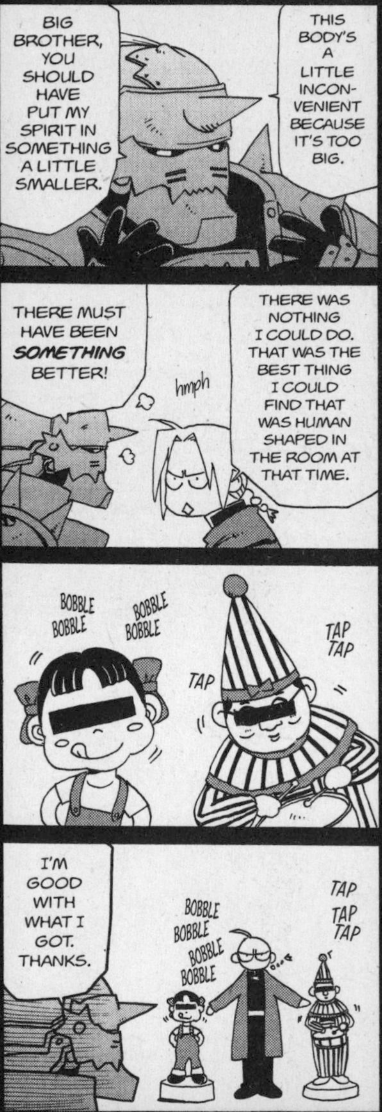
THIS BODY'S A LITTLE INCON-VENIENT BECAUSE IT'S TOO BIG.
BIG BROTHER, YOU SHOULD HAVE PUT MY SPIRIT IN SOMETHING A LITTLE SMALLER.
THERE WAS NOTHING I COULD DO. THAT WAS THE BEST THING I COULD FIND THAT WAS HUMAN SHAPED IN THE ROOM AT THAT TIME.
THERE MUST HAVE BEEN SOMETHING BETTER!
hmph
TAP TAP
BOBBLE BOBBLE
BOBBLE BOBBLE
TAP
TAP TAP TAP
I'M GOOD WITH WHAT I GOT. THANKS.
BOBBLE BOBBLE BOBBLE BOBBLE

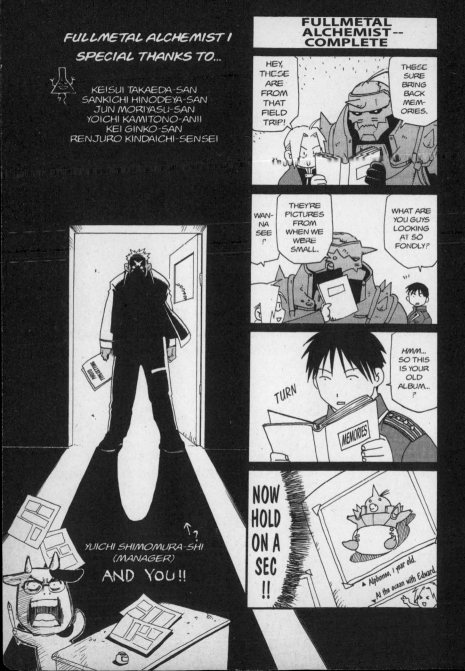

FULLMETAL ALCHEMIST -- COMPLETE

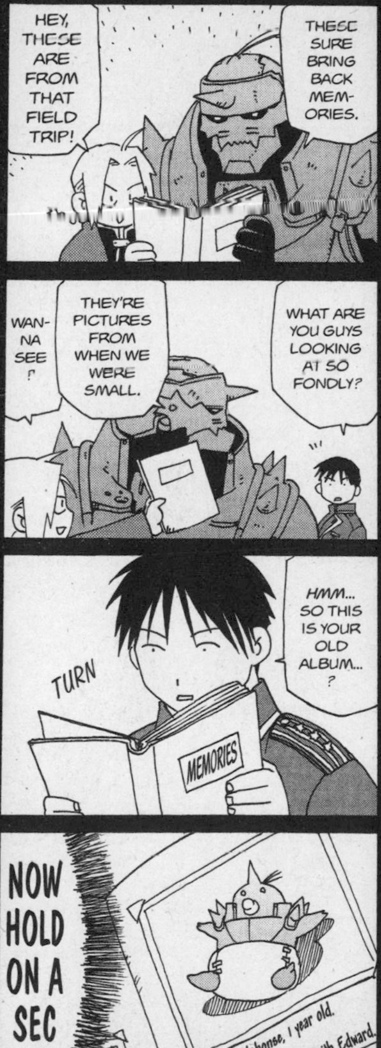
THESE SURE BRING BACK MEMORIES.
HEY, THESE ARE FROM THAT FIELD TRIP!
WHAT ARE YOU GUYS LOOKING AT SO FONDLY?
THEY'RE PICTURES FROM WHEN WE WERE SMALL.
WANNA SEE?
HMM... SO THIS IS YOUR OLD ALBUM...?
TURN
MEMORIES
▲ Alphonse, 1 year old.
▼ At the ocean with Edward.
NOW HOLD ON A SEC!!

FULLMETAL ALCHEMIST 1 SPECIAL THANKS TO...

KEISUI TAKAEDA-SAN
SANKICHI HINODEYA-SAN
JUN MORIYASU-SAN
YOICHI KAMITONO-ANII
KEI GINKO-SAN
RENJURO KINDAICHI-SENSEI

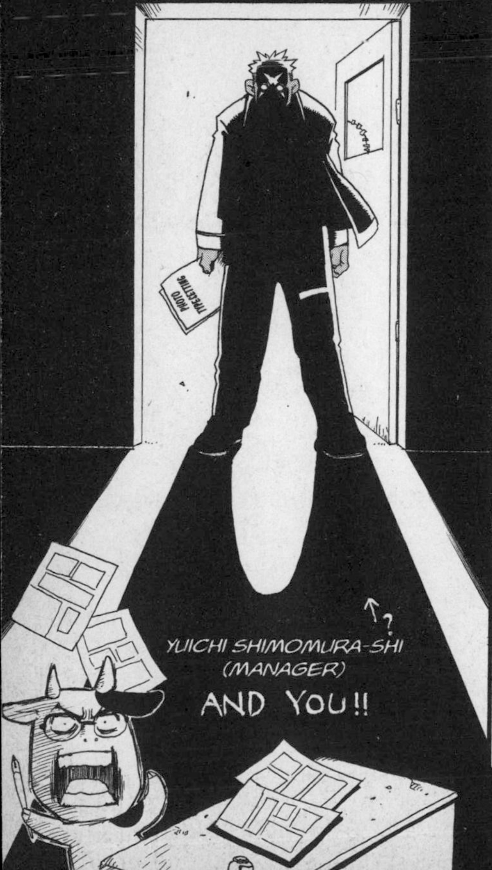
PHOTO TYPESETTING

YUICHI SHIMOMURA-SHI (MANAGER)

AND YOU!!

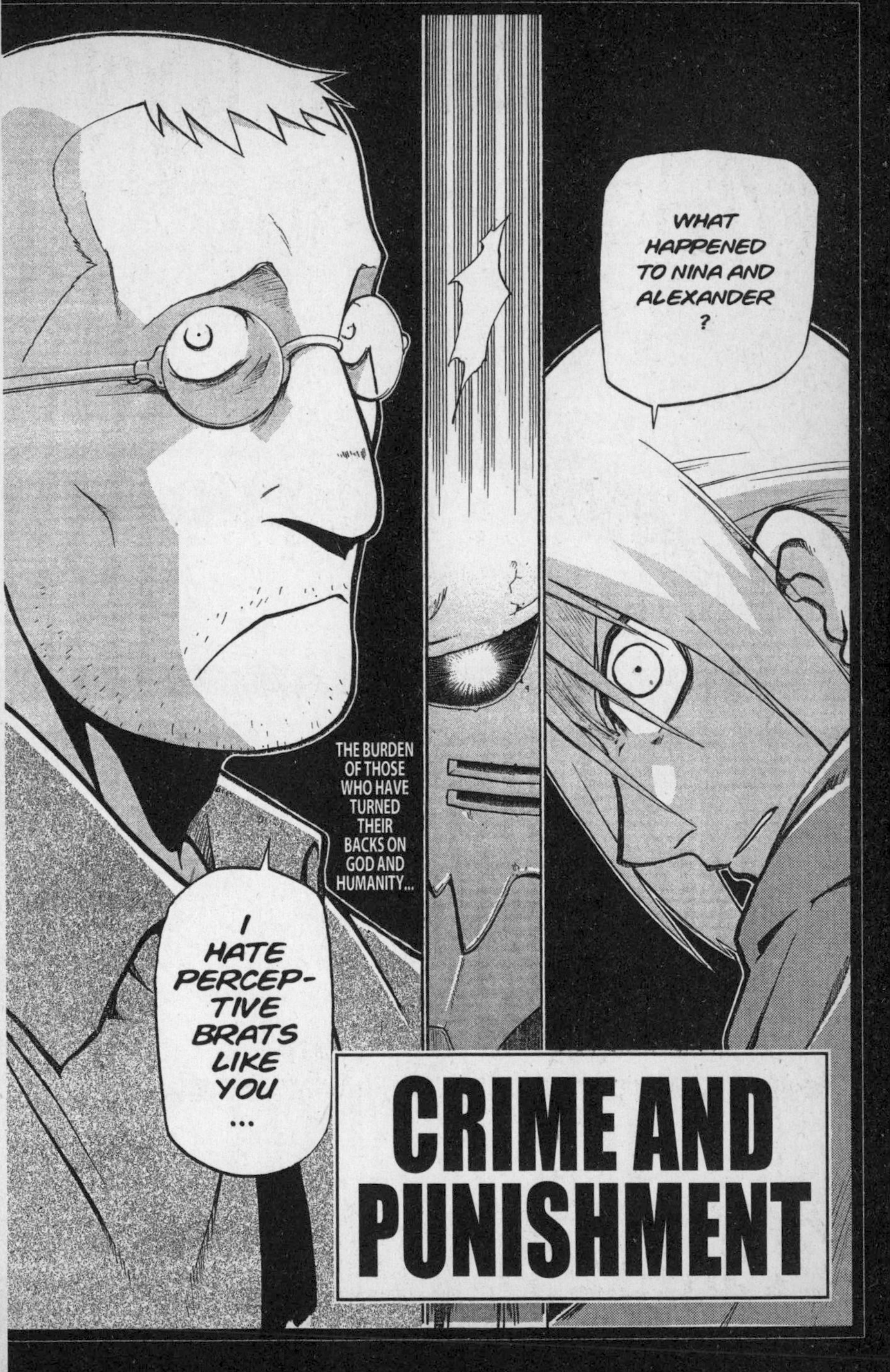
WHAT HAPPENED TO NINA AND ALEXANDER?
THE BURDEN OF THOSE WHO HAVE TURNED THEIR BACKS ON GOD AND HUMANITY...
I HATE PERCEP-TIVE BRATS LIKE YOU...
CRIME AND PUNISHMENT

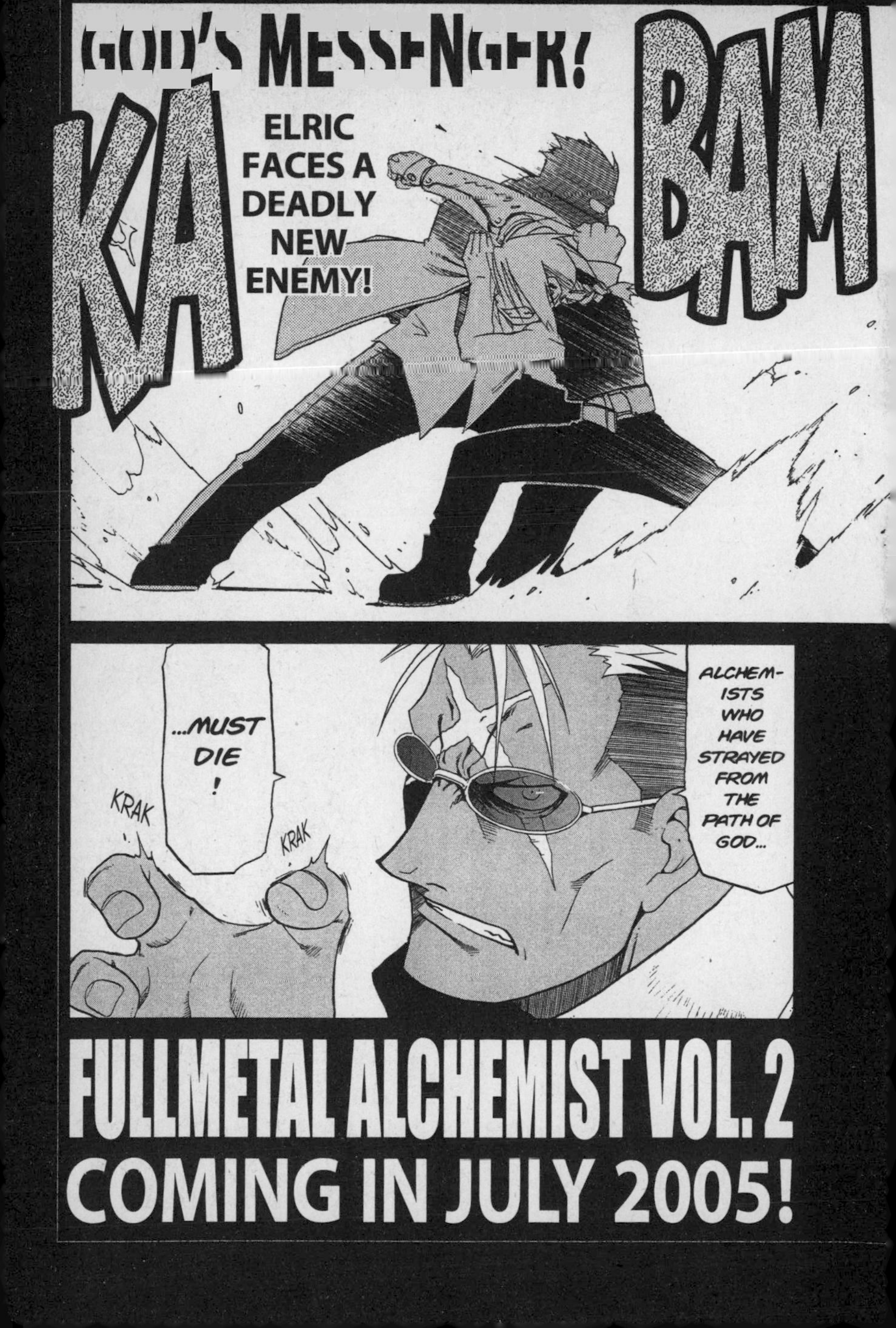
GOD'S MESSENGER!
ELRIC FACES A DEADLY NEW ENEMY!
KA BAM
ALCHEMISTS WHO HAVE STRAYED FROM THE PATH OF GOD...
...MUST DIE!
KRAK
KRAK

FULLMETAL ALCHEMIST VOL. 2
COMING IN JULY 2005!

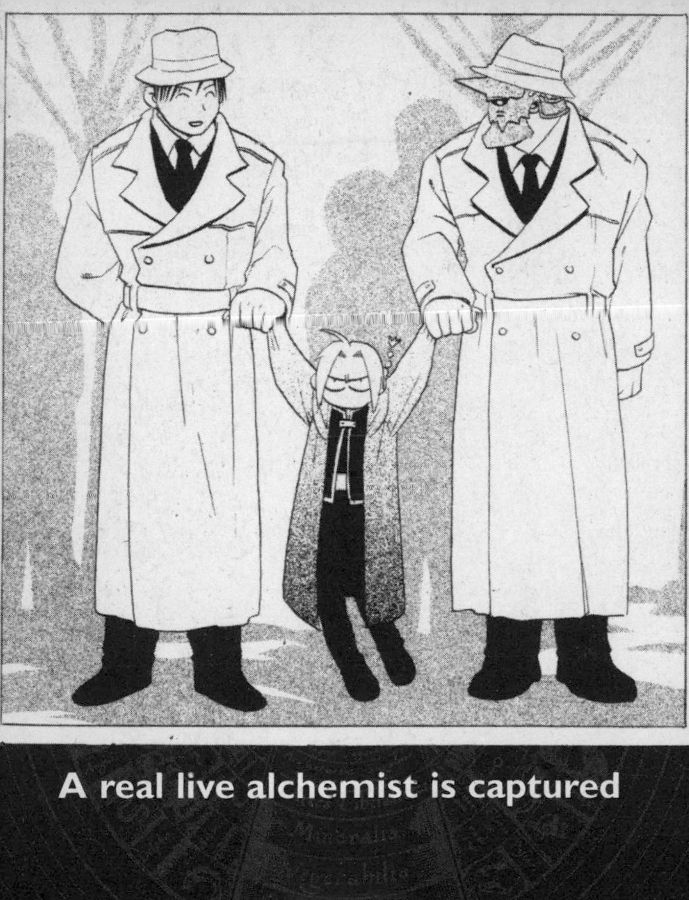

A real live alchemist is captured

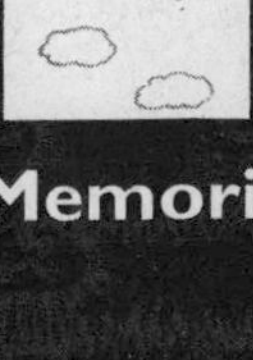

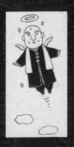

In Memoriam

EDITOR'S RECOMMENDATIONS

Many cultures have an alchemical tradition. In ancient China, the search for the elixir of immortality was the obsession of Daoist sages and emperors. In Europe, the earliest inklings of alchemy started with the ancient Greeks, then progressed through the Middle Ages. Medieval European alchemists (from which **Fullmetal Alchemist** draws some of its ideas) were more economically motivated than their Chinese counterparts: they wanted to change worthless metals into gold. But if the motivating factor of alchemy was ever "to make a lot of money," it didn't stay that way for long. The pseudo-science of alchemy went beyond materialism, and soon developed an almost religious meaning. Changing base metals into gold became a metaphor for changing base matter into something greater…something spiritual. Alchemy, like gnostic philosophy, became a "knowledge is power" quest whose motives could be either the grandest or the most selfish. To understand the nature of the universe, and possibly control it…to "know god," and maybe attain god's power.

In manga terms, though, alchemy is just a great weird element to base your story around, like Buddhism in Hiroyuki Takei's untranslated manga **Butsu Zone**, or Christianity in **Neon Genesis Evangelion**. The world of **Fullmetal Alchemist** resembles our world, sometime in the last hundred years or so, but the combination of alchemy and cybertechnology make it very different. As the series progresses, we'll learn more about both the science and the "magic" of the world of the Elric brothers…but in the meantime, here's some other excellent sci-fi manga with a philosophical twist.

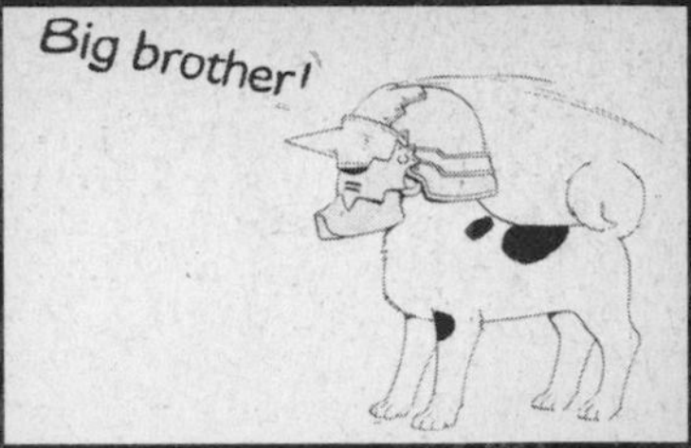
Big brother!

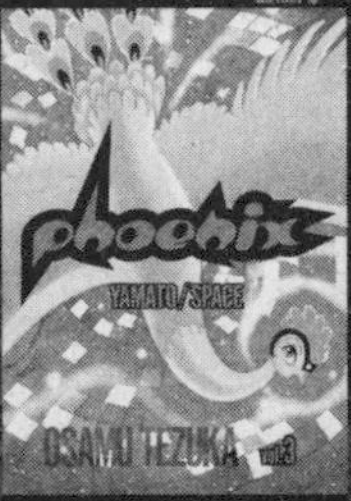
phoenix
YAMATO/SPACE
OSAMU TEZUKA
©2003 Tezuka Productions

Phoenix
by Osamu Tezuka: A classic manga combining stories of the historical past and science-fiction future.

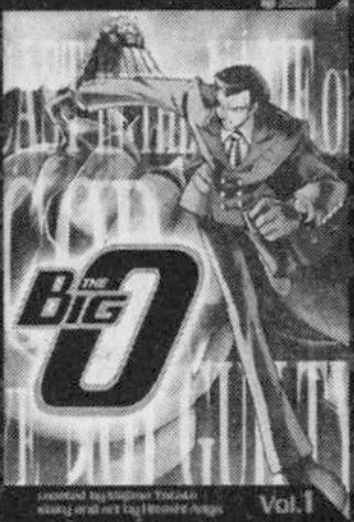
THE BIG O
Vol.1
© 1999 Hajime Yatate, Hitoshi Ariga © 1999 Sunrise/Kodansha Ltd.

The Big O
by Hajime Yatate and Hitoshi Ariga: Giant robots and film noir stylings in an urban world recovering from an apocalypse of mass amnesia.

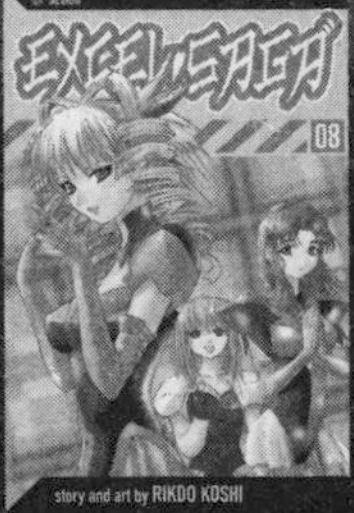
EXCEL SAGA
08
story and art by RIKDO KOSHI
© 1997 Rikdo Koshi/ SHONENGAHOSHA

Excel Saga
by Rikdo Koshi: Okay, this isn't really very philosophical. And it's only technically science fiction. But it's one of the funniest manga ever!

"Entertaining, heart-breaking & thought-provoking.
One of—if not the—greatest anime ever."
-Zac Bertschy, Anime Insider

AIRING SATURDAYS
[adult swim]
CARTOON
NETWORK
adultswim.com

FULLMETAL
ALCHEMIST™

www.fullmetalalchemist.com

Available Now

Available April 5th

©HIROMU ARAKAWA/SQUARE ENIX, MBS, ANX, BONES, dentsu 2004. Licensed by FUNimation® Productions Ltd. All Rights Reserved.
CARTOON NETWORK, ADULT SWIM and logos are trademarks of and © 2005 Cartoon Network. A Time Warner Company. All Rights Reserved.

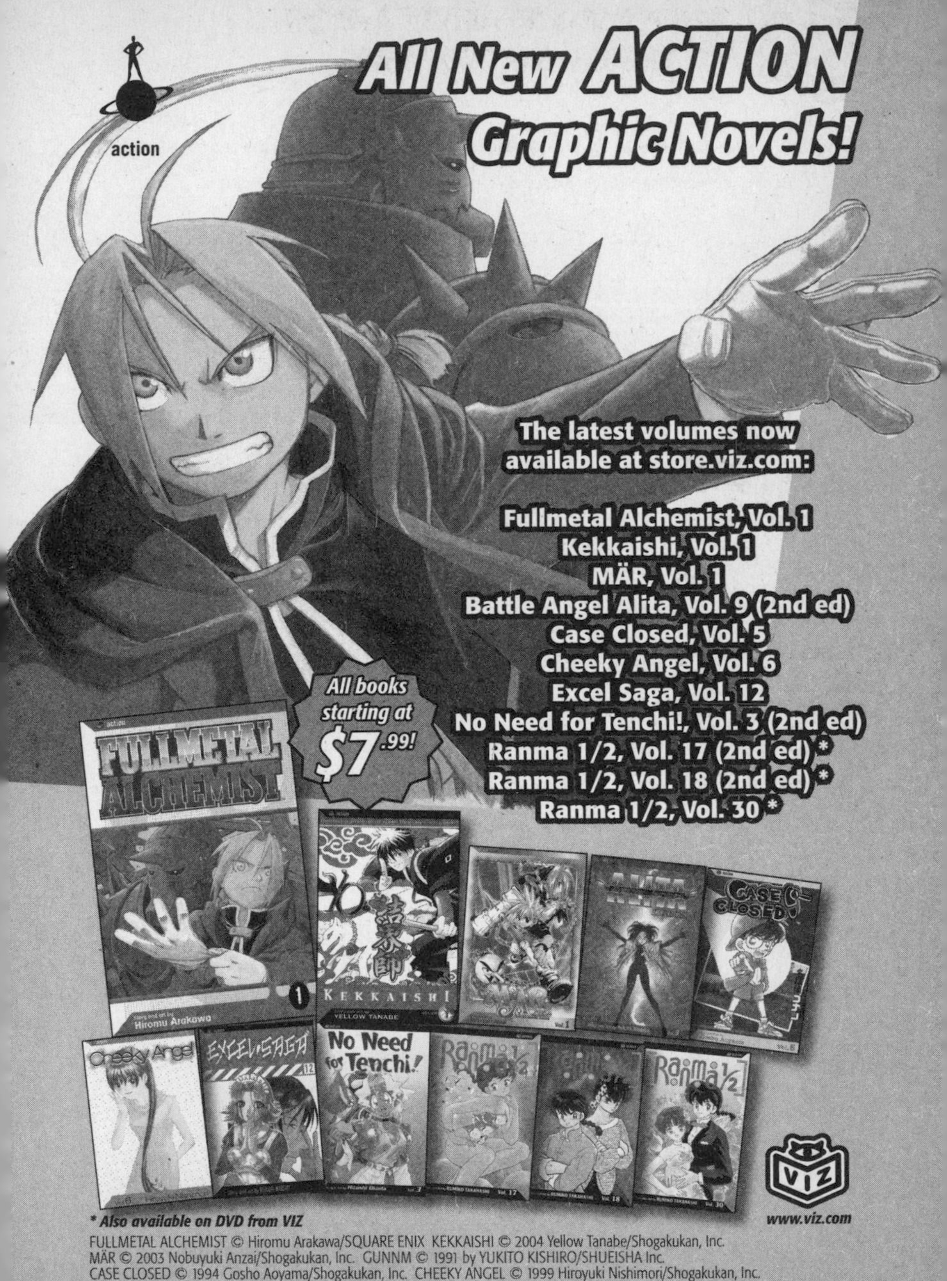
action
All New ACTION Graphic Novels!
The latest volumes now available at store.viz.com:
Fullmetal Alchemist, Vol. 1
Kekkaishi, Vol. 1
MÄR, Vol. 1
Battle Angel Alita, Vol. 9 (2nd ed)
Case Closed, Vol. 5
Cheeky Angel, Vol. 6
Excel Saga, Vol. 12
No Need for Tenchi!, Vol. 3 (2nd ed)
Ranma 1/2, Vol. 17 (2nd ed) *
Ranma 1/2, Vol. 18 (2nd ed) *
Ranma 1/2, Vol. 30 *
All books starting at $7.99!
FULLMETAL ALCHEMIST
Hiromu Arakawa
KEKKAISHI
YELLOW TANABE
CASE CLOSED
Cheeky Angel
EXCEL SAGA
No Need for Tenchi!
Ranma 1/2
VIZ
* Also available on DVD from VIZ
www.viz.com

How many anime and/or manga titles have you purchased in the last year? How many were VIZ titles? (please check one from each column)

ANIME	MANGA	VIZ
☐ None	☐ None	☐ None
☐ 1-4	☐ 1-4	☐ 1-4
☐ 5-10	☐ 5-10	☐ 5-10
☐ 11+	☐ 11+	☐ 11+

I find the pricing of VIZ products to be: (please check one)

☐ Cheap   ☐ Reasonable   ☐ Expensive

What genre of manga and anime would you like to see from VIZ? (please check two)

☐ Adventure   ☐ Comic Strip   ☐ Science Fiction   ☐ Fighting

☐ Horror   ☐ Romance   ☐ Fantasy   ☐ Sports

What do you think of VIZ's new look?

☐ Love It   ☐ It's OK   ☐ Hate It   ☐ Didn't Notice   ☐ No Opinion

Which do you prefer? (please check one)

☐ Reading right-to-left

☐ Reading left-to-right

Which do you prefer? (please check one)

☐ Sound effects in English

☐ Sound effects in Japanese with English captions

☐ Sound effects in Japanese only with a glossary at the back

THANK YOU! Please send the completed form to:

NJW Research
42 Catharine St.
Poughkeepsie, NY 12601

All information provided will be used for internal purposes only. We promise not to sell or otherwise divulge your information.

NO PURCHASE NECESSARY. Requests not in compliance with all terms of this form will not be acknowledged or returned. All submissions are subject to verification and become the property of VIZ, LLC. Fraudulent submission, including use of multiple addresses or P.O. boxes to obtain additional VIZ information or offers may result in prosecution. VIZ reserves the right to withdraw or modify any terms of this form. Void where prohibited, taxed, or restricted by law. VIZ will not be liable for lost, misdirected, mutilated, illegible, incomplete or postage-due mail. © 2003 VIZ, LLC. All Rights Reserved. VIZ, LLC, property titles, characters, names and plots therein under license to VIZ, LLC. All Rights Reserved.

COMPLETE OUR SURVEY AND LET US KNOW WHAT YOU THINK!

☐ Please do NOT send me information about VIZ products, news and events, special offers, or other information.

☐ Please do NOT send me information from VIZ's trusted business partners.

Name: _____

Address: _____

City: _____ State: _____ Zip: _____

E-mail: _____

☐ Male ☐ Female   Date of Birth (mm/dd/yyyy): ___ / ___ / _____   (Under 13? Parental consent required)

What race/ethnicity do you consider yourself? (please check one)

☐ Asian/Pacific Islander   ☐ Black/African American   ☐ Hispanic/Latino

☐ Native American/Alaskan Native ☐ White/Caucasian   ☐ Other: _____

What VIZ product did you purchase? (check all that apply and indicate title purchased)

☐ DVD/VHS _____

☐ Graphic Novel _____

☐ Magazines _____

☐ Merchandise _____

Reason for purchase: (check all that apply)

☐ Special offer   ☐ Favorite title   ☐ Gift

☐ Recommendation   ☐ Other _____

Where did you make your purchase? (please check one)

☐ Comic store   ☐ Bookstore   ☐ Mass/Grocery Store

☐ Newsstand   ☐ Video/Video Game Store ☐ Other: _____

☐ Online (site: _____)

What other VIZ properties have you purchased/own? _____